14 DAY BOOK

**This book is due on or before
the latest date stamped below**

CALIFORNIA STATE UNIVERSITY, NORTHRIDGE LIBRARY

THE DYNAMICS OF KNOWLEDGE REGIMES

Science, Technology and the International Political Economy

Series Editor: John de la Mothe

The upheavals of the international political economy during recent decades have fundamentally altered the relationships between firms and states, citizenship and management, social institutions and economic growth. The changing pace of competition, firm performance and geo-economics is shifting the pressures on public policy and corporate strategy alike. As a result, our conceptual frameworks for analyzing key events, emerging trends and driving forces are being challenged. As unclear as the future is, what remains certain is that science, technology and innovation will occupy a central place. By looking at a wide array of issues – ranging from security and foreign affairs, the environment, international institutions, corporate strategy and regional development to research policy, innovation gaps, intellectual property, ethics and law – this series will critically examine how science and technology are shaping the emerging international political economy.

Published titles in the series:

The Complexity Challenge, by Robert W. Rycroft and Don E. Kash

Developing Innovation Systems, edited by M. Cimoli

Evolutionary Economics and the New International Political Economy, edited by John de la Mothe and Gilles Paquet

Global Change and Intellectual Property Agencies, by G. Bruce Doern

The Governance of Innovation in Europe, by Philip Cooke, Patries Boekholt and Franz Tödtling

Regional Innovation, Knowledge and Global Change, edited by Zoltan Acs

Science, Technology and Governance, edited by John de la Mothe

Services and the Knowledge-Based Economy, edited by Ian Miles and Mark Boden

Systems of Innovation, edited by Charles Edquist

Universities and the Global Knowledge Economy, edited by Henry Etzkowitz and Loet Leydesdorff

Proposals for books can be sent directly to the series editor:
John de la Mothe
Program of Research on Innovation, Management and Economy (PRIME)
Faculty of Administration
University of Ottawa
275 Nicholas Street
Ottawa, Canada KlN 6N5
delamothe@admin.uottawa.ca

The Dynamics of Knowledge Regimes

Technology, Culture and National Competitiveness in the USA and Japan

Dengjian Jin

CONTINUUM
London and New York

Continuum
The Tower Building, 11 York Road, London SE1 7NX
370 Lexington Avenue, New York, NY 10017-6503

First published 2001

British Library Cataloguing-in-Publication Data
A catalogue record of this book is available from the British Library.

ISBN 0–8264–5453–4 (hardback)

Library of Congress Cataloging-in-Publication Data
Jin, Dengjian.
      The dynamics of knowledge regimes: technology, culture, and competitiveness in the
USA and Japan / Dengjian Jin.
            p. cm. — (Science, technology, and the international political economy)
      Includes bibliographical references and index.
      ISBN 0–8264–5433–4
         1. Research, Industrial—Economic aspects—United States. 2. Research,
Industrial—Economics aspects—Japan. 3. Technological innovations—Economic
aspects—United States. 4. Technological innovations—Economic aspects—Japan. 5.
United States—Foreign economic relations—Japan. 6. Japan—Foreign economic
relations—United States. I. Title. II. Science, technology, and the international political
economy series

HC110.R4 J56 2001
338′.064′0952—dc21   00–069377

Typeset by YHT Ltd, London
Printed and bound in Great Britain by The Cromwell Press, Trowbridge, Wilts.

Contents

List of Figures   viii
List of Tables   ix
Preface   xiii
Acknowledgments   xiv

1. Introduction   1

Part I   The Sectoral Approach   7

2. Sectoral Patterns of National Competitiveness   9
    Japanese export competitiveness in high-tech sectors   10
    US export competitiveness in high-tech sectors   13
    Japanese strength and US weakness in the export competitiveness
        of automobiles, mechatronics, and opto-electronics   15
    US strength and Japanese weakness in biotechnology,
        chemicals, food and beverages, and petroleum products   22
    Sectoral patterns of patenting advantage   27
    US strength and Japanese weakness in software, information
        services, and other service sectors   32
    American exceptionalism and Japanese uniqueness in the
        sectoral patterns of national competitiveness   39
    Discussion: the challenge of persistent sectoral patterns   42

Part II   The Knowledge Regime Perspective   45

3. The Knowledge Regime Framework   49
    The primacy of knowledge creation   49
    Beyond path-dependence   50
    Axial organizing principles as attractors: culture's impact   51
    Independent vs. interdependent models of organizing   52
    Contractual vs. connectual cultural paradigms   53
    From axial to derivative principles: dominant patterns of
        knowing and competitiveness   55
    The isomorphic structure of knowledge regimes   60
    Contractual vs. connectual governance   61
    Organizing principles and incentive structures   65
    Organizing principles and task structures   69
    Isomorphism and sectoral patterns of competitiveness   71

Discussion: the evolution and coevolution process reconsidered   72

4. Culture and Knowledge Creation   73
    Contractual man: the American pursuit of autonomy and
        separateness   73
    Connectual man: the Japanese pursuit of interdependence
        and mutual obligations   76
    Separate knowing vs. connectual knowing   81
    Trust and knowledge creation   89
    Discussion: dominant vs. complementary forms of human
        relations and human knowing   97

Part III Governance Mechanisms for Knowledge Creation   101

5. Contractual Governance for Knowledge Creation   105
    Contractual markets and knowledge creation   106
    Contractual hierarchies and knowledge creation   112
    Contractual networks and knowledge creation   118
    Contractual clans and knowledge creation   122
    Contractual governance as an attractor   124
    The state as enforcer of contractual governance   127
    Conclusion   128

6. Connectual Governance for Knowledge Creation   129
    Connectual governance and stakeholder capitalism   130
    Exogenous vs. endogenous enforcement of knowledge exchange   133
    Connectual hierarchies and knowledge creation   135
    Connectual markets and networks and knowledge creation   149
    Connectual government and knowledge creation   154
    Discussion: hybrid forms and the synergy of governance
        mechanisms   155

**Part IV Organizing for Competitiveness: Isomorphism and
        Sectoral Patterns   157**

7. Quantification vs. Contextualization   160
    Objectification as a means of autonomy and independence:
        the US advantage and disadvantage   162
    Contextualization as a means of connectual knowing:
        the Japanese advantage and diaadvantage   171
    The Japanese competitive advantage of synergy   182
    Conclusion   185

8. Spontaneous vs. Organized Fusion   186
    Organizing for spontaneous technology fusion: the US
        advantage   189
    The garbage can model of spontaneous fusion   195

Organized technology fusion: the Japanese advantage   204
Conclusion: the entrepreneurship debate reconsidered   211
9.   Modularity and Connectivity   214
    Two ways of dealing with complexity: the impact of culture   214
    The dominance of modularization in the American life   219
    Modularization as a double-edged sword for US
      competitiveness   224
    Contextual connectivity: the Japanese advantage and
      disadvantage   231
    Two types of modularization and connectivity: learning and
      cultural synergy between the USA and Japan   237

10. Systems Integration: People-independence vs. People-dependence   238
    Two ways of systems integration: the impact of cultural
      paradigms   238
    People-independent systems integration: the US way of
      systemization   249
    Complexity, modularization, and people-independent systems
      integration   254
    Systems integration in large-scale complex technological
      systems   257
    Explicit connectivity and shared database: software and
      information systems as integrators   261
    People-dependent systems integration: the dominant Japanese
      way of systemization   269
    Japanese competitive advantage in CNC, FMS, and CIM   276
    Discussion: Taylorism reassessed   278

11. The Great Synergy of Civilizations   280
    The sectoral perspective as a solution to linear thinking   280
    Coevolution and the problem of overdetermination   282
    Organizing principles and the synergy of civilizations   282
    The synergy of civilizations as the theme for the twenty-first
      century   285

References   290
Index   315

Figures

2.1   The relationship between US exports and FDI to the EC, by industry, 1989   25

2.2   The relationship between Japanese exports and FDI to the EC, by industry, 1989   25

2.3   The sectoral pattern of US and Japanese general competitiveness   40

2.4   The sectoral pattern of US relative competitiveness with Japan and other major competitors   41

3.1   Two-dimensional structures of value systems   54

3.2   Organizating principles and national competitiveness   55

3.3   Organizing principles and the broad-scope isomorphism of knowledge regimes   60

3.4   The dominance of contractual governance in the USA   63

3.5   The dominance of connectual governance in Japan   65

3.6   The dominance of the contractual incentive structure in the USA   68

3.7   The dominance of the connectual incentive structure in Japan   68

3.8   The US knowledge regime   71

3.9   The Japanese knowledge regime   72

4.1   Patterns of human relations in different economies   98

4.2   Patterns of human knowing in different economies   99

6.1   Sequential engineering as dominant in the USA   145

6.2   Concurrent engineering as dominant in Japan   146

8.1   The linear model of innovation   194

8.2   The garbage can model of spontaneous technology fusion   196

10.1   The relationship of complexity and knowledge creation   255

10.2   The relationship of complexity and modularization   256

10.3   The relationship of complexity and systems integration   257

11.1   The Japanese dynamic learning path in modularity   284

11.2   The US dynamic learning path in connectivity   285

Tables

2.1   The export/import ratio of Japanese high-tech sectors, 1981–1992   11

2.2   Japan's export/import indices of revealed comparative advantage in high-tech sectors, 1981–1992   11

2.3   Japan's export indices of revealed comparative advantage in high-tech sectors, 1981–1992   12

2.4   Japan's export/import ratios in high-tech products, 1967–1983   13

2.5   Japan's export indices of revealed comparative advantage in high-tech products, 1967–1983   14

2.6   Japan's global export share and export indices in high-tech sectors, 1995–1998   15

2.7   Japan's export/import ratio of high-tech manufacturing sectors, 1995–1998   16

2.8   The export/import ratio of US high-tech sectors, 1981–1992   17

2.9   US export/import indices of revealed comparative advantage in high-tech sectors, 1981–1992   17

2.10   US export indices of revealed comparative advantage in high-tech sectors, 1981–1992   18

2.11   Export/import ratios of US and Japanese high-tech sectors, 1980–1995   18

2.12   Export indices of comparative advantage of US and Japanese high-tech sectors, 1980–1995   19

2.13   World export share of top six countries in high-tech sectors (percentages)   20

2.14   US export/import ratio of top manufacturing sectors, 1995–1998   21

2.15   US global export share and export indices of top manufacturing sectors, 1995–1998   22

2.16   Major clustering Japanese and US manufacturing sectors with high world export shares   23

2.17   Cumulative Japanese and US FDI in Europe, by industry, early 1990s   24

2.18   Revenues generated by US outward and inward FDI, 1987–1994   25

2.19   Numbers of firms and percentages of consolidated sales accounted for by the twelve largest companies worldwide in each industry, by country of corporate headquarters, 1993   26

2.20   US export/import performance in high technologies   26

2.21   Country share of OECD exports, by technology, 1994   27

2.22   US trade performance in high technologies, 1995–1996   27

2.23   Patenting index of revealed comparative advantage, 1963–1968;

	1985–1990	28
2.24	Patenting indices of comparative advantage, 1985–1990	29
2.25	Top fifteen most emphasized patent classes for inventors in the USA and Japan, 1995	30
2.26	Correlation between countries in their patenting indices of revealed comparative advantage across 34 sectors	31
2.27	Number of firms within the top 20 of manufacturing sectors in US patenting, 1985–1990	31
2.28	Accumulative number of international patent families, 1990–1994	32
2.29	Accumulative number of highly cited international patent families, 1990–1994	32
2.30	US trade performance in software product, 1990–1996	33
2.31	Japanese trade performance in software, 1994–1996	33
2.32	Top 20 software companies worldwide, 1990 and 1996	34
2.33	Market share of US firms in prepackaged software, 1993 (percentages)	35
2.34	US domination in the global market for software and related services, 1990	35
2.35	Revenues of software and computer-related services sectors, 1990–1995	36
2.36	Trade performance in goods, services, and computer services, 1994 and 1996	38
2.37	US and Japanese trade performance in services, 1987–1996	38
2.38	US export/import ratios of service sectors, 1986–1998	39
4.1	Desirable patterns of relationships in Japan (percentages)	80
4.2	Percentage of products that succeeded	89
4.3	Amount of training for production workers in automobile assembly plants	94
4.4	Ph.D. ratio in US and Japanese laboratories	95
4.5	Dominant vs. complementary human relations in the USA and Japan	97
4.6	Dominant vs. complementary human knowing in the USA and Japan	98
5.1	The rise of the US management industry	110
5.2	Structure of R&D expenditure: sources and users, percentage of total national R&D expenditure	112
5.3	Clustering of connectual work practices in the USA, 1992 (percentages)	125
6.1	Percentage of managers choosing (a) 'the only goal a company has is to make a profit'	132
6.2	The priority rank of corporate goals: a US–Japan comparison	132
6.3	The production and transaction costs of the two types of knowledge	135
6.4	Percentage choosing (a) 'company as a set of tasks', rather than (b) 'company as relations'	136
6.5	Estimates of the number of jobs held by males over a lifetime in Japan and the USA	137

6.6	Job classification and multimachine operations of blue-collar workers at automotive components plants in Japan, the USA, and Europe, 1987–1989	138
6.7	Member composition of Japanese and American Marketing Associations	138
6.8	Job rotations to areas outside specialty: Japan and US comparison	139
6.9	Improvement of inventory reduction in US and UK manufacturing	143
7.1	Adoption of quantitative techniques in cost and managerial accounting practices: a US–Japan comparison	173
7.2	Ranks of perceived barriers to adopting quantitative methods	173
7.3	Ranks of top 25 global market/advertising/opinion research firms	178
7.4	Comparison of production technology	179
7.5	Adoption of marketing strategies to the UK market: a US–Japan comparison (percentages)	180
7.6	Comparison of improvement suggestions: a US–Japan comparison, 1990	181
8.1	Top ten Japanese electric machine makers, excluding appliances, 1970–1990	188
8.2	Concentration ratio of top ten firms in patents: 1963–1999	188
8.3	Number of establishments in software and computer-related services	198
8.4	How US venture capitalists spend their time	198
8.5	Venture capital under management in the USA and disbursements: 1983–1995	199
8.6	Top ten patenting corporations in the USA	207
8.7	Bilateral US–Japanese trade in patents and other proprietary inventions and technology, 1987–1995	210
9.1	Problems in getting design information from customers	225
9.2	Design for assembly (DFA) ranking	227
9.3	Packaged and customized software product as percentage of total software sales	228
10.1	Adoption ratio of formalized and standardized managerial systems: US–Japan differences in descending order, 1980 (percentages)	241
10.2	Methods of deploying improved technology: a comparison of US and Japanese SMEs in the manufacturing sector, 1994, percentage of firms	243
10.3	Biggest problems facing product and process development: a comparison of US and Japanese SMEs in the manufacturing sector, 1994, percentage of firms	244
10.4	Density of various technology systems and tools, by number of units per thousand employees in manufacturing	245
10.5	The use of computer systems in Japanese and US SMEs in the manufacturing sector during the past ten years, 1994, percentage of firms	245

10.6   Knowledge structure of R&D integrators in the semiconductor
        sector   252
10.7   The experimentation capability in the semiconductor sector: a
        US–Japan–Korea comparison   253
10.8   The adoption of a specific tool to transmit purchase orders to
        suppliers: 1987–1990 (percentages)   264
10.9   Use of computers for production planning and scheduling:
        1987–1990 (percentages)   266
10.10   Number of computers per 100 persons, 1994   266
10.11   Number of PCs per 100 white-collar workers, 1994   267

Preface

This book systematically analyzes the persistent disparity in the sectoral patterns of American and Japanese technological competitiveness. After revealing the limits of various existing approaches, it presents the knowledge regime perspective to explain this disparity. A knowledge regime of a nation consists primarily of *the dominant organizing principles and governance mechanisms of knowledge creation, transformation, diffusion, and appropriation.* The central hypotheses state that the American penchant for autonomy and independence and the resultant cultural paradigm of contractual man has led to the predominance of separate knowing, contractual governance, and the organizing principles of standardization, depersonalization, decontextualization, quantification, modularization, systemization, people-independent systems integration, and spontaneous fusion for knowledge creation. On the other hand, the Japanese zeal for interdependence and mutual obligations and the resultant cultural paradigm of connectual man has resulted in the preponderance of connectual knowing, connectual governance, and the organizing principles of customization, synchronization, harmonization, contextualization, connectualization, organized fusion, and people-dependent systems integration for knowledge creation. The former has contributed to the American competitiveness in the modular and loosely coupled technological sectors of prepackaged software, biotechnology, aircraft, chemicals, information processing, fast foods, banking, and other professional services. The latter has given rise to the Japanese competitive advantage in the non-modular and tightly coupled technological sectors of automobiles, electronics, opto-electronics, and mechatronics. In tracing the dynamics of knowledge regimes, the book attributes the rise of the American system of manufactures, Taylorism, Fordism, McDonaldization, and most recently, the Silicon Valley model to the contractual cultural paradigm and organizing principles. It further explains the rise of the flexible manufacturing system by the Japanese synergistic effort of combining the very best of transplanted American systems and endogenous organizing principles. Finally, the book asserts that the new information revolution has tilted the pendulum of competitive advantage back to the US side, and therefore, it is high time for Japan to learn the American way once again.

Acknowledgments

This study has been the result of an academic journey of more than ten years. During the process, I have greatly benefited from interaction with such great scholars as Seymour Martin Lipset, James M. Buchanan, Ambrose Y. C. King, Francis Fukuyama, and Don Lavoie. I am especially indebted to my Ph.D. advisor Don E. Kash. Without nearly five-year continuous and insightful interaction with him, this book would have been unimaginable. My academic dialogue and debate with him has stimulated many of the ideas presented here. Without his support and encouragement, I would not have been able to pursue a topic as broad as this book. The same debt is due to Dr. Roger R. Stough, who provided not only the much needed financial support, but also academic stimulation and encouragement throughout my Ph.D. years. Both Dr. Kash and Dr. Stough have painstakingly helped improve my skills in English writing. Although I was shy interacting with him, Dr. Seymour Martin Lipset has greatly influenced my research agenda and my thinking through his theories of American exceptionalism and Japanese uniqueness. I have also received advice from Professor Christopher T. Hill and David T. Roessner. I am especially indebted to Professor Hill in terms of the notion of micro vs. macro fusion. My thinking has also been stimulated by my fortunate interaction with other professors at the George Mason University, especially Kingsley Haynes, Louise White, and John Warfield. My colleagues at Dickinson College provided much needed encouragement for the completion of the book. Dickinson College also offered financial supports.

Denghui Jin provided detailed comments on the manuscript. Since English is not my native language, I am very grateful for the heroic efforts of freelance copyeditor Gillian Andrews and House Editor of Continuum, Neil Dowden, in making detailed editorial suggestions. I am especially grateful for the encouragement and support of John de la Mothe, the editor of the Science, Technology and the International Political Economy series and Caroline Wintersgill, Senior Commissioning Editor at Continuum, who made the publication of this book a reality.

My wife Dongmei and daughter Menghan provided the most important support that made the completion of this book possible. I owe them my greatest appreciation.

To my wife Dongmei
and daughter Menghan

CHAPTER ONE

Introduction

Few events have surprised more scholars in recent history than the two successive upside-down turns in the popularly perceived fortunes of the USA and Japan. Beginning in the late 1970s and running until the mid-1990s, a widely held perception of US economic and technological dominance since the beginning of the century was challenged by Japan's superior performance. A chain of bestselling books such as *Japan as Number One* (Vogel, 1979), *MITI and the Japanese Miracle* (Johnson, 1982), and *Trading Places* (Prestowitz, 1988) portrayed Japan as a rising economic and technological superpower while at the same time lamenting the American decline. Serious scholars from almost every discipline found sources of Japanese competitive advantages in almost every aspect, from culture, national character, to education, management, technology, to economic structure, enterprise governance, manufacturing system, to human resource management, innovation styles, knowledge creation pattern, and to industrial policy, technology policy, and trade policy. The American business community has also taken great pains to learn from the Japanese by importing such best Japanese practices as lean production, total quality management, just-in-time production and delivery, cross-functional teams, and incremental improvement. However, beginning in the mid-1990s, with the revival of the US economy and after a prolonged recession of the Japanese economy, especially at the height of the East Asian financial crisis of 1997 and 1998, people's perceptions turned upside down again. Once more, the USA was acclaimed as an unparalleled economic superpower that would dominate the next century (Zuckerman, 1998), while Japan was described as sinking toward the abysmal (*Business Week*, May 18, 1998, cover story).

This sea change of popular views on national competitiveness has a fundamental impact on both academic debates and policy discussions regarding the true driving forces for the wealth and poverty of nations. Indeed, while most agree that the speed of knowledge creation and innovation has become the sole source of competitive advantage, historically public deliberations regarding the issue of national competitiveness have been polarized into uncompromising camps charged with strong ideological commitments. Whereas neoliberals argue that the market is the best governance mechanism for knowledge creation, industrial policy advocates and many students of East Asian political economy believe that supportive government policies and public–private collaboration are indispensable (Johnson, 1982; Amsden, 1989). The revival of the US economy and the prolonged recession in Japan have bolstered the arguments by the former. Many scholars, journalists, and business leaders quickly jumped into a chorus to celebrate the triumph of the Anglo-American model of 'free-market' economy, while at the same time, declaring the death of the East Asian model, deriding it as 'statism,' 'authoritarianism', and 'crony capitalism.'

Just as the proponents of communitarian capitalism went too far in trumpeting the sweeping superiority of the Japanese system and the East Asian model (e.g. Vogel, 1979; Johnson, 1982; Lodge and Vogel, 1987; Prestowitz, 1988; Fallows, 1994; Dore, 1994), so the neoliberals' broad claim of the triumph of the Anglo-American model is premature and overgeneralized. If this episode of history could teach us anything, it is the need to refute *universal* propositions on national competitiveness that disregard sectoral disparities. If we move our attention from the national to the sectoral level, we find that, underneath the seemingly changing fate of national wealth, the distinct sectoral patterns of national competitiveness have persisted during the last two decades for both the USA and Japan. Judging by all the indicators of trade performance, foreign direct investment (FDI), global market share, productivity, and patenting activities, Japan has consistently not been competitive in the sectors of aircraft, biotechnology, software, information services, electronic business (e-business), and other professional services, in which the USA has held a leading position. Conversely, although there have been some improvements after a decade's long effort of learning from Japan, the USA is still not as competitive as Japan has been in the sectors of automobile, home electronics, opto-electronics, machine tools, and flexible manufacturing systems. What have changed during the 1990s are not the sectoral patterns of national competitiveness but rather the relative weights of sectors in the economy. While the importance of traditional manufacturing sectors of automobiles, home electronics, and opto-electronics has relatively declined, offsetting many of Japan's competitive advantages, the newly emerging sectors of information services, software, e-business, and biotechnology have gained in importance, favoring many American firms. Nevertheless, even with a rejuvenated economy and indisputably the most competitive position in these rising sectors, according to the US Department of Commerce the USA still ran a total trade deficit of 181.5 billion US dollars in 1999, of which 78 per cent came from trading with Japan and other East Asian nations. In 1999, the US trade deficit in goods reached a record of 345.6 billion US dollars, while its trade surplus in services also achieved a record of 80.6 billion US dollars.

This continued stability and disparity in the sectoral patterns of US and Japanese competitiveness calls for sobriety and a dose of reckoning. It challenges the millenium mania that tried to put an end to everything old while proclaiming the beginning of a completely new paradigm for every aspect of the world. Underlying such broad claims as 'Japan as Number One' (Vogel, 1979; Johnson, 1982; Prestowitz, 1988; Fallows, 1994), and 'the new American century' (Zuckerman, 1998) is the tendency of Anglo-American universalism that strives to extrapolate observations of one specific case to all situations. Sweeping overgeneralization seems to have become such an infectious virus that even the most shrewd futurists and dialectical thinkers are affected.

Such a drive for overgeneralization is also evident in the most recently American-generated management fads about knowledge management and in the mainstream economists' hypothesis of convergence. Underpinning those carefully packaged management fads such as reengineering, strategic outsourcing, and virtual integration rests an implicit assumption that their proposed way of organizing business process and the underlying task of knowledge creation is best, disregarding socio-economic and technological contingencies. Similarly, at the core of the convergence hypothesis in economics is a belief that the drive for efficiency and the mechanism of market competition will push firms in various nations to adopt 'the best way' of organizing resource allocation despite socio-cultural differences. This 'one best way' mentality has caused failure in the formulation of business strategy and economic policy regarding competitiveness both at firm and national levels. It has also given rise to unjustified arrogance in assuming the superiority of the Anglo-American model and, as a result, in pushing other nations to adopt the same business systems and macro-economic policies as those legitimated by the so-called 'Washington Consensus.'

This book postulates that most overgeneralization during the last two decades resulted from a failure to adopt *a sectoral approach* that takes into account a great variety of sectoral, technological, and cultural differences in understanding the dynamics of national competitiveness. At the core of such dynamics are the coevolution and the resultant broad-scope isomorphism of cultural paradigms, governance mechanisms, technological trajectories, and dominant organizing principles for knowledge creation, transformation, integration, diffusion, and appropriation.[1] Such a dynamic process of isomorphic coevolution is the very force underlying the emergence, dominance, and lock-in of specific governance mechanisms, particular technological trajectories, unique ways of knowing, and idiosyncratic configurations of organizing principles for knowledge creation in a nation.

Although most people admit the paramount importance of knowledge creation for competitiveness in this new age, there are many misconceptions and overgeneralizations as to how the process of knowledge creation should best be organized. From the sectoral perspective, the knowledge needed for competitive success differs from sector to sector and from technology to technology. The way knowledge is created, transformed, integrated, diffused, and appropriated also varies among nations. In other words, instead of following the myth of 'one best way,' *different societies handle knowledge creation differently according to their different cultural premises and organizing principles*. The national differences in the organizing principles of knowledge creation are persistent because they are embedded and locked into other isomorphic structures of cultural paradigms, patterns of knowing, governance mechanisms, and technological trajectories. This ecology of coevolving isomorphic structures in a nation constitutes what I call the national 'knowledge regime,' which is the major contributor for the persistence of the nation's sectoral pattern of competitiveness.

While there are theories that address some aspects of knowledge creation, most fail to adopt a sectoral perspective, nor are they able to recognize the primary importance of national organizing principles for generating fundamentally different systems of knowledge creation. New growth theory and new trade theory (Romer, 1990; Krugman, 1991) mainly focus on the stock and flow of knowledge and their impact on national economic growth and trade performance. Most literature on organizational learning (Senge, 1990) deals with learning problems at the firm level. Students of national innovation systems (Nelson, 1993) generally limit their attention to some specific aspects of knowledge regimes, notably national R&D and educational institutions. Except for some limited work by such authors as Kogut (1993), Kodama (1991), and Nonaka and Takeuchi (1995), most existing theories of knowledge management have not systematically investigated dynamic interaction between culture, technology, governance, and dominant organizing principles of knowledge creation.

Similarly, most studies of organization, institution, and governance fail to focus on the central issue of knowledge creation. They are often unable to take a sectoral perspective in discussing comparative advantages of various institutions and governance mechanisms. Except for some limited works, most also fail to investigate the impact of cultural paradigms and axial organizing principles on the evolution of institutions, organizations, and governance mechanisms.

This book tries to develop a conceptual framework for a systematic comparison of the dynamics of US and Japanese 'knowledge regimes.' It will first examine the persistent sectoral disparities of US and Japanese competitiveness. After pointing out the limitations of existing approaches to national competitiveness, it will offer a knowledge regime perspective for understanding the dynamics of national knowledge creation systems and their differential impact on the sectoral competitiveness of nations. The choice of Japan and the USA as the primary focus of this study is based on two factors. First, they are the two most economically and technologically competitive nations. Second, they represent two archetypal poles of *Yin* and *Yang* in cultural paradigms, governance mechanisms, and organizing principles of knowledge creation. When we are able to fully analyze these two extremes, it is relatively easy to explore other nations in between. By investigating the coevolution of cultural paradigms, governance mechanisms, organizing principles, and technological trajectories in these two countries, this book intends to provide an integrative framework on the dynamics of institutional evolution, technological development, on the emergence, dominance, adaptation, and persistence of national systems of knowledge creation, and on the role of national culture, industrial policy, international trade policy, generic technology, and business strategy in either facilitating or hindering national technological competitiveness in different sectors.

This book will investigate the following questions:

- What are the dominant organizing principles of knowledge creation in the USA and Japan?
- How have these organizing principles emerged, become dominant, and been institutionalized in these nations?
- What are the dominant cultural paradigms in the USA and Japan? How have they facilitated the predominance of differing ways of knowing?
- How have the differences in national culture, ideology, and history impacted the institutionalization of different organizing principles of knowledge creation, embedded mostly in different governance mechanisms for knowledge creation?
- How do differences in the knowledge inter-linkage of the subsystems of a technology require different ways of knowing and different organizing principles for knowledge creation?
- How have the differences in the institutions of knowledge creation impacted the sectoral competitiveness of different nations?
- How will information technology and the emerging digital economy likely impact the future of knowledge regimes and consequently national competitiveness in the twenty-first century?

- How can public policy tools be used to exploit comparative advantages and overcome comparative disadvantages in a nation's system of knowledge creation?

In striving to answer the above questions, we will reexamine various existing theories of institutionalization, of technological change, of knowledge management, and of competitive advantage of nations. We will reinterpret and reexamine the development of the American system of manufactures, the historical origins and dominance of Taylorism and Fordism, the Japanese synthesis between its native ethos and imported Taylorism in forming Toyotarism (Jin, 1995), and the emergence of digital economy and e-business in the USA. We will especially focus on the investigation of the divergent configurations of the organizing principles of knowledge creation in the USA and Japan, and consequently their differential impact on the sectoral competitiveness of these two nations.

Essentially, the book postulates that differences in the following factors are primarily responsible for the persistent sectoral disparities in national competitiveness:

- Knowledge structure in different sectors.
- The role of different types of knowledge in fulfilling different tasks.
- National differences in the organizing principles of knowledge creation.
- The incentive structures embedded in national culture and dominant governance mechanisms.
- The coevolution and resultant isomorphism among cultural paradigms, governance mechanisms, organizing principles, and technological trajectories.

These factors and their dynamic interplay will be examined from rational, evolutionary, and institutional perspectives.

The structure of the book

The book is composed of four parts. Part I contains chapter 2 which provides systematic analyses of the sectoral patterns of US and Japanese competitiveness.

Part II offers a framework for the knowledge regime perspective. Chapter 3 elaborates on the basic framework and concepts. Chapter 4 further explores the connection between culture and knowledge creation, examines the distinction between separate and connectual knowing, and discusses differing socio-cultural constructions of trust and knowledge creation.

Part III examines in detail various governance mechanisms for knowledge creation in the USA and Japan respectively in chapters 5 and 6. Unlike the conventional studies of governance mechanisms that deal primarily with the issues of *opportunism* and *transaction costs*, our study focuses on the governance mechanisms for *knowledge creation and appropriation*. Instead of a conventional treatment of the markets, hierarchies, networks, and clans as unitary and universal across cultural boundaries, we differentiate contractual governance and connectual governance as two generic and fundamentally different mechanisms within the same governance structures of the markets, hierarchies, networks, and clans. Such a treatment not only provides a new understanding of governance mechanisms, but also enables us to search for the causal links among dominant cultural paradigms, governance mechanisms, and the sectoral patterns of national competitiveness.

While Parts II and III elaborate on the dominant cultural paradigms and governance mechanisms in the USA and Japan respectively, Part IV explores the relationships between the dominant organizing principles of knowledge creation, technological paradigms, and the persistent US and Japanese sectoral patterns of national competitiveness. Chapter 7 discusses how the US contractual cultural paradigm has led to the predominance of the organizing principles of quantification, depersonalization, and decontextualization and the resultant US competitiveness in consulting, information services, e-business, and other professional services. After challenging the conventional dichotomy between *technological breakthrough* and *technology fusion*, chapter 8 systematically elaborates on a conceptual model that differentiates between *spontaneous* and *organized* technology fusion as being dominant in the USA and Japan respectively. It further discusses how this disparity has contributed to US competitiveness in the biotechnology and software sectors and Japanese competitiveness in opto-electronics and mechatronics. Chapter 9 discusses two fundamentally different sets of organizing principles in dealing with complexity. In the USA, the cultural penchant for autonomy and independence has led to the adoption of division, *modularization*, and encapsulation as the dominant principles organizing the increasingly complex tasks of technological innovation. By contrast, the Japanese penchant for connection, interdependence, and mutual obligation has given rise to the use of connectualization, customization, and contextualization as the dominant principles organizing the increasingly complex tasks of technological innovation. As a result, the USA is competitive in loosely coupled and modular technological sectors whereas Japan is competitive in tightly coupled and non-modular technological sectors. Chapter 10 differentiates two vastly different ways of systems integration: people-independent vs. people-dependent. In the USA the pursuit of autonomy and independence has led to the dominance of the former, while in Japan the preference for interdependence has given rise to the preponderance of the latter. The focus on people-independent systems integration has contributed to US strength in the innovation of technological systems of large-scale complexity such as aircraft, nuclear technologies, weapons, and large-scale logic semiconductors. On the other hand, the emphasis on people-dependent systems integration has provided Japanese firms competitive advantage in technological systems of middle-scale complexity such as opto-electronics, numerical control machine tools, robots, and flexible manufacturing systems. The concluding chapter discusses the great synergy of civilizations as the theme of the twenty-first century based on the knowledge regime perspective. It further explores the policy implications of the knowledge regime perspective, for example, how Japan can learn once again from the USA.

Note

1.   For simplicity, from now on, I will use 'knowledge creation' to mean the whole process of knowledge creation, transformation, integration, diffusion, and appropriation.

PART I

The Sectoral Approach

Sectoral Patterns of National Competitiveness

As I have frequently argued, it is impossible to understand a country without seeing how it varies from others. Those who know only one country know no country.
Seymour Martin Lipset (1996, p. 17)

The sectoral patterns of American and Japanese competitiveness in international markets are routinely evident to people all over the world. People watch Japanese-brand TVs, use Japanese cameras, play games on Japanese machines, and drive Japanese-brand cars, while drinking American-brand Cola, eating American fast food, using American software products, and riding on American-made airplanes. When Americans go shopping in Wal-Mart or when a Chinese enters department stores in Shanghai, the persistent image of a division between Japanese and American products is too obvious to go unnoticed. As will be systematically investigated in this chapter, the persistence of US and Japanese sectoral patterns of international competitiveness is supported by the following facts:

- The persistent sectoral patterns of trade performance.
- The stable sectoral patterns of outward and inward foreign direct investment (FDI).
- The consistency in the sectoral patterns of patenting and productivity.
- The failure of national industrial policy and technology policy in promoting certain types of technological sectors in both Japan and the USA.
- The consistent failure of business strategies to gain competitive advantage in certain segments of technologies and products for both US and Japanese firms.

After applying all of the indicators of competitiveness to the USA and Japan over time, we found persistent patterns of their sectoral competitiveness in both high-tech and non-high-tech sectors. The USA has been, and continues to be, globally competitive in aircraft, drugs and medicines, chemicals, scientific instruments, biotechnology, life science, weapons, nuclear technology, prepackaged software, consulting, information services, banking, retailing, food, entertainment, and other services. Japan has been very competitive in automobiles, consumer electronics, opto-electronics, game software, machine tools and robotics, flexible manufacturing systems (FMS), and computer-integrated manufacturing (CIM). Japan is not competitive in the sectors where the USA is strong; likewise, the USA is relatively weak in the areas where Japan is strong.

In a comprehensive study using a United Nations' database of multilateral trade flows, Gagnon and Rose (1995) also found, astonishingly, *persistence* in the patterns of sectoral trade balances over the past thirty years in the USA, Japan, Korea, the UK, Brazil, and Turkey. Intriguingly, this persistent disparity has been largely ignored by most existing literature. Studies on the rise and decline of nations (e.g. Lodge and Vogel, 1987; Chandler, 1990; Kennedy, 1993; Fukuyama, 1995; Landes, 1998) fail to appreciate the differential sectoral impact of their chosen explanatory variables. The industrial policy and competitiveness debates (Johnson, 1982; Okimoto, 1989; Thurow, 1992; Tyson, 1993) often ignore the limits of national policies in advancing certain sectors. Students of comparative capitalism, Japanese economic institutions, and East Asian dynamism (Dore, 1987; Berger and Hsiao, 1988; Tai, 1989; Biggard, 1991; Gerlach, 1992) neglect the persistent weakness of some Japanese sectors. New growth theory (Romer, 1990) and various theories of comparative and competitive advantages (Vernon, 1966; Imai, 1986; Porter, 1990; Kodama, 1991; Kogut, 1993; Nelson, 1993; Nonaka and Takeuchi, 1995) are also unable to provide a satisfactory explanation on the issue. The failure to take a sectoral approach is also evident in most theories of organization, knowledge management, digital economy, and e-businesses, as well as debates on international competitiveness. This failure has contributed to overgeneralization of organizational designs and business strategies and the bipolar arguments concerning both industrial policy and comparative capitalist systems.

Contrary to the claims of the advocates of both industrial policy and free markets, neither industrial policies nor business strategies have been generally successful in changing the persistent sectoral patterns of trade balance since 1960 (Gagnon and Rose, 1995). Examples of such failure range from the efforts of the Japanese Ministry of International Trade and Industry (MITI) in promoting the aircraft, biotechnology, and software sectors (Okimoto, 1989; Callon, 1995), to the endeavor of US government-backed Sematech to enhance photolithography technology (Bottoms, 1993). In the area of firm strategy, General Motors' determination to fight back the Japanese challenge by investing US$77 billion in automation and other high-tech equipment resulted in unexpected failure, while Ford and Chrysler's effort to emulate the Japanese practices of flexible production and total quality management have achieved only limited success (Smith, 1995). Similarly, the successive efforts of Japanese PC makers to penetrate the US market, and of Japanese biotechnology and software companies to gain international competitiveness, have all failed.

This chapter tries to provide detailed analyses of sectoral patterns of US and Japanese competitiveness by using various measures and indicators. Such a comparison does indeed reveal systematic sectoral disparity in the international competitiveness of these two leading countries, revealing American exceptionalism and Japanese uniqueness.

Japanese export competitiveness in high-tech sectors

The high-tech sectors as defined by OECD include aircraft (ISIC 3845), communication equipment (ISIC 3832), drugs & medicines (ISIC 3522), electrical machinery (ISIC 383 less 3832), office & computing machinery (ISIC 3825), and scientific instruments (ISIC 385). When trade performance is considered, as shown in Table 2.1, from 1981 to 1992, Japan's exports averaged about twenty times its imports in communication equipment, four times in electrical machinery and office & computing machinery, and two times in scientific instruments. On the other hand,

Table 2.1 The export/import ratio of Japanese high-tech sectors, 1981–1992

Year	Aircraft	Communication equipment	Drugs & medicines	Electrical machinery	Office & computing machinery	Scientific instruments
1981	0.09	33.97	0.28	5.59	4.00	4.17
1982	0.19	30.58	0.25	5.13	4.44	3.63
1983	0.10	32.93	0.27	5.43	6.18	3.60
1984	0.13	35.74	0.26	5.31	6.51	3.40
1985	0.07	36.07	0.27	5.23	5.89	3.46
1986	0.05	21.80	0.20	4.27	5.59	2.83
1987	0.08	13.54	0.18	3.84	5.19	2.51
1988	0.09	9.24	0.17	3.43	4.25	2.12
1989	0.15	6.99	0.18	3.20	3.44	1.97
1990	0.11	10.57	0.22	2.87	3.26	1.97
1991	0.12	7.96	0.22	2.66	3.20	2.12
1992	0.13	6.57	0.21	2.59	3.13	1.99

Source: Calculations based on Appendix 6.4, *Science & Engineering Indicators 1993*.

Japan's exports in the drugs and medicines sector were only about 20 per cent of its imports despite its relative closed domestic markets. Its exports in the aircraft sector were merely about 10 per cent of its imports.

Table 2.2 Japan's export/import indices of revealed comparative advantage in high-tech sectors, 1981–1992

Year	Aircraft	Communication equipment	Drugs & medicines	Electrical machinery	Office & computing machinery	Scientific instruments
1981	0.06	64.21	0.19	4.39	3.78	3.25
1982	0.12	60.98	0.16	4.01	4.37	2.86
1983	0.07	68.82	0.19	4.43	6.23	2.89
1984	0.08	83.99	0.19	4.70	6.77	2.79
1985	0.05	75.82	0.20	4.72	6.14	2.86
1986	0.04	42.85	0.17	4.19	6.22	2.67
1987	0.06	26.22	0.16	3.93	5.91	2.44
1988	0.08	19.67	0.16	3.63	5.00	2.09
1989	0.12	13.71	0.17	3.37	4.23	1.95
1990	0.09	15.86	0.20	3.07	4.31	1.97
1991	0.11	14.71	0.20	2.85	4.39	2.16
1992	0.12	11.71	0.20	2.77	4.40	2.07

Source: Calculations based on Appendix 6.4, *Science & Engineering Indicators 1993*.

Turning our attention from competitive advantage to comparative advantage of export, when we calculate the export/import indices and the export indices of Japan's revealed comparative advantage, more astonishing evidence for the persistence of the Japanese sectoral pattern appears. As Table 2.2 shows, the export/import indices of revealed Japanese comparative advantage, calculated against all manufacturing sectors in all OECD countries, had been nearly *constant* for all high-tech sectors except communication equipment during 1981–1992. The drastic change in the latter reflects not so much the decline of Japanese competitiveness as the fact that, since the 1980s, Japan has increasingly moved its production facilities of home electronics overseas, to the EU, China, South East Asia, and the USA (Yamashita, 1991; Belderbos, 1995).

Table 2.3 Japan's export indices of revealed comparative advantage in high-tech sectors, 1981–1992

Year	Aircraft	Communication equipment	Drugs & medicines	Electrical machinery	Office & computing machinery	Scientific instruments
1981	0.03	3.53	0.17	1.46	1.14	1.43
1982	0.05	3.46	0.15	1.40	1.27	1.36
1983	0.05	3.56	0.17	1.54	1.48	1.41
1984	0.04	3.59	0.16	1.64	1.52	1.35
1985	0.03	3.61	0.16	1.55	1.49	1.35
1986	0.03	3.46	0.17	1.53	1.63	1.36
1987	0.05	3.28	0.17	1.57	1.67	1.36
1988	0.05	3.22	0.17	1.61	1.70	1.37
1989	0.05	3.02	0.18	1.63	1.69	1.36
1990	0.06	2.40	0.19	1.56	1.76	1.34
1991	0.06	2.62	0.19	1.56	1.82	1.32
1992	0.06	2.49	0.18	1.56	1.87	1.30

Source: Calculations based on Appendix 6.4, *Science & Engineering Indicators 1993*.

Excluding the impact of trade protection on trade performance, as shown in Table 2.3, the export indices of Japanese revealed comparative advantage show similar persistence of the sectoral patterns. Some people, especially those revisionists of international trade (Prestowitz, 1988), may argue that this is due to Japan's prolonged structural trade barriers. A careful calculation refutes this argument. Tables 2.2 and 2.3 combined indicate that the patterns of Japanese comparative advantage in high-tech sectors, as revealed by both the export indices and the export/import indices, were stable and persistent throughout the period 1981–1992. The idiosyncrasies of import protections had little impact here. It is especially important to point out that this astonishing stability of both sectoral competitive and comparative advantages and disadvantages occurred during the period of volatile Japanese exchange rates in the 1980s and 1990s. According to conventional macro international economics, net export, and therefore export/import ratio, is a function of exchange rate, inflation rate, interest rate, and money supply. The relative stability of both export/import ratios and export indices of revealed comparative advantage in Japanese high-tech sectors is too important a fact to be unexplained. It is even more so when we consider all the idiosyncrasies and contingencies of government fiscal and monetary policies, trade and industrial policies, US campaigns to reduce Japanese trade barriers, and the rapid changes in the nature of international competition and industrial organization.

As a late industrializer, Japan has undergone a process of building up its

Table 2.4 Japan's export/import ratios in high-tech products, 1967–1983

Sector/Year	1967	1971	1975	1979	1983
Cellulosic fibers	499.00	1999.00	499.00	180.82	665.67
Calculating & accounting machines	0.58	3.16	15.13	38.22	89.91
Typewriters	1.77	2.14	3.67	8.43	34.71
Internal combustion engines	4.75	9.42	11.58	13.18	23.69
Telephone & telegraphic equipment	5.37	32.90	15.95	17.35	19.41
Synthetic fibers	249.00	82.33	75.92	4.31	12.89
Optical instruments	25.67	18.23	11.74	11.90	10.24
Photographic equipment & supplies	5.87	4.49	5.02	6.60	8.66
Platework & boilers	2.87	2.07	5.60	11.58	6.17
Electronic components	2.72	1.88	2.55	3.56	4.57
Computers	0.53	0.40	0.28	1.44	4.17
Steam engines & turbines	1.42	2.42	2.46	6.17	3.54
Agricultural chemicals	2.07	1.24	1.60	1.65	3.52
Office machinery	0.24	0.34	1.00	1.93	3.12
Scientific instruments	1.30	1.18	1.71	1.87	1.81
Medical instruments	1.79	2.23	1.31	1.31	1.62
Drugs	0.36	0.34	0.27	0.28	0.28
Aircraft engines	0.08	0.03	0.09	0.13	0.17
Aircraft	0.06	0.09	0.03	0.06	0.04

Source: Calculation from Balassa and Noland (1988: 212).

competitive advantages in many sectors, but its disadvantages in some other sectors have continued. As shown in Tables 2.4 and 2.5, in as early as 1967, Japan had obtained both competitive and comparative advantage of export in electronics, optical instruments, and opto-electronics. From 1967 to 1983, in both absolute and comparative terms, Japan successfully transformed its sectors of computers, calculating & accounting machines, and office machinery from a position of disadvantage to that of advantage. Conversely, its weakness in drugs, aircraft, and aircraft engines had continued over the same period. In fact the trade performances in the sectors of drugs and aircraft actually worsened both in absolute and comparative terms. As shown in Tables 2.6 and 2.7, measured in global export share, export indices of revealed comparative advantage, and export/import ratios, Japan has maintained its sectoral patterns of trade performance up to 1998.

The astonishingly stable sectoral pattern from 1967 to 1998 raises fundamental questions as to why such a persistence exists and how Japan has successfully transformed its competitive disadvantage in some sectors, but could not improve its weak position in some others, despite all the coordinated efforts that took place in both the private and public sectors.

US export competitiveness in high-tech sectors

The US export performances in high-tech sectors are somewhat the opposite of Japan's. As shown in Table 2.8, the export/import performances of US high-tech sectors show a similar pattern of persistence. In 1992, US exports were 4.08 times its imports in aircraft, 1.67 times in drugs and medicines, 1.38 times in scientific

Table 2.5 Japan's export indices of revealed comparative advantage in high-tech products, 1967–1983

Sector/Year	1967	1971	1975	1979	1983
Calculating & accounting machines	0.99	4.33	7.18	10.76	10.98
Optical instruments	11.45	8.82	8.08	9.10	7.00
Photographic equipment & supplies	4.65	3.43	4.03	5.73	6.20
Typewriters	1.94	2.11	1.70	2.61	5.58
Cellulosic fibers	5.50	4.51	5.01	4.20	3.83
Electronic components	2.08	1.68	2.07	3.16	3.45
Telephone & telegraphic equipment	1.01	1.90	1.99	2.49	3.35
Computers	0.84	0.42	0.68	0.96	2.97
Synthetic fibers	4.73	3.61	5.17	3.27	2.86
Internal combustion engines	1.02	1.48	1.77	2.48	2.69
Platework & boilers	2.06	2.62	2.53	2.33	2.27
Scientific instruments	1.38	1.10	1.19	1.95	1.65
Medical instruments	1.28	1.44	1.42	1.57	1.51
Office machinery	0.89	0.73	0.75	1.37	1.39
Agricultural chemicals	1.37	0.91	0.82	0.74	1.06
Drugs	0.67	0.62	0.43	0.52	0.44
Aircraft engines	0.10	0.04	0.07	0.09	0.15
Aircraft	0.38	0.17	0.04	0.06	0.05

Source: Balassa and Noland (1988: 210).

instruments, but were only about 30 per cent in communication equipment, 66 per cent in office & computing machinery, and 75 per cent in electrical machinery.

Turning from competitive advantage to the comparative advantage relative to OECD countries, as shown in Table 2.9 the US sectoral pattern of competitiveness continued. Compared with other OECD countries, however, the USA's comparative export/import advantage in the aircraft sector is smaller than its absolute level, largely owing to the competitiveness of the British and French aircraft sectors (Jin, 1998). Similarly, the US comparative export/import disadvantage in communication equipment is also smaller than its absolute level, owing to a similar competitive disadvantage in Italy, Germany, the UK, and France (Jin, 1998).

As shown in Table 2.10, US comparative export performances in all high-tech sectors are better than its comparative export/import ratios, largely owing to the high propensity of imports, low transaction costs, and the ease of market penetration in its domestic market. Except for a disadvantage in communication equipment, the USA has a comparative export advantage in most other high-tech sectors. Using data from *Science & Engineering Indicators 1998*, Tables 2.11 and 2.12 show US and Japanese export/import ratios and export indices of revealed comparative advantage in high-tech sectors during 1980–1995. In the calculation, a total of 68 countries and all manufacturing are used for world total exports and sectoral exports. Although slightly different in value from our previous results owing to different sectoral definitions and comparison bases, the distinct patterns of sectoral competitiveness continued up to 1995. A notable exception is the difference in the export comparative advantage of the *communications* equipment sector, which is defined more broadly than the *communication* equipment sector of the 1993 edition, which is limited to ISIC 3832.

Table 2.6 Japan's global export share and export indices in high-tech sectors, 1995–1998

Industrial sector	STIC code	Global export share				Rank (1998)	Export indices		
		1995	1996	1997	1998		1996	1997	1998
Sound/TV recorders etc.	763	28.8	25.1	27.2	36.7	1	3.22	3.53	5.13
Photo equipment	881	40.6	37.8	33.6	31.5	1	4.85	4.36	4.41
Machine tools remove mtrial	731	33.9	32.6	33.6	31.1	1	4.18	4.36	4.35
Office machines	751	27.4	25.3	26.9	24.7	1	3.25	3.49	3.45
Photo supplies	882	24.7	23.3	22.5	21.5	1	2.99	2.92	3.01
Optical instruments	871	32.0	28.4	25.2	21.3	1	3.65	3.27	2.98
Optical fibers	884	22.8	20.6	20.1	20.1	1	2.64	2.61	2.81
Electrical equipment	778	19.4	18.1	18.3	18.0	1	2.32	2.37	2.52
Passenger cars etc.	781	18.3	16.5	18.6	18.5	3	2.12	2.41	2.59
Transistors/valves etc.	776	25.0	21.3	18.4	15.9	2	2.73	2.39	2.22
Internal combust engines	713	24.2	20.8	18.1	15.2	2	2.67	2.35	2.13
Special indust machn nes	728	19.4	17.9	18.2	15.0	3	2.30	2.36	2.10
Non-electrical tools/acc mach	749	19.7	18.1	17.5	14.7	2	2.32	2.27	2.06
Office equipment parts	759	19.5	17.9	16.2	14.6	2	2.30	2.10	2.04
Mtl m-tools w/o mtl-rmvl	733	22.8	21.5	19.9	14.4	3	2.76	2.58	2.01
Electrical circuit equipment	772	18.6	16.4	15.8	13.9	3	2.11	2.05	1.94
Metal machine tool parts	735	11.3	11.0	12.2	11.0	3	1.41	1.58	1.54
Mechanical handling equip	744	15.8	15.0	14.0	10.7	3	1.93	1.82	1.50
Measure/control app nes	874	14.6	13.7	13.2	10.7	3	1.76	1.71	1.50
Computer equipment	752	14.4	11.9	12.2	10.5	3	1.53	1.58	1.47
Motor veh parts/access	784	16.5	14.4	12.1	10.3	3	1.85	1.57	1.44
Telecommunications equip	764	16.8	13.0	11.6	9.3	3	1.67	1.50	1.30
Medical equipment	872	12.2	10.1	9.8	8.8	4	1.30	1.27	1.23
Aircraft/spacecraft	792	0.9	1.1	1.5	1.6	7	0.14	0.19	0.22
Pharmaceut exc medicament	541	4.6	4.3	4.0	3.7	10	0.55	0.52	0.52
Weapons	891	1.2	0.9	0.9	1.1	11	0.12	0.12	0.15

Source: Calculation based on the COMTRADE databases of the United Nations Statistics Division.

When world export shares of the top six advanced nations are considered, as shown in Table 2.13, during 1980–1995, the USA maintained its leadership position in aircraft, office and computing machinery, and communications equipment. In drugs and medicines, it had been a solid second after Germany. On the other hand, although Japan had been second in communications equipment, and office and computing machines, its export shares in both sectors declined during 1990–1995 largely owing to the collapse of the bubble economy and the American revival. As expected, Japan's export share took last place in aircraft, and drugs and medicines.

Japanese strength and US weakness in the export competitiveness of automobiles, mechatronics, and opto-electronics

As the sector where the Fordist regime of mass production originated, the US automobile sector had been a symbol of American competitiveness until the late

Table 2.7 Japan's export/import ratio of high-tech manufacturing sectors, 1995–1998

STIC – Industrial sectors	1995	1996	1997	1998
713 – Internal combust engines	23.994	20.946	16.446	13.130
731 – Machine-tools remove mtrial	11.664	9.186	9.081	9.989
781 – Passenger cars etc.	4.215	3.943	6.143	9.130
784 – Motor veh parts/access	13.514	10.682	8.564	8.008
744 – Mechanical handling equip	11.122	9.651	8.779	7.442
737 – Metalworking machine nes	11.353	8.254	9.659	7.436
763 – Sound/TV recorders etc.	5.936	4.145	4.918	7.285
733 – Mattel machine-tools w/o mtl-rmvl	11.119	12.003	9.098	6.945
751 – Office machines	7.308	5.410	6.314	6.347
882 – Photo supplies	5.218	5.209	6.088	6.262
772 – Electrical circuit equipment	6.577	5.178	4.712	4.768
749 – Non-electrical tools/acc mach	8.152	6.592	5.435	4.495
778 – Electrical equipment	4.831	3.962	4.080	4.409
728 – Special industrial machn nes	6.735	5.012	4.660	4.055
881 – Photo equipment	5.044	4.373	3.825	3.904
884 – Optical fibers	3.616	2.859	2.841	2.669
776 – Transistors/valves etc.	3.332	2.693	2.611	2.634
735 – Metal machine tool parts	2.945	2.415	2.504	2.430
745 – Non-electrical machines nes	2.799	2.259	2.243	2.247
759 – Office equipment parts	3.082	2.450	2.313	2.228
764 – Telecommunications equip	3.133	2.105	2.308	2.099
874 – Measure/control app nes	2.197	1.829	1.882	1.641
762 – Radio broadcast receiver	2.277	1.668	1.663	1.623
752 – Computer equipment	1.646	1.278	1.538	1.595
872 – Medical equipment	0.828	0.672	0.701	0.667
541 – Pharmaceutics exc medicament	0.489	0.506	0.531	0.571
891 – Weapons	0.260	0.299	0.290	0.451
792 – Aircraft/spacecraft	0.219	0.346	0.363	0.332

Source: Calculation based on the COMTRADE databases of the United Nations Statistics Division.

1970s. Classic works by such authors as Chandler (1977, 1990) had acclaimed the automobile sector as an ideal model for the efficiency of the mass production paradigm. However, beginning in the late 1970s, this very sector has been used as an exemplar to typify the rise of lean production in Japan and the decline of US competitiveness (Womack *et al.*, 1990). According to Jin (1998), the export/import ratio of the US motor vehicles and car bodies sector plunged from 0.53 in 1975 to 0.07 in 1987, then recovered somewhat to 0.29 in 1992. Despite all the hype of revival, as shown in Table 2.14 from 1995 to 1998 the export/import ratio of the US passenger car sector actually declined from 0.244 to a mere 0.186, showing a sustained weakness.

When the global export share of passenger cars is considered, as shown in Table 2.15, in 1998 the USA was ranked only seventh, with a mere 5.6 per cent, down from 7 per cent in 1995. The export indices of revealed comparative advantage further indicate US weakness in passenger cars, which declined from 0.57 in 1995 to 0.44 in 1998.

Table 2.8 The export/import ratio of US high-tech sectors, 1981–1992

Year	Aircraft	Communication equipment	Drugs & medicines	Office & computing machinery	Electrical machinery	Scientific instruments
1981	5.21	0.42	2.46	2.67	0.99	1.68
1982	4.28	0.41	2.60	2.31	1.06	1.74
1983	5.80	0.32	2.21	1.67	0.91	1.48
1984	3.59	0.24	1.82	1.30	0.72	1.20
1985	3.96	0.22	1.62	1.25	0.67	1.09
1986	3.34	0.21	1.54	1.02	0.64	0.73
1987	3.95	0.24	1.34	0.98	0.64	0.96
1988	3.87	0.29	1.28	1.02	0.68	1.05
1989	4.02	0.33	1.71	0.88	0.71	1.18
1990	4.92	0.35	1.74	0.82	0.75	1.28
1991	4.51	0.36	1.68	0.75	0.76	1.36
1992	4.08	0.29	1.67	0.66	0.75	1.38

Source: Calculations based on Appendix 6.4, *Science & Engineering Indicators 1993*.

Table 2.9 US export/import indices of revealed comparative advantage in high-tech sectors, 1981–1992

Year	Aircraft	Communication equipment	Drugs & medicine	Electrical machinery	Office & computing machinery	Scientific instruments
1981	3.54	0.79	1.69	0.78	2.53	1.30
1982	2.68	0.82	1.64	0.83	2.27	1.37
1983	4.12	0.68	1.59	0.74	1.68	1.19
1984	2.35	0.56	1.35	0.64	1.35	0.99
1985	2.73	0.46	1.23	0.60	1.30	0.90
1986	2.59	0.41	1.33	0.63	1.13	0.92
1987	2.84	0.46	1.22	0.66	1.12	0.94
1988	3.26	0.62	1.21	0.72	1.20	1.03
1989	3.22	0.64	1.57	0.74	1.09	1.17
1990	3.94	0.53	1.60	0.80	1.09	1.28
1991	3.96	0.66	1.58	0.81	1.02	1.39
1992	3.89	0.51	1.58	0.80	0.92	1.44

Source: Calculations based on Appendix 6.4, *Science & Engineering Indicators 1993*.

The US weakness in the passenger car sector is also reflected in the productivity gap with its Japanese counterpart. According to the McKinsey Global Institute (1993), in 1987 Japanese productivity in auto parts was 4 per cent higher than that of the USA, increasing to 24 per cent in 1990. In auto cars, the productivity gap also enlarged from 14 per cent in 1987 to 16 per cent in 1990. According to another estimate by Pilkington (1998), in 1990 value-added per motor-vehicle employee in Japan was $107,874, 20.9 per cent higher than the US figure of $89,219.

Tables 2.7, 2.8, 2.14, and 2.15 combined reveal persistent Japanese strength and US weakness of export performance in TV receivers, sound/TV recorders, office machines, photo equipment, optical equipment parts, and machine tools. When

Table 2.10 US export indices of revealed comparative advantage in high-tech sectors, 1981–1992

Year	Aircraft	Communication equipment	Drugs & medicine	Electrical machinery	Office & computing machinery	Scientific instruments
1981	3.45	0.71	1.01	1.10	2.17	1.39
1982	2.99	0.78	1.00	1.32	2.26	1.51
1983	3.53	0.76	1.19	1.40	2.25	1.49
1984	3.09	0.68	1.20	1.42	2.21	1.43
1985	3.89	0.69	1.17	1.28	2.10	1.37
1986	4.17	0.70	1.20	1.29	1.98	1.36
1987	4.41	0.72	1.06	1.28	1.89	1.27
1988	3.45	0.78	1.04	1.23	1.81	1.21
1989	3.20	0.83	0.83	1.23	1.65	1.29
1990	3.49	0.64	0.84	1.26	1.64	1.32
1991	3.26	0.72	0.84	1.22	1.60	1.33
1992	3.22	0.64	0.84	1.24	1.54	1.37

Source: Calculations based on Appendix 6.4, *Science & Engineering Indicators 1993*.

Table 2.11 Export/import ratios of US and Japanese high-tech sectors, 1980–1995

Year	Aircraft USA	Aircraft Japan	Office & computing machinery USA	Office & computing machinery Japan	Communications equipment USA	Communications equipment Japan	Drugs & medicines USA	Drugs & medicines Japan
1980	5.45	0.08	3.37	2.71	0.72	16.7	3.79	0.34
1981	4.26	0.10	2.91	2.87	0.58	19.0	3.10	0.32
1982	3.60	0.19	2.38	3.55	0.54	18.9	2.69	0.29
1983	3.80	0.12	1.63	5.30	0.52	16.5	2.52	0.33
1984	2.48	0.14	1.37	6.49	0.42	16.6	2.21	0.32
1985	2.42	0.09	1.31	5.80	0.39	18.5	1.99	0.34
1986	2.49	0.08	1.18	6.21	0.44	14.5	2.24	0.31
1987	3.50	0.11	1.14	6.01	0.50	10.6	2.12	0.29
1988	3.10	0.14	1.13	5.47	0.61	8.84	2.23	0.26
1989	3.54	0.19	1.00	4.83	0.61	7.07	1.86	0.29
1990	3.55	0.12	1.03	4.62	0.76	6.18	1.89	0.35
1991	3.85	0.15	1.00	4.29	0.80	6.26	1.72	0.37
1992	3.75	0.14	0.90	4.36	0.75	5.79	1.62	0.38
1993	3.27	0.14	0.77	3.68	0.77	4.24	1.38	0.32
1994	3.21	0.14	0.77	2.87	0.82	3.34	1.32	0.29
1995	2.84	0.16	0.79	2.50	0.88	2.87	1.26	0.30

Source: Calculation based on Appendix 6.4, *Science & Engineering Indicators 1998*.

labor productivity is compared, according to the McKinsey Global Institute (1993), in 1990 Japanese labor productivity in consumer electronics was 15 per cent higher than that of the USA. Comparing our findings with Porter's (1990) findings of Table

Table 2.12 Export indices of comparative advantage of US and Japanese high-tech sectors, 1980–1995

Year	Aircraft		Office & computing machinery		Communications equipment		Drugs & medicines	
	USA	Japan	USA	Japan	USA	Japan	USA	Japan
1980	3.43	0.03	2.53	0.92	0.87	1.50	1.08	0.20
1981	3.24	0.03	2.62	0.90	0.85	1.65	1.07	0.19
1982	2.78	0.05	2.69	1.07	0.92	1.73	1.09	0.17
1983	3.23	0.04	2.66	1.32	1.18	2.03	1.31	0.19
1984	2.83	0.04	2.61	1.40	1.15	2.30	1.35	0.17
1985	3.61	0.03	2.52	1.32	1.10	2.22	1.31	0.18
1986	3.83	0.03	2.38	1.53	1.14	2.17	1.40	0.19
1987	4.32	0.05	2.24	1.60	1.11	2.10	1.26	0.20
1988	3.84	0.06	2.16	1.70	1.17	1.99	1.25	0.20
1989	3.55	0.07	1.85	1.67	1.12	2.07	1.02	0.22
1990	3.69	0.06	1.79	1.67	1.17	1.77	0.99	0.23
1991	3.25	0.06	1.74	1.66	1.17	1.79	0.94	0.24
1992	3.36	0.07	1.67	1.72	1.21	2.10	0.94	0.26
1993	3.29	0.07	1.59	1.73	1.30	2.28	0.88	0.24
1994	3.20	0.08	1.57	1.65	1.31	2.39	0.84	0.23
1995	2.58	0.09	1.59	1.55	1.39	2.53	0.80	0.24

Source: Calculation based on Appendix 6.4, *Science & Engineering Indicators 1998*.

2.16 we notice a mirror image of the persistence of sectoral patterns throughout the 1980s and 1990s. Following Kodama (1991) and Adams (1995), the term opto-mechatronics is used to summarize the major technological characteristics for products of the sectors of microelectronics, communications equipment, and machine tools and robotics, whose technological competitiveness is increasingly the result of the technology fusion of optical, mechanical, and electronic technologies. Table 2.16 further shows Japanese dominance in opto-mechatronics and US strength in aircraft, chemicals, and weapons.

The composition of direct foreign investment (FDI) reveals similar patterns of Japanese and American comparative advantage. As shown in Table 2.17, in the early 1990s Japanese investment in transport equipment was 17.2 per cent of its total accumulative FDI in the EC as compared to a mere 11.1 per cent for the USA. In the electrical and electronics machinery sector, the numbers were 31.7 per cent vs. 6.7 per cent. Conversely, in the processing industries of food products and chemicals, the Japanese FDI shares are only 36 per cent and 50 per cent respectively those of the USA.

Calculating FDI ratios of various sectors of information technology, which is the division of sales of outward FDI by that of inward FDI, we get a similar sectoral pattern of US competitive rates. As shown in Table 2.18, the annual growth rate of revenues generated by US outward FDI was only 0.94 per cent in consumer electronics and communications during 1987–1994, as compared to 6.8 per cent of its inward FDI, of which Japanese firms accounted 26 per cent of sales (OECD, 1997: 84). US FDI ratio in this sector actually declined from 0.58 in 1987 to 0.39 in 1994.

Table 2.13 World export share of top six countries in high-tech sectors (percentages)

Aircraft

Year	USA	UK	France	Germany	Italy	Japan
1980	49.0	25.3	5.1	8.0	1.5	0.35
1985	37.6	21.7	8.2	15.4	3.6	0.40
1990	46.8	13.2	9.2	10.6	3.8	0.67
1995	32.4	15.6	15.4	12.7	3.0	0.69

Office & computing machines

Year	USA	Japan	UK	Germany	France	Italy
1980	36.2	10.7	8.3	11.3	6.2	6.5
1985	26.3	17.4	8.7	11.3	5.5	4.6
1990	22.8	18.5	7.9	6.6	3.9	3.0
1995	20.0	12.3	7.3	4.9	3.4	2.4

Communications equipment

Year	USA	Japan	Germany	UK	France	Italy
1980	12.5	31.2	10.1	3.5	3.6	2.2
1985	11.5	36.4	8.9	3.8	4.0	2.3
1990	14.8	25.8	6.9	4.8	3.6	1.8
1995	17.6	15.3	5.9	5.2	3.3	1.6

Drugs and medicines

Year	Germany	USA	UK	France	Italy	Japan
1980	15.7	15.5	9.8	9.4	4.7	2.4
1985	16.4	13.7	9.9	9.7	5.5	2.3
1990	15.1	12.5	10.2	9.2	3.7	2.5
1995	14.6	10.0	9.4	8.7	4.7	1.9

Source: Calculation based on Appendix 6.4, *Science & Engineering Indicators 1998*.

Conversely, during the same period, US FDI ratio increased from 5.26 to 7.86 in computers, 2.21 to 2.69 in electronic components, and 0.69 to 3.10 in computer services, reflecting increasing US strength in these sectors. Comparing these FDI ratios with the export/import ratio in Table 2.8, it is clear that the decline of US trade performance in the office & computing machinery was partly caused by its strong outward FDI.

Buigues and Jacquemin (1994) provided a much broader comparison of US and Japanese export share and FDI share in the EC markets. As summarized in Figures 2.1 and 2.2, in the EC market, the USA has a high export share in chemicals, machinery, and data processing, and a high FDI share in food products, but it was low in terms of both export share and FDI share in metal products, electrical/ electronic equipment, and transport equipment. Conversely, Japan had a high export share in electrical and electronic equipment and a high FDI share in automobiles and machinery, but was low in both export share and FDI share in the processing industries of food products, chemicals, and papers.

The comparisons of Japanese strength and US weakness in automobiles and opto-mechatronics discussed above constitute a refutation of both the trade protection argument advanced by some mainstream neoclassical economists, such as Edward Lincoln (1990, 1993), and the structural barrier argument put forward by the

Table 2.14 US export/import ratio of top manufacturing sectors, 1995–1998

STIC – Industrial sectors	1995	1996	1997	1998
891 – Weapons	5.909	7.020	5.141	4.165
792 – Aircraft/spacecraft	3.854	4.063	4.017	3.921
874 – Measure/control app nes	1.793	1.812	1.858	1.699
872 – Medical equipment	1.686	1.780	1.851	1.626
541 – Pharmaceut exc medicament	1.516	1.289	1.339	1.448
774 – Medical etc. el diag equi	1.497	1.635	1.550	1.412
735 – Metal machine tool parts	1.118	1.333	1.260	1.244
728 – Special indust machn nes	1.346	1.428	1.390	1.177
784 – Motor veh parts/access	1.100	1.115	1.240	1.164
745 – Non-electrical machines nes	1.083	1.078	1.127	1.055
882 – Photo supplies	0.899	1.076	1.093	1.032
764 – Telecomms equipment nes	0.910	0.993	1.104	0.935
776 – Transistors/valves etc.	0.607	0.673	0.817	0.913
744 – Mechanical handling equip	1.057	1.161	1.116	0.901
772 – Electric circuit equipment	0.810	0.874	0.884	0.888
749 – Non-electrical tools/acc mach	0.488	0.643	0.711	0.851
737 – Metalworking machine nes	0.862	0.684	0.958	0.833
713 – Internal combust engines	0.762	0.724	0.856	0.816
871 – Optical instruments	0.736	0.858	0.937	0.813
778 – Electrical equipment	0.836	0.857	0.870	0.778
884 – Optical fibers	0.505	0.579	0.669	0.685
759 – Office equip parts	0.656	0.751	0.759	0.645
733 – Mtl m-tools w/o mtl-rmvl	0.607	0.660	0.625	0.531
783 – Road motor vehicles nes	0.632	0.560	0.566	0.523
752 – Computer equipment	0.560	0.535	0.506	0.474
731 – Machine-tools remove mtrial	0.630	0.600	0.535	0.410
881 – Photo equipment	0.383	0.367	0.318	0.295
751 – Office machines	0.190	0.207	0.201	0.221
781 – Passenger cars etc.	0.244	0.242	0.223	0.186
761 – Television receivers	0.183	0.176	0.212	0.150
763 – Sound/TV recorders etc.	0.107	0.106	0.127	0.104
762 – Radio broadcast receiver	0.100	0.119	0.124	0.094

Source: Calculation based on the COMTRADE databases of the United Nations Statistics Division.

revisionists, such as Prestowitz (1988). The sustained bilateral US trade deficit with Japan in the automobile and home electronics sectors is more than the simple result of unfair Japanese practices of import protection and its unfair structural barriers against imports. Japan enjoys competitive advantage over the USA in these two sectors in almost all indicators of competitiveness, ranging from share of global export markets, productivity, share of export and FDI in the third market, export/ import ratio, export indices of comparative advantage, and FDI ratio.

Table 2.15 US global export share and export indices of top manufacturing sectors, 1995–1998

Industrial sector	STIC code	Global export share				Rank (1998)	Export indices		
		1995	1996	1997	1998		1996	1997	1998
Aircraft/spacecraft	792	35.7	41.0	43.6	46.6	1	3.47	3.46	3.70
Weapons	891	55.5	56.4	52.6	41.6	1	4.78	4.17	3.30
Medical equipment	872	36.6	37.8	39.2	38.4	1	3.20	3.11	3.05
Measure/control app nes	874	25.2	25.9	28.1	28.0	1	2.19	2.23	2.22
Metal machine tool parts	735	18.8	22.6	23.4	22.6	1	1.91	1.86	1.80
Motor veh parts/access	784	19.5	19.7	21.9	22.1	1	1.67	1.74	1.76
Office equipment parts	759	18.8	19.7	20.3	18.5	1	1.67	1.61	1.47
Pharmaceut exc medicament	541	16.3	16.5	17.3	18.0	1	1.40	1.37	1.43
Transistors/valves etc.	776	15.2	15.4	17.1	17.7	1	1.30	1.36	1.41
Internal combust engines	713	16.1	15.7	17.8	17.5	1	1.33	1.41	1.39
Telecommunications equip	764	15.7	15.4	16.4	15.5	1	1.30	1.30	1.23
Computer equipment	752	16.7	16.0	15.4	14.3	1	1.35	1.22	1.14
Special indust machn nes	728	15.5	16.2	17.9	16.6	2	1.37	1.42	1.32
Optical fibers	884	12.2	13.5	14.3	16.0	2	1.14	1.13	1.27
Photo supplies	882	13.7	15.5	15.8	15.4	2	1.31	1.25	1.22
Mechanical handling equip	744	12.5	13.2	14.9	14.6	2	1.12	1.18	1.16
Electrical circuit equipment	772	12.8	17.6	14.5	14.2	2	1.49	1.15	1.13
Electrical equipment	778	11.9	12.9	13.8	13.4	2	1.09	1.09	1.06
Optical instruments	871	13.9	16.3	15.5	13.7	3	1.38	1.23	1.09
Machine tools remove mtrial	731	12.3	11.8	12.5	10.4	3	1.00	0.99	0.83
Non-electrical tools/acc mach	749	8.2	8.4	9.3	10.4	3	0.71	0.74	0.83
Mtl m-tools w/o mtl-rmvl	733	8.4	9.1	9.7	9.7	4	0.77	0.77	0.77
Photo equipment	881	9.5	9.0	8.5	8.6	4	0.76	0.67	0.68
Office machines	751	6.1	6.9	6.6	7.7	5	0.58	0.52	0.61
Passenger cars etc.	781	7.0	6.7	6.4	5.6	7	0.57	0.51	0.44
Sound/TV recorders etc.	763	3.5	4.2	5.4	4.6	6	0.36	0.43	0.37

Source: Calculation based on the COMTRADE databases of the United Nations Statistics Division.

US strength and Japanese weakness in biotechnology, chemicals, food and beverages, and petroleum products

Table 2.19 lists the numbers of firms and percentages of consolidated worldwide sales accounted for by the twelve largest companies in manufacturing industries, by country of corporate headquarters in 1993. It reveals the same sectoral patterns of national competitiveness found above. In terms of both the number of firms and the share of global sales, Japan is Number One in electrical equipment and electronics, iron and steel, non-electrical machinery, textiles, and tires and rubber. It is second to the USA in autos and trucks, and computers and office equipment. Japan, however, has no firms listed among the top twelve in aerospace, food and beverage products, and petroleum products. Japan has only 6 per cent of sales in pharmaceuticals, 15 per cent in chemicals, and 17 per cent in paper and paper products.

Conversely, the USA is strong in almost all areas where Japan is weak. In terms of the numbers of firms and their sales, the USA is Number One in aerospace, food and

Table 2.16 Major clustering Japanese and US manufacturing sectors with high world export shares

Japanese share of world exports (1985)	(%)	US share of world exports (1985)	(%)
Automobiles		*Aircraft*	
Motorcycles	82.0	Commercial aircraft and helicopters	79.4
Motorcycle parts and accessories	53.4	Aircraft internal combustion	
Track-laying tractors	51.8	engines and parts	67.4
Self-propelled dozers	50.6	Aircraft gas turbine engines	62.4
Motor radio receivers	42.5	Aircraft parts	56.6
New buses or truck tiers	39.1	Aircraft engines and motor parts	41.6
Buses	38.7		
Self-propelled shovels, excavators	38.4	*Chemicals*	
Passenger motor vehicles	30.8	Photo film	81.9
		Other manufactured fertilizers	69.6
Opto-mechatronics		Nitrogen-phosphate fertilizer	57.3
TV image and sound recorders	80.7	Radioactive materials	57.1
Calculating machines	69.7	Piezoelectric crystals	50.7
Mounted optical elements	67.5	Pharmaceuticals other than medicaments	41.8
Photo and thermocopy apparatus	65.9	Polyethylene in rods	39.9
Still cameras and flash apparatus	62.2	Polyvinyl chloride in rods	39.1
Cash registers, accounting engines	62.0	Artificial fur products	38.9
Electric gramophones	59.0	Other inorganic chemicals	30.4
Microphones, loudspeakers	55.7		
Color TV receivers	49.5	*Weapons*	
Portable radio receivers	48.7	War firearms, ammunition	62.7
Other radio receivers	47.9	Warships and boats	53.1
Electric typewriters	45.0		
TV picture tubes	42.2	*Scientific/Professional Equipment*	
Prepared sound recording media	41.5	Measuring, drawing, instrument parts	60.0
ADP peripheral units	37.9	Electromedical equipment	46.6
Other electronic tubes	36.5	Medical instruments	20.1
Clocks, watch movements, cases	33.8		

Source: Adapted from Porter (1990).

beverage products, petroleum products, pharmaceuticals, and paper and paper products.

When another data set of high technology is used, as shown in Table 2.20, in 1994 the US worldwide exports were 68.9 times its imports in nuclear technology, 13.82 times in biotechnology, 6.95 times in software, 5.04 times in weapons, 3.06 times in aerospace, 1.80 times in CIM, and 1.37 times in material design. US exports in opto-electronics were, however, only 37 per cent of its imports. When bilateral trade between the USA and Japan in high technology is considered, the contrasting sectoral patterns are even more salient. In 1994, US bilateral export/import ratio with Japan was 356 in nuclear technology, 189 in biotechnology, 20.7 in weapons, 10 in software, 7 in aerospace, but was only 0.11 in opto-electronics, 0.30 in computer and telecommunications, 0.32 in electronics, 0.42 in CIM, and 0.62 in material design. The bilateral disparity of competitiveness here is even more polarized, which

Table 2.17 Cumulative Japanese and US FDI in Europe, by industry, early 1990s

	Japan (Mar. 1992)		USA (Dec. 1990)		Japan (%)/
	$m.	%	$m.	%	USA (%)
1. Manufacturing industries					
Processing industries					
Food products	573	3.8	9,437	10.6	0.36
Chemical & allied products	1,640	10.9	19,262	21.6	0.50
Metals	693	4.5	4,131	4.6	0.98
Textiles & clothing	1,022	6.7	1,042	1.2	5.58
Wood-related products	94	0.6	313	0.4	1.50
Fabricating industries					
Electrical/electronic equipment	4,823	31.7	6,013	6.7	4.73
Non-electrical machinery	2,362	15.5	19,105	21.4	0.72
Transport equipment	2,618	17.2	9,870	11.1	1.55
Other products	1,406	9.2	19,917	22.4	0.41
TOTAL MANUFACTURING	15,230	100.0	89,090	100.0	1.00
2. Other industries					
Services					
Wholesale trade & commerce	8,329	15.6	24,875	18.6	0.84
Banking, finance, insurance & real estate	35,415	66.3	74,370	55.7	1.19
Other services	5,583	10.5	6,159	4.6	2.28
Other industry	4,079	7.6	28,060	21.1	0.36
TOTAL OTHER INDUSTRY	53,406	100.0	133,464	100.0	1.00
TOTAL ALL INDUSTRY	68,636	100.0	224,554	100.0	1.00

Source: Dunning (1994, p. 60).

is further evidenced by US export/import ratios with the rest of the world excluding Japan. In the sectors of nuclear technology, US export/import ratio with the rest of the world excluding Japan is 34.7, much lower than US/world ratio of 68.9, indicating that the US strength with the rest of the world is weaker than its strength with Japan in nuclear technology. In other words, in this sector Japan is not only weaker than the USA, but is also weaker than the rest of the world. This is true in the sectors of biotechnology, software, weapons, and aerospace as well.

Conversely, while the US bilateral export/import ratio with Japan in CIM is only 0.42, its ratio with the rest of the world excluding Japan is a high 4.7, indicating that even though the USA is weaker than Japan in CIM, it is very strong in comparison with the rest of the world. Similarly, while weaker than Japan, the USA is competitive in material design, life science, and electronics with the rest of the world. It is only in opto-electronics that the USA is behind not only Japan but also the rest of the world. When country share of OECD export is considered, as shown in Table 2.21, the USA and Japan show contrasting patterns of export shares in various high technologies that are consistent with their patterns of export/import ratios.

Table 2.18 Revenues generated by US outward and inward FDI, 1987–1994 (billion US$)

	1987			1994			Outward FDI annual growth rate %	Inward FDI annual growth rate %
	Outward FDI	Inward FDI	FDI ratio	Outward FDI	Inward FDI	FDI ratio		
Computer & office machinery	22.1	4.2	5.26	79.4	10.1	7.86	20.0	13.4
Consumer electronics & communications	7.4	12.8	0.58	7.9	20.3	0.39	0.94	6.8
Electronic components	9.5	4.3	2.21	30.1	11.2	2.69	17.9	14.7
Computer services	1.1	1.6	0.69	18.3	5.9	3.10	49.4	20.5

Source: Calculation from OECD (1997a, pp. 80 and 84).

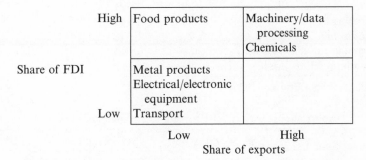

Figure 2.1 The relationship between US exports and FDI to the EC, by industry, 1989
Source: Adapted from Buigues and Jacquemin (1994).

	High	Textiles Machinery Transport	Electrical/electronic equipment
Share of FDI			
	Low	Chemicals Food Products Paper Non-ferrous metal	
		Low	High

Share of exports

Figure 2.2 The relationship between Japanese exports and FDI to the EC, by industry, 1989
Source: Adapted from Buigues and Jacquemin (1994).

Extending our observation to 1995 and 1996, Table 2.22 reveals a sustained US pattern of high-technology competitiveness.

In the chemical industry, according to Sachwald (1995), North America held 23.3 per cent of world production, while the EC represented 28.1 per cent and Japan 14.6 per cent. In 1990, the Japanese share in world chemical exports was only 5.5 per cent, lower not only than that of the USA, but also that of Germany, France, the UK, and

Table 2.19 Numbers of firms and percentages of consolidated sales accounted for by the twelve largest companies worldwide in each industry, by country of corporate headquarters, 1993

	USA		Japan	
	# of firms	% of sales	# of firms	% of sales
Aerospace	9	79	0	0
Computer and office equipment	7	65	4	32
Paper and paper products	7	63	2	17
Food and beverage products	7	56	0	0
Pharmaceuticals	6	50	1	6
Petroleum products	5	46	0	0
Autos and trucks	3	39	4	33
Textile	3	23	6	48
Non-electrical machinery	3	21	5	41
Tires and rubber	3	19	3	37
Non-ferrous metals	2	13	2	14
Electrical equipment and electronics	1	12	6	52
Iron and steel	0	0	5	49

Source: Adapted from Franko (1996).

Table 2.20 US export/import performance in high technologies

Sectors	USA/World					USA/Japan					USA/the rest
	1990	1991	1992	1993	1994	1990	1991	1992	1993	1994	1994
All technologies	1.60	1.61	1.49	1.34	1.23	0.63	0.63	0.59	0.49	0.5	
Nuclear technology	280	435	289	172	68.9	405	581	370	188	356	34.7
Biotechnology	20.6	14.5	15.3	14.8	13.8	128	93	96	107	189	11.4
Software	8.44	8.29	6.97	6.98	6.95	6.40	5.44	6.20	8.00	10.0	6.8
Weapons	5.30	5.07	5.00	4.54	5.04	41.9	38.7	32.3	32.3	20.7	4.5
Aerospace	3.45	3.46	3.35	3.24	3.06	8.37	6.10	7.59	6.05	6.99	2.9
CIM	1.85	1.82	2.03	1.80	1.80	0.54	0.53	0.43	0.36	0.42	4.7
Life science	1.42	1.28	1.21	1.32	1.42	0.92	0.81	0.8	0.94	1.12	1.5
Material design	6.13	5.92	1.49	1.45	1.37	0.91	1.08	0.67	0.79	0.62	2.2
Electronics	0.69	0.72	1.08	1.01	1.00	0.34	0.33	0.35	0.32	0.32	1.3
Computer & telecommunication	1.08	1.10	1.02	0.92	0.86	0.34	0.38	0.34	0.29	0.32	1.1
Opto-electronics	0.46	0.31	0.24	0.28	0.37	0.14	0.09	0.03	0.04	0.11	0.7

Source: Calculations based on data from *Science & Engineering Indicators 1996*.

the Netherlands. Its net export ratio in 1990 was even lower, a mere 0.02, as compared with 0.25 of the USA and 0.24 of Germany.

The productivity estimate by the McKinsey Global Institute (1993) also indicates US strength and Japanese weakness in the sectors of chemicals and food and beverages. According to the estimate, in 1990, Japanese labor productivity relative to the USA was only 33 per cent in food, 69 per cent in beer, and 94 per cent in soap and detergent. According to another estimate by van Ark and Pilat (1993), in 1990 while Japanese manufacturing productivity in machinery, electrical engineering, and

Table 2.21 Country share of OECD exports, by technology, 1994

Technology	USA	Japan	Germany
All technologies	25.2	17	11.7
Aerospace	44.2	1.4	11.3
Biotechnology	37	4.3	19.1
Weapon technologies	34.3	4.6	12.1
Advanced materials	28.6	9.3	15.1
Life science technologies	27.5	13.8	20.4
Nuclear technologies	20.8	0.2	9.6
Electronics	20.3	25.5	9.4
Information technologies	18.5	23	8.3
Manufacturing technologies	16.2	21.5	21.9
Opto-electronics	13.7	22.8	24

Source: *Science & Engineering Indicators 1996*: 6–8.

Table 2.22 US trade performance in high technologies, 1995–1996 (millions of US$)

	Exports		Imports		Trade balance		Export/ import ratio	
	1995	1996	1995	1996	1995	1996	1995	1996
Total	138,417	154,909	124,787	130,362	13,629.5	24,547.6	1.11	1.19
Biotechnology	1,055.5	1,197.4	444.8	548.8	610.7	648.6	2.37	2.18
Life science	8,571.5	9,255.5	6,607.2	7,291.6	1,964.3	1,963.9	1.30	1.27
Opto-electronics	1,164.6	1,418.6	2,816.6	3,172.8	−1,652.0	−1,754.2	0.41	0.45
Computers and telecommunications	47,890.5	52,780.1	58,865.6	61,346.1	−10,975.1	−8,566.0	0.81	0.86
Electronics	31,391.7	36,548.0	38,232.6	36,756.8	−6,840.9	−208.8	0.82	0.99
Flexible manufacturing	7,469.6	8,583.6	4,947.5	5,740.7	2,522.1	2,842.9	1.51	1.50
Advanced materials	4,519.5	1,693.6	1,527.6	1,219.8	2,991.9	473.8	2.96	1.39
Aerospace	30,983.1	38,088.7	10,540.5	12,805.4	20,442.6	25,283.3	2.94	2.97
Nuclear technology	1,040.5	1,466.9	205.0	265.5	835.5	1,201.4	5.08	5.53
Weapons	1,272.0	1,258.9	39.8	626.1	1,232.2	632.8	31.9	2.01
Software technology	3,057.9	2,617.7	559.8	588.0	2,498.1	2,029.7	5.46	4.45

Source: Calculation based on National Science Board (1998: A-367).

transport equipment was 114 per cent that of the USA, it was only 37 per cent in food products, beverages and tobacco, 48 per cent in textiles, wearing apparel and leather, 55 per cent in wood and paper products, 84 per cent in chemicals, petroleum, rubber, and plastic products, and 96 per cent in basic materials and metal products.

Sectoral patterns of patenting advantage

The divergent patterns of US and Japanese competitiveness in high-tech manufacturing sectors are further evidenced by their patenting indices of revealed

Table 2.23 Patenting index of revealed comparative advantage, 1963–1968; 1985–1990

	1985–1990			1963–1968		
	USA	Japan	Europe	USA	Japan	Europe
Electronics consumer goods	0.65	2.50	0.59	0.94	1.99	1.26
Vehicles	0.55	2.21	1.02	0.89	0.83	1.48
Electronics capital goods	0.97	1.65	0.61	1.02	1.47	0.92
Materials	0.95	1.42	0.83	1.04	1.02	0.86
Electric machinery	1.01	1.08	0.92	1.00	1.17	1.00
Telecommunications	1.04	0.97	0.94	1.03	1.06	0.91
Industrial chemicals	0.98	0.92	1.19	0.93	1.62	1.29
Mechanical engineering	0.99	0.85	1.13	1.01	0.77	0.99
Fine chemicals	0.97	0.72	1.33	0.89	2.95	1.34
Raw materials related	1.28	0.37	0.83	1.08	0.44	0.61
Defense related	1.15	0.09	1.40	0.99	0.36	1.14

Source: Adapted from Patel and Pavitt (1998: 298).

comparative advantage. As shown in Table 2.23, during 1985–1990, consistent with its trade performance, Japan's revealed comparative advantage of patenting was very strong in the sectors of vehicles, electronic consumer goods, and electronic capital goods and materials, whereas it has a revealed comparative disadvantage of patenting in chemicals, raw material related and defense related sectors. When the evolution of the comparative advantage of patenting is considered, it is interesting to observe how Japan's position in automobiles and electronics dramatically improved during 1963–1990, while its position in chemicals dramatically declined. In contrast, the USA had a strong comparative disadvantage of patenting in both vehicles and electronic consumer goods during 1985–1990, while at the same time it had a strong revealed advantage in the defense and raw material related sectors.

When more disaggregate sectors are included, as shown in Table 2.24, the contrasting patterns of national comparative advantage of patenting are even more salient. Consistent with its trade performance, Japan has a revealed comparative advantage of patenting in photography and photocopy, image and sound equipment, road vehicles and engines, calculators and computers, semiconductors, advanced materials, and instruments and controls, but has a strong revealed comparative disadvantage in mining and wells, aircraft, dentistry and surgery, induced nuclear reactions, drugs and bioengineering, chemicals, and food and tobacco. On the other hand, the US sectoral pattern is just the opposite.

Table 2.25 shows the top fifteen most emphasized patent classes for inventors in the USA and Japan in 1995. It reveals the same patterns of sectoral specialization in patenting as in earlier years. While the USA continues its strength in medical and surgical devices, electronic devices, telecommunications, and biotechnology, Japan keeps its prowess in opto-electronics, consumer electronics, information storage technology, and visual display systems for computers.

Indeed, in their statistical analysis of US patenting data, Patel and Pavitt (1998) found that the sectoral patterns of revealed comparative advantage of patenting in the USA, Japan, and most other OECD countries had maintained a statistically significant degree of stability during 1963–1989. As shown in Table 2.26, the

Table 2.24 Patenting indices of comparative advantage, 1985–1990

	Japan	USA	Germany
Photography and photocopy	3.01	0.51	0.57
Image and sound equipment	2.23	0.72	0.53
Road vehicles and engines	2.21	0.55	1.42
Calculators and computers	1.68	0.97	0.50
Semiconductors	1.60	0.97	0.54
Materials (glass and ceramics)	1.42	0.95	0.85
General elect. ind. apparatus	1.35	0.96	0.86
Instruments and control	1.25	0.94	0.91
Metallurgical and metal treatment proc.	1.23	0.87	0.93
Plastic and rubber products	1.21	0.86	1.26
Telecommunications	0.97	1.04	0.79
Organic chemicals	0.94	0.95	1.57
Chemical processes	0.89	1.04	1.08
Electrical devices and systems	0.86	1.10	0.85
Assembling and material handling app.	0.85	0.94	1.31
Metallurgical and metal working equip.	0.82	0.97	1.38
Power plant	0.82	0.99	1.25
General nonelectrical ind. equip.	0.80	0.91	1.39
Drugs and bioengineering	0.72	0.97	1.07
Other transport equip. (exc. aircraft)	0.72	1.08	0.86
App. for chemicals, food, glass, etc.	0.72	1.01	1.24
Inorganic chemicals	0.68	0.99	1.32
Agricultural chemicals	0.68	0.98	1.71
Food & tobacco (proc. & prod.)	0.59	1.12	0.72
Nonelectrical specialized ind. equip.	0.57	0.96	1.51
Bleaching, dyeing and disinfecting	0.51	0.73	2.42
Induced nuclear reaction	0.45	1.18	1.20
Textile, clothing, leather, wood products	0.45	1.23	0.64
Hydrocarbons, mineral oils, fuels, etc.	0.41	1.39	0.41
Dentistry and surgery	0.41	1.30	0.70
Other (ammunition and weapons)	0.27	1.30	0.61
Aircraft	0.12	1.29	1.19
Mining & wells: mach. and proc.	0.09	1.45	0.49

Source: Adapted from Patel (1996).

correlation over time between 1963–1968 and 1983–1989 is 0.56 and 0.45 respectively for the USA and Japan in their patenting indices of revealed comparative advantage. Using the patenting activity index data from *Science & Engineering Indicators 1998*, our calculation also shows that the correlation of revealed comparative advantage of patenting over time between 1985 and 1995 for the 51 most competitive patent classes in the USA and Japan are 0.67 and 0.83 respectively, which are all statistically significant at the 0.0001 level.

When correlations of the patenting indices of revealed comparative advantage across 34 sectors are calculated, Patel and Pavitt (1998) find that Japan had maintained a unique pattern of specialization in patenting, as evidenced by its negative correlations with most other OECD countries (Table 2.26). Interestingly,

Table 2.25 Top fifteen most emphasized patent classes for inventors in the USA and Japan, 1995

USA	Japan
1. Wells	1. Dynamic information storage or retrieval
2. Surgery (Class 606)	2. Photography
3. Surgery (Class 604)	3. Music
4. Surgery: light, thermal, and electrical applications	4. Photocopying
	5. Facsimile or television recording
5. Chemistry of hydrocarbons	6. Typewriting machines
6. Special receptacles or packages	7. Static information storage and retrieval
7. Surgery	8. Dynamic magnetic information storage or retrieval
8. Receptacles	
9. Supports	9. Active solid state devices
10. Cryptography	10. Radiation imagery chemistry: process, composition
11. Static structures (e.g. buildings)	
12. Processes, compositions for food or edible materials	11. Incremental printing
	12. Optics: systems and element
13. Amusement devices: games	13. Electrical generator
14. Cleaning and liquid contact with solids	14. Television
15. Chemistry: analytical and immunological testing	15. Metal treatment

Source: Adapted from National Science Board (1998, pp. 6–22).

while the USA maintained positive correlations with the other Anglo-American societies of Canada, the UK, and Australia, Japan had *statistically significant* negative correlations with the USA and Western Europe, with a value of -0.81 and -0.41 respectively during the 1985–1990 period. Such a negative correlation is further reflected in the number of firms among the top 20 of US patenting in various manufacturing sectors. As shown in Table 2.27, of the top 20 firms in US patenting, Japan has 14 in consumer electronics and 11 in motor vehicles, whereas the USA has merely 4 and 5 respectively.

On the other hand, of the top 20 patenting firms, the USA has 14 in defense related technologies, 16 in raw materials based technologies, 12 in fine chemicals, and 11 in industrial chemicals, as compared to merely 0, 1, 1, and 1 respectively for their Japanese counterparts. Western European firms are also major players in patenting in areas where Japanese firms are weak. The Japanese competitive advantage in advanced manufacturing, material design and the US advantage in biotechnology are also evidenced by their contribution to the total number of patents in these sectors. As Table 2.28 indicates, when the accumulated number of international patent families of the six countries of the USA, Japan, Germany, France, the UK, and South Korea during 1990–1994 are compared, Japan held 43 per cent in robot technology, and 39 per cent in advanced ceramic technology, followed by the USA with 24 per cent and 32 per cent respectively. Conversely, in genetic engineering, the USA generated an overwhelming 64 per cent of patents, followed by Japan with the distant second place of 13 per cent.

When only the highly cited patent families are considered, the USA has an absolute advantage of patenting in all the three advanced technologies, with Japan

Table 2.26 Correlation between countries in their patenting indices of revealed comparative advantage across 34 sectors

	Correlation over time 1963–1968 to 1983–1989	Correlation between countries	
		Japan	USA
USA	0.56*	−0.81*	
Japan	0.45*		−0.81*
Western Europe		−0.41*	−0.19
Norway	0.35*	−0.5*	0.5*
France	0.82*	−0.44*	0.23
Canada	0.67*	−0.44*	0.42*
Australia	0.28	−0.43*	0.22
Sweden	0.73*	−0.38*	0.13
UK	0.23	−0.34*	0.11
Finland	0.59*	−0.26	−0.01
Spain	0.53*	−0.23	−0.02
Denmark	0.47*	−0.22	−0.02
Germany	0.35*	−0.2	−0.37*
Portugal	0.25	−0.2	0.06
Switzerland	0.83*	−0.19	−0.26
Italy	0.32	−0.13	−0.09
Ireland	0.05	−0.13	0.25
Austria	0.76*	−0.07	−0.03
Belgium	0.54*	0.06	−0.2
The Netherlands	0.66*	0.24	−0.03

* Statistically significant at the 5% level.
Source: Adapted from Patel and Pavitt (1998: 300).

Table 2.27 Number of firms within the top 20 of manufacturing sectors in US patenting, 1985–1990

	USA	Japan	W. Europe
Defense related technologies	14	0	6
Fine chemicals	12	1	7
Industrial chemicals	11	1	8
Raw materials based technologies	16	1	3
Materials	13	4	3
Electrical machinery	10	6	4
Telecommunications	10	6	4
Electrical capital goods	9	8	3
Non-electrical machinery	8	9	3
Motor vehicles	5	11	4
Electronic consumer goods	4	14	2

Source: Patel and Pavitt (1998: 311).

being left behind in the far second or third position (Table 2.29). This reflects American strength in basic research and radical innovations in all advanced technologies. Tables 2.28 and 2.29 also reflect the fact that Japanese firms are good at incremental innovations but not so good at radical innovations (Imai, 1986).

Indeed, the sectoral patterns of patenting revealed here represent US exceptionalism and Japanese uniqueness not only in their competitiveness but also in their system of innovation and knowledge, which will be systematically investigated later in this book.

Table 2.28 Accumulative number of international patent families, 1990–1994

	Robot technology		Advanced ceramics		Genetic engineering	
	#	%	#	%	#	%
USA	411	23.9	310	32.0	2165	63.5
Japan	737	42.9	381	39.4	441	12.9
Germany	278	16.2	151	15.6	244	7.2
France	162	9.4	69	7.1	196	5.7
UK	72	4.2	47	4.9	344	10.1
South Korea	59	3.4	10	1.0	21	0.6
Total	1719	100.0	968	100.0	3411	100.0

Source: Adapted from National Science Board (1998, pp. 6–26, 6–28, 6–30).

Table 2.29 Accumulative number of highly cited international patent families, 1990–1994

	Robot technology		Advanced ceramics		Genetic engineering	
	#	%	#	%	#	%
USA	10	55.6	15	65.2	23	59.0
Japan	6	33.3	4	17.4	4	10.3
Germany	2	11.1	1	4.3	1	2.6
France	0	0	1	4.3	7	17.9
UK	0	0	2	8.7	4	10.3
South Korea	0	0	0	0	0	0
Total	18	100	23	100	39	100

Source: Adapted from National Science Board (1998, pp. 6–26, 6–28, 6–30).

US strength and Japanese weakness in software, information services, and other service sectors

The sharp contrast of sectoral patterns of US and Japanese competitiveness also extend to software, information services, and other services. According to the US Department of Commerce (1994), in 1993 US software vendors supplied 75 per cent of the $70 billion world prepackaged software market, 91 per cent of the $21 billion systems software market, and 77 per cent of the $20 billion application tool market. As Table 2.30 indicates, during 1990–1996, the USA had maintained a large trade balance in software product, with exports 4.45 times imports in 1996.

US strength in software is mirrored by Japanese weakness. As Table 2.31 indicates, during 1994–1996, Japan had run a trade deficit not only with the USA,

Table 2.30 US trade performance in software product, 1990–1996 (million US$)

Year	Exports	Imports	Trade balance	Export/import ratio
1990	1328	157	1171	8.46
1991	1625	196	1429	8.29
1992	2050	295	1755	6.95
1993	2526	360	2166	7.02
1994	3031	436	2595	6.95
1995	3058	560	2498	5.46
1996	2618	588	2030	4.45

Source: OECD (1997b, p. 33).

Table 2.31 Japanese trade performance in software, 1994–1996 (million US$)

	Exports			Imports			Average EIR, %
	1994	1995	1996	1994	1995	1996	1994–1996
Americas	18.7	8.8	13.2	2,458.8	3,840.3	3,273.7	0.43
Basic	8.0	5.3	7.7	1,823.5	2,489.8	2,201.2	0.32
Application	10.6	2.1	5.4	538.7	1,039.8	809.7	0.76
Custom	0.1	1.4	0.1	96.6	310.7	262.8	0.24
of which: *USA*	17.8	8.6	12.8	2,383.7	3,733.8	3,170.8	0.42
Basic	7.1	5.2	7.4	1,787.4	2,388.5	2,105.5	0.31
Application	10.6	2.0	5.3	531.5	1,035.3	802.5	0.76
Custom	0.1	1.4	0.1	64.8	309.9	262.7	0.25
Europe	10.9	9.5	7.9	33.7	101.3	220.9	7.95
Basic	7.5	7.2	6.9	20.6	30.4	39.6	23.8
Application	2.6	1.0	1.0	10.2	40.9	175.4	2.03
Custom	0.7	1.3	0.0	2.8	30.0	6.0	5.15
Asia	20.3	19.2	27.8	33.1	210.5	107.1	19.1
Basic	7.5	10.0	9.9	14.2	7.7	50.0	38.1
Application	12.3	7.8	15.2	3.1	192.0	41.0	14.9
Custom	0.5	1.3	2.7	15.8	10.8	16.2	10.5
Rest of the World	3.9	4.3	3.4	13.3	19.8	15.4	23.9
Basic	3.7	3.7	3.3	3.3	7.6	6.2	62.5
Application	0.1	0.1	0.1	2.2	3.3	3.3	3.41
Custom	0.1	0.5	0.0	7.7	8.9	5.9	2.67
World	53.7	41.8	52.2	2,538.9	4,171.9	3,617.1	1.43
Basic	26.6	26.2	27.8	1,861.6	2,535.5	2,296.9	1.20
Application	25.6	10.9	21.6	554.3	1,276.0	1,029.3	2.03
Custom	1.5	4.6	2.8	123.0	360.4	290.9	1.15

Source: OECD (1997b: 31).

but also with Europe, Asia, and the rest of the world. This is true in all categories of basic, application, and custom software. Its exports of all types of software to the world were only 1.43 per cent of its imports. In basic software and custom software, the numbers were even lower, with 1.20 per cent and 1.15 per cent respectively. The performance of Japan's bilateral software trade with the USA is even worse. During 1994–1996, its exports to the USA were only 0.43 of per cent of its imports from the USA. In the disaggregate categories of basic, application, and custom software, the numbers were merely 0.31 per cent, 0.76 per cent, and 0.25 per cent respectively.

US strength and Japanese weakness in software is also reflected in the overwhelming dominance of the USA in the number of the world's largest software companies. As shown in Table 2.32, of the top 20 worldwide software companies in 1996, fifteen were US firms, which accounted for 79.6 per cent of the total

Table 2.32 Top 20 software companies worldwide, 1990 and 1996

		Software revenues (million current US$)		Annual growth rate, %
		1996	1990	
IBM	US	13,502.0	9,842.6	5.4
Microsoft Corp.	US	9,247.0	1,289.9	38.9
Hitachi Ltd	Japan	3,960.0	956.3	26.7
Computer Associate International Inc.	US	3,945.0	978.2	26.2
Oracle Corp.	US	3,615.0	685.8	31.9
Fujitsu Ltd	Japan	2,000.0	1,820.8	1.7
SAP AG	Germany	1,692.0	190.4	43.9
Bull NH Information Systems Inc.	France	1,457.8	600.6	15.9
Digital Equipment Corp.	US	1,224.9	1,529.4	−3.6
Novell Inc.	US	1,208.0	433.1	18.6
Siemens Nixdorf	Germany	1,020.0	933.3	1.5
Sybase Inc.	US	1,011.5	76.7	53.7
Sun Microsystems Inc.	US	1,000.0	137.9	39.1
Informix Software Inc.	US	823.7	146.1	33.4
Hewlett-Packard Co.	US	798.5	442.3	10.3
Adobe Systems Inc.	US	786.6	303.7	17.2
SAS Institute Inc.	US	620.4	240.2	17.1
Unisys Corp.	US	600.0	758.3	−4.4
Parametric Technology Corp.	US	596.3	52.4	50.0
Cadence Design Systems	US	587.0	322.0	10.5
Total		49,695.7	21,740.0	
US total		39,565.9	17,238.7	14.8
Japan total		5,960.0	2,777.1	13.6
US total/Japan total		664%	621%	
US % of total consolidated revenue		79.6%	79.3%	
Japan % of total consolidated revenue		12%	12.8%	

Source: Adapted from OECD (1997b: 43).

consolidated software revenues, overwhelming the Japanese number of two firms and a mere 12 per cent respectively. The annual growth rate in software revenue was 14.8 per cent for the top fifteen US firms, which is larger than Japan's 13.6 per cent. As a result of this difference in growth rates, the gap of total consolidated software revenues between the USA and Japan grew from 621 per cent in 1990 to 664 per cent in 1996.

The overall global market shares of prepackaged software also exhibit similar patterns of US dominance. As shown in Table 2.33, in 1993 US firms had overwhelmingly dominant market shares for all categories of prepackaged software

Table 2.33 Market share of US firms in prepackaged software, 1993 (percentages)

Consuming regions	Tools	Applications	System-level software
USA	83.5	87.9	94.3
Japan	64.7	35.3	73.7
Western Europe	74.6	41.3	88.7

Source: Mowery (1996, p. 8).

not only at home but also in both Japanese and European markets. In that year, the market share of US firms in Japan reached 73.7 per cent in system-level software, 64.7 per cent in software tools, and 35.3 per cent in application software. US software market share in Europe was even higher, with 88.7 per cent in system-level software, 74.6 per cent in software tools, and 41.3 per cent in application software. In 1994, the USA held at least 75 per cent of world prepackaged software market, with 90 per cent in the USA, 63 per cent in Europe, and 55 per cent in Japan (OECD, 1998).

The overwhelming domination of US firms in software and related services is also reflected in Table 2.34. In 1990, US firms commanded 57 per cent of the $110 billion

Table 2.34 US domination in the global market for software and related services, 1990

Country	Sales revenue ($ billion)	Market share (%)
USA	62.70	57%
Japan	14.30	13%
France	8.80	8%
Germany	7.70	7%
UK	6.60	6%
Canada	3.30	3%
Others	6.60	6%

Source: Siwek and Furchtgott-Roth (1993, p. 28).

world market in software and related services. Although Japan's global market share in software reached 13 per cent, this largely reflects customized software sold only to Japan's large domestic market.

As in software, the USA also has a very strong position in information services. According to the US Department of Commerce (1994), in 1994 the USA controlled 46 per cent of the $282 billion world market in information services, followed by Europe, 32.5 per cent, and Asia/Pacific, 18.1 per cent. With an average annual growth rate of 13 per cent, the US information service sector is rated as one of the healthiest segments of the economy. According to the same source, the total international revenues of the US information service sector amounted to $40 billion in 1992. In 1994, US exports in information services, excluding shipment to foreign affiliates, grew 12 per cent and reached $3.2 billion, *7.54* times its import value of $424 million. If we were to include US shipments to its foreign affiliates, the export/import ratio would be larger.

According to the same source, US firms have about 50 per cent of the global market for professional services, including consulting, customer software develop-

Table 2.35 Revenues of software and computer-related services sectors, 1990–1995 (million US$)

USA	1990	1991	1992	1993	1994	1995
737 Computer programming, data processing, and other computer-related service	88,299	94,363	104,651	116,834	133,143	152,213
7371 Computer programming services	21,318	23,376	24,973	27,964	32,434	37,447
7372 Prepackaged software	16,523	18,306	21,236	24,648	27,597	31,087
7373 Computer-integrated systems design	12,916	13,751	15,177	17,084	18,953	20,592
7374 Computer processing and data preparation and processing services	17,820	18,824	20,447	22,604	26,641	31,144
7375 Information retrieval services	3,547	3,691	3,931	4,316	4,644	5,489
7376 Computer facilities and management services	1,994	2,206	2,608	2,638	2,814	3,110
7377 Computer rental and leasing	2,644	2,396	2,385	2,252	2,205	2,213
7378 Computer maintenance and repair	7,000	6,919	7,660	7,559	7,764	8,228
7389 Computer related services, n.e.c.	4,537	4,894	6,234	7,769	10,091	12,903
Japan						
841 Information service industry	4,056	5,226	5,628	5,858	6,043	6,764
Information processing	665	813	869	907	945	1,038
Soft. development & programming	2,388	3,193	3,392	3,429	3,410	3,931
Machine time sales	37	44	37	39	32	37
Database services	130	160	169	190	195	210
System management & operations service commission	191	229	287	323	351	379
Data entry	141	156	159	172	180	189
Various surveys/studies	180	233	219	223	242	255
Others	323	398	496	575	688	726

Source: OECD (1997b, p. 22).

ment, and systems integration. They also dominate global markets in databases. According to OECD (1993), in 1993 the USA produced 4,956 or 66 per cent of the 7,538 electronic databases around the world, followed by the UK, 641; Canada, 480; Germany, 342; and France, 288. Japan was not among the top five players in the global database market! Since the whole Asia/Pacific region has only 18.1 per cent of the global market share in information services, the weakness of Japanese firms in the information service sector is crystal-clear. As shown in Table 2.35, in 1995 the size of the US software and computer-related services sector had been much larger than that of Japan. Although the data are not directly comparable due to discrepancies in sectoral classifications, US revenues in the computer programming, data processing, and other computer-related services were 22.5 times that of the corresponding Japanese information service industry, a huge gap reflecting overwhelming US strength and a remarkable Japanese weakness.

In the new age of the Internet, this has translated into America's preponderance in emerging e-commerce and e-business. Of these blossoming trillion-dollar businesses, the USA has been the dominant player with such rising stars as America Online (AOL), Amazon.com, eBay, E*Trade, and Yahoo!. According to the OECD's Internet and e-commerce indicators (www.oecd.org/dsti/it/cm), the USA is ranked first in both the number of secure servers per million inhabitants and the number of Internet hosts per 1,000 inhabitants, whereas Japan is ranked only nineteenth and seventeenth respectively. In April 2000, the USA had about 190 secure servers per million inhabitants, ten times more than the Japanese number of about 18. In September, 1999, the USA had about 160 Internet hosts per 1,000 inhabitants, more than eight times the Japanese number of 19. More astonishingly, rather than Japan and the other countries catching up, the gap had actually enlarged since 1997 (www.oecd.org/dsti/it/cm). It seems clear that with the increasing importance of software, information services, and e-business in the global economy, US strength and Japanese weakness in these sectors has turned the competitiveness, and therefore wealth, of these two nations upside down – from Japanese success in the 1970s and 1980s to US dominance in the 1990s and early twenty-first century. A primary question that will be explored in this book is – will this pattern persist throughout this twenty-first century? While the detailed analysis is left to the whole book, the brief answer is yes. With the increasing importance of digital economy and e-business, US dominance in software and information services over Japan is likely to last for a long time, and therefore, reverse the fortunes of these two countries.

Looking at the situation broadly, in addition to software, information services, and e-business, the USA has been competitive in all categories of the service sector. As Table 2.36 indicates, in 1996 the US service sector had a trade surplus of $61.2 billion, as compared to its record merchandise trade deficit of $193 billion.

Conversely, while Japan had a net export of $63 billion in goods, it ran a $57.7 billion trade deficit in services. The US export/import ratio (EIR) of services in 1996 was 1.48, as compared to a mere 0.53 for Japan. As expected, the divergence is much larger in both software products and computer services. US exports of computer services in 1996 were 6.83 times its imports, while the Japanese ratio was a mere 0.03. Similarly, as Table 2.18 shows, US outward FDI in computer services is 3.10 times its inward FDI, once again revealing US strength in this sector.

Looking back to the 1980s, as shown in Table 2.37, the US export/import ratio in

Table 2.36 Trade performance in goods, services, and computer services, 1994 and 1996 (billion US$)

	1994				1996			
	Exports	Imports	Balance	EIR	Exports	Imports	Balance	EIR
US								
Total goods	512.5	689.2	−176.7	0.74	624.8	817.8	−193	0.76
Total services	178.2	120.7	57.5	1.48	189.5	128.3	61.2	1.48
Software products	3.0	0.4	2.6	7.5	2.6	0.6	2.0	4.33
Computer services	3.8	0.4	3.4	9.5	4.1	0.6	3.5	6.83
Japan								
Total goods	397.0	275.2	121.8	1.44	412.6	349.6	63.0	1.18
Total services	57.2	109.2	−52.0	0.52	63.9	121.6	−57.7	0.53
Computer services	0.1	2.5	−2.4	0.04	0.1	3.6	−3.5	0.03

Source: Calculation based on OECD (1997b: 28).

Table 2.37 US and Japanese trade performance in services, 1987–1996 (billion de $E-U)

	1987	1988	1989	1990	1991	1992	1993	1994	1995	1996
USA										
Export	97.7	110.1	125.8	146.4	162.5	175.0	184.3	199.2	217.8	236.7
Import	90.4	98.0	101.9	117.0	118.0	116.5	122.4	132.4	142.0	152.0
EIR	1.08	1.12	1.23	1.25	1.38	1.50	1.51	1.50	1.53	1.56
Japan										
Export	28.9	35.4	40.3	41.3	44.9	49.0	53.2	58.3	65.5	67.7
Import	49.2	65.7	77.0	84.1	86.7	93.0	96.2	106.2	122.8	130.0
EIR	0.59	0.54	0.52	0.49	0.52	0.53	0.55	0.55	0.53	0.52

Source: OECD (1998) (Service: International Transactions, p. 49).

services actually improved from 1.08 in 1987 to 1.56 in 1996, while Japan's ratio declined from 0.59 in 1987 to 0.52 in 1996. Other than performances in trade and FDI, US productivity in the service sector is also the highest in the world. According to the McKinsey Global Institute (1993), Japanese labor productivity was only 44 per cent that of the USA in general merchandise retailing in 1987, and 77 per cent in telecommunication service in 1989. Czinkota (1985) also finds strong evidence of low labor productivity of both Japanese wholesale and retail sectors. For example, despite its much smaller geographic size and population, Japan has about the same number of wholesalers as the USA, and only 10 per cent fewer retailers than the USA.

Table 2.38 shows US export/import ratios of various service sectors from 1986 to 1998. Consistent with Porter's (1990) findings, the USA has been persistently competitive in almost all service subsectors. In 1998, US export was 14.6 times its import in database and other information services; 5.58 times in computer and data processing services; 5.80 times in construction, engineering, architecture, and mining services; 4.98 times in industrial engineering service; 3.17 times in business,

Table 2.38 US export/import ratios of service sectors, 1986–1998

Service subsectors	1986	1988	1990	1992	1994	1996	1998
Total private services	1.18	1.24	1.39	1.62	1.56	1.61	1.49
Other unaffiliated services	13.14	12.43	13.49	14.74	15.70	15.44	18.70
Database & other information services	5.39	5.03	5.24	8.90	7.28	7.93	14.06
Operational leasing	7.68	6.97	3.97	2.53	2.31	4.56	12.38
Instll, maintenance, & repair of equip	2.21	2.07	2.84	14.37	21.32	15.26	8.49
Education	8.07	7.68	7.79	8.07	7.38	6.29	5.83
Constrct, engnrg, archtct, & mining services	2.52	2.57	5.10	7.41	8.84	7.64	5.80
Computer & data processing services	30.78	11.20	23.43	10.93	15.73	5.86	5.58
Human resource services			0.20	9.07	28.33	3.54	5.30
Industrial engineering service	1.31	2.09	6.39	1.89	5.75	4.42	4.98
Othr business, profess & techn services							4.40
Financial services	1.87	2.31	1.78	4.09	3.48	2.83	3.63
Legal services	2.43	2.78	4.06	4.37	4.22	3.16	3.56
Royalties and license fees	5.79	4.67	5.31	4.04	4.56	4.14	3.26
Business, profess, & technical services	3.69	3.08	3.70	3.78	3.96	3.51	3.17
Industrial processes		3.82	3.50	3.09	2.93	2.70	2.68
Training services	10.43	5.40	8.12	3.17	2.83	2.77	2.46
Management of health care facilities				1.69	1.50	2.25	2.40
Agricultural services	0.80	1.00		2.57	2.14	1.73	2.33
Management & consulting services	5.10	4.71	2.62	3.00	3.53	2.94	1.81
Research and development services	3.71	1.27	1.83	2.72	1.78	1.80	1.50
Port services	2.01	1.81	1.38	1.28	1.42	1.37	1.30
Travel	0.79	0.92	1.15	1.42	1.33	1.45	1.27
Accounting services	0.72	1.19	2.09	1.58	1.02	1.02	1.05
Passenger fares	0.86	1.16	1.45	1.57	1.30	1.29	1.01
Other transportation	0.87	0.92	0.88	0.91	0.91	0.95	0.84
Freight	0.39	0.47	0.56	0.62	0.60	0.67	0.58
Sports & performance arts	1.52		0.98	0.30	0.70	0.75	0.55
Advertising	1.22	0.77	0.53	0.70	0.67	0.56	0.55
Telecommunications	0.56	0.48	0.49	0.48	0.41	0.40	0.45
Insurance, net	0.63	0.32	0.12	0.52	0.42	0.56	0.41
Premiums	0.47	0.39	0.33	0.33	0.35	0.41	0.38

Source: Calculation based on US Department of Commerce (2000) Online Database.

professional, and technical services; in other business, 4.40 times in other business, professional, and technical services; 3.63 times in financial services; 2.68 times in industrial processes; 2.46 times in training services; 1.81 times in management and consulting services; 1.50 times in research and development services; revealing US strength in these areas.

American exceptionalism and Japanese uniqueness in the sectoral patterns of national competitiveness

Broadening our comparisons to include major European competitors of Germany, the UK, France, and Italy, we find that the USA and Japan always stand at the two extremes of the spectrum of competitiveness (Jin, 1998). Not only do US and

Japanese sectoral patterns constitute two contrasting extremes of competitive advantages and disadvantages, they are also consistent in all competitive indicators of export share, export/import ratios, export indices and export/import ratio indices of competitive advantages, FDI shares and ratios, labor productivity, and various patenting indices. They have also persisted in this way during the last two decades, despite heroic efforts by both governments and firms, and in spite of dramatic changes in economic conditions. All of these constitute US exceptionalism and Japanese uniqueness in the landscapes of national competitiveness, which pose a challenging question as to what are the fundamental underlying forces in shaping this persistence.

Summarizing our analyses, we can discern three types of sectors with regard to US and Japanese competitiveness. The first includes those sectors where the USA has maintained an absolute competitive advantage over all nations. They include nuclear technology, weapons, aerospace, aircraft, biotechnology, medical devices, software, information services, e-business, fast food, soft drinks, consulting, accounting, legal services, advertising, engineering/architectural services, credit cards, credit reporting, merchant/investment banking, insurance, leasing, money management, entertainment, car rental, and hotels. The second type includes those sectors where the USA has maintained competitive advantages over most European competitors, but has lost the leading position to Japanese firms. These include automobiles, electronics, office machinery, material design, machine tools & robotics, CIM, and FMS. The third type includes the sectors in which the USA has lost its competitive position not only to Japan, but also to the rest of the world. These include opto-electronics and consumer electronics (Jin, 1998).

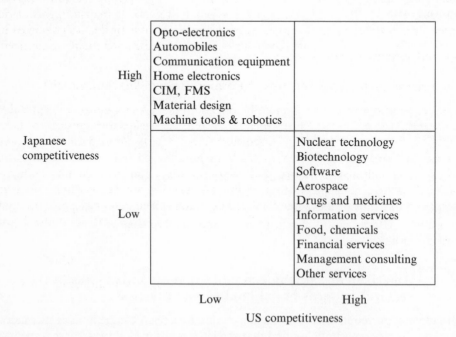

Figure 2.3 The sectoral pattern of US and Japanese general competitiveness

		Low	High
US competitiveness with Japan	High	Drugs and medicines Organic chemicals	Nuclear technology Biotechnology Software Aerospace Information services Food, chemicals Financial services Management consulting Other services
	Low	Communication equipment	Automobiles Opto-electronics Electronics Computer & telecom. CIM, FMS Material design Machine tools & robotics

Low   High
US competitiveness with other major EC competitors

Figure 2.4 The sectoral pattern of US relative competitiveness with Japan and other major competitors

The sectors where the USA has maintained its leading competitive position are also those where Japan has generally had a competitive disadvantage. Japan is less competitive than not only the USA, but also other major European competitors in aircraft, aerospace, drugs, chemicals, food, petroleum processing, packaged software, information services, and most other service sectors. Notwithstanding these weaknesses, Japan is the only country that has captured leading competitive positions from the USA in automobiles, electronics, opto-electronics, office machinery, material design, machine tools & robotics, CIM, and FMS. Figure 2.3 summarizes the sectoral pattern of competitiveness between the USA and Japan. Figure 2.4 reveals the US sectoral pattern of competitiveness as compared to Japan and other major competitors.

The USA is exceptional in the sense that, other than being second to Germany in organic chemicals and medicines, and having a general competitive disadvantage in communication equipment, it has maintained a large pool of very competitive sectors unmatched throughout the world. It is second only to Japan in automobiles, electronics, material design, machine tools & robotics, CIM, and FMS. It is also the overwhelmingly dominant player in the emerging sectors of information services, biotechnology, digital economy, and e-business. Japan is unique in the sense that any of its sectors that are more competitive than the USA are automatically more competitive than all other competitors in the world. In other words, other than organic chemicals and drugs, in which Germany successfully challenged the USA's leading positions, Japan is the only country that has been able to overtake the USA in many important high-tech manufacturing sectors. Japan is also unique because of a mythical bifurcation and polarization of its sectoral competitiveness. While Japan is very competitive in quite a few sectors, Japan is also hopelessly uncompetitive in most other sectors. The sectors that Japan is less competitive than the USA are also the ones in which Japan is less competitive than major European competitors.

As we will discuss later in the book, US exceptionalism and Japanese uniqueness in the sectoral patterns of competitiveness are also reflected in their exceptional capabilities in dealing with different types of *complex* technological systems, with various forms of manufacturing, and with divergent ways of knowledge creation and transformation. Where the scale and complexity of technology is concerned, the USA is generally competitive in technological systems of large-scale complexity such as nuclear technologies, aerospace, aircraft, and weapons that are batch produced. Japan is very competitive in technological systems of middle-scale complexity such as automobiles, electronics, machine tools, robotics, CIM, and FMS that can be flexibly produced in large quantities.

Where the nature of manufacturing is concerned, while the USA is superior in both *fabricating* and *processing* manufacturing, Japan is only superior in fabricating manufacturing in most cases. As a result, the USA is more competitive than Japan in the processing manufacturing sectors such as biotechnology, drugs, food, petroleum products, paper and paper products. On the other hand, Japan is superior to the USA in many complex fabricating manufacturing sectors such as automobiles, electronics, opto-electronics, machine tools & robotics, CIM, and FMS.

When the nature of knowledge creation and transformation is considered, the USA is superior in those sectors where knowledge can be codified, generalized, externalized, and marketized. This is reflected in their superior performance in information services, consulting, software, credit reporting, and fast food. On the other hand, as will be discussed in the remaining chapters, knowledge creation in automobiles and electronics involves less explicit knowledge and more tacit knowledge (Nonaka and Takeuchi, 1995).

Discussion: the challenge of persistent sectoral patterns

There are several concluding observations that can be made about the sectoral patterns we just analyzed in detail. First, the existence of persistent sectoral patterns between the USA and Japan pinpoints the limits of many economic, organizational, institutional, technological, and public policy approaches to national competitiveness. Most of them fail to take a sectoral approach in their analyses, leading not only to overgeneralization, but also to misguided policy prescriptions and false strategic recommendations. Second, the persistence of sectoral patterns also challenges both the convergence assumption of neoclassical economics and the statist propositions of revisionists such as Johnson (1982) and Amsden (1989). The free movement of capital, information, and knowledge cannot neutralize any first mover's advantage, as neoclassical economists assume, nor can state-directed industrial policy, technological policy, and trade policy completely transform any competitive disadvantage into competitive advantage, as the revisionists posit. Indeed, with all the forces of increasing pace of globalization, of free movement of information and knowledge, of international collaboration in research and development, and with all the state effort in promoting national competitiveness, yet the sectoral patterns of national competitiveness in both Japan and the USA have continued. In the sectors of service, software, drugs and medicines, biotechnology, Japan's competitive weaknesses have actually worsened in the last two decades of the twentieth century, even though the Japanese government has consistently targeted these sectors for government promotion.

Of more importance here is the fact that the US/Japanese sectoral patterns of competitiveness have continued in the last two decades despite volatile changes in exchange rates, dramatic reshaping of macro-economic conditions, increasing pace of globalization, giant leaps in technology, a paradigm shift of industrial organization, and sea changes in the nature of economy from that of industrial economy to digital economy. It is clear that more fundamental forces are at play that have contributed to Japanese and US sectoral patterns of competitiveness. To reveal these forces is the central purpose of this book.

PART II

The Knowledge Regime Perspective

At least six schools of explanations for the persistent sectoral patterns of national competitiveness can be derived from existing literature. The neoclassical approach explains them by using either the theory of comparative advantage or the theory of the international product cycle. As a new synthesis of the neoclassical approach, Porter's (1990) theory tries to account for sectoral patterns of national competitiveness by revealing differences in demand conditions, supply conditions, rivalry conditions, supporting and related sectors, and business strategies. The revisionist theory argues that Japanese success in certain sectors has largely been due to the combining advantage of active government industrial, trade, and technology policies and a specific business system that emphasizes production over consumption, export over import, and long-term market share over short-term profits (Johnson, 1982; Prestowitz, 1988; Fallows, 1994). The cultural approach attributes the sectoral patterns of national competitiveness to comparative cultural advantages and disadvantages of individualism and collectivism in different sectors and technologies (Dore, 1987; Vogel, 1987; Tai, 1989; Jin, 1995). The institutional approach proposes that it is differing forms of capitalism and divergent national systems of innovation, production, and organization that are responsible (Womack *et al.*, 1990; Gerlach, 1992). The technology approach emphasizes the importance of sectoral patterns of technological changes in causing disparity in competitiveness (Dosi, 1988; Pavitt, 1984; Kodama, 1991). And finally, the complexity approach attributes the persistent sectoral patterns either to the lock-in of divergent technological trajectories by the path-dependent impact of initial conditions and historical events (Mowery and Rosenberg, 1998) or to different degrees of complexity involved in product and process innovation in various sectors (Kash and Rycroft, 1999).

As elaborated elsewhere (Jin, 1998), while all the above approaches provide some insights into the sectoral patterns of national competitiveness, they are parochial, insufficient, and lack an integrative framework. This causes not only the fragmentation in theoretical development but also a danger of overgeneralization. Neglect of the problem of knowledge creation, which is the central concern for competitive advantage in this new age, further reduces the utility of existing approaches.

In this part, we will provide the knowledge regime perspective for explaining the sectoral patterns of US and Japanese competitiveness. This perspective does not deny the utilities of existing approaches, nor does it intend to substitute for them. It aims to provide a focus that links and integrates existing approaches into a coherent, meaningful, and systematic framework, and puts them into the right places and contingencies so that we can evaluate and appreciate both their advantages and shortcomings. In so doing, the knowledge regime perspective attempts to solve the controversies between adherents of the free market and proponents of industrial policy, between believers of individualism and advocates of groupism, and among supporters of the cultural, technological, institutional, and neoclassical approaches. Such a perspective will further provide a conceptual framework for both business strategists and policy analysts in making decisions concerning organizational, regional, and national competitiveness.

At the center of the knowledge regime perspective is the acknowledgment of the essential importance of the organizing principles of knowledge creation in shaping the persistent sectoral patterns of national competitiveness. The dominant organizing principles of a nation not only function as *attractors* that pull the constituting elements of the whole knowledge creation process into the 'iron cage' of a coherent system, but also put *isomorphic* pressures on both institutional and technological evolution to form a pervasive structure of isomorphism in which culture, technology, governance, and institutions coevolve into a mutually reinforcing and self-organizing system. Such a country-specific structure of isomorphism is the central cause for the formation and persistence of a robust country-specific system of knowledge creation that creates a persistent sectoral pattern of competitive advantages and disadvantages for each country.

The coevolution of culture, technology, governance, and institutions around specific organizing principles and the resultant isomorphic structure means that resorting to any single element as the explanatory variable for the persistent sectoral patterns of national competitiveness risks the fallacies of narrow focus and overgeneralization. To decode the nature of coevolution and the resultant isomorphic structures of a nation's system of knowledge creation, we need to focus on the underlying *dominant organizing principles* that shape the process of coevolution. Such a treatment will enable us to understand not only the coevolution of various elements of a country's knowledge regime, but also the resultant competitiveness implications. This part intends to provide a basic framework of the knowledge regime concept, and explore the relationship between culture and knowledge creation.

CHAPTER THREE

The Knowledge Regime Framework

Man does not know most of the rules on which he acts; and even what we call his intelligence is largely a system of rules which operate on him but which he does not know.

F. A. Hayek (1964: 461)

The U.S. and Japan clearly have distinct organizing principles and their values, institutions, and behavior fit into sharply different functional wholes.

Seymour Martin Lipset (1996: 212)

The primacy of knowledge creation

We have entered a knowledge society in which the sole source of sustainable competitive advantage is capability in the creation and appropriation of knowledge, rather than the traditional factors of production, such as unskilled labor, land, and physical capital (Drucker, 1993; Nonaka and Takeuchi, 1995). Notwithstanding its importance, people's perception of knowledge and its creation is still very much constrained by the narrow focus of various professional fields. Scholars and pratitioners from various disciplines emphasize different aspects of knowledge and thereby pinpoint different sources of competitive advantage. For Austrian economists, the foremost advocates for the importance of knowledge, the central problem is the effective discovery and utilization of dispersed knowledge at specific times and places (Hayek, 1945; Lavoie, 1985). For economists of human capital and specialists of human resource management, the focus is on knowledge imbedded in human skills and capabilities (Pfeffer, 1994). For resource-based theorists of business strategy, competitive advantages rest in firm-specific core competencies (Prahalad and Hamel, 1990). For evolutionary economists, what matters most is the kind of knowledge that is imbedded in organizational routines (Nelson and Winter, 1982). For new growth theorists, the key is the *stock* and *flow* of knowledge and their endogenous production (Romer, 1990). For students of technology policy, R&D and the resultant scientific and technological knowledge are the sole concern (Nelson, 1993). Consequently, according to various perspectives, the sources of competitive advantage can be attributed to human capital, knowledge stock and flow, R&D, organizational routines, core-competencies, and the market mechanism for discovery and appropriation of dispersed knowledge.

As analyzed by Jin (1998), neoclassical factors of production, including human capital and R&D, can hardly explain fully the sectoral patterns of national competitiveness. This is not only because human capital and R&D are, by themselves, only one aspect of the knowledge creation process, but also because different sectors may require different organizing principles for R&D and for the effective production and application of human capital. Furthermore, only through an examination of the whole process of knowledge creation can we effectively evaluate the role of human capital and R&D. The focus on the quantitative aspects of knowledge creation, including R&D spending, knowledge stock and flow, and aggregate human capital, is misleading because these variables are either the inputs for, or results of, the knowledge creation process. What really makes the difference in national competitiveness is the whole 'black box' of the knowledge creation process, which has not been systematically uncovered in the literature.

Such a knowledge creation process differs from one nation to another. Different countries have various stocks and flows of knowledge capital and human capital, attribute different weight to various forms of knowledge, adopt different patterns of knowing, build a distinct knowledge creation infrastructure, and organize the whole knowledge creation process according to dissimilar sets of organizing principles, constituting unique national systems of knowledge creation. The persistence of this uniqueness of national systems, which we will systematically investigate in this book, is indeed the very basis for the persistence of national sectoral patterns of competitiveness.

Beyond path-dependence

The persistent disparities of national sectoral patterns and national systems of knowledge creation challenge the convergence hypothesis of neoclassical economics or the rational school in general. Indeed, if economic institutions and governance mechanisms are formed purely as a result of rational consideration in minimizing either transaction costs or coordination costs as Williamson (1985) suggests, there should be no such persistent disparities. Instead, most national systems should have converged to make up the most efficient form.

As a response to this anomaly, scholars of technological innovation turn for help to evolutionary economics and the emerging science of complexity. Using such concepts as increasing returns, positive feedback, lock-in, and path-dependence, they explain the emergence and persistence of the specific trajectory of a nation's knowledge creation system through detailed accounts of historical conditions, events, players, and government policies, which are supposed to lock the evolutionary tractory into a path-dependent orbit (see e.g. Dosi *et al.*, 1998; Mowery and Rosenberg, 1998; Mowery and Nelson, 2000). Because of its emphasis on the impact of history on the evolution of technology and institutions, the approach is indeed a renewed historical school packaged with the new fad of complexity theory.

While the concept of path-dependence overcomes the fallacy of neoclassic economics, its oversimplified use and extension may create an even more dangerous trap that distracts people from the exploration of the in-depth forces shaping the evolution of technology and institutions. Indeed, if every technological trajectory, every governance mechanism, and every economic institution were only the result of lock-in and path-dependence of some seemingly whimsical historical conditions, events, and players, why would we be able to find so many consistencies of the sectoral patterns of national competitiveness, and of practices across different sectors and among different organizations within the same nation such as the USA and Japan (Biggart, 1991; Kogut, 1993; Westney, 1993; Jin, 1998)? Certainly different sectors and organizations within a nation have developed in different historical time, under different historical conditions, and being influenced by different players. Therefore, if trajectories of technologies and organizations were shaped only by the effect of path-dependence, they should have been quite dissimilar. Instead, overwhelming evidence indicates that the trajectories of technologies, business organizations, management practices, innovation patterns, human resource management, governance mechanisms, and sectoral competitiveness in either Japan or the USA are not only quite similar across various sectors but also isomorphic and mutually reinforcing among themselves (Jin, 1998). Such broad-scope isomorphism cannot be caused by simple path-dependence of accidental historical events or conditions, but by more fundamental forces that we will explore in this book.

From the view of epistemology, overreliance on historical events and the resultant path-dependence to explain the evolution and coevolution of technologies and institutions without exploring the deep forces shaping the process greatly reduces the explanatory power of any theory. In this chapter I will posit that, instead of being the path-dependent outcome of historical events and conditions, a nation's unique system of knowledge creation arises from the *attraction* of its axial organizing principles that act as *attractors* pulling the coevolution paths of culture, technology, governance, and institutions into an isomorphic system of knowledge creation, or what I have called the knowledge regime. By adopting this broad view of coevolution, the knowledge regime framework is able to integrate the fragmented institutional, cultural, technological, and complexity approaches to form an integrated perspective.

Axial organizing principles as attractors: culture's impact

What is missing in the *historical construction* of technological and institutional evolution by the path-dependence school is the human or socio-cultural construction. Both technological artifacts and social institutions are in essence constructed by human beings with purpose and values (Berger and Luckmann, 1966; Bijker *et al.*, 1989). What make people in different countries distinct are their fundamental assumptions about themselves, their relationship with nature, with other people, with society, and with the state, which constitute the core of national cultures. While anthropologists, sociologists, and organizational scientists have long recognized the important impact of national culture on the formation of national institutions and national business systems (Geertz, 1973; Hall, 1990; Lipset, 1990; Hofstede, 1991; Hampden-Turner and Trompenaars, 1993), students of technological innovation, influenced by mainstream economists' attitudes and the underlying rational school, have been reluctant to include culture as a major variable in their study of national innovation systems. If culture's impact is considered at all, it is treated as an *interfering* or *residual* factor that is marginal in its effect, just as many mainstream economics would suggest.

If we move away from formal rationality, centered on economists' narrow concern about efficiency and transaction costs, to substantial rationality, or the real purpose and value behind any human action (Polanyi, 1944/1957), we can find undeniable impact of national culture on the formation of institutions and organizations (Dore, 1987; Lipset, 1990, 1996; Fukuyama, 1995; Landes, 1998). Indeed, as decision scientists such as Simon (1957) and March (1988) reveal, value premises constitute the basis for both identifying a choice situation and choosing the preferred alternative. Therefore, when the issue is the choice of technologies or institutions, value premises should also be pivotal in shaping the final decision.

Notwithstanding the neoclassical bias, cultural theorists themselves have to take the blame for the failure to convince the mainstream of the important impact of culture on organizational, technological, and institutional evolution and coevolution. They tend to define culture in a too broad, too trivial, and too loose way to include anything that is not economic and not well-defined, ranging from culture as a system of habits, attitudes, values, and national characters, to culture as artifacts, arts, foods, novels, lifestyles, and idiosyncratic practices. If we redefine culture as human beings' fundamental assumptions about themselves and their relationships with others, and the underlying axial principles organizing both human relations and the human knowledge creation process, then it is much easier to understand that, in addition to economic rationality, these basic assumptions and organizing principles have a great impact on how we create technologies and institutions governing our relationships with nature, with other people, and with organizations, communities, and societies at large. When we shift from a pure economic concern for efficiency to the central issue of knowledge creation, the core value premises and axial organizing principles of a nation are found to be of pivotal importance.

Indeed, from the view of chaos theory and the theory of complexity, the axial cultural principles of a nation constitute the major *attractors* governing the evolution and coevolution of technologies, organizations, and institutions. When the process of knowledge creation is considered, while many students of technological innovation have focused on national disparity in various quantitative aspects of knowledge and its creation, such as patent statistics, R&D spending, and human capital, what are essential in understanding national systems of innovation are the axial principles that organize the whole knowledge creation process. The axial organizing principles of a nation define not only what kinds of R&D, knowledge, and capabilities are highly valued, but also how R&D is conducted, how different forms and types of knowledge are created, and how different kinds of knowledge capabilities are nurtured. Differences in the axial organizing principles of knowledge creation also determine in part how different knowledge infrastructures are created and sustained in various nations.

Independent vs. interdependent models of organizing

Nations differ in their culture largely as a result of their different basic assumptions about themselves and their relationships with others. Cultural theorists have developed various dimensions at which these assumptions may differ. For Hofstede (1991), they include individualism, power distance, uncertainty avoidance, masculinity, and long-term time orientation. For Hall (1990), they are high-context vs. low-context information processing, and monochronic vs. polychronic treatment of time. For Parsons (1937) and Trompenaars and Hampden-Turner (1993), they are universalism vs. particularism, affective vs. neutral, specific vs. diffused, and achievement vs. ascription. While all these dimensions are valid, they are not independent variables. Indeed, many of them are the derivatives of the axial principles of a cultural paradigm. In the USA, the axial principles organizing both human relations and human knowledge creation process are *autonomy* and *independence*. These principles lead to an individualist orientation in dealing with other people, the emphasis of low-context information processing, specificity and affective neutrality in role definition, and short-term and monochronic time orientation. Conversely, in Japan, the axial principles organizing both human relations and human knowledge creation process are *connection* and *interdependence*. These principles lead to groupism, high-context affectiveness, diffusedness, and polychronic time.

According to Markus and Kitayama (1998: 68), while the socialization process in the West has nurtured 'the independent model of personhood,' the same process in Japan has fostered 'the interdependent model of self.' The former treats individuals as being born free, equal, independent, separate, autonomous, and decontextualized, whereas the latter sees a person as 'an interdependent entity who is part of an encompassing social relationship' (p. 70). The independent model of self in the USA is consistent with its extreme individualism; it promotes separate, modular, and decontextual thinking in which individuals separate themselves from others and their surrounding social contexts, and make decisions according to objective calculation of self-interest and universal rules. Conversely, the interdependent model of self facilitates connectual and contextual knowing in which individuals connect themselves with others and with their surrounding environments and make decisions according to specific relationships and situations.

Contractual vs. connectual cultural paradigms

The axial organizing principles of a nation are derived from, and imbedded in, its dominant value structure, which determines the preferred ways of dealing with other people and the rest of the world. According to Lipset (1996), the USA and Japan are the two outliers that not only distinguish themselves from the rest of the world but also distinguish themselves from each other. In his words, the USA and Japan 'clearly have distinct organizing principles and their values, institutions, and behaviors fit into sharply different functional wholes' (p. 212). The most discussed distinction is between US individualism and Japanese groupism. As Lipset (1996: 20) summarizes:

> The emphasis in the American value system, in the American Creed, has been on the individual. Citizens have been expected to demand and protect their rights on a personal basis. The exceptional focus on law here as compared to Europe, derived from the Constitution and the Bill of Rights, has stressed rights against the state and other powers. America began and continues as the most anti-statist, legalistic, and rights-oriented nation.

Citing the work of psychologist Janet Spence, he (p. 218) further observes that individualism in the USA leads to 'a sense of self with a sharp boundary that stops at one's skin and clearly demarks self from non-self.' In sharp contrast, he remarks, 'for the Japanese, "*me* becomes merged with the we, and the reactions of the others to one's behaviors gains priority over one's own evaluations."' Quoting Spence's conclusion, Lipset (p. 218) comments:

These contrasting senses of self in the two societies are produced by and lead to differing emphases on rights versus obligations, on autonomy versus personal sacrifice, and on the priority of the individual versus that of the group – differences that have broad ramifications for the structure of political, economic, and social institutions.

Viewing the issue from a broader scope, the above descriptions by Lipset and Spence go beyond the dichotomy between individualism and groupism (or collectivism). The issue here is not just a concern for oneself vs. concern for others, but also a question of *how these concerns are fulfilled*. Both personal and collective interest can be achieved through either *contract* or *connection*. While the former cherishes the autonomy and independence of individuals, the latter values the connection and interdependence of members. While the former focuses on individual or collective *rights*, the latter emphasizes individual or collective *obligations*. While the former resorts to generalized rules of law to protect rights, the latter relies on the self-reinforcing nature of strong social ties and bonds to secure the fulfillment of obligations. In sum, other than the dichotomy between individualism and groupism (collectivism), we have another independent dichotomy between *contractual man* and *connectual man*. As a result, we have two dimensions in the value structures of nations (Figure 3.1).

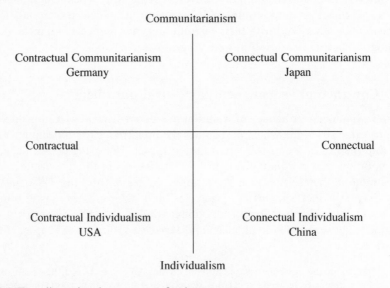

Figure 3.1 Two-dimensional structures of value systems

The dichotomy of contractual and connectual man is very much in line with Parsons's (1937) distinction between universalism and particularism, since contractual man resorts to universal and generalized rules of law to safeguard one's rights whereas connectual man relies on particular social networks in securing the fulfillment of obligations. Once we make this linkage, we can use the measurement of universalism vs. particularism as a proxy for the measurement of contractual vs. connectual man. In comparing country differences according to their empirical data, Hampden-Turner and Trompenaars (1993, p. 198) find that:

Germany and the United States are both highly universalistic, whereas Japan is particularistic. But in two other values, Germany has more in common with Japan than the United States. Where the United States is analytical, Germany is integrative. Where the United States is individualistic, Germany is communitarian.

In our terminology, German culture can be characterized as contractual communitarianism, whereas Japanese culture is connectual communitarianism. On the other hand, the USA belongs to contractual individualism, whereas China adheres to connectual individualism. By making these distinctions, we are able to differentiate the puzzling similarities and differences between these countries. Influenced by the same Confucian heritage, both Japan and China emphasize the connectual structure of human interactions (Jin, 1995). However, the Japanese connectual structure is directed *vertically* toward groups or communities, whereas the Chinese one is directed *horizontally* toward family members, kin, and friends (Nakane, 1972). Similarly, influenced by the same Judeo-Christian heritage, both the USA and Germany emphasize the importance of universal rules and contracts in governing human interaction. However, Germany with its communitarian tradition emphasizes contracts among *groups* whereas the USA with its individualistic creed stresses contracts among *independent individuals*.

From this point of view, the major differences between the West and the East, or more specifically between Christian culture and Confucian culture, is a distinction not so much between individualism and communitarianism as between contractual man and connectual man. The former seeks the universal and generalized rule of law and contracts to govern human interaction whereas the latter relies on some forms of connectual structures as the dominant governing mechanisms for human interaction.

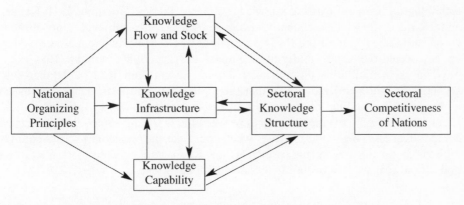

Figure 3.2 Organizing principles and national competitiveness

From axial to derivative principles: dominant patterns of knowing and competitiveness

Both cultural paradigms and the imbedding axial organizing principles have a fundamental impact on the way knowledge is created. Figure 3.2 shows the centrality of axial organizing principles in the constitution of a nation's knowledge creation system and in the formation of the sectoral patterns of national competitiveness.

Organizing principles and knowledge stock and flow

The stock of knowledge in a nation refers to the existing inventory of knowledge that the nation accumulated in all forms including scientific theories, technological knowledge, human capital, organizational routines, standards, patents, manuals, and books. The flow of knowledge is the net increase in the pool of knowledge. Both knowledge stock and flow are not solely the result of investment in education and R&D. Rather, their national disparities are shaped by the different axial organizing principles in various nations, which determine not only what types and forms of knowledge are highly valued, but also how they are produced, reproduced, stored, exchanged, and appropriated.

For example, because of its penchant for autonomy and independence, the USA values highly explicit, scientific, objective, quantitative, analytic, and professional knowledge. Antithetically, because of its strong inclination for connection and interdependence, Japan prefers highly tacit, intuitive, inter-subjective, qualitative, synergetic, firm-specific, and relation-specific knowledge. As a result, the nature of human capital and R&D is very different in the USA and Japan. While in the USA human capital is treated as being equivalent to formal training and professional experiences, in Japan it is centered on shop-floor experiences, cross-functional knowledge integration, and individual capabilities in contributing to the *group process* of knowledge creation (Koike, 1990). In the USA, the objective of R&D is scientific and technological breakthroughs, whereas in Japan it is focused on learning, incremental improvement, cross-functional integration, and cross-technological fusion of existing knowledge and capabilities (Kodama, 1991; Kenney and Florida, 1993). Consequently, while knowledge creation and innovation is considered the sole job of the R&D department in US firms, in Japanese firms they are considered the responsibility of all employees (Imai, 1986; Nonaka, 1994).

When such qualitative differences in human capital and R&D are taken into account, it is quite understandable that their quantitative aspects, measured in such terms as R&D spending, number of Ph.D.s, and average years of formal education, cannot account fully for the differences between the USA and Japan in their sectoral competitiveness (Jin, 1998). Only when we take into account cross-country differences in the organizing principles of R&D and skill formation can we understand real sources of national competitive advantage.

Organizing principles and knowledge infrastructure

Country-specific axial organizing principles shape the emergence of a nation's unique infrastructure for knowledge creation, including its systems of education, innovation, learning, and skill formation. First, its axial principles of independence and autonomy have led to the emphasis on explicit knowledge in the USA, which in turn has given rise to a knowledge creation system that is centered on formal education, independent R&D, and systematic codification of information. The stress on explicit knowledge in turn facilitates the formation of a plethora of consulting services trying to sell knowledge and skills in the market. Dimetrically, Japan's axial principles of connection and interdependence has led to its emphasis on tacit and contextual knowledge, leading to the formation of a system of knowledge creation that is centered on shop-floor learning and broad skill formation (Koike and Inoki, 1990).

Second, the US drive for autonomy and independence has given rise to the dominance of division and specialization in the knowledge creation process, characterized by separation of thinking from executing, of basic research from applied research, of R&D from production and marketing, and of one discipline of knowledge from another. It also causes the division of the knowledge creation processes between suppliers and producers, and between producers and users. The separation of disciplines contributes to the emphasis on specialists and the formation of strong professional organizations in the USA. In contrast, the drive for connection and interdependence in Japan has resulted in its stress on the organic integration of knowledge between thinking and doing, among R&D, manufacturing, and marketing, and between suppliers and producers (Clark and Fujimoto, 1991). The same inclination toward connection and interdependence has shaped the Japanese focus on fusion and integration among various scientific disciplines and technological domains. The result is a preference for generalists in Japan (Westney, 1993).

Third, the US axial principles of autonomy and independence have led to an emphasis on standardization, modularization, systemization, and people-independent systems integration as the dominant principles in organizing the knowledge creation processes. These principles have contributed significantly to the emergence of the US system of mass production, which is the main cause for US dominance in the twentieth century. Although it faced the Japanese challenge, the mass production system continues to give US firms a competitive advantage in the sectors where these organizing principles still work effectively. In the 1990s, the same organizing principles have also facilitated US dominance in digital economy and e-business.

By comparison, the Japanese drive for connection and interdependence has directed its emphasis on customization, contextualization, connectivity, and people-dependent systems integration as the dominant principles in organizing the knowledge creation processes. The fusion of these endogenous principles with transplanted US principles of division, standardization, modularization, and systemization has led to the emergence of a Japanese system of flexible production which combines the best of the two sets of organizing principles. This has given Japanese firms a competitive advantage in the sectors where the organizing principles of division, standardization, modularization, and systemization alone cannot work effectively without the complementary support of the organizing principles of customization, contextualization, connectivity, and people-dependent systems integration.

Finally, the US penchant for autonomy and independence has also created a sharp division between public and private knowledge. When the production and reproduction of knowledge have large positive externalities that are difficult to appropriate by the producers of knowledge, the USA tries to provide the knowledge as a public good. The public provision of knowledge enables the autonomy of individuals who are dependent on it for further knowledge creation and appropriation. In contrast, the Japanese way of appropriating the externalities of knowledge is through the establishment of a system of *corporate networks* that share the externalities of knowledge amongst themselves. As a result, the public portion of R&D investment in the USA is always much larger than that of Japan (Sternberg, 1996).

Organizing principles and knowledge creation capability

The differing organizing principles and the resultant disparate knowledge infrastructures have a great impact on the knowledge creation capabilities of nations. This is especially reflected in the disparity in the speed, quality, swiftness, agility, and capacity in engaging in effective knowledge creation to serve the objective of maintaining and enhancing national competitiveness. In the USA, an emphasis on individual autonomy and independence leads to a superior capability in individual entrepreneurship and the *spontaneous innovation* of new technologies. The dominant organizing principles of division and specialization also enable the formation and maintenance of well-developed professional capabilities in dealing with very delicate technological problems in depth. The preponderant organizing principles of modularization and systemization further facilitate a superior US capability in people-independent systems integration and in the design of large-scale technological systems such as aircraft and nuclear technologies. The USA's emphasis on standardization also nurtures its superior capacity in the production and marketing of standardized products such as Coca-Cola and McDonald's hamburgers. Finally, the US emphasis on explicit, objective, scientific, and quantitative knowledge also leads to its superior competencies in science-based sectors, in information services, and recently in e-businesses.

Conversely, the Japanese desire for connection and interdependence leads to the formation of a superior capability in the *fusion* of existing technologies (Kodama, 1991). Their preference for knowledge integration among R&D, manufacturing, and marketing, between suppliers and producers, and between producers and users enables the formation of core competencies in concurrent engineering, design for manufacturing, and in harnessing knowledge across disciplinary, task, and organizational boundaries. The emphasis on tacit, inter-subjective, relation-specific knowledge, together with the practices of just-in-time production and delivery (JIT), quality circles, and job rotation, contributes greatly to Japanese superiority in incremental improvement.

Organizing principles and knowledge structure

The structure of knowledge in a sector refers to the relevance and composition of various types and forms of knowledge for a firm's competitiveness in that sector. Different sectors require different capabilities for the creation of different types and forms of knowledge to achieve different competitive advantages. Several dimensions of knowledge structure need to be considered for understanding the dynamics of knowledge creation. The first is the possibility to digitalize, codify, quantify, standardize, depersonalize, and decontextualize knowledge that is of pivotal importance for competitiveness. When the possibility is high, US companies usually have a competitive advantage. Conversely, when the pivotal knowledge for competitiveness is difficult to make explicit, to quantify and decontextualize, but is rather imbedded in people's tacit skill, in contextual understanding, and in customized relations, Japanese firms usually have a competitive advantage. The sectors that belong to the first category include soft drinks, fast food, insurance services, financial services, consulting, formal marketing research, information processing, and most recently e-commerce and e-business. The sectors belonging to the second category include most complex fabricating manufacturing sectors of home electronics, opto-electronics, and mechatronics.

The second dimension is the extent to which the knowledge among various domains, functions, and specialties is interlinked. When the pivotal knowledge for competitive advantage can be generated within a given domain, or when each domain or division can successfully modularize and encapsulate its knowledge creation process, US firms are usually competitive. Conversely, when the organic integration of knowledge among various domains, functions, and specialties is pivotal for success, Japanese firms are usually more competitive. The very possibility of partitioning, modularizing, and encapsulating the tasks of knowledge creation into separate and independent domains enables US firms to harness their superior capabilities of individual entrepreneurship, technological breakthrough, and spontaneous technological innovation, constituting the keys for US competitive success in the sectors of biotechnology, prepackaged software, and information service. Conversely, Japanese firms are competitive in the sectors of mature, complex fabricating manufacturing sectors, in which the knowledge capabilities of *organized technological fusion*, incremental improvement, design for manufacturing, and organic knowledge integration across functional and organizational boundaries are pivotal for competitive success.

The disparity of US and Japanese competitiveness in the above sectors is further reinforced by the third dimension of their knowledge structures, i.e. the cumulativeness and continuity of knowledge over time. Because of the dominance of connectual governance mechanisms, which we will discuss later, the Japanese are more competitive in the sectors where the need for synthesizing the knowledge of the past with that of the present is high, which is typical in complex fabricating manufacturing sectors. Conversely, because of the dominance of contractual governance mechanisms, which we will also discuss later, US firms are more agile in generating technological breakthroughs that cause technological discontinuity, which is typical in biotechnology.

The final dimension is the nature of knowledge linkage among subsystems. While in some sectors such as prepackaged software, knowledge linkage can be articulated into explicit and prespecified system logic and systems architecture by systems designers and system integrators, other sectors such as FMS require the organic integration of knowledge by the people on the shop floor. The US advantage in prepackaged computer software is therefore facilitated by its organizing principles of standardization, modularization, systemization, and people-independent systems integration. Conversely, the Japanese competitive advantage in opto-electronics, CNC (numerical control machine tools), FMS, and CIM (computer-integrated manufacturing) is enabled by the organizing principles of connection, integration, fusion, contextualization, and customization.

In the design, production and application of CNC, FMS, and CIM, other than the importance of systems integration, the key issue is to harness the experiences of shop-floor operators to make flexible changes in the programming of the system to best suit the diverse requirements of various functions and operations. While the penchant for specialization and systemization does help Americans in the design of CNC, FMS and CIM, their preference for people-independent systems integration leads to a failure in integrating the important knowledge of shop-floor operators. By contrast, the Japanese emphasis on connection, contextual fusion, and people-dependent integration enables their firms to harness the knowledge of shop-floor operators as well as relation-specific knowledge across functional and organizational boundaries.

The isomorphic structure of knowledge regimes

Looking from a much broader angle, it is the case that not only the knowledge stock and flow, knowledge infrastructure, and knowledge capabilities of a nation are greatly impacted by its axial organizing principles, but so are the emergence and dominance of institutions of knowledge creation and trajectories of technological development. The coevolution of cultural paradigms, governance mechanisms, and technological trajectories around the attraction of axial organizing principles forms the broad-scope isomorphic structure of knowledge regimes. Within such a structure, the dominant national organizing principles of knowledge creation are facilitated and imbedded in the value structure, governance structure, task structure, and incentive structure of a nation's knowledge creation system. Reciprocally, the organizing principles of knowledge creation facilitate the realization of dominant cultural values, support the emergence and dominance of certain governance mechanisms, influence the structure of incentives, and enable the fulfillment of some tasks while hindering others, pulling technological trajectories of different sectors to an isomorphic path. As a result, as shown in Figure 3.3, culture, governance, technology, and institutions are all attracted by the same axial organizing principles to form a structure of broad-scope isomorphism in a nation.

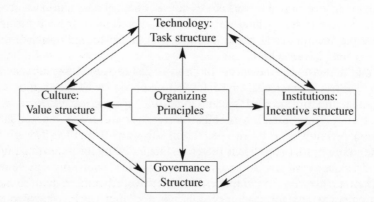

Figure 3.3 Organizing principles and the broad-scope isomorphism of knowledge regimes

It is important to point out that this broad-scope isomorphism is much more pervasive and encompassing than the concept of institutional isomorphism put forward by DiMaggio and Powell (1983). While the latter limits itself to an organizational field, the former encompasses all organizational fields in a nation; while the latter focuses only on similarity of organizational practices, the former extends the similarity across culture, technology, organization, and institutions. It is this mutually reinforcing nature of culture, technology, institutions, and governance mechanisms organized around axial organizing principles that enables the formation of an *iron cage* of a broad-scope isomorphism that makes a nation's knowledge regime and its evolution unique, consistent, and not conducive to change. It also hampers the adoption and transplantation of alternative organizing principles, governance mechanisms, and technological trajectories. The persistence of the sectoral patterns of national competitiveness is largely the result of the super-stable structure of isomorphism surrounding the dominant organizing principles.

Contractual vs. connectual governance

The differences in axial organizing principles and cultural paradigms lead to the divergence of the dominant governance mechanisms for knowledge creation among nations. While the cultural paradigm of contractual man enables the emergence and predominance of contractual governance in the USA, the cultural paradigm of connectual man facilitates the emergence and preponderance of connectual governance in Japan.

Acknowledgement of the existence of these two *generic* mechanisms of governance has profound theoretical ramifications. It places the cultural dimension back into our analysis of governance mechanisms. In the neoclassical theory of governance, as represented by Williamson's (1985) work, no place is reserved for the impact of culture on governance mechanisms. He talks about the governance structures of markets, hierarchies, and their hybrid forms as if they were generic and universally identical across different societies with distinct cultures. From our perspective, the Williamsonian governance structures of markets and hierarchies are only the *contractual* types that are prevalent in Anglo-American societies. The dominant forms of market and hierarchical governance in East Asian Confucian societies are those of the *connectual* type that are very different from the *contractual* type of Anglo-American societies. Furthermore, instead of focusing on economic transaction and transaction costs, our discussion of governance mechanisms is about knowledge creation and appropriation. By focusing on knowledge creation, we transform the definition of the firm from that of economizing transaction costs to that of maximizing knowledge creation, and the focus of governance mechanisms from economic institutions to national systems of innovation.

Contractual governance for knowledge creation in the USA

The contractual governance mechanisms as dominant in the USA attempt to align the interests of individuals through *formal contracts* in which the rights and interests of each participating individual are clearly delineated and demarcated. Contracts are implemented through the state enforcement of the universal rule of law. Under contractual governance, each individual is assumed to pursue the maximization of his or her self-interest. The design of contracts is also structured in such a way that possible opportunities for manipulation are minimized. In so doing, contractual governance mechanisms aim at maximizing autonomy and independence of individuals in both economic transactions and the knowledge creation process.

There are several contractual governance mechanisms that are dominant in Anglo-American societies. The contractual markets try to maximize the autonomy and independence of contracting partners through a system of competitive bidding which is impersonal and at arm's length. To maximize the *interchangeability* and *substitutability* of transacting partners, the trading subjects, including materials, labor, skills, capabilities, and knowledge, are standardized, quantified, modularized, encapsulated, and packaged.

The same is true for the contractual governance of hierarchies. To secure the maximal autonomy and independence of business owners and top managers, the operations of firms are routinized and systemized. Operational and financial information is systematically collected and analyzed so that the possibilities for opportunistic manipulation by middle-level management are minimized. Job tasks and their required skills are also standardized so that workers are interchangeable. Finally, divisional functions are made independent through the creation of profit centers or strategic business units (SBU) that modularize and encapsulate divisional task structures.

The contractual governance of markets and hierarchies in the USA has coevolved with the emergence and dominance of Taylorism and Fordism, and with the development of US capital markets, job markets, education systems, and R&D institutions. It has facilitated the McDonaldization, modularization, systemization, and digitalization of US society (Blair, 1988; Ritzer, 1995). It has enabled the marketization of knowledge creation and appropriation through business franchizing, information services, consulting, and professionalization. It underpins the US innovations of fast foods, supermarket and discount warehouse retailing, the linear model of innovation, M-form organization, venture capital institutions, object-oriented technology, e-business, and modular designs of production lines, business processes, cargo containers, buildings, automobiles, furnitures, musics, TV series, sports, and college curricula.

Contractual governance mechanisms even permeate the operation of clans and networks in the USA, the two structures thought to be Japanese inventions (Ouchi, 1980). Even though the clan structure in the USA has shared values among its members, as in the cases of US basketball teams and high-tech start-up firms, their formation is largely based on contracts that demarcate concrete rights and responsibilities for each member. Furthermore, contracts have limited time horizons so that there are opportunities for renegotiating terms and for exiting teams. The same is true for the network governance in the USA, which is very much contract-based. In sum, the dominant US governance structures of markets, hierarchies, clans, and networks follow the same contractual mechanisms derived from the US cultural paradigm of contractual man and axial principles of autonomy and independence (Figure 3.4).

The competitive advantages and disadvantages of contractual governance are sector-contingent. In the sectors where transactional terms for knowledge creation

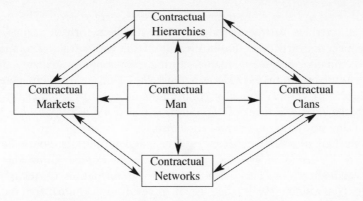

Figure 3.4 The dominance of contractual governance in the USA

and exchange are difficult to articulate in advance or where tasks are difficult effectively to partition, modularize, and encapsulate into independent tasks for individual transactions, contractual governance incurs both high transaction costs and loss of knowledge creation opportunities owing to a lack of exchange, integration, and fusion of knowledge across inter-linked tasks. These situations are typical in the complex fabricated manufacturing sectors. On the other hand, the very need for explicitly articulating transactional terms has facilitated US innovation in digitalization and codification. It has pulled the USA to the forefront in the codification, quantification, standardization, digitalization, and systemization of data and information involved in every economic transaction, making the USA a top innovator and dominant player in accounting services, formal marketing research, information processing and services, and most recently the emerging e-businesses. The need to sell various forms of created knowledge in contractual markets has also contributed to US dominance in technical and managerial consulting, and in business franchising. The penchant for appropriating knowledge through contractual markets, combined with a strong intellectual property protection regime and a strong tendency for voluntary association (Lipset, 1990), has stimulated the emergence of a plethora of individualistic entrepreneurs, start-up firms, and venture capitalists for the spontaneous innovation of new products and processes. The fast configuring and reconfiguring nature of contractual teams and networks further secures the agility in recruiting the best talents for swift innovations (Quinn *et al.*, 1996). This superior capability in spontaneous innovation and simultaneous experimentation has been the pivotal force underpinning the USA's strong position in biotechnology, information technology, and e-business.

Connectual governance for knowledge creation in Japan

In contrast to the preponderance of the contractual governance in the USA, the cultural model of connectual man in Japan has led to the dominance of connectual governance mechanisms of markets, hierarchies, and networks. The Japanese markets have been dominantly governed by various *connectual structures* that link suppliers with producers, producers with customers, businesses with banks, businesses with governments, and businesses with local communities. Such connectual relations are long-term oriented and cooperative. The connectual structures of markets between producers and suppliers form a *vertical keiretsu*, while the connectual structures that link a major bank with a trading company, a life insurance company, and many manufacturing companies specializing in various sectors constitute an *intermarket keiretsu* (Gerlach, 1992). Because Japanese markets are imbedded into various forms of connections among firms, banks, and trading companies, the Japanese form of capitalism is called *alliance capitalism* (Gerlach, 1992), or, using our term, *connectual capitalism.*

The connectual structures between producers and suppliers support the effective exchange and diffusion of various types of tacit and explicit knowledge between producers and suppliers. They also facilitate the formation of relation-specific knowledge (Asanuma, 1989) that is of pivotal importance for incremental improvements. The connectual structures between business and government, largely through industrial policy, technology policy, and trade policy, also enable the effective exchange and diffusion of knowledge and capabilities among business firms and between government and business (Samuels, 1994).

Connectual governance mechanisms also dominate relationships within Japanese firms. It is well known that in Japan the relationship between employers and employees is not contractual but relational (Nakane, 1972). Workers are not treated as dispensable factors of production but as both an asset and the most important stakeholder of the firm. Reciprocally, employees see the firm as an extended family and identify themselves with it. The lifetime employment policy that was prevalent in large Japanese firms until very recently is very much an imbodiment of, and a tool for, connectual exchange between employers and employees and among employees. The connectual structures thereby facilitate the emergence and dominance of a system of work organization characterized by broad job classifications, a lack of functional specialization, and an emphasis on generalists, shop-floor experiences, job rotation, cross-functional teams, horizontal information flows and coordination, quality circles, and decision by consensus (Lincoln, 1989; Aoki, 1994).

One of the competitive advantages of all these organizational arrangements is their ability to create and maintain knowledge links among various organizational functions and units. First, the connectual structure enables Japanese firms to encourage employees to create and master firm-specific, relational, and contextual knowledge and skills that are not saleable to external markets. This is further supported by practices of job rotation and cross-functional teams and the emphasis on generalists and long-term shop-floor learning. Second, the connectual structure enables the free exchange, diffusion, and organic integration of information, knowledge, and competencies across functional units and among co-workers (Aoki, 1990). The exchange of knowledge, especially tacit knowledge, is further institutionalized through quality circles, and cross-functional teams. Finally, when linked to the connectual structure outside the firm's boundaries, the connectual structure within the company can provide the kinds of knowledge that are tacit, firm-, relation- and context-specific to other firms, further appropriating the knowledge creation capability of connected firms.

An in-depth application of the connectual governance mechanisms to Japanese firms can produce clan-like organizations in which members share both their values and objectives (Ouchi, 1981). Such a clan structure vastly reduces the need for *economic* incentives to motivate employees for their commitment to knowledge creation. A clan structure also promotes a process of socialization that aids the sharing of tacit knowledge (Nonaka and Takeuchi, 1995). In summary, the connectual cultural paradigm in Japan facilitates the emergence and dominance of the connectual governance structures of markets, hierarchies, clans, and networks (Figure 3.5).

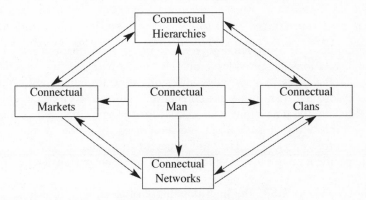

Figure 3.5 The dominance of connectual governance in Japan

Connectual governance mechanisms are not without disadvantages. First, by limiting the innovation effort within the boundaries of various connectual structures, the emergence of start-ups for spontaneous innovation are hindered. Second, by focusing on connectual exchange and the creation and sharing of tacit, relational, contextual, and firm-specific knowledge, it neglects the systematic codification, digitalization, quantification, and sharing of explicit data and information for contractual economic transactions. Third, by emphasizing people as the key connector for integrating technological subsystems, it neglects the development of capabilities in the design and integration of technologies of large-scale complexity, such as large-scale software systems and airplanes, whose operation can be people-independent. Finally, while connectual governance was a superior structure for knowledge creation and integration in the age of mass production in which the speed of technical change was moderate while the technological and economic uncertainties were low, it is increasingly showing a lack of flexibility and agility in the age of mass customization, increasing returns, hypercompetition, fast technical change, and great uncertainties. With the increasing pace of technological change and the accelerating significance of spontaneous innovation and e-business, the impact of these deficiencies has been greatly magnified during the 1990s.

Organizing principles and incentive structures

The most important impact of governance mechanisms on knowledge creation, and therefore on competitiveness, is the way in which they structure the incentives for knowledge creation. Under the dominance of contractual governance, US knowledge workers create knowledge primarily for contractual exchange. They secure the market value of their knowledge and skills by specialization and by identifying with their professions; and they maximize opportunities for employment and promotion by socializing within professional associations. Alternatively, under the dominance of connectual governance mechanisms, Japanese knowledge workers create knowledge for connectual exchange. They try to maximize the value of their knowledge and skills to the connected firms by socializing within the firms and by developing firm- and relation-specific knowledge (Koike, 1994).

Exit and knowledge creation

Under the dominance of contractual governance in the USA, the low cost of exiting a contractual relationship provides employee incentives for the creation and development of the types of knowledge and skills that are either useful for other firms or useful for their own future entrepreneurial ventures. As a result, employees are driven either by the development of knowledge for spin-off ventures, or by the generation and mastering of generalized and standardized knowledge and skills that are saleable to other employers. They are reluctant to master tacit, firm-, relation- and context-specific knowledge and skills that are useless when transferring from one firm to another.[1]

For employers in the USA, the high possibility of an employee exiting the firm lowers management motivation to provide on-the-job-training and increases the incentive to standardize and modularize the jobs and skill requirements so that management's reliance on a particular employee's skill and, therefore, the switching costs of changing employees, are minimized. For the educational institutions, the provision of explicit, standardized, modularized, and systemized knowledge and skills is always preferred to the development of tacit, relation-specific, and contextual knowledge, because the former enables the formation of distinct professions that are independent and autonomic. As a result, the education system in the USA has been dominantly organized by the principles of modularization and professionalization (Blair, 1988). This similar incentive structure of minimizing exit costs and switching costs for employers, employees and educators provides a strong isomorphic pull for the production and reproduction of standardized, modularized, and professionalized knowledge and skills, making professionals and knowledge workers interchangeable in the job market.

By contrast, in the Japanese system of connectual governance, the costs of exit for employees are so high that in most cases it is not a realistic option. The expectation of lifetime employment provides incentives for management to offer on-the-job training and incentives for employees to learn firm-, relation- and context-specific knowledge and skills. The emergence and dominance of the Japanese practices of on-the-job training, job rotation, cross-functional teams, and an emphasis on generalists (Koike, 1994) are very much the results of both management and employee incentives to learn tacit, firm-, relation- and context-specific, and cross-functional knowledge and skills.

Socialization and knowledge creation

The Japanese incentives for learning these types of knowledge and skills are further facilitated by the emphasis on socialization, a process in which shared organizational norms, rules, and routine are emerging and evolving through frequent interactions among group members. Ubiquitous in Japanese firms, socialization is imbedded in such practices as company slogans and ceremonies, company-sponsored sports and vocations, and after-work social gatherings at bars. It enables not only the alignment of individual values and behaviors with the norms of organizations and groups, but also the development of *inter-subjective* knowledge about the skills and capabilities of other members. It facilitates the diffusion of tacit knowledge (Nonaka, 1994); it helps the creation of relational and contextual knowledge and generates a common knowledge base for further knowledge creation.

While the socialization process is highly integrated into Japanese organizational and group life, it is less so in US firms. Instead, it often happens outside the firm, in families, churches, friend circles, and associations, and through mass media. The high turnover rate of employees further deteriorates the already thin common knowledge base for effective transfer of tacit knowledge within the boundaries of organizations. As a result, instead of a focus on relation-specific and inter-subjective knowledge, Americans tend to rely on objective, explicit, quantitative, standardized, and systemized knowledge that is people-independent.

Identification and knowledge creation

Different modes of identification further pull the USA to the organizing principles of standardization, specialization, modularization, and systemization, and draw Japan to those of customization, connection, contextualization, and integration. In assessing the deep-seated differences in the social attachments of Japanese and Westerners, Lincoln (1993: 57) notes:

> Westerners (perhaps Americans in particular) identify heavily with their occupational positions and roles, and only secondarily with the organizations and groups in which those positions and roles are imbedded; hence, the pervasive pattern in the U.S. economy of people pursuing careers within occupations that take them across a series of employing organizations. The Japanese ... link themselves first to groups and only secondly to functional positions within them. ... A strong affiliation with a group implies a willingness to take on any of the responsibilities arising from group membership.

This American tendency is derived from the cultural model of contractual man and the subsequent dominance of contractual governance mechanisms. In other words, occupational positions and roles become the subject of identification because the occupational knowledge and skills imbedded in their positions and roles are the only sources for US workers to contract with their firms. Once they lose their occupations they also lose their market value for employers. Therefore, the acquisition of professional knowledge and the development of occupational skills that can be sold in the professional market become the most important career objective for US knowledge workers. They further rely on professional reputation and professional networks in securing future employment and promotion opportunities.

On the other hand, the Japanese identification with their affiliated groups and organizations is also derived from its cultural model of connectual man and the resulting dominance of the connectual governance mechanisms. Connectual logic requires mutual identification and obligation between employers and employees. It is in connectual exchange of commitment where each side takes the values and interests of the other side as one's own and enlarges the bodily limited self to the extended self that includes connected group members.

The identification of Japanese employees with their firms has a profound impact on the dominant organizing principles of knowledge creation. While the knowledge creation process in US firms is individually based and therefore directed toward the development of professional knowledge and skills, in Japan it is group-based and therefore directed toward the development of firm-specific, relation-specific, and mission-specific knowledge and skills that can help achieve the ultimate goals of the firms (Cole, 1995b). The willingness of Japanese employees to master cross-functional knowledge and skills through job rotation and other forms of cross-functional training provides their firms with a competitive advantage in the fusion of existing knowledge, capabilities, and technologies. The identification of Japanese employees with their firms also helps the formation of a superior capability for incremental improvement. Underpinning the successful Japanese practices of quality

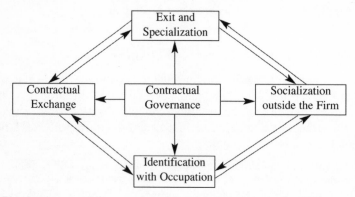

Figure 3.6 The dominance of the contractual incentive structure in the USA

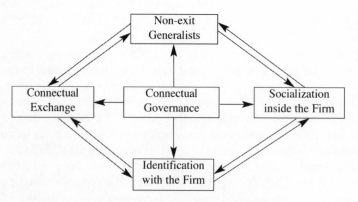

Figure 3.7 The dominance of the connectual incentive structure in Japan

circles, JIT production and delivery, concurrent engineering, and flexible production is the unending Japanese devotion to knowledge creation and skill formation.

Figures 3.6 and 3.7 summarize the two different dominant incentive structures for knowledge creation in the USA and Japan. In the USA, the contractual incentive structure promotes a frequent exit of knowledge workers to establish new start-up ventures. The socialization and identification with professional associations, together with various institutional arrangements, further facilitates the fast configuration and reconfiguration of a large number of innovative teams for spontaneous innovation. In Japan, the emphasis on generalists and on long-term socialization, identification, and exchange within connectual structures facilitates organized technological fusion and organic knowledge integration across task and organizational boundaries. While US superior capability in spontaneous innovation promotes its competitiveness in biotechnology and information technology, Japanese superior capability in organized technology fusion enhances its competitiveness in opto-electronics and mechatronics.

Organizing principles and task structures

The cross-national differences in cultural paradigms, governance mechanisms, and incentive structures would not cause sectoral differences in national competitiveness were there no sectoral differences in the task structure of knowledge creation. Like our discussion of knowledge structure, the task structure of a sector is characterized by several dimensions, which include complexity of scale, decomposibility, tightness of coupling, explicitness of coupling, linearity of coupling, and continuity of architecture.

When the task of knowledge creation and innovation is simple, as is typical in the simple products of soft drinks and fast food and in the simple processes of car rental and credit reporting, the US system of contractual governance usually works well (Kash and Rycroft, 1999). When the task is extremely complex, as is typical in the innovation and development of airplanes, telecomunications systems, and semiconductor chips on a large scale, the US system that emphasizes specialists, division, and people-independent systems integration works more effectively than its Japanese counterpart because the latter stresses generalists, organic connection, and people-dependent systems integration. The Japanese system is less effective because of the limited cognitive capacity of generalists in dealing with problems of extreme complexity. Conversely, when the scale of complexity is moderate, as in the case of automobiles, opto-electronics, and mechatronics, areas in which generalists have enough cognitive capacity to prosper through long-term on-the-job learning and job rotation, Japanese firms are usually more competitive.

The second dimension is decomposibility, i.e. the possibility of partitioning, modularizing, and encapsulating a complex task into relatively independent subtasks for independent individuals to deal with. When a complex task is completely decomposable, it can be partitioned effectively in order that specialists can attack each subtask independently without any need for organic integration or any loss of knowledge creation opportunities. This opens up great opportunities for division of labor and for simultaneous experimentation by a large number of independent innovators and knowledge creators. This situation certainly favors the USA with its high level of individualism. Conversely, when it is difficult to partition a complex task without compromising knowledge integration or losing knowledge creation opportunities, a connectual structure of generalists is required to cope with the complexity. In such a case, Japanese firms usually hold the competitive advantage. One good example of this is US competitiveness in the design and production of standardized auto parts and Japanese competitiveness in the design and production of auto engines. While the task of the former can be effectively partitioned and therefore accomplished by individuals, the task of the latter can only be accomplished by a holistic approach. Another example involves computers with open systems architecture and modular design. The modular design of computers enables spontaneous innovation of computer parts by US firms, leaving most Japanese firms desperately trying to catch up. With its object-oriented technology, the Internet provides the ultimate source for spontaneous innovation in all related areas, and it has thereby tilted the lever of competitive advantage to the US side.

The third dimension is the tightness of ties between parts in a technological system. When parts can be loosely coupled without affecting their best performance as a whole, the knowledge link among parts is also weak, and individual specialists can attack each problem independently with a minimal need for coordination and integration. In such a case, the USA is usually competitive. A good example of this is the design and production of a hamburger and other modular products. When a technological system requires tight coupling for best performance as in the cases of the design of automobiles, opto-electronics, and mechatronics, and of advanced manufacturing technologies, there is greater need for organic integration and seamless coordination. In such cases, Japanese connectual governance, with its emphasis on cross-functional teams and job rotations, has a great advantage.

The fourth dimension is the explicitness of coupling. The USA is more competitive than Japan when the interlinkage among subsystems can be effectively articulated explicitly, as in the case of the software systems for enterprise integration such as enterprise resource planning (ERP), customer-relation management (CRM), and supply-chain management (SCM), as well as in the case of software systems for design and manufacturing such as computer-aided design (CAD) and computer-aided manufacturing (CAM). At the center of all these software systems is the possibility of generalizing, standardizing, articulating, prespecifying, and externalizing all possible contingencies and logic relations connecting various functions, steps, and tasks. Here, the US emphasis on analysis, division, generalization, standardization, articulation, and codification play a significant role in its overwhelming dominance of various software packages. The same analysis can also be applied to information processing and chemical processing. Conversely, when the interlinkage among subsystems cannot be effectively generalized, standardized, and prespecified, but rather requires customization, personalization, contextualization, and real-time adjustment on the shop floor, Japanese firms usually have competitive advantage. The good example of this is the design and operation FMS. What is required for effectiveness here is the tight fit, organic integration, and seamless customization with the specific tasks. The flexibility of operation also requires the flexible programming by shop-floor workers (Jaikumar, 1986; Upton, 1995).

Underpinning the disparity between ERP, CRM, SCM, and CAD on one side and FMS on the other is the dynamics of interaction. While the former is linear and predesigned, the latter is non-linear and requires dynamic feedback from people. When the interaction of subsystems can be linearly predesigned, it is easy for individual specialists to attack each task sequentially; this fits in well with contractual governance. When the interaction of subsystems is non-linear and needs dynamic feedback, the design and operation of the whole technological system requires tacit and cross-functional knowledge for organic integration and seamless coordination; this is a situation to which Japanese connectual governance is best suited.

Finally, the task structure of a technological system can be differentiated by the continuity of its architecture and dominant design. In sectors where technological innovation makes old architecture and old core competencies obsolete, the USA is more competitive. Conversely, in sectors where technological innovation is based on the modification of existing architecture and the enhancement of existing core competencies, Japanese firms are more competitive.

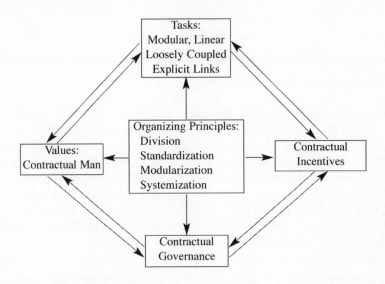

Figure 3.8 The US knowledge regime

Isomorphism and sectoral patterns of competitiveness

Figures 3.8 and 3.9 summarize the essential elements of US and Japanese knowledge regimes. In the USA, the broad-scope isomorphism of the contractual cultural paradigm, contractual governance mechanisms, contractual incentive structures, and the dominant organizing principles of division, standardization, modularization, generalization, and systemization have contributed to the persistent US competitive advantage in sectors where tasks of knowledge creation are either modular, or linear, loosely coupled, or explicitly connected. These include aircraft, pharmaceuticals, biotechnology, software, information services, and e-businesses.

Conversely, in Japan, the broad-scope isomorphism of the connectual cultural paradigm, connectual governance mechanisms, connectual incentive structures, and the dominant organizing principles of connection, fusion, contextualization,

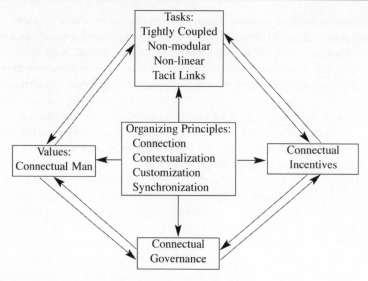

Figure 3.9 The Japanese knowledge regime

customization, and synchronization have contributed to its competitiveness in sectors where tasks of knowledge creation are non-modular, non-linear, tightly coupled, and organically linked. Isomorphically, the axial organizing principles of autonomy and independence in the USA have attracted the trajectories of technological sectors to the paths that are modular, linear, standardized, systemized, loosely coupled, and people-independent. Alternatively, in Japan, the axial organizing principles of connection and interdependence have pulled the trajectories of technological sectors into the paths that are non-modular, closely coupled, non-linear, customized, contextualized, and people-dependent.

Discussion: the evolution and coevolution process reconsidered

While the discussions above focus on the broad-scope *structural* isomorphism among axial organizing principles, cultural paradigms, technological trajectories, and governance mechanisms, the same framework can be used to understand the historical evolution and coevolution of these structures. Indeed, the isomorphic structure can be seen as an autocatalytic chain or ecosystem that governs the evolution and coevolution process. As will be elaborated later, most of US and Japanese organizational, institutional, and technological innovations can be understood within this framework.

Note

1.   For a framework of 'exit, voice, and loyalty,' see Hirshman (1970).

CHAPTER FOUR

Culture and Knowledge Creation

Naturally there are vast differences of convictions and behavior between and within individuals and groups, but the culture as a whole, in the interest of its own development, favors certain *organizing principles* whereas contrary movements are discouraged or contained. (*Italics added.*)

John G. Blair (1988: 8)

Culture has a great impact on the knowledge creation system of a nation, both in its emergence stage and in its further development. This impact is, however, caused less by national character and attitudes, as the conventional cultural approach holds, than by the underlying dominant organizing principles of human minds and human relations. From this perspective, the fundamental differences between Anglo-American and East Asian Confucian societies can best be summarized by the concepts of contractual man vs. connectual man, separate knowing vs. connectual knowing, and the relationship between trust and knowledge creation. In this chapter, I will elaborate on these fundamental differences in the hope of providing a much clearer picture of the interplay between culture and knowledge creation.

Contractual man: the American pursuit of autonomy and separateness

The dominant organizing principles of human minds and human relations in the West in general and the USA in particular can best be characterized by the notion of contractual man. Being the foundation of the Western concepts of self, society, state, economy, and polity, the notion of contractual man pinpoints the core values of Anglo-American cultures and summarizes many basic assumptions underpinning the Western design of human relations and institutions, including the Western systems of religion, the state, laws, property rights, civil rights, political rights, and civil organizations.

In the ideal model of contractual man, as imbodied in both the American creed and neoclassical economic and political theories, human beings are assumed to be born free, equal, autonomous, and independent. Individuals enter into complex relationships with others through the universal rule of law that protects individual rights and through consensual contracts that detail the rights and obligations of each transacting partner. Such contracts are presumably the results of the rational calculation of self-interest by all sides involved. To maximize individual autonomy and independence, contracts are contingent and specific, with a limited time-span, limited commitment, and many options for exit, and are enforced by the rule of law, not the rule of man.

Through a profound process of socialization, this cultural notion of autonomous and independent individuals has been ingrained into the American concept of self, shaping people's personality and behavior (Markus and Kitayama, 1998). The profound commitment to individual autonomy, independence, and separateness is of central importance to understanding the dominance of contractual cultural paradigm in the Western societies in general and the USA in particular. Under such a dominance, individuals are the sole source of all values. States, societies, communities, organizations, and groups exist not for any transcendent values imbedded in themselves but only as a result of consensual social contracts that serve the needs of individuals by protecting their freedom, autonomy, separateness, and other inalienable rights. In describing the pursuit of separateness in the modern West, Schmitt (1995: 1) observes:

> In the modern world contracts are the dominant examples of relationships. Contracts are specific and limited. One person contracts to perform a certain service if the other provides adequate compensation, agreed on beforehand. Contractual relationships are reciprocal and they are expected to benefit each partner. They are entered as a result of calculation concerning the satisfaction of one's own preferences. The relationships that are most common in our world are motivated by self-interest. Each person's responsibilities are limited to performing the action contracted for.

In tracing the origins of Western individualism, Biggart and Hamilton (1994: 483) note:

> The belief in individual autonomy, as applied to both people and their business, arose out of an intellectual tradition that is characteristically Western. The strands of this tradition can be traced to antiquity, particularly to the Roman legal system, which had decisive effects on modern Western European state structure, citizenship, commercial law, and to Christianity, which conceptualized each individual as a distinct soul-bearing entity.

The Western concept of autonomous and independent individuals was explicitly expressed and elaborated in the Enlightenment. In his *Second Treatise on Civil Government*, John Locke (1690/1986: 8) declares:

> To understand political power aright, and derive it from its original, we must consider what estate all men are naturally in, and that is, a state of *perfect freedom* to order their actions, and dispose of their possessions and persons as they think fit, within the bounds of law of nature, without asking leave or *depending upon* the will of any other man. (*Italics added.*)

He also said:

> MEN being, as has been said, by nature all *free, equal, and independent*, no one can be put out of this estate and subjected to the political power of another without his own consent. (*Italics added.*)

This Lockean ideal of classical liberalism was institutionalized in Western Europe through the establishment of a constitutional order based on the rule of law, the division, check, and balance of power, and various democratic processes designed to protect private property rights and individual autonomy.

According to theorists of *American exceptionalism*, notably Hartz (1955) and Lipset (1990, 1996), while most Western societies accept to some extent the Lockean notion of individual freedom and autonomy, the USA stands out as the exceptional outlier in its *pervasive* Lockean consensus of classical liberalism and individualism. In summarizing Hartz's theory of American exceptionalism, Greenstone (1986: 4) notes:

The people who settled the thirteen colonies represent only a liberal middle-class *fragment* of European society. Unencumbered by an entrenched aristocracy and a feudal past, these colonists built a political and social order in which European class antagonisms had no place. All white immigrants could freely pursue their individual goals and aspirations in a society dominated by the norm of '*atomistic social freedom*' – provided only they not interfere with the similar rights of others. (*Italics added.*)

According to Lipset and others, in addition to the lack of a feudal past, the American Revolution, Protestant sectarianism, and the immigrant and frontier experiences have all promoted the pervasive American commitment to and consensus on Lockean liberalism and individualism. As Lipset (1990: 8) comments:

Thus, the United States remained throughout the 19th and early 20th centuries the *extreme* example of a classically liberal or Lockean society, one that rejected the assumptions of the alliance of the throne and altar, of ascriptive elitism, of mercantilism, of noblesse oblige, of communitarianism ... The United States was 'purely bourgeois, so entirely without feudal past.'

As a result, in all major empirical studies of comparative cultures (Hofstede, 1991; Trompenaars, 1993), the USA is consistently at the extreme end of individualism, universalism, egalitarianism, and anti-statism. Its strong commitment to individual autonomy, independence, and separateness has led to antagonism to any forms of *dependence*, ranging from any monopoly of power by states, religious sects, parties, and corporations. This is reflected in a continued emphasis on limiting and dividing the power of the state, on the separation between religion and the state, on sectarianism of religions, on pluralism of political associations, and on the continued enforcement of anti-trust laws (Lipset, 1990, 1996).

In American social science and psychiatry, as Frank Johnson (1993: 31) notes, 'dependency is also connected to a spectrum of normatively *negative* performances involved with undesirable states of heightened needs, frequently defined as "maladaptive," "maladjustive," "age-inappropriate," or "deviant."' As a result, '"abnormal" conditions of dependency are represented in terms of adjustment disorders, development disorders, and personality disorders' (p. 32). Just as the Anglo-American theory of psychiatry overvalues independence and devalues dependency, so do neoclassical economical and political theories, which are dominated by Anglo-American scholars. From James Buchanan's theory of constitutional political economy to John Rawl's (1971) theory of justice, and from the economics of transaction costs and property rights to Austrian economics, the beginning point of any analysis and theoretical construction is always the Lockean notion of completely free, autonomous, independent, separate, and rational individuals. People enter into relationships with others through voluntary agreement and consensual contracts. This ideology is institutionalized pervasively in every aspect of American life (Lipset, 1990). It justifies 'an economic system that was premised on contractual relations between individuals' (Bowman, 1996: 6). At the same time, not only has the notion of contractual man become the cornerstone of the dominant Anglo-American theory of governance (Williamson, 1985), but the firm itself is defined as a 'nexus for a set of contracting relationships' in the agency theory of firm behavior (Jensen and Mechling, 1976).

Remarking the linkage between the cultural penchant for autonomy and the US economic system, Biggart (1991: 222) notes:

> The U.S. economy is based on an institutional logic of *autonomous* firms and *independent* actors. Accounting regulations, hiring practices, and anti-trust regulations – all are expressions of a belief in the correctness of individualism and *autonomy*. (*Italics added*.)

This penchant for individual autonomy and independence and its corresponding organizing principles are responsible for the emergence of the American system of manufactures, the Taylorist movement of 'Scientific Management,' the Fordist system of mass production, the American innovations of multi-divisional (M-form) business organizations, and the emerging digital economy and e-business.

Though a far less studied topic, the US penchant for individual autonomy and independence and the corresponding contractual cultural paradigm also facilitated the *emergence* and *dominance* of the American system of knowledge creation. Such a system is characterized by the sharp division between thinking and acting, between public and private knowledge, and between R&D and production; by the standardization and modularization of knowledge, skills, and capabilities; by the penchant for objective, quantitative, and decontextualized information and knowledge; and by the development, integration, and systemization of people-independent knowledge creation systems.

Connectual man: the Japanese pursuit of interdependence and mutual obligations

As an opposite to the Western penchant for individual autonomy and independence, East Asian societies have put priority on connection and mutual interdependence. This sense of interdependence is deeply ingrained in East Asian and Japanese philosophy, in its language, in its sense of self, in its psychology, in its models of relating to the rest of the world, in its way of knowing, and in its organization of corporation, society, state, and polity.[1]

In the ideal model of connectual man, as pervasively reflected in the moral teachings of Confucianism, in folklore, in civic religions, and in dominant political cultures, human beings are assumed to be born into five major connectual relationships between father and son, husband and wife, superior and subordinate, between elder and younger brothers or sisters, and between friends. Here the life-long mutual commitments and obligations between family members are of central concern. Indeed, because of the centrality of family in the Confucian connectual structure, friendship networks, communities, and even nations are modeled as extended families.

At the center of the Confucian emphasis on connectual relationships rests its design of human values. Individuals are not supposed to seek the values of life solely in themselves, but in their connections with ancestors, families, clans, friends, communities, and nations. Consequently, the ultimate goal of life is to maintain harmonious relationships within the connectual structures of individuals, in the forms of either family and connectual networks, as is the case in China, or corporations and communities, as is the case in Japan (Nakane, 1972).[2]

The dominant mechanism for maintaining harmony is the fulfillment of good will and mutual obligations (Dore, 1983). Here, maintaining harmony and fulfilling mutual obligations are not only a means to keep the connectual structure functioning, but also an end in itself. It is where the ideal value of life lies. Just as the value of life rests in the mutually exclusive rights, autonomy and independence of individuals in the Western ideal model of contractual man, the value of life in the Eastern ideal model of connectual man lies in the mutual obligation, connection, and interdependence of individuals within a connectual structure.

The East Asian emphasis on connections, interdependence, and mutual obligations has led to an exceptional eschewal from using contracts as a means to govern human relations. In tracing Japanese failure in the development of the modern contract system, the noted Japanese sociologist Chie Nakane (1972: 79) observes:

> The development of the modern contract system in the West, and its failure in Japan, seems to me to be traceable not to any differences in degree of industrialization but rather to the existence and persistence of native values manifested ever since the feudal age in the relationship between lord and subject. Plurality of lords, permissible in the west, was refused all countenance in Japan: 'a man cannot serve two masters,' it was said, and if the relationship continued from generation to generation so much the better. The nature of the relationship between lord and subject was also quite different. In the west the relationship involved an embryonic notion of the modern contract, while in Japan it means a life-long commitment, embodying an ideology far divorced from any sense of contract.

The sharp contrast between the USA and Japan in their use of contracts as a means of governing human relations is reflected by the fact that the former has 3.12 lawyers per 1,000 people, more than three times the latter's number of 1.02 per 1,000 (Lipset, 1996: 227). According to Gibney (1982) quoted by Williamson (1985: 123), 'the total number of civil actions in Japan in one year (1980) was about 500,000 – about half the number of cases in California. On a per capita basis, there is one lawsuit in Japan for every twenty in the United States.'

Parallel to the Confucian emphasis on emotional and moral connections, there is a stress on cognitive connections in Chinese and Japanese epistemology. To the East Asian mind of connectual man, Heaven, Earth, and Man, the three key constituting elements of the world, are all connected and in perpetual mutual adjustment to seek harmony among themselves. Here, the problem is not an unending search for the smallest, separable particle or the ultimate cause in the world, as is the case in Western epistemology, but a perpetual effort in linking everything to everything else.

The great historian of Chinese science, Joseph Needham (1956), contrasts Chinese 'associative thinking' with the Western 'billiard ball' concept of the cause–effect relationship. While the former sees the world as an organic and holistic system in which everything is related to everything else, the latter looks at the world as a linear chain of cause and effect among *separate* and *independent* objects. Citing the work of Joseph Needham, Biggart and Hamilton (1994: 485) comment:

> Chinese science did not rest on correlations based on cause and effect, on first principles, or on lawlike assertions. Instead, Chinese science rests on a conception of order. In the Chinese thinking, order rests on a *stable relationship* among things. There is order in a family when all the relationships in a family are obeyed; there is order in a country when all the reciprocal relationships between subjects and rulers are fulfilled; there is order in the universe when mankind fulfills its relationship with heaven and earth. (*Italics added.*)

Extending the Chinese influence to other East Asian societies, they (also p. 485) further note:

> In Asian societies the principle informing human behavior is not for people to obey the law, whether God's laws or natural laws or economic laws. Instead it is for people to create order by obeying the requirements of human relationships as these are manifest in a situational context. The person in Asia is always imbedded in ongoing relationships and is not an abstract entity that exists outside society, not even for the purposes of rational calculation.

The Confucian emphasis on connections and mutual obligations also leads to a parallel emphasis on mutual *dependency and dependability*. According to Lucian Pye (1985), a top scholar on Asian cultures and politics, Confucian ethics have given rise to the triumph of *dependency* in every aspect of social, economic and political life of East Asia. The mutual dependency structure lies not only in the relationship between father and son, superiors and subordinates, but also in the individual perception of self (Markus and Kitayama, 1998) and in all other connectual relationships (Yamada, 1997). In other words, the dominance of the interdependent relationship rests in the fact that not only the means of achieving individual values but also the individual values themselves are defined and fulfilled in the connectual structure of individuals. The lack of specificity, affective neutrality, and universalism in Confucian societies (Parsons, 1937; Trompenaars, 1993) is very much the result of the Confucian emphasis on dependable and mutually obligated connections. This has given rise to a sharp difference of human interactions between the insiders and the outsiders of a person's connectual structure. In comparing Western universalism and Confucian particularism, Parsons (1937: 550–551) brilliantly notes:

> One of the fundamentals of our modern Western social order is its ethical 'universalism.' To a very high degree both in theory and in practice our highest ethical duties apply 'impersonally' to all men, or to large categories of them irrespective of any specific personal relation involved ... In this respect the Puritan ethic represents an intensification of the general Christian tendency. It is an extremely powerful animus against nepotism and favoritism. To this the Confucian ethic stands in sharp contrast. Its ethical sanction was given to an individual's *personal* relations to particular persons – and with any strong ethical emphasis *only* to these. The whole Chinese social structure accepted and sanctioned by the Confucian ethics was a predominantly 'particularistic' structure of relationship. This left relationships outside this category in a realm of ethical indifferences, with a general unwillingness to assume ethical obligations. (*Italics in original.*)

The Confucian emphasis on the mutual obligation, connection, and interdependence of individuals has a profound impact on the emergence of the specific economic institutions in both China and Japan. In the latter case, it facilitated the establishment of a structure of *interdependence* in its systems of political economy (Okimoto, 1989) and business organization (Fruin, 1992; Oliver and Wilkinson, 1992). In describing the economies of both Japan and China, Biggart and Hamilton (1994: 485) observe that, 'the organization of these economies, like the organization of society, rested on principles quite different from those found in the West.' They (p. 474) further remark that:

> Asian economies espouse different institutional logics from Western economies, one rooted in *connectedness* and *relationships*: Asians believe that social relations between economic actors do not impede market functioning, but rather promote it. Just as

Western economies have institutionalized ways of maintaining *autonomy* between actors, Asian economies are rooted in institutions that encourage and maintain ties. (*Italics added.*)

In the same vein, in his comparison of Japanese communitarian capitalism with Anglo-American individualistic capitalism, Dore (1994) notes:

> The difference between the two types of economy is such that, in Japan, a much smaller proportion of economic transactions are of the pure cash nexus type; a much higher proportion are imbedded in social relationships of trust and mutual obligations.

Clarifying the non-contractual nature of Japanese society, Shichihei (1992: 41) argues:

> To say that Japan is not a contractual society means that contracts do not critically influence social structure; it does not mean that individuals lack faith or that they do not abide by decisions reached through group consensus. In Japan, the consensus system takes the place of contracts, which is why we are not identified as a contractual society.

Even when a contract is used in Japan, it serves the purpose of affirming and maintaining good will and mutual obligations, as Shichihei (1992: 47) puts it:

> In Japan, a contract might be said to contain only one provision of overriding importance: that in the event of disagreement, both parties will discuss the matter in good faith. If a contract is concluded at all, it is no more than a document affirming the tradition of dialogue.

Indeed, to the extent that Japan as well as other East Asian economies is rooted in connectedness, relationships, and the consensus built around them, we can call their economies *connectual*, as compared to the *contractual economy* of the USA. The major difference in various Asian economies lies in their differing ways of connection, and their emphasis on different types of connection. While in Japan, dominant forms of connections are *vertically* structured communities, clans, and firms, in China, they are family ties, friend circles, and various *horizontal* networks formed through connections to the same school, native birthplace, surname, and friends (Hamilton and Feenstra, 1998).

According to Nakane (1972) and Fukutake (1989), the Japanese emphasis on vertical relationships is inherited from its feudal system of family and village. In such a system, membership was automatic and exclusive only to villagers. While the parent–child relationship was essential and primary, it was somehow extended to the whole village. The landlord and tenant relationship was especially modeled after the family, where, according to Fukutake, the landowners played the father role, while the tenants played the children role. Such a mutually affective, obligatory, and interdependent relationship was crucial for both to survive the turbulent world of uncertainty. In modern times, this emotional and mutually obligatory bond has been extended to the firm organization in which members treat each other like an extended family in a traditional *ie* or clan (Nakane, 1972).

Table 4.1 shows the persistent patterns of desirable relationships in Japan. It indicates that while partial relationships with neighbors are preferred, still about half of the Japanese desires total and emotional relations in their workplace. Interestingly, in both the workplace and the neighborhood, less than 19 per cent of the Japanese prefer formal and impersonal relations. These results reflect not only

Table 4.1 Desirable patterns of relationships in Japan (percentages)

	Workplace relations			Neighbor relations		
	Formal	Partial	Total	Formal	Partial	Total
1973	11	26	59	15	50	35
1978	10	31	55	15	53	32
1983	14	32	52	20	48	32
1988	15	38	45	19	53	27

Source: Adapted from Fukutake (1989, p. 146).

the predominance of the connectual cultural paradigm in Japan, but also the centrality of the firm in the Japanese connectual structure. In a survey quoted by Fukutake (1989: 147), the Japanese were asked to choose between the following options:

> (a). 'A department chief who never expects you to work beyond what the regulations call for, but who never looks after you in matters not related to your work.'
> (b). 'A department chief who sometimes expects far more than you are supposed to do but who cares about what happens to people and looks after them in matters that have nothing to do with work.'

While in 1953, an overwhelming 80 per cent of people chose (b), in 1983 the number increased to 89 per cent. According to another survey by Takezawa and Whitechill (1981), while only 20 per cent of Americans think of their company as a part of their life that is at least of equal importance to their personal life, an overwhelming 64 per cent of the Japanese think so. These numbers further indicate the predominance of the connectual paradigm in the Japanese workplace.

In his study of trading relations between a large trading company and its affiliated small family firms in a Japanese town, Dore (1983) also finds that the relations are entirely particularistic, moralized, and obligated. Although following Williamson's (1979) lead, Dore (1983) mistakenly terms these relations as 'relational contracting,' the relations described are, nevertheless, of a connectual nature, which are based on communal solidarity, particularistic ties, affective commitment and identification, good will, and mutual obligations which are tacitly perceived, consciously followed, and not legally based. Indeed, as Fukuyama (1995: 187) notes, Japanese employers dislike the legalistic use of contracts to *explicitly* guarantee permanent employment. Instead, as Dore (1983) observes, both employment with a company and trading relations are much more like a marriage which requires fundamental commitment and personal affection, rather than being like a spot contract. The termination of these connections is like a traditional divorce that only happens either when mutual affection, obligation, and commitment no longer exist, or when severe economic conditions do not permit a continued alliance, a process that causes great pain on both sides.

The contrasting pursuit of independence vs. interdependence between Americans and the Japanese is reinforced by the socialization processes at various stages of life, especially the early age, as Rosenberger (1992: 7) states, quoting the work of Caudill and Weinstein (1969/1986): 'Japanese babies are trained to be other-oriented and interdependent, stressing emotion and intuition in decision making, whereas American babies are trained to be individual-oriented and independent, emphasizing the rationale in decision making.' Such a socialization process has led to the formation of the Japanese sense of self that is relational, interdependent, contextual, situational, particularistic, and group-oriented (Rosenberger, 1992; F. Johnson, 1993; Markus and Kitayama, 1998). This, in turn, strengthens the dominance of the connectual cultural paradigm in Japan.

Separate knowing vs. connectual knowing

The different cultural paradigms between the West and the East have a profound impact on not only how knowledge is created but also on what types and forms of knowledge are highly valued. The Western model of contractual man leads to the dominance of what Schmitt (1995) called *separate knowing*, whereas the East Asian model of connectual man gives rise to the dominance of *connectual knowing*, or knowing-in-relation in Schmitt's terms. While the former espouses and legitimizes explicit, objective, quantitative, context-free, and propositional knowledge as the only form of genuine knowledge, the latter regards tacit, inter-subjective, qualitative, contextual, and situational knowledge as indispensable for both understanding the world order and dealing with human relations.

The dominance of separate knowing in the USA

According to Schmitt (1995: Ch. 7), since the time of Descartes, separate knowing has been the only legitimate form of knowing in the West. Such a dominance can easily trace its origin to Western epistemology, which assumes the disembodiment of mind from body, the self from external environment, and the knower from known (Lakoff and Johnson, 1999). In my view, however, it is also reinforced and facilitated by the Western cultural paradigm of contractual man. Indeed, when individuals are assumed to be autonomous, independent, and separate, so must their ways of knowing be. Separate knowing means not just the separateness and independence of the knower and the known. It requires that the knower is totally free from any preexisting biases, convictions, affective commitment, and the influence of other people's opinions in the pursuit of knowledge. It also demands the independent discovery and verification of the knowledge discovered and convened by other knowers. It assumes the possibility of *isolating* and *separating* an object for knowing that is autonomous and independent from the impact of other objects. It also assumes the possibility of *separating* cause from effect and facilitators from impediments.

The emphasis on separate knowing leads to a parallel stress on division and analysis. In both R&D and management fields, Americans tend to divide and subdivide a problem into smallest domains so that individuals can attack them separately through independent investigation. Describing the division and analysis mentality of American management, Whitehill (1991: 155) notes:

> An American manager faced with a problem in his department typically tries to *isolate, define, and quantify* the issue. There is a strong feeling that problems cannot be resolved until they are clearly defined. Instead of a holistic approach, attention is devoted to breaking down the whole into parts, and submitting each part to intensive, rational analysis. (*Italics added.*)

Underpinning this compartmentalization process in problem solving is the dominantly Western notion that the whole is the sum of parts and each part either has a cause–effect relationship with others or is independent of all the other parts (Hayashi, 1988: 72). Indeed, the dominant Newtonian worldview treats the world as consisting of separate particles linked by universal laws of cause and effect. When it comes to human society as a whole, the social systems theory provided by the American sociologist Talcott Parsons treats it 'as one vast system divided into a series of distinct and relatively autonomous realms, or subsystems.' (See Piore, 1996: 743.) This perceived possibility of independence and autonomy of subsystems has not only legitimated division and analysis as a primary way of knowing, but also led to the proliferation of a system of professions in the USA, with each focusing on the separate knowing of a claimed 'independent' domain of a subsystem and a well-defined problem associated with it.

As a result of its pursuit of separateness and independence, separate knowing embodies and leads to a deeply held skepticism toward any form of personal and contextual knowledge, as Schmitt (1995: 126) notes:

> According to the assumption of separateness, the perceptions of others cannot count as evidence for me until I have satisfied myself that the others 'perceive' in the sense in which I perceive. Since I cannot know that, I also cannot know that the other perceives as I do, and hence I cannot know there is an 'external world.' I must remain a skeptic in that respect also as long as I hold my separate autonomy as knower ... As a *separate person*, I do not have the resources to answer all these questions. I am separate – philosophers assume – and can know only what I have assembled the evidence for ... The knowledge claims made by the separate knower always rest on what is evident for this separate person: Thus the Cartesian project comes into existence, that of founding all of human knowledge on evidence available to a single, separate person.

To overcome the skepticism imbedded in the logic of separate knowing, it is necessary to present any knowledge in impersonal, decontexted, and propositional forms so that a separate knower can *independently* either *verify* or *falsify* the knowledge explicitly stated by other separate knowers. Only when the knowledge of a person is expressed in explicit and more preferably propositional forms can it be independently verified or falsified by other *autonomous* observers and researchers. Only when autonomous individuals can independently discover or verify the same claimed knowledge by others can the knowledge be accepted as legitimate. Here the *detachment* among independent knowers and between knowledge and its discoverers provides not only the means to overcome the skepticism of other knowers but also the shields to preserve individual autonomy and independence in knowledge creation by preventing any *dependence* on the knowledge of others beyond the control of autonomous individuals.

The dominance of separate knowing in the West results in the legitimization of explicit, objective, and quantitative knowledge as the only genuine forms of knowledge. In particular, as Schmitt (1995: Ch. 7) brilliantly notes, the dominance of separate knowing in the West has led to the legitimization of *propositional knowledge* that links a cause and an effect explicitly and *in isolation*. Here, the isolation of a cause and an effect from the rest of its contextual environment and the explicit articulation of the causal link make it possible for independent verification or falsification of the knowledge presented. Because it guarantees the autonomy and independence of knowers, in the West in general and the USA in particular, propositional knowledge has always been highly valued whereas any forms of personal and contextual knowledge are dismissed, as Schmitt (1995: 134) observes:

> The conception of knowledge as propositional leads us very easily into a set of normative judgements: Theoretical science is the highest kind of knowledge, and only those who have scientific knowledge are genuine knowers. As a result, knowledge that is not propositional is denigrated.

The result of the American penchant for propositional knowledge has been the dismissal of the knowledge of *insiders* and *shop-floor workers*, and an acknowledgment of the superiority of outside observers equipped with professional credentials. From the position of a separate knower, insiders blind themselves through too great a commitment, and too close a connection, to the subject of knowing. This situation impairs the very requirement of objectivity and affective-neutrality in the process of separate knowing. On the other hand, outside observers can bring about objectivity and neutrality to the revelation of genuine knowledge. In the words of Schmitt (1995: 136):

> That leads to the further conclusion that outside observers, if equipped with the proper research tools, are in a position to know the lives and problems of people quite different from themselves better than the members of those groups themselves.

As will be discussed later in detail, such a fundamental trust in outside observers as the genuine knowers has contributed to the preeminent role of external consultants, external change agents, and external marketing firms in the creation and diffusion of knowledge in the USA.

When the emergence of professions is considered, the dominance of separate knowing in the West in general, and the USA in particular, has led to the development of *modularized* academic disciplines in which each separates an object from all others as the independent subject of knowing. The dominant notion of a separate object for knowing and the resultant specialization process enables the profession within the discipline to hold a special claim for the knowledge of the subject and establish barriers to prevent other knowers from entering. As Schmitt (1995: 131) further notes:

> Separate knowers have systematically *insulated* themselves as a consequence of two other aspects of separate knowing. They have defined knowledge as a relation to a *separate* entity, such as a proposition, and thereby excluded all those from the domain of science whose knowledge is not only propositional. They have thereby protected themselves against possible criticism of their work by all those who lack university credentials. The knowledge of the uncredentialed has been uniformly disparaged; their criticism of intellectual work of intellectuals therefore has not been heard. Separateness has, in addition, also been extended to the relation between knowers and what they are studying. Knowing is not a joint accomplishment of the inquirer and the subjects of a given study, but the accomplishment of the knower *alone* in which the subjects are more or less passive. (*Italics added.*)

The American emphasis on separate knowing has thus contributed a pervasive professionalization process of knowledge creation and diffusion that endorses specialists and dismisses generalists. The notion of separate knowing enables specialists to legitimately claim the knowledge of a specific domain that is presumably well defined, separate, self-contained, autonomous, and independent. On the other hand, generalists fail to claim the legitimacy of their knowledge, skill, and capabilities since these are based on the connectual knowing of many interconnected domains and subjects. By nature, such knowledge, skills, and capabilities are difficult to break down into self-contained domains for independent knowers to verify or falsify. Even when it is possible to partition the knowledge of a generalist into small pieces, the very utility of the generalist's knowledge is accordingly lost. Furthermore, the very existence of, or a need for, the knowledge of generalists imposes a *dependency* relationship that threatens the autonomy and independence of the individuals in the West. A reliance on generalists' knowledge means the inability to separate out a self-contained domain for separate knowing by separate knowers. It also leads to the inability (or a prohibitively high cost) to independently verify or falsify the knowledge of a generalist by the separate knowers who need it. While the credentials and utilities of specialists can always be examined through their track records of formal education and professional experiences, the qualifications of generalists cannot be effectively evaluated without resorting to personal and contextual knowledge about their idiosyncratic knowledge and skills and how they match with the specific needs of a job.

In summary, just as the American preference for explicit and propositional knowledge is the result of their penchant for individual autonomy and independence, so also is their admiration for the knowledge of specialists. On the other hand, the American dismissal of tacit, subjective, qualitative, and generalist knowledge is also very much the result of their high valuation of individual autonomy and independence.

The dominance of connectual knowing in Japan

In sharp contrast, the dominant form of knowing in East Asian Confucian societies in general, and Japan in particular, is *connectual knowing*, or what Schmitt (1995) called 'knowing-in-relation' and what Needham (1956) called 'associative thinking.' The emphasis on connectual knowing underpins all East Asian and Japanese philosophies and religions, including Confucianism, Taoism, and Zen Buddhism (Suzuki, 1959). The central assumption of all these is the ubiquitous connections and interdependence among individuals and among Heaven, Man, and Earth. When individuals are assumed to be interdependent of each other and of the rest of the world, so are their ways of knowing. Connectual knowing implies an organic interdependence and integration between the knower and the known, between knowing and acting, between knowers, and among known objects.

First, connectual knowing involves the organic connection and integration of the knower and the known. In the words of Eastern epistemology, to know and understand an object is a process of merging oneself totally with, or projecting oneself completely into, it to become a unified whole in which a distinction between the self and the object is blurred. It is believed that only through such a unifying effort can one grasp the utmost intricacies of the objects. In describing the process of *mediance* and *trajection* in the Japanese ways of knowing and relating to environments, Berque (1992: 94) notes:

The logic of the Japanese medial process, or mediance, tends to blur the identity of the self and, at the same time, to enhance the identification of the self with what is not self: environment, both social and natural. These processes involve not only psychological, social, and ecological relations as such (e.g., self and others, self and environment) but, more generally, the relation of the subject with the object.

When the relationship between men and machine is considered, Japanese artisans not only recognize interconnectedness with the machines they used, but also identify with and humanize them, as Kondo (1992: 53) observes the Japanese artisanal tradition:

> Becoming a full-fledged artisan and a full-fledged human being at the workplace means engaging with the world in a particular way, cultivating a close relationship between men and the material and natural worlds ... The penchant for humanizing the machine implies that human beings and machines partake of a same world, and that people are very intimately identified with the process of production, for every machine they use in creating their products – even if the product is made on an assembly line – can be thought of as parts of, or representative of, themselves.

It is through the identification and humanization process that shop-floor workers at Japanese firms create knowledge specially tailored for the best performance of a special machine.

Here, the differences of principles and processes between separate knowing and connectual knowing cannot be sharper. Rather than an objective observation of the object by the former, the latter requires a passionate trajection into it. Instead of the former's affection-neutral and rational investigation of the object, the latter involves a compassionate and empathetic 'feeling' for it. In place of the former's explicit revelation of the knowledge as the end product of separate knowing, most products of the latter are the types of knowledge that are highly tacit, intuitive, contextual, and subjective. Indeed, Eastern epistemology usually assumes that knowledge that is articulated is no longer genuine because it cuts away many contextual and tacit links and connections that are difficult to articulate. Just as what Lao Zi, the founder of the Taoism, says, '*the Tao that is articulated is no longer a genuine Tao.*'

The Eastern legitimization of tacit, personal, contextual, and intuitive knowledge and its skepticism toward explicit, impersonal, decontextual, and propositional knowledge is in sharp contrast to Western epistemology. At the center of this difference rests the East Asian conviction that *genuine* knowledge exists in innumerable contextual and organic connections among things and between men and the material world. Since it is impossible to articulate all the intricacies of contextual relationships, any effort of articulating genuine knowledge from its tacit and contextual forms to the explicit and abstract forms will inevitably sever some crucial but inarticulatable contextual links, and, therefore, reduce the genuine knowledge into one that is partially true and partially false.

Second, unlike the separation of knowing from acting in the case of separate knowing, connectual knowing requires their integration and unification. Here acting is also a process of knowing in which the knower *empathetically* 'feels' how the enforced action has caused the reaction of the acted object. Reciprocally, knowing is also a process that tacitly directs acting. Such a unification of knowing and acting is very much like Michael Polanyi's (1958/1964) notion of tacit knowing. However, there are two major differences here. First, tacit knowing is only one form of connectual knowing. The latter also includes empathetic knowing, mediated knowing, and other forms of knowing. Second, while the notion of connectual knowing has always been dominant in East Asian Confucian societies, Michael Polanyi's (1958/1964, 1969) works on tacit knowledge and tacit knowing are indeed the *protest* of an exceptionally sensitive intellectual against their being totally neglected and delegitimated in the West.

Third, unlike the separation, autonomy, and independence of knowers in the Western preponderance of separate knowing, connectual knowing requires connection, integration, and mutual dependence of all elements involved in the process. Indeed, the requirement to tacitly 'feel' the needs of other connected people, including their desires, emotions, and affections, is the central task of knowing for the connectual man of East Asia. After all, in Japan, the value of an individual's life is tied to his or her connectual structures of family, friends, clans, firms, and communities, forming 'the empathetic self' that is far larger than is the case with Americans, who tend to limit the bonded self within their nuclear family (Lebra, 1992). Such an enlargement of 'the empathetic self' is reinforced by the principle of reciprocity in which the needs of individuals, their desires, emotions, and affections are empathetically 'felt' by the people in their connectual structure so that their cares and favors can be reciprocated. Here, knowing is an empathetic learning and socialization process in which one individual 'takes the role of others' by casting oneself in the attitudes, values, feelings, situations, and contexts of others in order to know their needs, expectations, and possible responses (Lincoln *et al.*, 1998).

In the Western cultural paradigm of contractual man, beyond the nuclear family in which the empathetic self identifies, there is less of a need to tacitly know other people since individuals are supposed to take care of themselves and to seek self-interest in interacting with others. By contrast, under the dominance of the cultural paradigm of connectual man in East Asia, people within a connectual structure of family, friends, clans, firms, and communities have mutual obligations to take care of each other and to adopt the interests of others as their own. Knowing other people becomes the central task of people dominated by the cultural paradigm of connectual man. A person who has the ability to know tacitly and empathetically the needs and expectations of connected others and properly offers help is seen as mature and well respected. On the other hand, one who only cares for his or her own self-interest, or a person who knows neither the needs and expectations of others nor how to offer help is seen as selfish, immature, and not worthy of the caring of others. While the former type of people will have a large and effective connectual structure, the latter will have only a very limited one. Under the logic of connectual man, this means the former will be more successful than the latter.

The huge importance attached to the ability in tacitly and empathetically knowing others makes the nurturing of this ability the central task of a person's life in East Asian societies. People begin to learn their ability of empathetic knowing from socialization in the family at their early age. While the ability of separate knowers is very much determined by both their cognitive capacities and their stock of knowledge and skills, the ability for connectual knowers to anticipate the needs of others rests very much on the capacity to project oneself into another person's position in order to empathetically feel the needs of others. The nurturing of the capabilities in connectual knowing also requires an intensive socialization process with one another within a connectual structure so that there is a common knowledge base, common contextual experiences, and common habits of thinking and acting. Indeed, the socialization process in East Asia is a process of establishing the *inter-subjectivity of knowing* among closed networks of individuals who are both emotionally and structurally connected. As Nakane (1972: 123) rightly points out, a strong in-group feeling with a high emotional content is the primary reason for the Japanese disregarding objective observation and rational analysis.

This East Asian need of *inter-subjectivity* in the knowing process is diametrically opposed to the Western demand of objectivity. In the cultural model of contractual man, there is no need to know and understand a person as a whole with his or her emotional needs and idiosyncrasies. On the contrary, what is needed is a *detachment* and *separateness* between work and family life and between coworkers so that individual autonomy and independence can be maximally preserved. In such a case, inter-subjectivity is as much an evil as objectivity is a virtue. On the other hand, in the cultural model of connectual man, there is a deep need for knowing and understanding a person as a whole in all contextual connections and with all emotional needs and all idiosyncrasies. In such a case, inter-subjectivity is a virtue because it helps one to grasp personal and contextual knowledge about the connected person. The reluctance of the Japanese as well as others in East Asia to deal with people outside one's connectual structure, therefore, reflects not only the *incentive gap* between the connected and the unconnected but also the *knowledge gap* between the known and the unknown. It is much easier to know the needs and expectations of people within a connectual structure than to know those of outsiders.

Finally, the need for knowing other people is also the result of the East Asian penchant for knowing other things. In East Asian epistemology, everything is connected to everything else. As a result, any isolated knowing of an isolated object has less value than connectual knowing that grasps the relationship between many interconnected objects. As a result, knowing is dominantly the *broadening* of the scope of knowledge and the enriching of knowledge linkages among interconnected objects. There are primarily two ways of doing so. The first is to foster *generalists* through such practices as job rotation and on-the-job training. The second is to develop knowledge links among peoples within a connectual structure. These links are created by the overlap of knowledge held by connected knowers, and by relational and contextual knowledge about the knowledge of other connected knowers. The group processes of knowledge creation that are prevalent in Japan, such as quality circles, cross-functional teams, and job rotation, are precisely the sort of institutional innovations that fulfil the needs for developing an overlapping scope of knowledge and for nurturing relational and contextual knowledge of one another. These have helped immensely the effective fulfillment of connectual knowing. In line with my notions of separate vs. connectual knowing, Nonaka (1990: 29) notes:

> In the innovation generation process of Japanese organizations, the concept of division of labor, in the sense that areas of activities are clearly specialized, is not completely adopted. Rather, in what is also termed 'a shared division of labor,' every phase of innovation generation is loosely connected and overlaps, expanding and contracting with the unrestricted elasticity of diversity.

In the areas of corporate management and governance, the Japanese emphasis on connections and connectual knowing is further evidenced by the fact that while most board directors in US companies are outsiders with part-time devotion to securing independence as a way of ensuring effective checks and balances and for independent knowledge input into important decisions, most directors in Japanese firms are full-time insiders who have both a fundamental commitment to and knowledge about the firm. Moreover, while most Anglo-American managers have a financial background, their Japanese counterparts come mainly from technical backgrounds, having undergone long-term cross-functional training (Odagiri and Goto, 1993; Kusunoki and Numagami, 1997).

Competitive implications

The sharply different ways of knowing in the USA and Japan have a great impact on their sectoral patterns of national competitiveness. The Western penchant for explicit, objective, quantitative, and propositional knowledge has contributed greatly to the rise of not only modern sciences, but also Taylorism, Fordism, accounting, financial management, all the other disciplines of modern management and the social sciences, and most recently digital economy and e-business. As we will see in chapter 7, the zeal for separate knowing has also contributed to US international competitiveness in such sectors as information processing and e-business where the codification and quantification of information is the key for competitive success. On the other hand, since the dominance of separate knowing leads to skepticism toward tacit, subjective, qualitative, relational, contextual, and situational knowledge, the USA is usually less competitive in sectors where the creation and application of these forms of knowledge are crucial for competitive success.

In contrast, the Japanese competitive advantages and disadvantages are opposite to those of the USA. Because of its emphasis on, and legitimization of, tacit, inter-subjective, connectual, contextual, and situational knowledge, Japan is competitive in the complex manufacturing sectors in which the creation and application of these forms of knowledge is the key for competitive success (Lincoln *et al.*, 1998). Conversely, Japan is not competitive in the sectors of information processing and information services where the codification and quantification of transactional information is the primary means toward competitive success. Furthermore, the US emphasis and Japanese de-emphasis on propositional knowledge has contributed to US strength and Japanese weakness in such science-based sectors as chemicals and pharmaceuticals.

Separate knowing leads to the *deepening* of knowledge about an isolated object, whereas connectual knowing leads to the *widening* of knowledge about the relationship of interconnected objects.[3] As a result, the predominance of separate knowing in the USA has contributed, in part, to US technological superiority in most advanced technologies. On the other hand, the dominance of connectual knowing in Japan has led to Japanese competitiveness in design for manufacturing and concurrent engineering that aims at improving quality and reducing costs through creating knowledge about the connectual relationships involved in the various processes (McKinsey Global Institute, 1993). Finally, the US endorsement of outside observers as a better source of knowledge than insiders also contributes to the high demand for, and supply of, consulting services, which has led to US competitiveness in various sectors of consulting. By contrast, the Japanese reluctance to trust the knowledge of outsiders has led to the relative underdevelopment of consulting services.

There are at least two empirical studies that support my dichotomy of separate vs. connectual knowing. In their survey of all publicly traded Japanese manufacturing firms in 1993, Kusunoki *et al.* (1998) found with statistical significance that Japanese firms have superior capabilities in creating knowledge on the dynamic interaction of units, but poor capabilities in creating isolated and individual knowledge units. They further statistically proved that while the former contributed to Japanese competitiveness in the 'system-based' industries of machinery, electronics, automobiles, and precision machinery, the latter played a significant role in Japan's poor performance in the 'material-based' industries of paper, general chemicals, other chemicals, and petroleum/rubber. From my perspective, while connectual knowing is good at creating knowledge about the interaction of units, separate knowing is superior at creating knowledge about independent units. In their systematic comparison of US and Japanese product development, Souder *et al.* (1998) found that when any stage of development, manufacturing, and marketing is scrimped in the new product development process, US firms have more than double the percentage of success rate of their Japanese counterparts. Conversely, when all stages of new product development are implemented, Japanese firms have a higher percentage of success rate (Table 4.2). This result is also evident from the knowledge regime perspective. While connectual knowing requires the involvement of all stages and all units, separate knowing can target individual stages and units for effective knowledge creation.

Table 4.2 Percentage of products that succeeded

	USA	Japan
All-stages thorough	70%	83%
Development scrimped	35%	14%
Manufacturing scrimped	40%	21%
Marketing scrimped	40%	18%

Source: Adapted from Souder *et al.* (1998: 52).

Trust and knowledge creation

The contrasting cultural paradigms also lead to divergent social constructions of trust in the USA and Japan. While some authors such as Fukuyama (1995) believe that both the USA and Japan are high trust societies, the bases for trust are, nevertheless, quite different. Whereas the logic of contractual man requires and facilitates trust in individuals, contracts, abstract systems, universal rules, and anything objective and impersonal, the logic of connectual man requires and facilitates trust in groups, personal connections, holistic and contextual ties, and inter-subjective sharing of values and knowledge. The former has led to the emergence and predominance of a US system of knowledge creation that is rule-based, modular, system-oriented, and people-independent, whereas the latter has contributed to the emergence and preponderance of a Japanese system that is group-oriented, connection-based, and people-dependent.

Trust in individuals vs. trust in groups in knowledge creation

At the center of the cultural paradigm of contractual man is the belief in separate individuals, as Kash (1989: 60) observes: 'In the American social paradigm, the individual has a role analogous to that assigned to the atom by physicists in the early part of this century. That is, the individual is the indivisible building block of society.' Consequently, as he further notes: 'The American success story is commonly construed as the story of exceptional individuals.'

The US emphasis on individuals, combined with the central belief in separate knowing, leads to the trusting of individualistic entrepreneurs as the primary knowledge creators. The heavy reliance on exceptional scientists, independent inventors, brilliant technologists, and heroic entrepreneurs for technological breakthroughs and business innovations has been the hallmark of US capitalism (Hughes, 1989b). According to the Anglo-American theory of entrepreneurship, entrepreneurs are those whose driving motivation is independence, who are self-confident and self-reliant, are willing to take risks, are dependent on individual power and resolution, are defiant to group norms, and are resistant to bureaucratic structures and rules (Longenecker *et al.*, 1988). When it comes to the implications of knowledge creation, according to Kirzner (1979, 1985), the foremost advocate of the primacy of entrepreneurial discovery process, entrepreneurs are those who are always alert to new ways and opportunities for doing business. To Austrian economists, notably Schumpeter, Hayek and Kirzner, such an entrepreneurial *alertness* is the very source of the discovery of dispersed economic knowledge at specific times and places. In emphasizing the primacy of entrepreneurial discovery, Kirzner (1985: 22) notes:

> Entrepreneurship is thus not something to be deliberately introduced into a potential production process: it is, instead, something primordial to the very idea of a potential production process awaiting possible implementation. Entrepreneurial alertness is not an ingredient *to be deployed* in decision making; it is rather something in which *the decision itself is imbedded* and without which it would be unthinkable.

From the perspective taken here, what Kirzner calls 'entrepreneurship' is only the Anglo-American type of individualistic entrepreneurship. While early students of Austrian economics, like most early American social scientists, ignored the cultural origin and context of their theory and concepts, scholars since the mid-1980s have recognized the different socio-cultural constructions of entrepreneurship. In other words, what they conceived of as a universally valid concept of 'entrepreneurship' is only the Anglo-American type, which depends solely on heroic, independent, and autonomous individuals for the discovery of knowledge (Lavoie and Chamlee-Wright, 1997). What they perceived as a lack of 'entrepreneurship' in Japan is actually the lack of the American type. What is dominant in Japan is a kind of communitarian entrepreneurship that emphasizes group involvement in the discovery, creation, and transformation of knowledge. In contrast to the American type that relies on exceptional individuals for the creation of knowledge, the

Japanese type emphasizes groups consisting of *mediocre but dedicated* engineers and shop-floor workers as the dominant creators of knowledge. In comparing organizational learning in US and Japanese industry, Cole (1995b: 374) notices that Japanese firms focus on group and organizational learning, whereas US firms 'focus on individual learning for selected employees; assume it is translated into organizational learning.'

As discussed above, underpinning the Japanese emphasis on groups as the primary creators of knowledge is their belief in the importance of connectual and inter-subjective knowing. The process of quality circles, as developed in Japan, is one type of *connectual* knowing in which a group of shop-floor workers share tacit knowledge, transform it into explicit knowledge, and integrate the dispersed knowledge of individuals into a meaningful and connected whole for grasping the opportunities for improving the manufacturing processes linking the tasks of group members. Using the terminology of Henderson and Clark (1990), the group process of knowing creates *architectural knowledge* that is crucial for improving the architectural structures of both products and processes and for achieving effective implementation of design for manufacturing and concurrent engineering.

The competitive implications of knowing based on individuals vs. knowing based on groups are contingent upon the nature of technological sectors. In sectors such as biotechnology and software, individualistic entrepreneurship and exceptional technological talents are still the key for competitive success. In biotechnology, for example, Liebeskind *et al.* (1996) find that only a few star researchers in the world have made discoveries of significant commercial value. In the relatively mature fabricating manufacturing sectors such as automobiles and consumer electronics, however, the driving force behind competitiveness is not so much individual talent as *group intelligence*, which harnesses the dispersed knowledge of group members for incremental improvement.

Trust in contract vs. trust in connection

Another fundamental difference in the socio-cultural construction of trust caused by divergent cultural paradigms rests in the varying confidence toward contracts and connections. In the contractual cultural paradigm, the predominant means for people to trust each other is through a fundamental belief in effective implementation of contracts, whereas in the connectual cultural paradigm, the primary way for people to trust each other is through the existence of multiple ties between one another. While the former is able to extend trust far beyond personal connections, the latter still relies on personal and communal ties as the primary means for establishing trust. While the former leads to the emergence of *extended orders* such as impersonalized and generalized markets and bureaucracies, the latter gives rise to the emergence of *bounded governance* structures such as networks and clans (Jin, 1995). While the former trusts impersonalized rules and procedures, the latter can only trust people within the connectual structure.

To some extent, the rise of trust in contracts in the West has been the result of the emergence of constitutional orders in which the generalized rules of law, especially those concerning the enforcement of contracts and the protection of freedom of choice and private property rights, are effectively enforced by the states (Rosenberg and Birdzell, 1986; Jones, 1987). Here, there exists a positive feedback loop in the rise of modern constitutional states and the cultural model of contractual man. The cultural model of contractual man needs the state to protect individual rights and to enforce contracts. Reciprocally, the effective protection of individual rights and enforcement of contracts by the state further strengthen the cultural model of contractual man.

By contrast, in East Asian Confucian societies the logic of connectual man leads to a positive feedback structure that strengthens both trust in and dependence on connections as the primary mechanisms for securing the reciprocity of mutual obligations. As a result, the state in East Asian Confucian societies was traditionally less of a tool to enforce contracts than a means to guarantee the moral requirements for the reciprocity of obligations (Pye, 1985). In linking the Confucian emphasis on connection and East Asian distrust of outsiders, Pye (1985: 80) notes:

> The Confucian valuing of family relationships no doubt contributed to the strong sense of division between in-group and out-group which characterized all four of the East Asian cultures. In China, Japan, Korea, and Vietnam the basis of social relations was the feeling that trust should automatically be extended to family members and to those in analogous groups, while all others should be viewed with suspicion. Clannishness was understood and accepted as normal behavior.

The central issue here is not family relationships, but rather the logic of connectual man that puts fundamental trust in connectual structures. The dominant connectual structures in China, Japan, Korea, and Vietnam may vary, but in all of them, one tends only to trust people who are specifically connected.

The difference between trust in contracts and trust in connections has a profound impact on the mechanisms of knowledge creation. When contracts are the dominant facilitators for trust, knowledge is created and transformed in a manner that can be appropriated through contracts that detail the terms of exchange. Consequently, the development of saleable knowledge becomes the primary focus of knowledge creation in the West. The commodification of knowledge can be achieved through its standardization and encapsulation. The standardization of knowledge enables the objective and competitive evaluation of its value, while its encapsulation enables the establishment of separable, unique, and saleable units of knowledge as goods for market transactions. While the former leads to the professionalization and specialization of knowledge and its creation, the latter gives rise to a system of knowledge creation that focuses on the production of patents and copyrights as well as a system of laws in securing their appropriation. On the other hand, the trust in connections leads to a focus on the creation of firm- and relation-specific knowledge and on the diffusion and fusion of knowledge within the connectual structures of the firm in Japan. While the trust in contracts in the USA is evidenced by the primary role played by lawyers and financial experts, the very lack of such a primacy in Japan represents a vastly different emphasis.

The competitiveness implications of trust in contracts vs. trust in connections are sector-contingent. In the US case, the penchant for the specialization and professionalization of knowledge and its creation has provided a competitive edge in professional services and in technological deepening, while a focus on patents and copyrights has contributed to US competitiveness in technological breakthroughs. Conversely, the US preference for the commodification of knowledge has led to its neglect in the creation of the types of knowledge, such as ones that are relation-specific, that have prohibitively high transaction costs in selling to competitive markets under the logic of contractual man. The US emphasis on contract as the dominant form of exchange also leads to prohibitively high costs in transacting firm-specific and tacit knowledge developed within the firm. The result has been inefficiency in both creating and appropriating tacit, firm-specific, and relation-specific knowledge in corporate America. On the other hand, while the Japanese competitive advantage rests in its superior ability in creating, fusing, diffusing, and therefore appropriating tacit, firm- and relation-specific knowledge across firm boundaries, Japan has great competitive disadvantages in the professionalization and commodification of knowledge. All are derived from the same logic of connectual man.

Trust in specialists vs. trust in generalists

While the preponderance of trust in individuals and contracts facilitates trust in specialists and professionals in the USA, the predominance of trust in groups and connections fosters trust in generalists in Japan (Aoki, 1988; Westney, 1993). Knowing based on individuals, as preeminent in the USA, not only means a focus on individual separate knowing but also the full responsibility of individuals in acquiring necessary knowledge, skills, and capabilities. While Japanese firms take the responsibility of training their workers, in the USA this is primarily left to formal educational institutions and individuals (Sakakibara and Westney, 1992). Indeed, in order for individuals to exchange their knowledge and skills for wages and salaries, they need to acquire the forms of knowledge and skills that are *saleable* in the job markets. This requires that knowledge and skills be specialized and professionalized.

From a contractual viewpoint, in order to keep maximal freedom and independence from specific employers, the best thing employees can do is to develop standardized and encapsulated knowledge and skills that can be used elsewhere. The same is true for employers. In order to keep maximal freedom and independence, they also seek to hire professionals whose knowledge and skills are interchangeable with others. This combined effect of demand pull and supply push for standardized knowledge and skills has led to the legitimization of, and a focus on, the formal training of specialists and professionals in the USA. Even for the blue collar workers, according to a 1991 Bureau of Labor Statistics Survey, of the 57 per cent of workers who reported needing training in order to qualify for their current jobs, the major source of training came from schooling (32 per cent), as well as informal on-the-job training (27 per cent), with a minimal role of formal company training (12 per cent) (Brown and Reich, 1997: 127). Lynch (1990) estimates that only 14.7 per cent of young employees in the USA had received off-the-job training, and found an even lower 4.2 per cent and 1.8 per cent for company training and apprenticeship training respectively.

By contrast, the logic of connectual man in Japan requires both a trust in generalists and a focus on their production through on-the-job-training and job rotation. Furthermore, an emphasis on the *organic* mutual dependence of individuals also requires interdependence of their knowledge base and knowledge structure. On the demand side, the need for connectual knowing requires the development of mutually overlapping knowledge. On the supply side, the lifetime employment practice for core workers in Japan, which has emerged from the logic of connectual man, provides the incentives for both employers to offer and employees to participate in broad on-the-job-training (Koike, 1990). This is especially evidenced by the large amount of training provided by Japanese firms for their production workers in automobile assembly plants as compared with that provided by their US counterparts (Table 4.3). When compared with the rest of the world, while Japanese auto firms provide the greatest number of hours of training for both new and experienced workers, their US counterparts offer almost the least. (Australia comes bottom of the league.)

More significant than the gap in the amount of training is the scope of the training provided by the different countries. In their empirical study, Kusunoki and

Table 4.3 Amount of training for production workers in automobile assembly plants

Ownership/location	Hours of training in the first six months for new workers	Hours per year for those with > 1 year experience
Japanese/Japan	364	76
Japanese/North America	225	52
US/North America	42	31
US/Europe	43	34
European/Europe	178	52
Newly industrialized countries	260	46
Australia	40	15

Source: Adapted from MacDuffie and Kochan (1995: 156).

Numagami (1997) identified a pattern of frequent intra-firm transfers of engineers in Japanese firms as a systematic way of creating and sharing cross-functional knowledge. This supported the finding of Lynn *et al.* (1993) that while US engineers increase their specialization through time, their Japanese counterparts continue intra-firm transfer uniformly throughout their careers. Similarly, Nishiguchi (1994) found a systematic intra-firm transfer of engineers and others between connected suppliers and producers. Indeed, Kusunoki and Numagami (1997) found that, as a result of the emphasis on cross-functional knowledge, the possibility of promotion for Japanese engineers is highly linked to the scope and speed of intra-firm transfer they experienced.

In addition to the sharp contrast in the extent of on-the-job training and job rotation, the Japanese emphasis on generalists and the US stress on specialists is best evidenced by the stark differences in the proportion of researchers with a Ph.D. in laboratories. As shown in Table 4.4, the Ph.D. ratio in Japanese industrial R&D labs is only 17 per cent, less than one third of the US number. In university and government labs, the Japanese ratios are only about half that of the USA.

The competitiveness implications of trust in specialists vs. trust in generalists are also sector-contingent. In such sectors as biotechnology, software, aircraft, nuclear technology, and other large-scale complex technological sectors, separate knowing and therefore specialists are often the key factors for competitive success. Iansiti and

Table 4.4 Ph.D. ratio in US and Japanese laboratories

	Japan (n = 27)	USA (n = 20)	Japan/USA US = 100
Universities	18%	38%	47
Industry	17%	57%	30
Gov't labs	33%	61%	54

Source: Adapted from Cutler (1991: 73).

West (1997) attribute the US revival of the semiconductor sector to its heavy reliance on Ph.D. researchers with specialized capability of technology integration. Similarly, the dearth of formally trained computer programmers is partly responsible for the Japanese lack of competitiveness in prepackaged software (Duvall, 1995; Baba *et al.*, 1996). On the other hand, in the relatively mature fabricating manufacturing sectors such as opto-electronics and mechatronics, generalists are usually the major contributors to competitive success.

Trust in universal rules and abstract systems vs. trust in people and contextual situations

American zeal for autonomy and independence and the corresponding logic of contractual man leads to an emphasis on trust in universal rules and abstract systems, whereas the Japanese penchant for mutual connection and interdependence gives rise to the predominance of trust in people and contextual situations. Many scholars of modernity categorize trust in abstract systems as a characteristic of modernity irrespective of cultural differences (Giddens, 1990). An abstract system is one that applies abstract rules and procedures universally to all peoples. While trust in abstract systems has gradually diffused to non-Western societies, it is still predominantly a Western phenomenon. Trust in persons is still the norm in most East Asian societies.

According to the American theorist of modernity Anthony Giddens (1990: 88), '*Trust in systems* takes the form of *faceless commitments*, in which faith is sustained in the workings of knowledge of which the lay person is largely ignorant.' On the other hand, '*Trust in persons* involves *facework commitments*, in which indicators of the integrity of others (within given areas of action) are sought.' Such definitions are still very much based on the implicit Anglo-American cultural paradigm of contractual man, since the major criterion here for judging the trustworthiness of individuals is their 'integrity' rather than their personal connections. Furthermore, trust in abstract systems also means a fundamental belief in people's willingness to follow the rule of universal laws and procedures. Because of its contractual cultural paradigm, the USA is consistently ranked among the highest in all measures of universalism, whereas such a willingness to follow universal rules is low in East Asian societies (Trompenaars, 1993).

In East Asian societies, a focus on *trust in persons* means confidence in the *good will* of persons within a connectual structure and the *enforceability of tacitly perceived and expected mutual obligations among connected persons*. It sometimes also implicitly means a lack of confidence in anything that is not under the control of a person's connectual structure. The latter is especially true in China where abstract rules are applied differently to people according to their connections to the enforcers of the rules. Under the logic of connectual exchange, the trust in connected persons, the high cost of losing the trust of the connected, and the penchant for mutual interdependence constitute a loop of positive feedback in which all elements reinforce each other. By contrast, the penchant for autonomy and independence in the USA leads to the predominance of trust in abstract systems of generalized rules and impersonalized procedures for the protection of individual freedom and separateness. Since *trust in persons* leads to dependence upon other people's good will, it is not preferred in the USA.

The difference between trust in abstract systems and trust in persons has fundamental implications for knowledge creation. Using the terminology of Giddens (1990: 21), the predominance of the former in the USA leads to the emergence and predominance of many *disimbedding mechanisms*. These mechanisms try to exclude any personal factors and contextual links from the knowledge creation process so that the dependence on any given individual or special situations in knowledge creation is minimized. There have been many US institutional innovations that serve as disimbedding mechanisms in the knowledge creation process. These include the standardization of knowledge and skills, the establishment of an independent R&D department, the setup of independent quality check units, the hiring of outside consultants, the use of specialists for both product and process designs, the functional division of labor, the M-form organization, the competitive bidding for modularized parts, the setup and maintenance of a corporate management control system, the use of such technologies as robots and automatically paced assembly lines as a means for either getting rid of workers or controlling the pace of work, and so on. They constitute inter-linked parts of the US knowledge creation system with the dominant organizing principles of systemization, depersonalization, decontextualization, and people-independent system integration at the core.

In Japan, however, the dominance of trust in persons leads to the emergence and primacy of *imbedding mechanisms* that aim at maximizing the use of personal knowledge, skills and capabilities in the knowledge creation process. JIT production and delivery systems, quality circles, job rotation, on-the-job-training, lifetime employment, long-term subcontracting relationships, cross-functional teams, design for manufacturing, concurrent engineering, and so on are all Japanese institutional innovations that try to organically integrate and imbed people into the knowledge creation process. Underpinning these innovations is the Japanese desire for mutual connections and interdependence and the resultant dominant organizing principles of connection, recontextualization, customization, and people-dependent system integration.

The competitiveness implications of these differences are sector-contingent. In the sectors where the organizing principles of systemization, depersonalization, decontextualization, and people-independent system integration can work well, the stress of trust in abstract systems provides a competitive advantage for US firms. Conversely, in the sectors where the organizing principles of connection, recontextualization, and people-dependent system integration function best, the emphasis on trust in people and contextual situations provides Japan with a competitive advantage.

Discussion: dominant vs. complementary forms of human relations and human knowing

In summary, culture paradigms and national systems of knowledge creation are inherently intertwined. In the USA, the dominant cultural paradigm of contractual man has facilitated the preponderance of *separate knowing* as the major form of knowledge creation. The contractual cultural paradigm further fosters American fundamental trust in individuals, contracts, specialists, numbers, explicit and objective knowledge, universal rules, and abstract systems. On the other hand, in Japan the predominant cultural paradigm of connectual man has facilitated the primacy of *connectual knowing* in its system of knowledge creation. It further promotes the profound Japanese trust in groups, connections, generalists, tacit and inter-subjective knowledge, and contextual situations and persons. These fundamental differences in knowing and trust are major causes for the persistent sectoral patterns of national competitiveness.

It should be noted, however, that the preponderance of contractual relations in the USA does not mean the non-existence of non-contractual relations in US business practices. To the contrary, connectual relations have always been an indispensable complement to the dominant contractual governance in the USA (Macaulay, 1963). The same is true for the Japanese cultural paradigm. While connectual relations are dominant in human interactions, contracts are often used as a complement to deal with people both inside and outside a connectual structure. Its use can even be predominant in dealing with strangers. Here, the most important question is not so much whether both forms of human relations exist but rather which one is dominant and therefore has played the role of attractor in shaping human behaviors and human organizations? These dialectic relationships between dominant and complementary human relations in the USA and Japan are shown in Table 4.5.

By extending a specific form of human relation into a more discrete scale from dominant to fair to weak and by including more economies, we arrive at Figure 4.1. Here, culture synergy happens when Japan and the four little dragons in East Asia

Table 4.5 Dominant vs. complementary human relations in the USA and Japan

	USA	Japan
Dominant human relations	Contractual	Connectual
Complementary human relations	Connectual	Contractual

learn to incorporate rules of law and contracts into their value and economic systems. And from the 1980s, in their attempts to learn from Japan, US companies tried to incorporate more connectual relations and strategic alliances into their industrial organizations (Smith, 1995). Albeit with a traditional lack of rule of law, China is moving toward more reliance on contractual mechanisms in governing human interactions (Jin, 1995).

The same dialectical structures and synergistic processes exist in the country patterns of knowing. Aside from the predominance of separate knowing, some forms of connectual knowing exist as a complement in the US system of knowledge

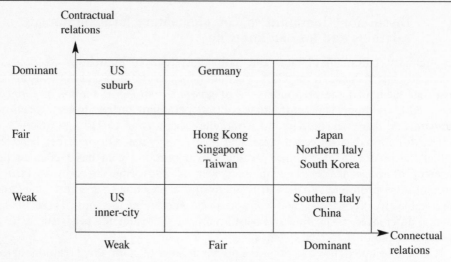

Figure 4.1 Patterns of human relations in different economies

creation. Similarly in Japan, various forms of separate knowing exist to complement the predominance of connectual knowing (Table 4.6).

Notwithstanding this, the extent of the complementary forms of knowing varies among countries. While Japan and, to a lesser extent, South Korea, Singapore, Taiwan, and Hong Kong have been willing to learn and adopt Western science and

Table 4.6 Dominant vs. complementary human knowing in the USA and Japan

	USA	Japan
Dominant human knowing	Contractual	Connectual
Complementary human knowing	Connectual	Contractual

implicitly its dominant methodology of separate knowing, Americans have been weak in connectual knowing until the discovery of its importance in the 1980s through such revealed Japanese best practices as total quality management, *kaizen* (incremental improvement), job rotation, JIT production, and concurrent engineering. Despite such an effort of learning, the dominant patterns of knowing can hardly change and the need for synthesis and synergy can never end. As a result, as shown in Figure 4.2, although with an increasing emphasis by both scholars (Kash and Rycroft, 1999) and practitioners (Smith, 1995), because of the isomorphic pull of the contractual paradigm, the US pattern of knowing is still characterized by the predominance of separate knowing, or in Cole's (1995b) terms, individual learning.

On the other hand, while connectual knowing is still predominant in the East Asian economies of Japan, South Korea, Singapore, Hong Kong, and Taiwan, the efforts of learning from Western science and technology in general and US management fads in particular have led them to adopt a fair extent of separate knowing. It is clear that there is still room for both sides of the East and the West to overcome the isomorphic pull of their dominant paradigms of knowing to adopt and synthesize the increasing extent of the complementary form of knowing.

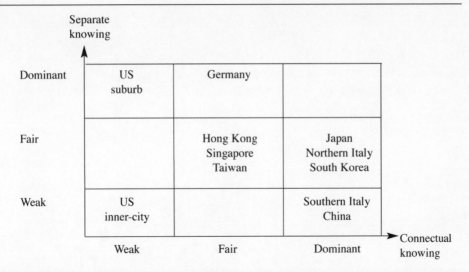

Figure 4.2 Patterns of human knowing in different economies

This process of synergy can also happen in the differing socio-cultural construction of trust with regard to knowledge creation and exchange. Although Americans still put greater emphasis and therefore trust on individual entrepreneurship, contracts, specialists, universal rules, and abstract systems, there are always synergistic opportunities to nurture increasing trust in cooperation, connections, generalists, contexts, and particular situations. Similarly, Japan can benefit greatly if they can incorporate a much greater emphasis on individual entrepreneurship, specialists, and people-independent systems integration.

Notes

1. For the Japanese psychology of *amae*, or dependency, see Doi (1971/1981) and Frank Johnson (1993). For a comparison of the rule of independence in the USA vs. the rule of interdependence in Japan in their communication styles, see Yamada (1997). For analysis of the East Asian political system of dependency, see Pye (1985). For the interdependent iron-triangle of businessmen, politicians, and bureaucrats, see Okimoto (1989). For the elaboration of the Japanese organization system as fostering dependency, see Oliver and Wilkinson (1992: 70–87), and Fruin (1992: 30–49).
2. For the influence of Confucianism in Japan, see Tu (1996); Dore (1987).
3. For the concept of technology deepening and widening, see Malerba and Orsenigo (1996).

Governance Mechanisms for Knowledge Creation

As we have seen in Part II, cultural paradigms have a profound impact on the dominant governance mechanisms for knowledge creation in various nations. While the paradigm of contractual man has facilitated the emergence and dominance of a flock of contractual governance mechanisms for knowledge creation in the USA, the paradigm of connectual man has fostered the emergence and dominance of a cluster of connectual governance mechanisms for knowledge creation in Japan.

This part will examine in detail various governance mechanisms in the USA and Japan. Unlike the conventional focus on the issues of *opportunism* and *transaction costs*, our study will concentrate on the governance mechanisms for *knowledge creation and appropriation*. Instead of the conventional treatment of the markets, hierarchies, networks, and clans as unitary and universal across cultural boundaries, we will differentiate each of them into two generic and fundamentally different mechanisms: contractual vs. connectual governance. Such a treatment enables us to understand the issue of governance from the perspective of knowledge creation. It also provides the possibility for us to search for the causal links among dominant cultural paradigms, governance mechanisms, and the sectoral patterns of national competitiveness.

By its focus on transaction costs and opportunism and its treatment of hierarchies and markets as universal, Williamson's theory of governance reveals not only the fundamental Anglo-American mentality of contractual man, but also the Newtonian belief in the existence of a unique equilibrium as the optimal point. As a result, while the Newtonian system of diminishing returns reaches its optimality when the force of friction is reduced to zero, the Williamsonian governance structure achieves efficiency when the economic force of friction – transaction costs – is minimized. This could be the case if there were neither a need for learning and evolution, nor the possibility for knowledge creation and synthesis.

As conceptualized in the complexity literature, the assumption of optimality and universality collapses once we acknowledge the existence and importance of learning and coevolution, and, more importantly, of increasing returns and positive feedback generated through the creation and application of knowledge (Arthur, 1989; Kash and Rycroft, 1999). As a result, the most pivotal problem in organizational governance is neither that of economizing transaction costs, as Williamson (1985) assumes, nor that of exploiting economies of scale and scope, as Chandler (1990) posits; nor that of best utilizing dispersed economic knowledge at specific times and places, as Hayek (1945) suggests. Instead, the key issue is how knowledge creation, transformation, diffusion and appropriation can best be organized so that all existing knowledge is mobilized and synthesized, all potential knowledge is created and appropriated, and all acquired knowledge, expertise, and capability is effectively maintained and enhanced. In other words, the effectiveness of knowledge creation, diffusion, transformation, and appropriation is the primary force of competitive advantage, which will in turn lead to high quality, low costs, and long-term profitability.

When the central concern of governance is shifted from transaction costs to knowledge creation, cultural paradigms enter into play through the isomorphic pulls of organizing principles. In chapter 5, I will elaborate on the *contractual* governance mechanisms of the markets, hierarchies, networks, and clans for knowledge creation. I will explain how the US penchant for autonomy and independence and the resultant cultural paradigm of contractual man have enabled and facilitated the emergence and dominance of various organizational, institutional, and technological innovations that have formed a specific system of knowledge creation in the USA. By discussing their comparative advantages and disadvantages, I will be able to link these mechanisms to the persistent sectoral pattern of US competitiveness.

In chapter 6, we will explore various *connectual* governance mechanisms for knowledge creation in Japan. I will link their emergence and preponderance to the Japanese cultural paradigm of connectual man. I will also explain the persistent sectoral pattern of Japanese competitiveness through discussions of the comparative advantages and disadvantages of various Japanese connectual governance mechanisms for knowledge creation and by linking them to the sectoral structure of knowledge and knowledge creation.

It is important to point out that the knowledge creation systems of such advanced nations as the USA and Japan are so complex that any effort of generalization will result in some exceptions. As a result of the dynamic interplay of *Yin* and *Yang*, there are always minor opposing patterns accompanying the dominant ones as an important complement. This acknowledgment, however, does not diminish the value of exploring and revealing the dominant patterns underpinning the complex economic and technological landscapes of nations. On the contrary, the increasing complexity of our current world of organizational and technological advancement poses a great cognitive challenge for us to identify meaningful patterns of cause and effect and structures of interdependence, self-organization, and isomorphism underlying the seemingly chaotic surfaces of the complex world. Regrettably, the Anglo-American tradition of emphasizing analysis and narrow specialization has created the Tower of Babel in which each profession explores a narrowly defined domain with separately created jargons and terminology. It creates more confusion than understanding. It floods readers with numerous, tiny, unrelated, and sometimes contradictory details of unconnected domains, which only 'see trees without any proper vision of the whole forest.'

The identification of underlying patterns of dominant governance mechanisms overcomes these problems. Such a task, however, cannot be realized through the mentality of analysis, nor can it be achieved through putting together all the statistics. It needs both an imaginary jump and a conceptualization process that capture the deep structures and underlying logics linking the seemingly disconnected subsystems. Here, the Weberian ideal-typical methodology is of great help. As has happened in physics and sociology, what we need is to identify pure forms in ideal situations and then extend them to the real world of complexity. From this point of view, it is better to treat the dominant governance mechanisms as kinds of *attractors* toward which many real practices are pulled. Therefore, even though there are exceptions, as is the case in chaos theory, these do not undermine the impact of the dominant mechanisms as attractors.

CHAPTER FIVE

Contractual Governance for Knowledge Creation

Thus, the United States remained throughout the 19th and early 20th centuries the extreme example of a classically liberal or Lockean society, one that rejected the assumptions of the alliance of the throne and altar, of ascriptive elitism, of mercantilism, of noblesse oblige, of communitarianism ... The United States was 'purely bourgeois, so entirely without feudal past.'

Seymour Martin Lipset (1990: 8)

According to scholars of American exceptionalism (Lipset, 1996), the USA has been an outlier because of its extreme pursuit of Lockean liberalism and its strong antagonism toward any form of dependency, ascriptive status, and particularism. This has led to the development of exceptional political and social systems, which are characterized by pluralism, egalitarianism, anti-statism, voluntarism, and spontaneous sociability (Lipset, 1990). Strikingly, while the impact of the USA's exceptional cultural values on the development of its social and political systems are well established, most scholars in economics, organizational science, and technological innovations have failed to take into consideration such an impact in their studies of US systems of capitalism, management, and innovation.

The most notable example of this is Chandler's (1977, 1990) account of the managerial revolution and rise of mass production in US business. Inheriting a bias from the economic profession that explains everything based on economic factors, Chandler (1977) attributed the rise of US mass production to such economic factors as large and unified markets facilitated by railway expansion, a lack of skilled labor, sustained investment in physical capital and management, and so on. While no one denies the importance of these factors, what is missing in such an account are the motivational forces that *pulled* Americans out of the '*lock-in*' of the craft production system which had lasted for thousands of years. Anyhow, as Piore and Sabel (1984) brilliantly show, mass production was only among one of many possible trajectories under the economic conditions of nineteenth-century America.

In this chapter, I intend to prove that the emergence of US capitalism in general, and its mass production trajectory in particular, was neither the lock-in of historical events, nor a pure result of economic factors. It was, rather, facilitated by *the isomorphic pull* of the US contractual cultural paradigm and the underlying drive for autonomy and independence. Instead of adopting a historical approach that traces the origins of the US system through detailed documentary studies, I choose the structurist approach that focuses on the revelation of *the deep logical* links between the contractual cultural paradigm and various contractual governance mechanisms emerged in the USA. In so doing, I try to integrate the seemingly fragmented evolutionary stages of US capitalism – from US System of Manufactures in the mid-nineteenth century, to Taylorism and Fordist mass production in the early and mid-twentieth century, to the Silicon Valley model of innovation and e-business in the 1990s – into a consistent framework on contractual governance mechanisms for knowledge creation.

Contractual markets and knowledge creation

The markets as described in neoclassical economics are solely the Anglo-American types that are contract-based, competitive, short-term oriented, and at arm's length. This system has emerged and become predominant in the USA in order to maximize individual autonomy, freedom, separateness, and independence in transacting with others. This is true especially with regard to the creation and exchange of knowledge, the primary human activity in the knowledge society.

Neoclassical economics as the revealer

The contractual governance mechanisms of the market as predominant in the USA are best revealed by neoclassical economics. In the neoclassical model, the markets are competitive and at arm's length. The ideal economic transactions are conducted through competitive bidding and secured through the state enforcement of contracts. While the former makes economic transactions independent of any particular transacting partners, the latter reduces the risks of relying on the good will of others for contract implementation. The impersonal and arm's length relationship between buyers and sellers enables the maximal freedom of both in seeking new transactional opportunities. The competitive process also minimizes the need for information exchange. In fully competitive markets, both buyers and sellers are price takers so that the buyers need not worry about the costs of sellers, nor need the sellers worry about the concrete utility functions of the buyers. All they need to be concerned with is the maximization of profits and their utility functions. As a result, *the neoclassical market becomes the best tool in securing individual autonomy and independence*. From this point of view, it is understandable why the neoclassical model of a completely competitive market has been so enthusiastically embraced by Anglo-American societies. In pointing out the *autonomic* and *independent* nature of the contractual market governance, Knight (1957: 78) notes that in perfect competition:

> Every member of the society is to act as an individual only, in entire independence of all other persons. To complete his independence he must be free from social wants, prejudices, preferences, and repulsions, or any values that are not completely manifested in market dealing. Exchange of finished goods is the only form of relation between individuals, or at least there is no other form which influences economic conduct. And in exchanges between individuals, no interests of persons or parties to the exchange are to be concerned, either for good or for ill.

The neoclassical model of market governance has a profound impact on the ways in which knowledge is created, transformed, and appropriated. Because the neoclassical model requires *minimal* interdependence of knowledge, any forms of knowledge involved in a transaction must be *modularized* and *encapsulated* so that their utility can be independently evaluated by separate buyers and they can therefore be traded in the markets with low transaction costs.

Standardization of demand

One form of modularization and encapsulation is the standardization of demand. By offering a succession of homogeneous and standardized goods and services that aim at serving specified segments of customers, mass production firms in the USA not only can exploit economies of scale, but they can also achieve great autonomy by reducing the interdependence between producers and customers that was prevalent in the age of craft production. Through the standardization of demands, the knowledge links between producers and customers were also decontextualized and depersonalized. The idiosyncratic tastes and preferences of individual customers that were typical in the age of craft production were transformed into various segments of standardized tastes that represent the means of a given segment of consumers. The process is further enhanced by various forms of mass marketing aimed at establishing brand loyalty and standard tastes.

Historically, the drive for standardization of demand was the very force enabling the emergence and dominance of mass production in the USA. Currently, it is through the standardization of demands that corporate America dominates the world by exporting American-style consumerism. This is achieved through mass marketing of the image of a superior American lifestyle imbedded in a preference for such standardized goods as soft drinks, fast food, and consumer chemicals.

Franchising and standardization of supply

Parallel to the standardization of demand is the standardization of supply. If it were not for the latter and a franchising strategy that supported its geographical expansion, the US fast food industry, hotel-chain industry, and other service sectors would not have dominated the world. As Shook and Shook (1993) note, the strategy of franchising that emerged in the USA has fundamentally changed the business landscape of the world. According to them, in 1993, there were more than 540,000 franchised business in the USA alone, generating more than $758 billion revenues and employing more than 7 million Americans. While 65 per cent of all business start-ups fail within five years of their operation, less than 5 per cent of franchised outlets face the same fate each year. In addition to the advantageous economies of scale and scope, underpinning this phenomenal success is the standardization of every aspect of the business.

Through such a process, the knowledge about customers, operations, and services that is entrenched in the success of a once local business is explicitly articulated and encapsulated into a saleable package. The strategy of franchising is, to some extent, the selling of successful business models by exactly *copying* the practices to other geographic locations. By carefully dividing customer base in the geographical dimension and granting a special segment exclusively to a franchisee, franchising guarantees enough potential demand for the services. By providing standardized business plans, operational procedures, inputs, logistics, and advertising, and by offering standardized training, franchising generates economies of scale and scope, and guarantees certainty in service quality, and therefore attracts enough demand for profit-making.

Standardization of parts and their supply

When it comes to the supplier relationship, one way to minimize interdependence of knowledge is by the standardization of transacted parts. By so doing, the knowledge links between producers and suppliers are either artificially severed or truly minimized. It therefore enabled US firms, such as GM and Ford, to keep arm's length relationships with their suppliers before the mid-1980s. They can use the competitive bidding process to choose the suppliers with the best prices to deliver standard parts. Car-makers can also change suppliers with low switching costs.

Historically, the standardization of parts was the very force leading to the rise of the American System of Manufactures in the nineteenth century and the Fordist mass production in the twentieth century, which has given rise to US dominance in the world until it was challenged by the Japanese in the 1980s (Best, 1990; Hounshell, 1984; Marcus and Segal, 1989; Staudenmaier, 1989). It is also the reason for US large export shares in metal machine tool parts, auto parts, office equipment parts (see Table 2.14, p. 21). The same principles of standardization and modularization have been the very force for US competitiveness in e-business and the digital economy.

Standardization of knowledge and skills

The fourth form of modularization and encapsulation is the standardization of knowledge, skills, and expertise that can fulfil standard tasks and solve standard problems. According to Mintzberg (1989: Ch. 10), this standardization process leads to professionalization in the production and reproduction of knowledge and skills. Through standardization, the knowledge and skills of a profession become *interchangeable* and therefore directly saleable to the competitive market, where both buyers and sellers of knowledge and skills may achieve maximum autonomy and independence. Because of this causal linkage, the USA has been exceptional in its maximum extension of professionalism. As the efforts to modularize tasks and skills intensify through time, the division and specialization among various professions also explodes. In the process, the problem of knowledge links among professions is solved through the *spin-off* of new professions that specialize in the creation, standardization, and application of newly developed knowledge and skills that attack newly separated and isolated problem domains. This has given rise to the proliferation and compartmentalization of professions in the USA. Professions permeate every aspect of American society. And almost everyone claims a specialist of a narrowly defined and self-contained domain that aims at some specific tasks or problems.

By dividing and isolating ever increasingly narrow fields of specialization, professionalization has the comparative advantage of creating in-depth knowledge and capabilities. The standardization process that is imbedded also reduces the transaction costs in the diffusion and exchange of knowledge and skills. The very action of dividing and isolating problem domains may, however, *sever* the dynamic and complex knowledge links involved in some non-modular, tightly coupled, and complex tasks. The standardization process may also leave many forms of contextual and tacit knowledge untapped. Consequently, the competitiveness implications of professionalization are also sector-contingent. In the sectors where major tasks can be effectively partitioned, modularized, and encapsulated *without* the loss of knowledge creation opportunities, the USA has a competitive advantage. Otherwise, it is possible that the USA will face a competitive disadvantage.

Consulting services and the externalization of knowledge

The fifth form of modularization and encapsulation of knowledge is the creation of new fads. Once a set of coherent insights and knowledge is explicitly articulated and encapsulated into an operationable tool kit that has earned a successful track record and a reputation in solving certain problems, it creates a separate identity and attaches to itself a measurable value that is *saleable* to the market. The market value is further promoted by external consultants who package it into a new fad that promises universal applicability and validity. The widespread awareness of its value, combined with the conformist nature of American individualism, makes it possible that such a fad could create a huge market for consulting services. The American ability to continuously push out new management fads – from one-minute-management, to total quality management, lean production, organizational learning, downsizing, reengineering, and to e-business, mass customization, supply chain management, enterprise resource planning, and customer relationship management – contributes significantly to the superior competitiveness of the US management consulting sector. According to O'Shea and Madigan (1997), management consulting has become one of the most successful businesses in American history, with an annual revenue of $25 billion in the USA alone, about *one-half* of the global share. According to the London-based journal *Accountancy* (March, 1998: 14), the Big Six US accounting firms alone took a 23 per cent slice of the $62 billion global management consultancy market. Table 5.1 indicates the rapid rise of the US management industry broadly defined, which includes business schools, management consulting, corporate training, and business media.

In addition to its own competitive advantage as an independent sector, the superior management and technical consulting sectors have also contributed greatly to the competitiveness of US firms in other sectors. Not only have external consultants of various expertise and capabilities played a pivotal role in the restructuring and reengineering of corporate business processes, they have also been primary sources of knowledge for engineers inside corporate America. According to Lynn *et al.* (1993: 67), while only 42.8 per cent of Japanese engineers have ever used external consultants as sources of knowledge, 70.8 per cent of US engineers have done so. Consulting services have the competitive advantage of providing the best skills, insights, and intellectual services to reshape the structure and strategy of both firms and economies. Historically, external consultants of industrial engineering had facilitated significantly the rapid diffusion of Taylorism and therefore the rise of mass production in the USA (Nelson, 1995). Under the challenge of Japanese flexible production in the 1980s, external consultants have also greatly helped the explicit articulation and diffusion of such best Japanese practices as total quality management (TQM), JIT production and delivery, cross-functional teams, producer–designer collaboration, and concurrent engineering (Cole, 1998). They therefore contributed significantly to the moderate comeback of the US automobile and semiconductor sectors in the late 1990s (Macher *et al.*, 1998). Most importantly,

Table 5.1 The rise of the US management industry

	1982	1992	Growth
Management schools and MBAs			
Number of management schools	545	670	23%
Number MBAs granted	60,000	80,000	33%
Consulting industry			
Number of consulting firms	780	1,533	97%
Number of consultants	30,000	81,000	170%
Total consulting revenues	$3.5 billion	$15.2 billion	334%
Corporate training			
Number of people trained	33.5 million	40.9 million	22%
Total training hours	1.1 billion	1.3 billion	18%
Total corporate expenditure	$10 billion	$45 billion	350%
Business media			
Number of business stories	125,000	680,000	444%
Number of new business books	1,327	1,831	38%
Sales of business books	$225 million	$490 million	118%

Source: Nohria and Berkley (1994: 130).

external consultants with the most advanced technologies and expertise have played a pivotal role in the formation of the USA's superior capability in leading and riding the new waves of information technology in general, and Internet technologies and e-business in particular.

The tendency of US firms to rely on consulting services, however, has some negative impacts. First and foremost, an overreliance on external knowledge, skills, and capabilities in the restructuring and reengineering of firms may deprive them of the opportunities for an endogenous growth of knowledge, skills, and capabilities. In many cases, an overreliance on external consultants for inputs of knowledge, skills, and capabilities is the result of a deeply entrenched division between thinking and acting. As a result, while the most challenging tasks of thinking are assigned to external consultants, the work of internal employees is reduced to routine operation and maintenance. This certainly reduces the capability for organizations to learn, especially on the shop floor. Another disadvantage rests in the inability of external consultants to develop and apply firm-specific knowledge. More often than not, they try to apply *universal* concepts and tool kits to attack problems in specific firms without considering the need for fitting and adapting them to the specific realities and missions of the specific firm. Indeed, as Nohria and Berkley (1994) point out, by resorting to external consultants for a successive series of fads with off-the-shelf solutions, many US managers in the 1980s abdicated their responsibility for creatively adapting new ideas to the strategic, organizational, and technological context of their firms. In many cases, external consultants are used to avoid responsibility, to 'lend credibility and packaging to decisions that have already been made,' and for staff to use their recommendations as the best defense policies (Shapiro *et al.*, 1993: 94).

The rapid rise of the consulting sector and US heavy dependence on it reveals not only the predominance of separate knowing but also the fact that US firms have difficulty in retaining employees with superior knowledge, skills, and capabilities. This is due to the low cost of exit and the inability of US firms fully to appropriate the value of the superior knowledge of their specialists other than through the contractual markets. In other words, US firms usually fail to pay superior knowledge workers the full value of their potential capabilities because they are unable fully to appropriate their values beyond the firm boundary. The result is the transformation of the best knowledge workers into external consultants who sell their services directly to the contractual markets.

Patents and copyrights as forms of knowledge appropriation

In order to be saleable in the contractual market, knowledge and skills can also be contained, imbedded, and encapsulated in certain patents and copyrights. Although a patent may be infringed upon by inventing around it, the knowledge imbedded in it has a higher degree of appropriability than one that is not patentable. As a result, technological breakthroughs that can lead to patents have always been preferred in the USA to incremental improvements that are difficult to patent. Partly because of this, the USA is competitive in sectors where patent and copyright protections are effective ways of appropriating the benefits of knowledge.

Knowledge as public vs. private goods

As the dominant conceptual models in the USA, both the dichotomy of knowledge between public and private goods, and the linear model of innovation serve as powerful tools for modularization and encapsulation. The distinction of knowledge as public goods from knowledge as private goods enables the separation of knowledge that is difficult to appropriate from one that is easy. By the public provision of the former, the market failure of knowledge creation is partly solved. It enables profit-seeking firms to focus on the creation of appropriable knowledge based on the availability of public knowledge.

The linear model of innovation delineates the innovation process as separable, independent, and sequential steps moving from basic research to applied research to commercialization (Kline and Rosenberg, 1986). It serves not only to distinguish knowledge as a public good from knowledge as a private good, but also to arrange its creation in a modularized and sequential way. According to this model, basic research as a public good is the only source of *genuine* knowledge and critical breakthroughs. Applied research intends to find useful applications for the findings of basic research, and the following commercialization process appropriates the results of applied research by creating new products and processes that are saleable to the markets. As a result of the dominance of this linear model, the US system of knowledge creation had emphasized basic research and its public provision in the period from 1945 to the 1980s. As shown in Table 5.2, in 1988 the government share of total national R&D expenditure in the USA was 48 per cent, far larger than the figure of a mere 18.4 per cent in Japan.

Huge public R&D spending in the USA since 1945 has created the largest number of best-research universities and institutions in the world, which has in turn provided

Table 5.2 Structure of R&D expenditure: sources and users, percentage of total national R&D expenditure

	Government		Industry		Universities		Private institutes	
	Provided	Spent	Provided	Spent	Provided	Spent	Provided	Spent
USA (1988)	48.0	11.5	47.9	71.8	2.8	13.8	1.4	2.9
Japan (1988)	18.4	9.3	76.3	73.9	4.5	12.6	0.7	4.3
W. Germany (1987)	36.6	3.4	62.3	73.1	*	12.9	*	10.6
France (1983)	53.8	26.4	42.0	56.8	0.2	15.9	0.4	0.9
UK (1987)	38.7	15.1	49.7	67.0	0.6	14.2	1.9	3.7

* Information not available in the original.
Source: Westney (1994: 157).

a rich knowledge base for spontaneous innovation and fusion.

It should be noted that, although the linear model of innovation has been widely discredited since the mid-1980s (Kline and Rosenberg, 1986), it is still useful in sectors such as biotechnology and chemicals. According to Liebeskind *et al.* (1996), US success in biotechnology is still very much the result of a superior research infrastructure. On the other hand, in mature fabricating manufacturing sectors such as automobiles and consumer electronics, the linear model of innovation is vastly inappropriate. This is confirmed by the negative correlation between R&D intensity and the revealed comparative advantage of export in these two sectors (Jin, 1998). The mistaken emphasis on R&D is part of the reason for US firms failing in the automobile and consumer electronics sectors, while the Japanese have succeeded.

Knowledge as commercial secrecy

Finally, when all the above methods of knowledge appropriation fail, US firms seek to appropriate created knowledge by keeping it in 'secrecy.' The treatment of knowledge as 'secrecy,' however, fails to appropriate its full potential benefits and therefore represents a type of market failure. This partly contributed to the 'Not-Invented-Here' syndrome in the USA, causing many wasted efforts in the creation of knowledge already owned somewhere by other firms. Furthermore, the high mobility of knowledge workers in the USA makes the strategy of 'secrecy' vulnerable because other companies can hunt knowledge workers mastering the secrecy.

Contractual hierarchies and knowledge creation

When the contractual market still fails in knowledge creation with all the institutional innovations discussed above, Americans resort to the contractual governance structure of hierarchies. Although Williamson (1985) treats the markets and the hierarchies as two separate, discrete, and mutually exclusive governance structures, from the knowledge regime perspective they are mutually complementary and isomorphic. They are attracted to the same contractual cultural paradigms, share similar organizing principles, and complement one another in maximizing individual autonomy and independence.

Parallel to the autonomous and independent markets are autonomous and independent firms. As Biggart and Hamilton (1994: 483) describe the characteristics of Western firms in general and US firms in particular:

> The legal assignment of private property rights requires a clear delineation of who claims ownership and what is owned. When non-state businesses in the West were subdued under the legal definition of private property, business firms became in principle *separate, distinct, and independent*. They became conceptualized as a person – as *autonomous*, legally indivisible units that could form *contractual* links with people and with other firms. (*Italics added.*)

There have been many institutional innovations in the USA to keep the maximal autonomy and independence of firms. These include, the doctrine of management prerogative; the codification of information; the centralization of management information and control systems; the standardization, modularization and sequentialization of tasks; the separation between thinking and executing; the specialization of functional units; the creation of separate quality control units and separate R&D departments; the use of buffers and inventories; the adoption of profit centers and M-form organization; and the centrality of financial knowledge in corporate governance. The central purpose of all these arrangements is to maintain the autonomy in knowledge creation and the independence of one knower on the knowledge and skills of others. In so doing, the American cultural paradigm of contractual man has facilitated the emergence and dominance of a specific corporate system of knowledge creation.

'Stockholder capitalism' and the prerogative of owners and managers

The logic of contractual man leads to the Anglo-American treatment of firms as private properties that are fully at the disposal of their owners. As a result, owners have full rights in the control, management, and disposal of their firms and, within them, the factors of production including physical capital, intellectual property rights, land, and labor. As Weinstein and Kochan (1995: 3) put it:

> In the United States, both blue- and white-collar employees have neither *de jure* nor *de facto* stakeholder rights by virtue of their employment with the firm. Underpinning this traditional conception is the distinctly American notion that the firm is a bundle of tradable assets owned by shareholders whose sole agents are the managers and officers of the enterprise. In the United States, employers have neither the juridical nor socially expected responsibility to involve employees in the daily strategic decisions of the firm.

This distinctly American notion of the exclusive ownership of firms has given rise to 'stockholder capitalism' in the USA. In such a system, profits and returns on investment are the sole concern of stockholders and management. Investors freely sell and buy stocks in search of profits and capital gains. Firms are constantly merged, bought out, and spun off according to the same calculation. Workers are not treated as stakeholders who have a legitimate voice in the firm but as a fungible factor of production.

In the ideal US labor markets, workers exchange the control of their labor and services for wages through contracting with the firm. In so doing, labor becomes another factor of production fully at the command of managers. Indeed, the persistent US commitment to the doctrine of the management prerogative over workers (Bowman, 1996) is shaped by its dominant cultural paradigm of contractual man and the resultant economic paradigm of contractual exchange. It is derived from management perception of complete *ownership* of the services derived from labor.

The management prerogative, however, has been constantly challenged by the opportunistic behavior of labor. One persistent theme in US management–labor relations has been the consistent tension between management's attempt to fully control the labor process and labor's effort to nullify such control through opportunistic manipulation. In so doing, both sides want to keep full autonomy and be maximally independent of one another. The result has been the emergence and dominance of US corporate governance mechanisms that maximize the autonomy and independence of stockholders and management on the one hand and the independence and autonomy of workers on the other. Ironically, the autonomy and independence of both sides relies heavily on the same process of division, separation, and standardization.

Standardization of job tasks

One way to keep the maximal autonomy and independence of both management and employees is the standardization of job tasks and skill requirements. Combined with the standardization of knowledge and skills discussed before, this enables the interchangeability and substitutability of skilled labors and professionals. Such interchangeability not only helps management to substitute external for internal knowledge workers with low transaction costs and sunk costs, but also makes the turnover of knowledge workers from one firm to another less costly. In other words, the interchangeability realized through the standardization process vastly reduces the mutual dependence between employers and employees concerning both the demand and supply of knowledge and skills.

Here, firm-specific knowledge, or using Williamson's term, 'asset-specific knowledge,' is not welcome by both management and workers because it creates an uncomfortable mutual dependency structure between them. For management, a reliance on the non-substitutable knowledge of workers means the possibility of being held up by the latter's opportunistic manipulation. For employees, the development of firm-specific knowledge and skills also means being too dependent on their current employers in the appropriation of knowledge and skills. Workers with firm-specific knowledge and skills may risk the inability to sell their knowledge and skills to other firms. As a result, interchangeable knowledge and skills become a sort of *attractor* that exerts isomorphic pull for both employers and employees.

Standardization of rules, routines, and procedures

Parallel to the standardization of tasks is the standardization of rules, routines, and procedures that aims at eliminating any idiosyncratic or personal effects on the operation of organizations. In addition, this has the function of safeguarding the rights and responsibilities of both management and employees, of securing the quality of products, and of minimizing any form of uncertainty or dependency on other people's personal incentives and good will. When applied to the interfaces among various procedures, standardization also makes each procedure autonomous in its operation and in its knowledge creation process.

The pervasive process of standardization has led to the rise of US-style bureaucracy in which both government and the private sector rely on a system of universal rules and measures to substitute impersonal calculations for personal judgment (Porter, 1995: 195). Indeed, according to Wilson (1989), the USA depends on formal rules to control the exercise of power to a greater extent than any other advanced nation. Similarly, the pervasive use of formal rules and routines in the private sector has led to the 'McDonaldization' of American society (Ritzer, 1995).

Standardization of costs

Once parts, jobs, tasks, and procedures are standardized it becomes possible to standardize the costs in producing parts, hiring workers, fulfilling tasks, and implementing procedures. When this is achieved, it is possible to allocate the various costs involved to individual business units and to calculate their efficiency, productivity, and other performance criteria. Top managers can accordingly use these objective measures to motivate middle-level managers through pay for performance. On the shop floor, standard costs can be used as benchmarks for middle-level managers to measure labor productivity, control labor process, and motivate workers. Because it enables the autonomy and independence of individual business units in performance measurement, the standard cost system is more widely used in the USA than in Japan (Hiromoto, 1988).

The codification of information

More broadly, the standardization of parts, tasks, skills, procedures, and costs enables the codification and quantification of information of business processes and job performance, which has become the central tool for management to prevent opportunistic manipulation from employees. In other words, an information system systematically recording data about work flow and job performance enables management to exert control over the labor process without dependency on the good will of employees. Nelson *et al.*'s (1992) research confirms that US firms are more reliant on management information systems for corporate governance than are their Japanese counterparts.

Separate quality control and performance evaluation units

Parallel to the pervasive use of management information systems is the establishment of separate quality control and performance evaluation units. Both enable management to monitor the work of employees without depending on direct employee feedback, therefore reducing the possibility of opportunism. Obviously, the separation of quality control function from shop-floor operation (Cole, 1998) is also a result of the American penchant for separate knowing.

The separation of thinking from executing

To further reduce management's dependence on the knowledge of shop-floor workers, the tasks of thinking and executing were separated in the USA until recently (Sabel, 1987). Historically, this trend began with Frederick Taylor's Scientific Management movement that emphasized the use of external consultants and in-house industrial engineers to determine the 'best' methods of operation (Nelson, 1995). By moving the locus of knowledge creation away from the shop floor to the management and professionals, the practice vastly reduces management reliance on the knowledge of craft masters, shop-floor workers, and foremen in the operation of firms.

The functional division and the specialization of tasks

The American penchant for autonomy and independence is embodied not only in the relationships between management and employees but also in the interaction among organization units. To increase their autonomy, individual tasks are divided into near-independent functional units. Consequently, different tasks of knowledge creation, such as R&D, product design, and process design, are made independent functional divisions.

The modularization and sequentialization of tasks

The independence of tasks can be achieved through the process of modularization and encapsulation of all units so that the knowledge links and the need for knowledge exchange among them are minimized. There are several ways to make functional divisions more independent of one another in the knowledge creation process. The first is to sequentialize the knowledge creation process. Here, the linear model of innovation as dominant in the USA plays a key role. The second is to use buffers to decrease or totally eliminate the interdependence between adjacent processes. The buffers can be time, in the case of product development, or inventory in the case of production lines. Third, an independent department can be established to coordinate the work of divisions. By setting aside the special task of coordination, the structural interdependence among divisions is transformed and imbedded into the newly created planning and coordinating division. The horizontal information flow among divisions is also transformed into a vertical flow between headquarters and their divisions. As a result, in contrast to the Japanese emphasis on horizontal information flow, US firms focus on vertical information flow (Aoki, 1986). Finally, the interdependence of functional divisions can be imbedded into organizational architecture, rules, and routines so that the need for direct knowledge exchange among functional divisions is minimized.

M-form organization as a form of modularization

The autonomy and independence of functional divisions can be further enhanced through the design of profit centers in an M-form organization. This practice minimizes the need for knowledge exchange between headquarters and organizational divisions. It enables top managers independently to evaluate the financial performance of each division without the need to monitor intensively its concrete operations. As a result, US firms pioneered M-form organization, and they have also adopted it more pervasively than all other nations. According to Kagono *et al.* (1984: 50), in 1979, while only 59.8 per cent of Japanese firms have adopted divisional forms, the US number is an overwhelming 94.4 per cent.

Competitiveness implications

The dominance of contractual governance mechanisms of hierarchies has competitiveness implications that are sector-contingent. In processing sectors such as soft drinks, fast food, chemicals, and services, the standardization of products and procedures enables US firms to establish a global image and consumer loyalty owing to the desirability and certainty in the quality of products. The standardization process and the resultant mass production also enables the effective exploitation of economies of scale and scope. When the problem of knowledge creation is considered, in most processing sectors, the linear model of innovation and the separation between thinking and executing can still work well. In these sectors, once knowledge is discovered, it can be encapsulated into standardized procedures so that it can be reproduced *identically* elsewhere through such practices as franchising and the expansion of branches. The American success stories of Coca-Cola, McDonald's, Wal-Mart, and even Microsoft are still derived from American contractual governance mechanisms of hierarchies and the imbedded dominant organizing principles of division, standardization, specialization, and modularization.

From this point of view, the recent academic debate about Fordism and post-Fordism (Scott and Storper, 1990) and the resultant total dismissal of the former is misleading. First, the Fordist mode of mass production still provides competitive advantages for the USA in the processing manufacturing sectors of chemicals, soft drinks, fast food, paper products, and even health care. Second, even though many US firms have undergone a tremendous transformation from Fordism to various forms of post-Fordism, many once dominant organizing principles such as standardization and modularization have found new ground in the sectors of computers, semiconductors, software, information services, and e-business, which will be elaborated on later in Part IV.

The contractual governance mechanisms of hierarchies as dominant in the USA do have a negative impact on the relatively mature fabricating manufacturing sectors of automobiles and consumer electronics. The central problem here is the importance of relation-specific knowledge and dispersed technological knowledge for the continuous improvement of products and processes in these sectors. The Fordist penchant for standardization and the separation of thinking from executing fails effectively to harness the dispersed technological knowledge on the shop floor for incremental improvement of products and processes. The Fordist penchant for modularization and specialization, its lack of horizontal knowledge exchange among divisions, and its narrow job descriptions also contribute to the inability of Fordist firms in the USA to create and appropriate relation-specific knowledge for continuous shop-floor learning.

Contractual networks and knowledge creation

One way to overcome the failure of the contractual markets and hierarchies is to resort to networks as the governance mechanism for knowledge creation and appropriation. The establishment of network structures both within and across firm boundaries enables firms to overcome the lack of knowledge exchange and synergy across organizational boundaries and functional lines. In recent years, the emergence of the network governance in the USA has been greatly facilitated by the management fads of strategic alliance, R&D consortia, and the widespread recognition of the network nature of the new economy and the ecological nature of new competition (Moore, 1996).

Notwithstanding all the new fads, the dominant mechanism for the governance of networks in the USA is still of a contractual nature. Although some connectual types always exist as a complement, most networks in the USA are formed through explicit or implicit contracts. They are aimed at specific objectives with limited time horizons, are open for entry and exit, and have low entry and exit costs (Aldrich and Sasaki, 1995).

In other words, many contractual networks in the USA respect the rights and freedom of entry and exit for all eligible members. They are operated according to explicitly or tacitly agreed upon universalistic rules and procedures. They emerge, reconfigure, and dissolve rapidly according to changing environments and changing needs of members. In Granovetter's (1973) words, the dominant networks in the USA have only *weak ties*. Unlike the *strong ties* of networks in Japan, those in the USA do not involve strong personal and organizational affections and emotional identification. Instead, they only involve professional common interests and are governed impersonally by contracts. In describing the nature of inter-company relationships in the USA, Kanter (1994: 97) observes: 'North American companies, more than others in the world, take a narrow, opportunistic view of relationships, evaluating them strictly in financial terms, or seeing them as barely tolerable alternatives to outright acquisition.'

In comparing Japan and the USA in terms of the organization of innovation in the semiconductor equipment industry, Bolton *et al.* (1994: 653) also note:

> In the United States, relations between firms in vertically related industries correspond closely to the neoclassical contracting, characterized by arm's length, spot contracting on the open market. In Japan, inter-firm relations are more likely to involve relational contracting, characterized by stable bonding mechanisms and a dense historical network of economic ties between the parties to the exchange.

Here, of interest to us is not whether networks exist in the USA, but how they are socially constructed and governed, and how they operate. In his survey of market networks in the USA, Baker (1990) finds that:

> Real market ties are the result of deliberate management. They are products of intentional efforts to reduce *dependence* and exploit *power* in interorganizational relations. Corporations directly manipulate the number and intensity of market ties to pursue the objective of *independence*, uncertainty reduction, and efficiency. (*Italics added.*)

This finding confirms my hypothesis on the isomorphic pull of the US contractual cultural paradigm that pursues maximum autonomy, independence, and self-interest.

Voluntary associations as networks

Historically, the dominant forms of networks in the USA have been voluntary associations such as professional associations and local chambers of commerce. The proliferation of various networks are very much the result of the American penchant for civic engagement and civic sociability (Bellah *et al.*, 1986; Lipset, 1990). They constitute what Putnam (1995) and Fukuyama (1995) have called 'social capital' that nurtures the norms of cooperation and reciprocity, and that overcomes the problems of free riding and opportunism. Where the problem of knowledge creation is concerned, networks of voluntary associations facilitate knowledge exchange among members and enable the collective provision of a common knowledge base for them all to benefit from.

Notwithstanding this, the nature of civic engagement in the USA is still very much of a contractual type. Unlike the one-to-one contracting in the governance of markets and hierarchies, contracting in civic engagement is social and collective, in which every individual takes *universal* responsibilities as a member of a society, a community, a profession to fulfill civic duties and follow the pre-agreed on *universal* rules and norms. In exchange, the individual achieves a membership status that holds *universal* rights of benefiting from the service provided.

Here, the distinction between the contractual governance of US voluntary associations and the connectual governance of East Asian networks could not be sharper. Whereas the membership of the former is *universally open* to certain groups of people who share certain characteristics or identities, that of the latter is open only to those with *particular* ties and connections. Whereas the entry and exit costs of the former are low, those of the latter are very high. Whereas rights are still the central concern of the former, mutual obligations are the focus of the latter. Whereas the former has limited time horizons and aims at *specific* objectives, the latter usually covers long-term commitment and shares *diffused* values and goals. Whereas the former is pluralistic in nature, the latter is unitary. Whereas the former has only *weak ties* among members so that it secures their maximal autonomy and independence, the latter usually has *strong ties* that require interdependence and mutual obligations.

The most important US civic associations in the governance of knowledge creation are professional organizations, local chambers of commerce, and other business and technical associations. Scientists and engineers join professional associations to share ideas, keep informed of the latest new developments in knowledge, seek professional reputations, look for future job opportunities, and achieve professional identity. Industrialists join local chambers of commerce and other business associations to share information, seek support, and exert influence. In so doing, professional journals, newsletters, and conferences all play important roles. In addition to information sharing and knowledge exchange, professional associations also play the role of standard setting, training, and quality assurance. Networks of professions also reinforce academic standards, norms of reciprocity, and trustworthiness (Liebeskind *et al.*, 1996).

Social and professional networks of knowledge workers

Within professional and other voluntary associations, knowledge workers can create their own *informal* social networks of friends, classmates, former colleagues, and other acquaintances that facilitate information sharing and knowledge exchange. While the ties of informal social networks are stronger than those of professional associations, they are still much weaker than those in Japanese network structures. Social networks in the USA are constantly evolving, dissolving, and reconfiguring. The most important link is not affective commitments and obligations, as is the case in Japan, but simply an *acquaintance* with each other and a trust in the good character and integrity of one another. While in Japan it is the mutual commitments and obligations that bind networks together, in the USA it is mutual interests and potential benefits. Once such a shared interest disappears, the network itself also dissolves, while new networks emerge as a result of newly found shared common interests.

The constantly *emerging, dissolving, and reconfiguring* nature of weak ties can best characterize the dense networks of professionals and associations in Silicon Valley (Saxenian, 1994). These spontaneously emerged networks have the competitive advantage of effectively and swiftly harnessing and configuring the best talents in pushing forward innovative ideas and new technologies. They also help firms swiftly to adapt to the new environments of technologies and international competition. They have contributed greatly to the success of computer and software firms in Silicon Valley (Saxenian, 1994) and other high-tech regions in the USA. According to Liebeskind *et al.* (1996), the constantly emerging and reconfiguring networks have also contributed to US competitiveness in the biotechnology sector.

Strategic alliance and the business ecology

According to Langlois (1992) and Moore (1996), the increasing emergence of strategic alliances and firm networks in the USA is also facilitated by the changing nature of international competition, from a focus on individual firms to a reliance on business ecologies. In other words, the unit of competition and market selection is no longer individual firms but groups of firms linked together by their complementary competencies to form business ecologies. Firms achieve competitive advantage by establishing strategic alliances in which core competencies of individual firms mutually reinforce one another to achieve great synergy and symbiosis.

The best example of the power of business ecology is the Wintel ecology of computers' hardware and software products centered on the Intel-Microsoft alliance. Here, two sets of interlinked technical standards, Intel microprocessors and Microsoft operating systems, play the role of *abstract technical systems* that link the communities of computer hardware vendors and software developers. By aggressively pushing forward successively new generations of microprocessors with vastly increased speeds, Intel has generated a huge demand not only for increasingly advanced computer parts but also for more sophisticated software products. By designing increasingly sophisticated operating systems that serve as the new standards, Microsoft enables the spontaneous development of compatible software products. Because of its uniquely designed compatibility, the increasing popularity of

Microsoft operating systems simultaneously promotes the popularity of Intel processors. It also induces a supplementary huge demand for Microsoft-compatible software products, forming a symbiotic ecology of prosperity.

The competitiveness implications of weak ties

The weak ties of voluntary associations overcome the failure of the contractual markets and hierarchies in the exchange of knowledge, and at the same time preserve the autonomy and independence of members in pursuing their self-interest. The competitive advantage of weak ties rests in their capability of swiftly and agilely reconfiguring networks with a new set of core competencies and complementary capabilities to fit the needs of new tasks and new environments. The US system of contractual networks, therefore, is especially advantageous in those sectors such as information technology and biotechnology where the constant and spontaneous emergence of new technologies, new products, and new processes is the norm.

According to Cole (1998), the establishment and expansion of rich networks of professional association, government-sponsored consortia, industrial sponsored groups, and regional organizations focusing on the adaptation and diffusion of Japanese best practices of TQM have greatly contributed to the revival of many US firms. This was achieved through the efforts of these 'innovation and diffusion communities' in facilitating the creation and sharing of knowledge about TQM.

The weak ties of contractual networks, however, are not without competitive disadvantages. First, while the constantly emerging and reconfiguring nature of weak ties facilitates radical innovations, it sometimes hampers the *preservation, reproduction, and maintenance* of knowledge and capabilities for the effective commercial exploitation of innovations.[1] Where the follow-up process innovation is pivotal for successful commercialization, the innovating networks in the USA sometimes fail to appropriate the benefits of product innovations simply because of the easy collapse of weak ties due to the exit of key participants. This is especially true when crucial knowledge is imbedded in human capital. Second, the governance of weak ties is not conducive to the creation and preservation of tacit, firm- and relation-specific knowledge that is crucial for the incremental improvement of existing innovations. Indeed, although weak ties are good at exchanging explicit knowledge, they are poor at exchanging tacit knowledge (Sarah, 1998). This has caused the failure of some US innovating firms to compete with following-up Japanese firms. Third, the governance of weak ties usually fails to make a substantial commitment to huge investment in both physical capital and core capabilities required for competitive success in manufacturing technology. The short-termism of the US capital budgeting system and capital markets can further hinder investment in capability-building (Porter, 1992; Badwin and Clark, 1994).

In the biotechnology as well as the software sector, knowledge is imbedded in patents and copyrights. Incremental improvement is not the key for competitive success, nor is there a need for large-scale physical investment in manufacturing. As a result, in these two sectors, while the competitive advantage of weak ties plays a pivotal role for US success, its competitive disadvantage is circumvented. Conversely, because of the tightly coupled and non-modular sectoral knowledge structure in sectors such as opto-electronics, the competitive advantage of weak ties in spontaneous radical innovation is sometimes outweighed by its competitive disadvantage in incremental improvement.

Contractual clans and knowledge creation

In the 1980s, with the increasing realization of their superior performance in many sectors, Japan's governance mechanisms of clans were emulated in the USA (Ouchi, 1981, 1984). As a result, there has been a vast reconstruction of business vocabulary and value structures in corporate America. Collaboration substitutes for competition. Long-term alliances are preferred to arm's length relations. An emphasis on shared value overtakes the old focus on impersonal economic exchange. Teamwork is more desirable than individual endeavor. Decision by consensus replaces decision by command, and the experiment of empowerment challenges the conventional mentality of control (Schonberger, 1994).

The result has been the increasing legitimacy and desirability of clannish governance, with many US business firms trying to reshape their workplace and their relationship with suppliers and customers (Appelbaum and Batt, 1994). While many US firms were busy hiring external consultants to implement new forms of governance mechanisms, Ouchi (1981, 1984) even argued that the best performing US firms such as IBM had practiced clannish governance similar to that of Japanese firms all the time. There also have been many stories about successful workplace transformation at Motorola, Xerox, and Saturn in business media and academic journals (Smith, 1995).

While examples of similar practice are possible, the underlying universalistic assumptions about them are questionable. Just as the Christian family is vastly different from the Confucian family, the clannish governance as practiced in the USA is drastically different from that in Japan. While the former is still very much built on contracts, the latter is based more on consensus. In a contractual clan, although there are shared values, they are only *specifically* related to the clan's missions, rather than the *diffuseness* in connectual clans. Although there is intense communication among members, they are work-related, task-oriented, impersonal, and mostly affection-neutral. Although there are various forms of teamwork in contractual clans, they rely on professional codes and universal ethics rather than personal commitment and identification. Indeed, in the Anglo-American cultural contexts, as Mintzberg *et al.* (1996) note, collaboration works best when relations among team members are neither too close nor too remote. Unlike the long-term and stable nature of Japanese connectual clans, the clans predominant in the USA are short-term, mission-oriented, and contract-based. Members do not expect a long-term commitment to and identification with one another and with the clan. The option of exit is always available, and the cost of exit is also low when contracts expire. As a result, clan members in the USA tend still to focus on the development of skills and knowledge within their own professions. There is still little incentive to develop relation-specific knowledge and an overlapping knowledge base.

One good example of this is cross-functional design and development teams in the USA. Management brings *specialists* from different functional divisions together to form a team in order to fulfil a mission in design and development. Each member is expected to contribute specific professional skills, knowledge, and capabilities to the team. However, like US professional basketball teams, there is high pressure to measure individual performance rather than team performance, even though the latter is the only useful outcome.[2] As a result, collaboration among team members still stays very much at the professional and impersonal level.

Another form of contractual clans in the USA can be found in the start-up venture business. The well-known examples include the start-up clans of Intel, Apple, Microsoft, Sun Microsystems, Netscape, AOL, and Yahoo! in their early years. The start-up clans of venture business usually consist of a few entrepreneurs and technologists who share the same vision of new products or new business models. A shared vision, however, does not mean a lifelong personal commitment and identification. Often, members of start-up clans make clear through contracts the share of benefits each member will have in the new business.

Like the case of contractual networks, the competitive advantage of contractual clans in the USA lies in their constantly emerging, evolving, and reconfiguring nature and in their collaborative entrepreneurship. Under the logic of contractual man, US entrepreneurs can be quite collaborative when they share a very clear vision. This logic has given rise to the emergence and dominance of such internationally prominent firms as Intel, Microsoft, Cisco, Sun Microsystems, Oracle, Apple, and AOL within a short period of time. The rapid rise of these US firms is unimaginable to the Japanese because the logic of connectual governance inhibits the constant emergence and reconfiguration of totally new clans and networks.

The competitive advantage of contractual clans usually evaporates once a start-up firm realizes its vision and begins to harvest its fruit. The time of harvest is also when members cash in the fruits and leave the clan in search of new opportunities. It is also the time for formulating new visions in which clan members may not find consensus. As a result, original clans may fall apart, team spirit may evaporate, and the same advantageous contractual clan governance may turn out to be a liability in maintaining the momentum of growth. In addition, the constantly emerging, evolving, dissolving, and reconfiguring nature of contractual clans also makes it hard to preserve and maintain capabilities and expertise, especially when the vision is not agreed upon by all members.

This alternative impact of the competitive advantage and disadvantage has contributed to the uniquely US drama of the rise and fall of corporations. The most recent examples are the rise and fall of Digital Equipment Corporation (DEC) and Silicon Graphics. Just as their rapid rise is unthinkable in the Japanese business environment, so is their precipitous decline. In contractual governance, any sign and promise of success can rapidly reinforce itself through a positive feedback loop in the infusion of the brightest minds and huge capital. On the other hand, any sign of vulnerability will rapidly incur more weakness through the exodus of capital and the best talent.

In the case of Silicon Graphics, according to *Business Week* (August 4, 1997), the turnover rate doubled to 20 per cent in 1996 as turmoil grew, and at least 16 of 43 top executives left the company in the years 1995 to 1997. According to the same source, the exodus had reached such a level that one executive recruiter in April 1997 stopped trying to tap talent from Silicon Graphics. The drama here is that the co-founder of Silicon Graphics, Jim Clark, left his firm and set up the hugely successful

Netscape Corporation with technical genius Marc Andreessen (*Forbes ASAP*, August 28, 1995).

While it is natural for a founder to leave the company he created and begin another under the logic of contractual governance, it is almost unthinkable under the logic of connectual governance. In the Japanese case, the dominance of connectual governance means the stability not only of connectual structures but also of firm ranking. There are few newly emergent firms that can rise to the top in Japan, just as there are few companies that will incur precipitous decline. Under the logic of connectual governance, leaving a firm when it faces hardship is unthinkable and unforgivable. The reconfiguration and dissolution of new clans and new networks is rare because trust is based on long-term relationships. While the impossibility of exodus makes Japanese firms less vulnerable to external shocks and internal mistakes, the inability for fast reconfiguration also makes it difficult for the dramatic rise of such new corporate stars as Microsoft and AOL in Japan.

Contractual governance as an attractor

It is worth admitting that many companies in the USA have tried to escape the *isomorphic pull* of contractual governance. Theoretically, from Maslow's theory of need hierarchy to McGregor's Theory Y, many Western theories of human motivation recognize the needs for affiliation and connection. In practice, the best performing US firms such as IBM, Microsoft, and Intel have always tried to build an organizational culture that encourages collaboration, teamwork, commitment, and identification. It is not an exaggeration to say that the successful operation of networks and clans in the USA always needs complementary support from some forms of connectual governance mechanisms. Indeed, as Barley and Kunda (1992) illustrate, the history of managerial discourse in the USA since the 1870s has exhibited recurrent waves alternating between the trajectory of scientific management and the concern for human relations, and between the individualistic ideology and the desire for community.

Notwithstanding this, under the dominance of the contractual cultural paradigm, there has always been an *isomorphic pull* and tremendous pressure to *retreat* to contractual governance mechanisms when problems arise in the operation of networks and clans. Often a practice of connectual governance originated in Japan is transformed to a different style when transplanted to the USA, largely because of the isomorphic pull of both the contractual cultural paradigm and the contractual governance mechanisms. In their systematic study of the US workplace, Appelbaum and Batt (1994) find that, although a series of new 'management fads' derived from the study of the best practices of Japanese firms, such as cross-functional teams, quality circle (QC), JIT, lean production, and concurrent engineering, have helped many US firms to adopt some reforms, such reforms are often short-lived and affect only a minority of the workers. They further note that the widely publicized cases such as the successful transformation of Xerox and Saturn are highly exceptional, and that the percentage of firms that have radically transformed their governance mechanisms is very small. Many firms have not even experimented with any reforms. In another study, Henke *et al.* (1993) also find that, although the idea of cross-functional teams is considered a good concept, its implementation in the USA is poor. Often the functional mind-set that is predominant in traditional US firms is difficult to break and needs help from an organizational culture of collective responsibility, which is at odds with American individualism (Majchrzak and Wang, 1996). At the top management level, cross-functional teams also face the problem of fragmentation in incentives and in knowledge base (Hambrick, 1995). As a result, many firms that have experimented with the concept of cross-functional teams for years have questioned the idea's value in the end (Henke *et al.*, 1993).

In his survey of the workplace transformation in the USA, Osterman (1994) finds that in 1992 only about 35 per cent of private sector establishments had involved more than 50 per cent of their employees in some form of Japanese practice such as teams, job rotations, TQM, and QC. The clustering of these workplace practices with 50 per cent or greater employee participation is even lower (Table 5.3). Although accompanied by tremendous efforts in learning the Japanese system of flexible work organization, as late as 1992 only about 5 per cent of Osterman's (1994) sample engaged all connectual workplace practices with an employee participation rate of 50 per cent or more.

Table 5.3 Clustering of connectual work practices in the USA, 1992 (50% or greater penetration) (percentages)

Description	Entire sample	Manufacturing/blue-collar
None	36.0	33.2
All	4.8	5.0
Teams only	14.4	5.5
Rotation only	7.0	11.7
QC only	3.1	2.4
TQM only	2.6	4.5
Team/rotation	4.8	4.6
Team/QC	4.3	3.3
Team/TQM	4.6	4.2
Rotation/QC	3.0	3.3
Rotation/TQM	1.5	4.5
TQM/QC	4.4	4.9
Team/TQM/QC	3.6	4.2
Team/rotation/TQM	1.2	1.6
Team/rotation/QC	2.3	3.4
Rotation/TQM/QC	1.4	2.9

Source: Osterman (1994: 177).

As regards producer–supplier relationships, although companies such as Chrysler (Dyer, 1996) have adopted the Japanese form of long-term subcontracting, the US Congressional Office of Technology Assessment (1990: 135) concludes that:

It is longstanding custom for American manufacturers to discourage – even forbid – design engineers from developing close relationships with suppliers. Direct approaches to suppliers are known as 'going around the purchasing department,' and are against company rules. Purchasing agents are frequently re-assigned to different types of suppliers, so they won't develop overtly cozy relations with suppliers. The ideas behind all this are, first, that maintaining arm's length, impersonal, strictly contract-based relations with suppliers is the best way to get a good price and keeps costs down; second, that it is unfair to give any supplier a privileged position and deny the others an equal chance. Some company officials even believe that they might be subjects to lawsuits if their suppliers were deprived of the chance to bid for contracts (quoted in Harrison, 1994: 181–182).

Here, the central issue is that the very practice of long-term supplier relationship is in sharp contradiction with the logic of contractual governance. Such a contradiction also leads to a high vulnerability of suppliers to be held up and opportunistically manipulated by major equipment producers because of the dependency structure inherent in the long-term relationship. After interviewing many auto parts suppliers in the USA, Harrison (1994: 182) observed that the typical US supplier is wary of 'being blindsided by his large business customers, whether by being forced to take a sudden large price cut or being expected to upgrade his technology without the financial wherewithal to do so.' Harrison (1994: 182) further notes that:

> The majority of suppliers continue to report that their customers are 'not trustworthy' and that they still do not provide much assistance to suppliers to reduce costs or adopt new technologies. Most disturbingly, there is a definite trend toward a practice in which GM, Ford, and Chrysler 'obtain improvements in quality and delivery by forcing suppliers to adopt methods, such as JIT delivery without JIT productions ... that provide better service to customers at the expense of supplier profit margins.

In 1992, GM did revoke its long-term contracts with existing suppliers and put them into a competitive bidding process with all other suppliers, disregarding the fact that many suppliers had borrowed heavily to invest in technical capabilities to fit GM's needs (Harrison, 1994). According to Milkman (1997), GM's effort of adopting Japanese workplace practices also met with great difficulty because of workers' mistrust of management, foremen's resistance to give up control, and the orientation of the conventional production system that maximizes output with the minimum of workers.

Notwithstanding the misguided incentives in implementing the Japanese practice of connectual governance, many US firms that have sincerely tried to implement connectual governance mechanisms also faced great isomorphic pressures from the dominance of both the contractual cultural paradigm and contractual governance mechanisms. It is therefore not surprising that the successful adoption of connectual governance, or in conventional terms, flexible workplace practices, was highly related to the extent of exposure to international competition, especially from the Japanese, and to management willingness to adopt a value structure that accepted responsibility for the personal and family well-being of the employees (Osterman, 1994). Using the terminology employed in this book, Osterman's findings confirm that the adoption of connectual governance requires the support of a connectual value structure. Even with the support of such a value structure within an organization, there is still an isomorphic pull from the dominantly contractual cultural paradigm to return to the conventional form of contractual practices. This is why historically the high rate of experimentation with new forms of workplace practices of a connectual type has been accompanied by a similarly high rate of abandonment (Weinstein and Kochan, 1995). In his case study of the Intel Corporation, Adams (1995) observes that its managers have had to insulate their firm from the erosion of American individualism by the establishment of what he called an 'organizational cultural island' for collaboration and teamwork in the sea of the competition mentality. Even in such a case, Adams notes that the management in Intel is under tremendous pressure to keep its 'cultural island' from being eroded.

Using the terminology of chaos theory, the cultural paradigm of contractual man, together with the correspondent contractual governance mechanisms, functions as an *attractor* that sustains the core values of autonomy and independence and induces both individuals and firms to take a contractual perspective in dealing with one another. The existence of such attractors is the major reason for the *persistence* of cultures and institutions. Alternatively, the national differences in cultural and institutional attractors are the major causes for the difficulty in diffusing organizing principles across national boundaries, and therefore in the national differentiation of sectoral competitiveness.

The state as enforcer of contractual governance

The role of contractual governance as an *attractor* in American society is further facilitated by the American state as the impartial third-party enforcer of contracts. Indeed, the penchant for autonomy, independence, and equal opportunity is so deeply ingrained in the American soul that any forms of dependency structure, from religious, political, to economic dependency, are suspiciously viewed as the ultimate cause of tyranny and the evil force of corruption that should be avoided by various constitutional, institutional, and democratic means. These include the separation of religion from the state, religious sectarianism, a division and balance of legislative, executive, and judicial powers, pluralism of political associations and interest groups, democratic processes and populist movements, anti-trust laws, the state provision of education to secure equal opportunity, and state laws against discrimination.

As a result, the state takes the role of the impartial third-party enforcer of contractual governance. It enforces consensual contracts and protects the intellectual property rights of knowledge creators; it provides knowledge as a public good so that the market failure in knowledge creation is overcome; it enforces anti-trust laws so that people's choice is not limited and their incentives for knowledge creation are not stifled by any monopoly.

This notion of the state as an impartial third-party contract enforcer is the direct result of the American cultural paradigm of contractual man. It creates tremendous resistance from academic, business and policy communities to industrial policy and strategic trade policy. Because of a lack of legitimacy, industrial policy in the USA is often disguised under the banner of defense, social, and tax policies (Kash, 1989; Graham, 1992). These were often the results of lobbying from interest groups and therefore, according to Graham (1992), were inconsistent, futile, and bad. Notwithstanding this, US industrial policies imbedded in the defense policy were pivotal for US strength in aircraft, aerospace, telecommunications, computers, new materials, nuclear technologies, and most other advanced technologies (Flamm, 1988; Kash, 1989). Especially, as Kash (1989) points out, the military–industry–university complex that was built to fit the needs of the Cold War overcame the barriers of American individualism and facilitated cooperation among scientists, business firms, and government to push forward *synthetic innovations* far beyond the reach of individualism.

Indeed, the central issue here is not industrial policy or technology policy *per se*, but how the scope, methods, and processes of industrial policy or technology policy face isomorphic pulls and are constrained by the dominant cultural paradigms of nations. To the extent that a democratic state cannot formulate an industrial policy that is in sharp contradiction to its dominant cultural paradigm, we can say that public policy is more an *endogenous variable* than an *exogenous* variable that is at the disposal of policy-makers. From this point of view, the problem with the industrial policy approach in explaining national competitiveness rests in its failure to recognize the socio-culturally constructed nature of public policy in general and industrial policy in particular.

This recognition, however, does not deny the possibility of using public policy to overcome the inherent deficiencies of the organizing principles of a nation. First, as happened in the USA during the Cold War, the imperative to fight against communism can legitimate a defense policy that overcomes the isomorphic pull from the dominant cultural paradigm and organizing principles. Second, the consensus of a nation in realizing the shortcomings of the existing system and the need for fundamental reforms, as happened in South Korea and Japan during the East Asian financial crises in 1997–1998, can trigger national support for public policy transforming the existing governance mechanisms.

Conclusion

It is clear from the analysis here that many organizational, institutional, and technological innovations in the USA since the second industrial revolution have been the results of the American penchant for autonomy and independence and the dominant cultural paradigms of contractual man. These innovations themselves constitute the mechanisms of contractual governance dominating the knowledge creation process in the USA. Although these mechanisms have been emerging, unfolding, evolving, dominating, and persisting from the second industrial revolution to the new revolution in information and communication technologies, the underlying organizing principles have been astonishingly similar. Their competitive advantages and disadvantages, to a large extent, shape the sectoral patterns of US competitiveness, and this is something we will discuss in detail in Part IV.

Notes

1. For the case of how US firms failed to commercialize the US invention of active–matrix display technology and how they failed in competition with Japan, see Florida and Browdy (1991).
2. Schuler and Rogovsky (1998) find that compensation practices based on individual performance are highly correlated to the extent of individualism in national culture.

CHAPTER SIX

Connectual Governance for Knowledge Creation

> Societies have distinct social structures based on unique traditions. Each operates according to its own principles, reflecting the attitudinal and behavioral patterns of its members. Although enterprises in these countries share certain outward features of capitalism, their modes of operation differ from one culture to another. While the principles by which they operate may be invisible to those outside the culture, they are self-evident to those within – every one knows exactly what they are.
>
> Yamamoto Shichihei (1992, pp. 6–7)

Few nations in the world have presented a greater intellectual puzzle and challenge than Japan in the last five decades. When few put much faith in its ability to survive its defeat in World War II, Japan rose rapidly to become an economic and technological powerhouse such that in the 1980s it challenged US leadership in the economic sphere and pushed many giant US companies to the edge of bankruptcy. Ironically, after Western scholars tried for more than two decades to uncover the secrets of its phenomenal success, the Japanese economy plunged into a prolonged recession in the 1990s, which has led to the declaration by many of the death of the Japanese model.

As a result, any serious study about Japan has to simultaneously address the causes for both its success and its failure. From the knowledge regime perspective, the spectacular success and 'unexpected' failure of Japanese firms in international markets represent two sides of the same coin of the dominant connectual governance in Japan, which exerts sector-contingent impact on competitiveness. The first part of this chapter makes it clear that the two sides of Japanese competitiveness, with one set of very competitive sectors and another of very uncompetitive ones, are not a surprise. They have been consistent throughout the post-World War II period.

The negative side of Japanese competitiveness is only an 'unexpected' surprise because of most scholars' lack of sectoral perspective. The weakness of many Japanese sectors has been persistent during the last several decades. The shortcomings of the Japanese system, however, did not manifest themselves until the fundamental change of economy from an industrial economy to the new digital economy in the mid-1990s. This paradigm shift has not only *nullified* many sources of Japanese competitive advantage but also *magnified* the negative impact of many existing competitive disadvantages of the Japanese system of knowledge creation.

From the positive side, ever since the late 1970s, superior Japanese performance in manufacturing has triggered a continuous search for an explanation. Like nearly any reaction to an anomaly in an early stage of paradigm change (Kuhn, 1962/1970), the initial reactions to the Japanese challenge had been framed within the neoclassical paradigm. Consequently, numerous factors were found to be responsible for their success, which include low labor and capital costs, high saving rates, heavy investment in human capital, cooperative labor unions, unfair entry barriers and government and business conspiracies, and Japanese free riding on the US provision of international security and open markets. Conversely, an opposite attribution of all the above factors was found to be the cause for the US decline (Dertouzos *et al.*, 1989).

It was not until the mid- and late 1980s, after more in-depth studies of the Japanese organizational system, that people in the USA realized that, rather than the discrete neoclassic factors listed above, the most important contributor for Japanese success has been their system of manufacturing. This has been called variously Toyotarism, the Toyota mode of production, just-in-time (JIT) production and delivery, lean production (Womack *et al.*, 1990), and flexible production (Macduffie, 1995).

As Kuhn's (1962) original concept of paradigm indicates, the new manufacturing paradigm originated in Japan cannot be fully understood in its individual constituent parts but *in its totality and the mutually reinforcing nature of its subsystems*. From the knowledge regime perspective, this totality rests in the *isomorphic structure* of the connectual cultural paradigm, connectual governance mechanisms, and the flexible manufacturing paradigm. This isomorphism has not only contributed to Japan's superior performance in the mature fabricating manufacturing sectors but also to its weakness in prepackaged software, biotechnology, information processing, and e-businesses.

From this point of view, I dispute many pundits' attribution of the prolonged Japanese recession simply to its enterprise system, government mismanagement, as well as the collapse of the bubble economy. Instead, I would argue that it could be caused partly by the fundamental deficiencies of the Japanese system for effective knowledge creation in the sectors of information technology, software, and information services, which are the driving forces for the rise of the digital economy. This acknowledgment does not, however, deny Japan's superior knowledge creation capability in the tightly coupled technological sectors of automobiles, opto-electronics, and mechatronics.

This chapter intends to solve the dilemma of the sharp division in the sectoral pattern of Japanese competitiveness by examining various connectual governance mechanisms of knowledge creation and their competitive implications. In so doing, we constantly compare Japan to the USA with regard to their dominant organizing principles and practices. We further explore the dynamic emergence, dominance, and transplantation of various Japanese governance mechanisms. In so doing, we reveal the socio-cultural isomorphism among cultural paradigms, governance mechanisms, organizing principles, and technology trajectories.

Connectual governance and stakeholder capitalism

From a knowledge regime perspective, the Japanese manufacturing system can best be understood as a set of mutually reinforcing attributes (Aoki, 1994) as well as connectual governance mechanisms for knowledge creation, aimed at continuous improvements, organic knowledge integration, organized technology fusion, and in-house capability building. These attributes include:

1. A coherent system of corporate goals and strategies (Dore, 1983).
   - Focus on long-term capabilities and market shares as compared to the US focus on short-term profit.
   - The welfare of employees as the first priority.
   - Mutual obligations to various stakeholders, including suppliers and banks.
   - Focus on quality and customer satisfaction.
   - Emphasis on mutual dependence, obligations, and trust.
2. A coherent system of human resource practices (Macduffie, 1995).
   - Lifetime employment for core workers.
   - Internal promotion and job rotation.
   - Work teams and quality circles.
   - On-the-job training (OJT).
   - Broad job classification.
3. A coherent system of R&D, production, delivery, and marketing (Nonaka, 1994).
   - Just-in-time production and delivery (JIT).
   - Total quality management (TQM).
   - Cross-functional integration in product and process development
   - Emphasis on technology fusion (Kodama, 1991).
   - Emphasis on knowledge creation, rather than information processing.
   - Integration among R&D, manufacturing, and marketing
   - Concurrent engineering, design for manufacturing (DFM), and design for assembly (DFA).
   - A combination of standardization and continuous improvement.
4. A system of inter-industry and intra-industry business groups (Gerlach, 1992).
   - Inter-linking shareholding among banks, producers, and suppliers.
   - Long-term cooperative relationships between producers and suppliers.
   - Geographical proximity in the location of suppliers to their producers.
5. A system of government–business relations.
   - The role of MITI.
   - The role of national labs.

While correctly noticing the inter-linked nature of the Japanese system of attributes, Aoki (1994) fails to explain the linkage in a sufficiently detailed way. Similarly, while correctly pointing out the puzzling similarity of the Japanese logic of intra-organizational and inter-organizational relations, Kenney and Florida (1993) were not able to explain the causes of such a similarity.

From the knowledge regime perspective, both the Japanese system of attributes and their isomorphic intra- and inter-organizational logic are the characteristics of the connectual governance mechanisms that are dominant in Japan. First, the coherent system of corporate goals and strategies reflects the value structure of the connectual cultural paradigm. Unlike the US firms who are considered to be 'owned' by their shareholders, the Japanese firm is a community of connected 'stakeholders' with shared values and goals (Dore, 1994). As shown in Table 6.1, when asked about the primary purpose of firms, 40 per cent of US managers believed that making a profit is the only goal, as compared to a mere 8 per cent of their Japanese counterparts. The USA and Japan clearly constitute the two extremes of the contractual vs. connectual view of the firm among twelve developed nations. Indeed, as early as the 1970s, a noted Japanese anthropologist Chie Nakane (1972: 14) had pointed out the connectual nature of the employment relationship in Japan:

Table 6.1 Percentage of managers choosing (a) 'the only goal a company has is to make a profit'

USA	AUS	CAN	UK	IT	SWE	NL	BEL	GER	FRA	SIN	JAP
40	35	34	33	28	27	26	25	24	16	11	8

> The relationship between employer and employee is not to be explained in contractual terms. The attitude of the employer is expressed by the spirit of the common saying, 'the enterprise is the people'. This affirms the belief that employer and employee are bounded as one by fate in conditions which produced a tie between man and man often as firm and close as that between husband and wife. Such a relationship is manifestly not a pure contractual one between employer and employee; the employee is already a member of his own family, and all members of his family are naturally included in the larger company 'family' … This trend can be traced consistently in Japanese management from the Meiji period to the present.

As a result, the most important stakeholders in Japanese firms are core workers who devote their lifetime to the firm's goals and who treat the firm as their extended family. In reciprocity, the Japanese firm also considers the welfare of employees, instead of the profit of shareholders, as its most important goal. The other stakeholders of a Japanese firm include the bankers that offer credit, suppliers that deliver major components and services, customers that buy the products, the state and local governments that provide public goods, and local communities that support many indispensable community services. Since the stakeholders have a long-term commitment to the firm, they take priority over the firm's long-term knowledge creation capabilities and market shares, rather than its short-term profits and return on investment (see Table 6.2).

Table 6.2 The priority rank of corporate goals: a US–Japan comparison*

Corporate goals	USA	Japan
Return on investment	2.43	1.24
Rising stock price	1.14	0.02
Market share	0.73	1.43
Improved product portfolio	0.50	0.68
Rationalization of logistic system	0.46	0.71
Improved net worth	0.38	0.59
New product development	0.21	1.06
Increased company recognition	0.05	0.20
Improved working conditions	0.04	0.09

*3 = most important, 0 = least important
Source: Kagono (1980).

Second, the connectual relations between the firm and its employees lead to a coherent system of human resource practices in Japan. These include lifetime employment for core workers, broad job classification, on-the-job training (OJT), job rotation, and internal promotion based on accumulated experiences and skills (Itoh, 1994; Koike, 1994). While lifetime employment is the natural result of the logic of connectual man and connectual governance, the practices of broad job classification and job rotation are the result of the Japanese emphasis on connectual knowing and organic knowledge integration among various tasks.

Third, the Japanese capability of connectual knowing is further facilitated by the coherent Japanese systems of R&D, production, delivery, and marketing. These include JIT, TQM, the integration of R&D, production, and marketing, DFM/ DFA, concurrent engineering, a synergy between standardization and learning, and an emphasis on *organized technology fusion*.

Fourth, under the same logic of connectual governance, the creation of mutually *interdependent* structures is extended outside the firm to govern its interaction with major suppliers, users, customers, and bankers (Fruin, 1992; Gerlach, 1992). These inter-firm arrangements include close producer–customer interaction; the interlocking mutual shareholding among banks, producers, and suppliers; long-term strategic alliances; JIT delivery; joint product and process development; and geographical proximity between producers and suppliers. In essence, all of these institutional innovations aim at creating mutually *interconnected* and *interdependent structures* both within and across firm boundaries to exploit the opportunities for creating and appropriating relation-specific and cross-functional knowledge across firm boundaries.

Finally, the logic of connectual governance is extended to business–government relations. While the US state plays primarily the role of the exogenous enforcer of contracts to safeguard private property and individual freedom, the state in Japan plays the essential and indispensable roles of an enabler, organizer, and connector that furthers interdependence and interconnections among business firms, especially with regard to information sharing and knowledge creation (Okimoto, 1989). Indeed, industrial policies in Japan are essentially indispensable parts of the connectual governance mechanisms aimed at assisting and coordinating the efforts of Japanese firms in building superior infrastructure for knowledge creation in specific sectors to gain international competitiveness.

As a result of these densely intertwined connectual structures, it is very difficult for mergers and acquisitions to happen in Japan (Gerlach, 1992). The same can be said about the low mobility of employees, because their skills are highly tailored to the specific needs of the employing firm.

Exogenous vs. endogenous enforcement of knowledge exchange

It is interesting to note that while any dependency structure is seen as a threat to individual autonomy and therefore is maximally avoided under the logic of contractual governance, interdependence among key processes and key players is strengthened under the logic of connectual governance. This explains the following observation by Fruin (1992: 31).

The concert of *interdependence* between factory, firm, and network suggests some of the ways in which Japanese corporations differ in structure, function, and meaning from those of the West where, for any number of reasons, such high levels of *organizational interdependence* have not appeared. (*Italics added.*)

Similarly, as Oliver and Wilkinson (1992: Ch. 3) rightly note, while American organizational theorists such as Galbraith (1973) see any dependency as the root of uncertainty, conflicts, and disruption and, therefore, propose the creation of slack resources and self-contained tasks to minimize it, the Japanese production system, especially its practices of JIT and TQM, intends to strengthen the dependency relations. The Japanese system of subcontracting (Nishiguchi, 1994) also strengthens the interdependence between producers and key suppliers. Such a dramatic difference is caused not only by a sharp contrast of value judgment between the desire for autonomy and the need for interdependence, but also by the fundamentally different nature of exchange relations and their different enforcement mechanisms. Whereas contractual exchange is prevalent in the USA, connectual exchange is predominant in Japan. While the former is *exogenously* enforced by a third party – the state, the latter is *endogenously* enforced by the *interdependency* structures themselves.[1] In other words, while *the abstract system* of the state and the rule of law enforce the fulfillment of contracts between *autonomous* parties, various *contextual* interdependency structures are used as tools to *endogenously* enforce the norm of reciprocity and the fulfillment of mutual obligations.

The knowledge creation implications of exogenous vs. endogenous enforcement are tremendous. The exogenous enforcement of contractual exchange requires that knowledge involved in exchange be separate, explicit, objective, impersonal, quantitative, context-free, and modularized. In other words, the involvement of any tacit, subjective, qualitative, contextual, and relational knowledge will inevitably make the transaction costs of both bargaining and enforcing contractual exchange prohibitively high. Conversely, because of the possibility of separate knowing, the contractual exchange of explicit, objective, quantitative, context-free, and modularized knowledge has low transaction costs both in negotiation and in implementation. In addition, the dominance of *trust in contracts* and *separate knowing* also facilitates demand for externalized, explicit, quantitative, and decontextual knowledge.

By contrast, the connectual governance mechanisms as dominant in Japan have relatively low transaction costs in the creation, exchange, and appropriation of tacit, qualitative, relational, and contextual knowledge. It is not only because the connectual structure enables the creation of these types of knowledge, but also because it endogenously enforces the norm of reciprocity for their exchange within it. Therefore, while an external enforcement of the exchange of tacit, qualitative, relational, and contextual knowledge is costly, its endogenous enforcement within a connectual structure is low. Furthermore, through a process of socialization, connectual governance is best for achieving an empathetic understanding of other members' knowledge and of their contributions to the knowledge creation process. Indeed, as Fruin's (1997) case study of Toshiba indicates, the need for interdependent governance increases with the increasing level of asset-specificity and the increasing need for sharing tacit and site- and relation-specific knowledge.

Conversely, the creation of explicit, objective, and context-free knowledge usually incurs high costs of production within the connectual governance. The existence of and preference for knowledge in highly tacit, subjective, contextual, and relational forms hampers the externalization of knowledge into explicit, objective, context-free, and modularized forms. The preponderance of trust in connections and in connectual knowledge, and of socialization as a dominant form of knowledge creation further suppresses the need for externalized, explicit, qualitative, and contextual knowledge. Table 6.3 summarizes the production costs and transaction costs of two categories of knowledge under contractual vs. connectual governance. As a result of the sharp differences in the production costs and transaction costs of different types of knowledge, Japanese firms rely more on subjective judgment than objective measures in evaluating the performance of their employees, whereas US firms do just the opposite (Itoh, 1994). Similarly, Japanese firms depend more on subjective and contextual knowledge in market research than do their US counterparts (Johansson and Nonaka, 1993, 1996).

Table 6.3 The production and transaction costs of the two types of knowledge

	Explicit, objective, quantitative, and encapsulated knowledge	Tacit, firm- and relation-specific, contextual knowledge
Endogenous enforcement: connectual governance	High	Low
Exogenous enforcement: contractual governance	Low	High

The sharp differences in the production costs and transaction costs of the two categories of knowledge under the two generic governance mechanisms give rise to profound competitiveness implications. With the dominance of connectual governance, Japanese firms have a comparative advantage in the production, transformation, exchange, and appropriation of the categories of knowledge that are tacit, subjective, qualitative, relation-specific, cross-functional, and contextual. By contrast, under the dominance of contractual governance, US firms have a comparative advantage in the production, transformation, exchange, and appropriation of explicit, objective, quantitative, context-free, generalized, professionalized, and modularized knowledge.

Connectual hierarchies and knowledge creation

While the competitive markets are at the center of the contractual governance in the USA, connectual hierarchies and clans are the primary structures in Japan. When the nature of the firm is considered, Americans see the firm as a system of contracts, whereas the Japanese see it as a group of people working together. As shown in Table 6.4, while 74 per cent of Americans take the task-based view of the firm, only 29 per cent of Japanese do so. Conversely, while 71 per cent of Japanese take the relation-view of the firm, only 26 per cent of their American counterparts do so. Once again, the USA and Japan represent the two extremes of the cultural paradigms of contractual man vs. connectual man among the twelve advanced nations.

Table 6.4 Percentage choosing (a) 'company as a set of tasks,' rather than (b) 'company as relations'

USA	AUS	CAN	UK	IT	SWE	NL	BEL	GER	FRA	SIN	JAP
74	69	68	61	59	56	55	46	41	39	35	29

Source: Hampden-Turner and Trompenaars (1993: 32).

Connectual human resource management and knowledge creation

In Japanese firms, the knowledge, expertise, and capabilities of employees are systematically nurtured, maintained, and harnessed through a set of human resource practices. As opposed to the treatment of labor as a fungible factor of production in the USA, the Japanese treat employees as their most valued assets as well as the most important stakeholders and partners of all. The high status of the human resource department in Japanese firms as compared to its low rank in the USA reflects this dramatic difference (Sullivan, 1995).

These two ways of conceptualizing labor have overwhelming implications for competitiveness. Deming (1986) attributes the US decline in the 1980s to US treatment of workers as fungible costs. Lazonick (1990a,b) also believes that such a practice leads to the deskilling of labor; adversarial and combative business–labor relations; low worker loyalty and commitment to corporate goals; low incentive for employers to provide on-the-job-training (OJT); and low incentive for workers to develop firm-specific skills and expertise. In his empirical study, Osterman (1995) finds a clear increase in skills for technical/professional positions but not for blue-collar jobs in US firms. One explanation of this finding rests in the US separation of thinking and execution. As a result, while technical/professional knowledge is generally enhanced through formal education and highly demanded in the job market, the skill and knowledge of blue-collar workers is less nurtured. This in turn has led to a sharp income gap between professionals and blue-collar workers.

Contrary to the deskilling of the US shop floor, Japanese human resource practices try in every way to enhance and maintain firm-specific skills and capabilities (Itoh, 1994). Lifetime employment motivates employees to develop firm-specific knowledge, expertise, and capabilities; job rotation makes possible the effective cross-functional integration of knowledge; TQM harnesses dispersed knowledge on the shop floor for continuous improvement.

Lifetime employment and firm-specific knowledge

Lifetime employment for core knowledge workers is at the root of Japanese connectual governance and the resulting human resource practices. As shown in Table 6.5, job tenure is much longer in Japan than in the USA. This is true not only for large Japanese firms but also for small firms (Hashimoto and Raisian, 1985).

Through lifetime employment, the values of core employees are connected to the fate of the firm. Employees have incentives to develop firm- and relation-specific knowledge solely for the mission of the firm, and the firm also has incentives to

Table 6.5 Estimates of the number of jobs held by males over a lifetime in Japan and the USA

Age groups	OECD		Hashimoto and Raisian	
	Japan 1977	USA 1981	Japan 1977	USA 1978
16–19	0.54	1.07	0.72	2.0
20–24	1.19	2.54	2.06	4.4
25–29	1.54	3.69	2.71	6.15
30–34	1.75	4.57	3.11	7.4
35–39	1.92	5.35	3.46	8.3
40–44	2.05	5.98	4.21	10.25
45–49	2.15	6.45	4.91	10.95
50–54	2.26	6.9		11.15
55–64	2.62	7.5		11.16

Source: OECD Employment Outlook, September 1984, p. 63. Hashimoto and Raisian (1985: 724), reprinted in Lipset (1996: 231).

provide OJT for employees. Lifetime commitment and socialization also enables the *formation and preservation of a firm-specific common knowledge base*, often in its tacit form, for effective knowledge exchange and synergy among employees across firm boundaries. The competitive advantage of lifetime employment, therefore, rests in the ability of firms to create, transform, preserve, and appropriate the types of knowledge that are tacit, and firm- and relation-specific, which are of crucial importance for *organized* technology fusion and incremental improvement.

Lifetime employment policy is, however, not without competitive disadvantages. First, it often suppresses the standardization, specialization, and marketization of knowledge. Second, when the growth rate of the economy slows down, as has happened since 1990, the policy has been a substantial drag on efficiency owing to inflexibility in cutting labor forces. Third, when the pace of technological change is so fast in the emerging sectors of information technology, biotechnology, and e-business, the policy greatly constrains the Japanese ability to compete with their US counterparts who are free to replace outdated workforces with ones who have mastered the most advanced knowledge and skills.

Broad job classification, job rotation, and cross-functional knowledge

Lifetime employment enables the formation and preservation of not only firm-specific knowledge but also relation-specific, connectual, and cross-functional knowledge. By removing the *market pressure* for the specialization, professionalization, and marketization of skills and knowledge, the Japanese policy of lifetime employment enables the practices of broad job classification and job rotation that further facilitate the formation, preservation, and application of relation-specific and cross-functional knowledge. As James R. Lincoln (1993: 57) observes:

> Japanese factories avoid narrow delineation of job boundaries, job proliferation, and a rigid one-to-one matching of workers and jobs. They screen for talented generalists fresh out of school and invest heavily in training them for a wide array of responsibilities. In so doing, they insure that workers develop broad skills and can be

flexibly adapted to variations in production scheduling and demand.

He (p. 58) further notes that:

> The Japanese propensity to reject Western habits of organizing around functional specialties is not confined to job design. Narrow specializations are likewise typical neither of organizational subunits nor management careers. Japanese companies rarely have the array of specialist staff departments – finance, planning, law, and so on – found in U.S. firms.

This contrast is evidenced in Table 6.6. While the average number of job classifications of blue-collar workers at Japanese automotive components plants is less than one-third of their US counterparts, the average number of machines Japanese workers operated was about three times that of their US counterparts.

Table 6.6 Job classification and multimachine operations of blue-collar workers at automotive components plants in Japan, the USA, and Europe, 1987–1989

Nationality/region	No. of job classification	No. of machines per worker
Japan/Japan	2.9	7.4
Japan/USA	3.4	4.1
USA/USA	9.5	2.5
Europe/Europe	5.1	2.7

Source: Adapted from Nishiguchi (1994: 201–202).

When it comes to functional fields, the Japanese emphasis on generalists vs. the American mentality on specialization still prevail. In their comparison of membership structure of the Japanese Marketing Association vs. American Marketing Association, Kotabe and Lanctot (1998) find that while 69 per cent of members of the Japanese Marketing Association are either top executives or non-marketing personnel, an overwhelming 71 per cent of members of the American Marketing Association are from marketing professionals (Table 6.7).

Table 6.7 Member composition of Japanese and American Marketing Associations

	Japan		USA	
	Number	Percentage	Number	Percentage
Top executive	400	35	39	4
Marketing	340	30	580	71
Non-marketing	388	34	196	24
Total	1128		815	

Source: Kotabe and Lanctot (1998: 166).

In the engineering field, as shown in Table 6.8, while only 16.9 per cent of American engineers of outside specialty had been sent by their firm to research/ design/development areas for training, 47.5 per cent of Japanese engineers had had such an experience. Similarly, 34.6 per cent of Japanese engineers of outside specialty had job rotation experiences in the area of production, as compared to a mere 19.6

per cent in the USA. Overall, 61.9 per cent of Japanese as compared to a mere 40.4 per cent of Americans reported having experienced job rotation. These sharp differences reflect a contrast between trust in generalists and trust in specialists, between an emphasis on shop-floor experiences and a reliance on professional knowledge, and between integration of knowing and acting in Japan and a stress on division and specialization in the USA.

Table 6.8 Job rotations to areas outside specialty: Japan and US comparison

Area assigned to	Percentage of respondents	
	USA (N = 455)	Japan (N = 426)
Research/design/development	16.9	47.5
Production	19.6	34.6
Marketing/sale	10.3	15.3
Purchasing	5.1	1.4
Public relations	2.6	1.4
Finance	4.0	1.0
Personnel	3.7	1.0
Other	12.1	8.8
At least one of the above	40.4	61.9

Source: Lynn, Piehler, and Kieler (1993: 63).

The Japanese avoidance of narrow specialization is to a large extent derived from its connectual cultural paradigm and its preference for connectual knowing that suspects the utility of separation and division and honors the value of connection and integration. In other words, both the practices of broad job classification and job rotation are simultaneously the institutional expression of the Japanese cultural penchant for connection and interdependence and the governance mechanisms that facilitate the creation, preservation, and appropriation of relational, cross-functional, and contextual knowledge, skills, and capabilities.

By contrast, under the dominance of separate knowing and the cultural paradigm of contractual man, there are very strong incentives for both employers and employees to avoid the development of firm-specific, relational, cross-functional, and contextual knowledge, skills, and capabilities that are neither saleable nor substitutable in the market. These types of knowledge, skills, and capabilities create a *dependency structure* that leaves both contracting partners vulnerable to the opportunistic manipulation of the other side. For management, a reliance on relational and contextual knowledge, skills, and capabilities of employees that are not substitutable in the market means a loss of bargaining power and monitoring capability, as it was so prominently prevalent in pre-Taylorist craft production. For the employees the development of firm- and relation-specific knowledge, skills, and capabilities means a dependence on the current employer for their effective appropriation. Once employees lose their jobs, the firm-specific knowledge they have developed will have little value in the market. This is the reason underpinning the fact that in Japan firm-specific experience (tenure) has a greater effect on an employee's wage than general experience (total years of experience), while in the

USA the opposite is true (Kalleberg and Lincoln, 1988).

In the Japanese case, broad job classification facilitates the realization of the cultural need for connections and the governance requirement for connectual knowing. Conversely, since broad job classification makes the assignment of individual responsibilities and performances impossible, it runs counter to the American cultural penchant for autonomy and independence and the governance needs for contractual incentives and separate knowing. As a result, broad job classification is rare in the USA.

Hamada and Yaguchi (1994) provide a good example of the incompatibility of the Japanese practices of broad job classification and the American cultural paradigm of contractual man. In their case study of a Japanese transplant in the USA, they found that the Japanese practices of broad job classification and job rotation finally had to be abandoned and changed to the American system of narrow job description and narrow specialization, even though Japanese managers desperately tried to make the former work. Kenney and Florida (1993: 288) also found that 'American managers have experienced serious problems adapting to the Japanese rotation system.'

The competitive advantage of broad job classification and job rotation lies in their facilitation of the creation of relation-specific knowledge for organized technology fusion and for incremental improvement. The competitive disadvantage of such practices, however, lies in their impeding the process of specialization and professionalization in knowledge creation. Therefore, it is ironic but not surprising that while broad job classification and job rotation have been cited as major contributors to Japanese success in the automobile and consumer electronics sectors, the same practices are considered as the major causes of backwardness in the Japanese banking industry (Dattel, 1994) and software sector (Nakahara, 1993).

TQM and knowledge creation

Total quality management (TQM), especially quality circles (QC), has been an indispensable part of the Japanese system of connectual governance. It is aimed at harnessing, integrating, and synthesizing *dispersed* and *inter-linked* knowledge about incremental improvement on the shop floor. In some sectors, such as automobiles, opto-electronics, and mechatronics, there are tremendous improvement opportunities. However, the types of knowledge effective for harnessing improvement opportunities in these sectors are generally those that are position-specific, relation-specific, and cross-functional. Although the practices of broad job classification and job rotation facilitate the formation of these types of knowledge, their further appropriation requires the integration and synergy of various forms of knowledge by a group of employees. The group process and the overlapping knowledge bases of members in the QC ensure that dispersed pieces of the knowledge held by shop-floor employees can be integrated and synthesized to form insights about incremental improvement. Here, while the existence and overlap of relational, cross-functional, and contextual knowledge provides a common knowledge base for incremental improvement, the connectual value structure ensures that employees have strong incentives to participate in the creation and application of knowledge for incremental improvement.

Because of the incompatibilities between the predominant American penchant for knowledge specialization and the requirement of relational knowledge for TQM, as well as between the American cultural value of autonomy and the group-interdependent structure of TQM, the transplantation of TQM to the USA has been traumatic (Cole, 1995a). As a result of the desire for autonomy and independence, the dominant quality paradigm in the USA that originated from Taylor's Scientific Management movement endorses *separate knowing* and propositional knowledge. Consequently, quality is secured by the separation of thinking and executing, by the standardization of procedures, and by the separation of quality inspection from shop-floor workers as an independent function (Cole, 1995a, 1998). These practices fail to harness the dispersed knowledge of shop-floor workers for quality inspection and quality improvement.

In contrast, TQM as dominant in Japan is a new quality paradigm that emphasizes the involvement of all employees and departments in harnessing dispersed knowledge for incremental improvement (Cole, 1998). It requires employees to develop knowledge and skills far beyond the traditional narrow definition of jobs and professions. It further requires a group process where team members share, integrate, and transform their dispersed knowledge into knowledge for incremental improvement. In sum, the effective operation of TQM requires US firms to adapt some connectual governance mechanisms that were foreign to them until recently. In their study of Japanese transplants to the USA, Kenney and Florida (1993: 227) observe that: 'Most transplant electronic facilities have not implemented quality-control, *kaizen*, or other work improvement initiatives. Only one plant we visited tried to implement QC circles; however, this attempt failed.' Choi and Behling (1997: 37) summarize the disappointing results of the Anglo-American effort of transplanting TQM in the 1980s and early 1990s thus:

> The 1990s have not been good to TQM: A survey of 500 executives in U.S. manufacturing and service firms indicated that 'only one-third believe that TQM made them more competitive;' a survey of 100 British firms that implemented quality programs found that only one-fifth believed that their programs had 'a significant impact;' an American Electronics Association survey revealed that use of TQM by member firms dropped from 86 percent in 1988 to 73 percent in 1991 and that 63 percent of the firms reported that TQM failed to reduce defects by 10 percent or more, even though they had been in operation for almost two and one-half years on average; McKinsay & Company found that two-thirds of the TQM programs it examined had simply ground to a halt because they failed to produce expected results.

The difficulty in transplanting TQM and other Japanese human resource practices to the USA lies in the fact that they are integral parts of the system of connectual mechanisms of governance. Therefore, an imitation of only a single part of the whole system is vulnerable to failure. Using an international data-set from a 1989–1990 survey of 62 automotive assembly plants, Macduffie (1995: 197) found that human resource (HR) practices affect performance not 'individually but as interrelated elements in an internally consistent HR "bundle" or system.' He (p. 197) further found that 'these HR bundles contribute most to assembly plant productivity and quality when they are integrated with manufacturing policies under the "organizational logic" of a flexible production system.' From the perspective of knowledge regimes, both the 'organizational logic' of the flexible production system and the coherent system of HR practices are integral parts of the whole system of connectual governance mechanisms that aim at harnessing dispersed and inter-linked knowledge for incremental improvement.

JIT and knowledge creation

Just as TQM is a form of connectual governance, the Japanese innovation of JIT (just-in-time) production and delivery can also be seen as a connectual governance mechanism that facilitates the creation and appropriation of relational, cross-functional, and contextual knowledge. Sabel (1994) conceptualizes the learning effect of the Japanese JIT production system through his concept of learning by monitoring. This is a practice in which deficiencies of products and processes are identified and eliminated on the spot by easing the bottlenecks of production flow. It is also a process in which the knowledge links between adjacent steps are revealed through the tightening of flows among procedures. By minimizing buffers of all kinds, including inventories and slacks of time and space, task and organizational interdependence among the various agents involved in the production process is maximized (Oliver and Wilkinson, 1992: 76). At the same time, knowledge links among tasks are revealed to the greatest extent, and deficiencies and flaws in products and processes are forced to the surface and eliminated (Womack *et al.*, 1990; Sabel, 1994).

As Oliver and Wilkinson (1992) and Macduffie (1995) correctly point out, the JIT production system creates a high level of *dependency* among functional lines. Such a dependency structure is a logical result of the Japanese penchant for connection and mutual obligation. It will not work effectively unless it has the support of a coherent system of human resource practices that reinforce connectual governance. JIT delivery would also not be effective without the proximity of suppliers to producers, which in turn depends on long-term subcontracting relations (Nishiguchi, 1994).

In contrast, the US contractual governance of firms as represented in their system of mass production had used all forms of buffers such as inventories, additional time and spatial slacks, and separate coordinating and controlling units to make each function independent to the greatest degree. Although it promoted specialization and decreased transaction and coordination costs in organizing the production process, it buried the precious information about potential improvement opportunities that would otherwise have been detected in JIT production and delivery systems. Underpinning the US use of all forms of buffers maximally to eliminate task interdependence is the fear of any interdependency structure that reduces individual autonomy and freedom. It is, therefore, understandable that US workers complained of the loss of separate team identity and individual freedom when buffers were removed between and within work teams (Klein, 1989). Indeed, the incompatibility between the American pursuit of independence and the interdependency structure of JIT production and delivery is the major cause for the traumas experienced when US firms experimented with JIT and when Japanese firms transplanted it to the USA (Kenney and Florida, 1993; Harrison, 1994). Anyhow, judged from the conventional Anglo-American theory of conflict and conflict resolution, any interdependent structures are seen as sources of conflict while the use of any buffers to minimize interdependence is seen as an effective way of avoiding potential conflict.

Notwithstanding the difficulty, the Japanese challenge did generate a process of

'Japanization' in the Anglo-American societies of both the USA and the UK (Oliver and Wilkinson, 1992; Pilkington, 1998). During the 1980s and early 1990s, companies in both countries rushed to implement the best Japanese practice of JIT. As indicated in Table 6.9, the results are mixed. From 1975 to 1992, while in the heavily contested automobile industry, both the USA and the UK had significantly reduced the inventory of parts and increased value added to work-in-process, the stock level in all manufacturing sectors had not seen much improvement. In most cases, companies simply shifted the burden of inventory to suppliers and sales networks without JIT production (Pilkington, 1998).

Table 6.9 Improvement of inventory reduction in US and UK manufacturing

	Value added to work-in-process (1973 as base level)				Finished goods stocks as percentage of all stocks			
	All manufacturing sectors		Automobile manufacturing		All manufacturing sectors		Automobile manufacturing	
	USA	UK	USA	UK	USA	UK	USA	UK
1973	1.0	1.0	1.0	1.0	30.5	22.2	8.4	27.8
1975	0.9	1.0	0.7	0.9	31.3	25.9	8.5	31.3
1977	1.0	0.9	0.9	0.9	31.5	27.5	9.3	34.6
1979	0.9	0.9	1.0	1.0	30.1	27.3	10.0	39.3
1981	0.9	0.8	1.1	1.0	31.5	28.3	11.1	47.2
1983	0.9	0.9	1.1	1.3	32.8	28.9	12.9	54.3
1985	0.9	1.0	1.4	1.6	32.5	29.7	13.2	58.0
1987	1.0	1.1	1.7	1.6	31.7	30.4	17.1	57.1
1989	0.9	1.2	2.4	2.2	31.6	32.0	19.5	62.9
1991	1.0	1.3	2.2	1.9	32.9	33.0	16.2	60.6
1992	1.1	1.3	2.2	2.2	34.3	32.6	15.7	59.6

Source: Pilkington (1998: 39).

Integration of R&D, manufacturing, and marketing

In the Japanese practice of flexible production and connectual governance, a more specific type of knowledge fusion and integration happens among the R&D, manufacturing, and marketing departments. The routine practice of the job rotation of engineers among these divisions enables product designers to take into consideration both consumer's needs and manufacturability (Lynn *et al.*, 1993). The frequent use of cross-functional teams in product and process development also makes knowledge integration and technology fusion more effective (Kodama, 1991). The mutually reinforcing nature in the sharing and integrating of cross-functional knowledge forms positive feedback in organizational learning and knowledge creation (Susman, 1992).

In the old paradigm of mass production and contractual governance, the Taylorist organizing principle requires that the tasks of thinking be assigned to industrial engineers who design standard operating procedures through objective 'scientific' methods, while the task of blue-collar workers is to execute these predesigned operating procedures. Underpinning this principle is the assumption that there is only one best way of doing things and it can only be found through the scientific method (Ayres, 1992). This linear view of knowledge creation led to the inability for the old leaders within the mass production paradigm to grasp the essence of learning and knowledge creation in manufacturing. It treats learning as something that either happens in engineers' efforts in isolated R&D, or is automatically realized through running down the so-called 'learning curve.' The importance of locational and relation-specific knowledge, the dispersed and tacit nature of improvement knowledge, and the mutually reinforcing nature of different sources of knowledge across functional lines are neglected in both theory and practice. The result has been a handicap in learning on the shop floor.

Consistent with the studies by Womack *et al.* (1990) and Clark and Fujimoto, (1991), Song and Parry (1992) find that Japanese marketing managers are more inclined than their US counterparts to recognize the importance of R&D-marketing cooperation to analyze customer preferences. They also 'place more emphasis on integration in the initial stage of the new product development process' (p. 110). Similarly, according to Mansfield's (1988a) survey, in Japanese firms, one-third of total R&D projects were proposed by the production line and customers, twice the number of their US counterparts.

Concurrent engineering and knowledge creation

The Japanese advantage in the integration of R&D, manufacturing, and marketing is best reflected in the practice of concurrent engineering. According to Clark and Fujimoto (1991), in traditional *sequential engineering* as dominant in the USA, there is a great degree of specialization and sequentialization among product design, process design, manufacturing, and marketing (see Figure 6.1). In the USA, as Clark *et al.* (1992: 201) observe, 'design and manufacturing tasks have traditionally been thought of as distinct, radically different activities.' Design engineers seldom consulted manufacturing engineers and marketing personnel in their design effort, nor did they elaborately incorporate the criteria of manufacturability and assembly into their design.

Observing the relationship between design and manufacturing engineers, Francis (1994: 63) also notes:

> There has been a wall between them. Over this wall the designers have thrown their drawings and specifications and production engineers have taken a pride in their ability to work out how to manufacture anything the designers could throw at them.

From a knowledge regime perspective, this 'throw-it-over-the-wall' mentality is very much the result of the American pursuit of autonomy and independence. In the automobile sector, the artificial modularization and encapsulation of the product development process not only severs the knowledge links and consequent knowledge exchange between design and manufacturing tasks but also artificially sequentializes product and manufacturing design processes that are inherently non-linear. The

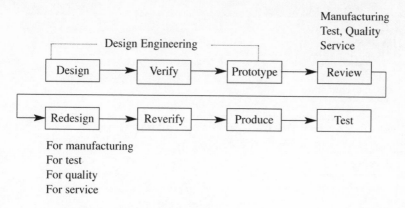

Figure 6.1 Sequential engineering as dominant in the USA
Source: Rosenblatt and Watson (1991: 31).

results have been a lack of manufacturability and assembly and a prolonged development cycle (Clark and Fujimoto, 1991).

As opposed to the American wall mentality, and facilitated by the cultural paradigm of connectual man, leading Japanese firms such as Toyota have tried to 'tear down the walls' that separate R&D, manufacturing, and marketing and integrate them into a system of concurrent engineering in which overlaps in knowledge exchange and product development are abundant. In concurrent engineering, instead of a one-way and one-to-one sequential process, product development is an *overlapping problem solving process* (Clark and Fujimoto, 1991). Instead of a lack of horizontal communications among functional divisions, knowledge flow, exchange, and integration across divisional lines are the norm (Aoki, 1990). Like the JIT production system, concurrent engineering creates an *interdependency structure* in which no task can function independently without considering the needs of others and seeking knowledge inputs from others. There are several institutional means to construct an interdependent structure for concurrent engineering. First, it is created by incorporating the objectives conventionally assigned to an individual task group to all task groups. By so doing, each task group is forced to maximally utilize the knowledge of others in the fulfillment of the objectives of the whole product design process. For example, the objectives of manufacturability and assembly are not the sole responsibility of manufacturing engineers but are also that of design engineers. Second, the interdependent structure is further strengthened by shortening and tightening the development schedule so that only a strategy of overlapped problem solving and a process of simultaneous project development can fulfil the goal. Like the incorporation of systemic goals, such a tightened development schedule further facilitates knowledge flow, exchange, and fusion among task groups. Finally, the overlap in the knowledge base of project teams, which is acquired through job rotation, facilitates not only knowledge sharing but also knowledge integration and fusion across functional boundaries. A typical concurrent engineering process is shown in Figure 6.2.

There are many competitive advantages associated with concurrent engineering. First, by incorporating the criteria of the whole product development process to

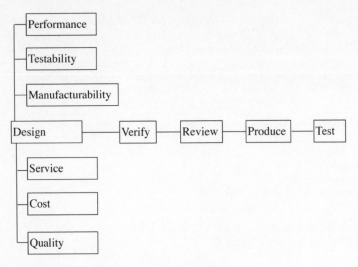

Figure 6.2 Concurrent engineering as dominant in Japan
Source: Rosenblatt and Watson (1991: 31).

every task group, it facilitates the achievement of what Clark and Fujimoto (1990) called 'product integrity', which is characterized by the products with coherent and integrated concepts, values, and attributes. According to them, product integrity has provided Japanese auto companies such as Honda and Mazda a competitive edge in the artistic values, soundness, incorruptibility, quality, and completeness of their automobiles.

Second, by the simultaneous development of all stages, concurrent engineering vastly reduces the whole product development cycle. In their detailed study of the world auto industry, Clark and Fujimoto (1991: 217) find that concurrent engineering is a major cause for the competitive advantage of the Japanese auto industry in engineering lead-time over the US competitors. While US car-makers spend an average of 34 months to launch new cars, their Japanese counterparts take just an average of 24 months.

Third, by incorporating the criteria of manufacturability and assembility into the whole product development process, concurrent engineering vastly reduces the cost in manufacturing and assembling. According to the McKinsey Global Institute (1993), concurrent engineering and its subsets – design for manufacturability (DFM) and design for assembly (DFA) – are the major reasons for high Japanese productivity in metalworking, automobiles, automobile parts, and consumer electronics. Although design accounts for only 5 per cent of total product cost, it influences about 70 per cent of total product cost (Boothroyd, 1988).

Discussion: cultural paradigms, organization evolution, and technological trajectories

While the competitive implications of concurrent engineering are clear, the central issue here is the cause of the two drastically different technical trajectories for engineering design and product development between the USA and Japan.

Ironically, it was the US auto makers, Ford, General Motors, and Chrysler, who pioneered concurrent engineering during World War II (Ziemke and Spann, 1993). After the war, however, US auto makers 'mystically' abandoned the practice and retreated to the pre-war routine of sequential engineering, just as most US firms abandoned Demings' teachings in quality control, and the US government terminated the very successful Training Within Industries (TWI) program (Robinson and Schroeder, 1993). Just as the failure in adopting Deming's teaching and the demise of the TWI programs led to American backwardness in quality control, training, and TQM, the abandonment of concurrent engineering caused competitive disadvantages in product and process design in relatively matured fabricating industries. In describing the 'mysterious' demise of concurrent engineering in the USA, Ziemke and Spann (1993) note with disbelief:

> Despite the success achieved through the use of wartime concurrent engineering teams and a concentration on DFM and DFA techniques to maximize production volume, the concurrent engineering design team concept virtually disappeared until about 1979 and the emphasis on DFM and DFA was greatly reduced ... It took the Ford Company about thirty years to reinvent an engineering philosophy pioneered by founder Henry Ford and demonstrated so capably during the World War II ... Ford managers and engineers forgot their concurrent and DFM/DFA heritage and competencies fairly quickly and rather completely until desperation brought them back to the founder's knee (pp. 37–38).

From the knowledge regime perspective, the 'mysterious' disappearance of concurrent engineering in the USA is largely due to its *incompatibility* with the logic of the contractual cultural paradigm and contractual governance. The highly interdependent structure imbedded in concurrent engineering is at odds with the American penchant for autonomy, separateness, and independence.

World War II was a special period in which the clannish feeling of unity and common fate might somehow have suppressed the dominance of the contractual cultural paradigm and contractual governance. Together with the high stakes, extreme time pressure, and pervasively tight resource constraints that characterized the war effort, the clannish environment promoted institutional innovations beyond the limits of conventional contractual governance. These innovations include cross-functional teams, Deming's quality management, concurrent engineering, and the US government's TWI program.

The end of World War II saw the end of both the clannish spirit and the high pressures of time and resources for connectual governance. The war transformed the USA into an unmatchable superpower. US firms also overwhelmingly dominated world business. All these conditions contributed to the return of the predominance of the contractual cultural paradigm and contractual governance, leading to the unnoted demise of not only concurrent engineering, but also quality management, and the TWI program. In the new environment, these practices were aberrations that fitted the needs of war but were at odds with the dominant cultural needs for autonomy, separateness, and independence.

Unlike its disappointing fate in the USA, the TWI program received tremendous success when the American occupation force introduced it to Japan (Robinson and Schroeder, 1993), which has brought a pervasive diffusion of Deming's philosophy of quality control. Because of this episode, many Americans totally dismissed

Japanese originality in creating the new quality paradigm. The case of concurrent engineering in Japan provides a counter-argument for such a judgment. Although the USA pioneered concurrent engineering, there has been no evidence of any American influence on the emergence and dominance of concurrent engineering in Japan. Because of the quick disappearance of concurrent engineering and the rapid resurgent dominance of sequential engineering in the USA, the impact of the USA on the emergence and dominance of concurrent engineering in Japan must be negative. This is especially true when Japanese firms enthusiastically imitated American practices after World War II. From the knowledge regime perspective, the endogenous emergence and dominance of concurrent engineering in Japan are very much facilitated by the dominant Japanese cultural paradigm of connectual man. Its emphasis on cross-functional connections in objectives and in knowledge flows, its stress on simultaneous and overlapping development, and most importantly, its imbedded interdependency structure are all facilitated and reinforced by the Japanese cultural tendency toward connection and mutual obligations.

The case of concurrent engineering elucidates the importance of cultural paradigms and organizing principles in shaping the emergence and predominance of certain management practices and institutions. After World War II, US superiority and dominance in technology, organization, production, and management put huge pressure on other nations to learn from the USA. The Japanese were especially keen to imitate American success. The Japanese dominant cultural paradigm of connectual man and its imbedding organizing principles, however, exerted an *isomorphic pull* and *synthesizing* effect that induced a creative fusion between the exogenous American system of mass production and endogenous Japanese connectual governance. TQM, JIT, and concurrent engineering are only three cases of such a successful fusion. From this viewpoint, it is quite possible to assume that even without the influence of Deming and the TWI program, the logic of connectual governance in Japan would have induced a similar kind of quality paradigm as practiced in present day Japan. In fact, many elements of the Japanese quality paradigm, such as lifetime employment, job rotation, QC, cross-functional teams, continuous incremental improvement, and JIT have gone far beyond Deming's original concept of statistical quality control.

Where the evolution of governance mechanisms is concerned, as the works by Gordon (1985), Baron *et al.* (1986), and Aoki (1997) show, even in the case of war, the American and Japanese responses to the challenge for increasing production of munitions were divergent. In the Japanese case, Akio (1997: 241) notes:

> Because of acute labor and material shortages, various emergencies had to be coped with on an *ad hoc* basis, by the collective efforts of workers, machine breakdowns had to be fixed without the expert help of scarce mechanics. Ways of dealing with shortages of parts and tools had to be improvised on the spot. Frequent absenteeism caused by workers' trips to the countryside to collect food was coped with by sharing jobs among the remaining workers.

In sharp contrast, in the US case:

> Facing the same challenge for increasing munitions production during the war, American industry began to adopt the scientific management method on an unprecedented scale. In this method, individual workers were trained to use their work times as efficiently as possible through the calculated division of tasks. It was also

designed to train workers to respond *individually* to minor random events relevant to their own tasks, such as routine adjustment of machines, regular material defects, etc., according to a *prescribed* manual. Major problems were assumed to be handled by problem-solving *specialists*, such as machinists, industrial engineers, and inspectors. The machinery and factory layout were designed – and the precautionary inventory of materials, parts, and half-products was planned – to *minimize the need for interaction among workers* and to control the occurrence of random events that might simultaneously affect their tasks. (*Italics added.*)

What is interesting here is how different societies respond differently to a similar crisis. It seems clear that they resort to the spirit, energy, and organizing principles that the transformative potential of their cultural paradigms can best offer.[2] Therefore, underneath the seemingly unintended emergence of specific practices and institutions (Akoi, 1997), there is the hidden role of cultural paradigms as attractors and catalysts. Indeed, such an isomorphic structure of organizing principles, governance mechanisms, and technology trajectories can only be overcome and transformed by either outside challenge or outright outside imposition of alternatives. In the case of Japan, as Baba *et al.* (1997) note, the Japanese did not fully adopt many practices of the US systems of manufacturing until the American occupation authority imposed them. In the US case, it was not until the Japanese firms drove them to near-bankruptcy that US firms began to put serious effort into transforming their governance mechanisms. Like the Japanese synergy of Taylorism and mass production with its endogenous organizing principles,[3] the transplantation of the lean production system has taken a hybrid form (Abo, 1994), synthesizing both Japanese practices and American mentalities.

Connectual markets and networks and knowledge creation

Japanese connectual governance mechanisms are not only predominant inside firm boundaries, but also extend to dominate firms' relations with major suppliers, customers, banks, trading companies, other related businesses, and finally government agencies (Gerlach, 1992; Nishiguchi; 1994). Indeed, many of the Japanese intra-firm connectual governance mechanisms would not have been effective if they were not supported by rich inter-firm connections. The first-tier suppliers of major equipment producers are actually actively involved in the practices of cross-functional teams, TQM, JIT delivery, concurrent product and process design, and DFM/DFA; so are Japanese trading companies, retail channels, customers, and government agencies.

Producer–supplier linkage and knowledge creation

In the case of supplier relationships, the connectual structures of mutual shareholding and of long-term cooperative subcontracting enable producers and suppliers to build meaningful relationships. The connectual knowing between producers and suppliers is facilitated through frequent planned communications, mutual technical assistance, intensive sharing of information, easy exchange of guest engineers, transfer of employees to suppliers, and involvement of suppliers in the design process (Dyer and Ouchi, 1993). These practices facilitate the effective exchange and diffusion of firm-specific knowledge regarding potential improvements in product and process design, a raising of standards, quality and delivery, and a reduction of costs. In addition, the long-term meaningful relationship also enables suppliers to invest in customized physical capitals (Dyer and Ouchi, 1993), and develop relation-specific knowledge and skills specifically tailored to the idiosyncratic needs of their major customers (Asanuma, 1989). The effective creation, exchange and synthesis of firm- and relation-specific knowledge between suppliers and producers provide a competitive advantage for Japanese firms (Dyer and Ouchi, 1993; Nishiguchi, 1994).

In contrast to long-term relations of mutual obligation and trust in Japan, producer–supplier relations in the old American system of mass production had been neoclassic contracting and adversarial bidding (Helper, 1991a,b; Bolton *et al.*, 1994). To avoid the possibility of being held up owing to asset specificity and opportunism (Williamson, 1985), mass production firms in the USA either vertically integrated suppliers into their firms, or encouraged and maintained multiple and competing suppliers as late as the mid-1980s (Helper, 1991a). To avoid being held up by the opportunism of the major producer, suppliers in the USA also seek multiple customers, and minimize dedicated investments specially customized to any individual customer. According to Dyer and Ouchi (1993), while 31 per cent of Japanese suppliers' total investment in capital equipment could not be redeployed to alternative customers, the nondeployable portion of US suppliers' total investment is only 15 per cent.

Intriguingly, before the Japanese challenge was widely acknowledged, this American practice of short-term and arm's length supplier relationship had not been seriously challenged either in theory or in practice. Instead, both neoclassic economics and transaction cost economics theoretically endorse it. When faced with the problem of choosing dedicated, nondeployable technologies vs. generic, deployable ones, Williamson (1996: 239) suggests that suppliers choose the latter to minimize transaction costs and opportunism.

Indeed, it is the focus on transaction costs rather than knowledge creation that has led to the legitimization of arm's length and adversarial supply relations in the USA. According to Helper (1991a), because of the Japanese challenge, there have been efforts in the USA to change the relationship between producers and their suppliers. Improved supplier relationships have contributed significantly to the revival of US companies such as Chrysler (Dyer, 1996). Empirically, it is well supported that both producers and suppliers benefit from adopting a strategy of maintaining long-term relationships with one another (Kalwani and Narayandas, 1995). But notwithstanding the well-publicized stories and the economic rationale, while the mentality of the adversarial supplier relationship has gone away to a certain extent, opportunism and lack of trust still persist (Helper, 1991a).

Producer–retailer–customer linkage and knowledge creation

Connectual governance mechanisms extend to dominate the producer–retailer–customer relationship in Japan. Instead of an arm's length relationship with both retailers and customers as is dominant in the USA, Japanese producers try to establish long-term connections and mutual trust and obligations with retailers and customers (Czinkota, 1985; Womack *et al.*, 1990). In describing the Toyota Corolla automobile distribution channel, Womack *et al.* (1990: 183, 185, 186) note:

> The prime objective of Japanese dealers is to keep the customer feeling that he or she is part of the dealer's 'family.' ... A key objective of every distribution channel is to build and nurture lifetime channel loyalty ... Once a new car is delivered, the owner becomes part of the Corolla family. This means frequent calls from the person selling the car – who henceforth becomes the owner's personal sales agent. The representative will make sure the car is working properly and ferret out any problems the owner may be having to relay back to the factory.

Intense, contextual, and connectual interaction with customers in Japan enables the salesperson to harness in-depth and delicate knowledge about consumer preferences and possible improvement opportunities. As a result of the dealer's in-depth knowledge about customers, Womack *et al.* (1990: 180–181) observe:

> The Corolla channel is directly tied into product-development process. During the entire period that new cars destined for sale through the channel are being developed, staff members from the channel are on loan to development teams. These channel representatives are in a position to make an invaluable contribution to product development.

This long-term and connectual relationship with retailers and customers is prevalent over all the Japanese distribution system. The sources of connections include business groups, financial ties, and personal relationships. The latter is of especially great importance in maintaining the connectual governance between producers and retailers and among channel members, as Czinkota (1985: 303) notes,

> The Japanese distribution system also relies heavily upon personal relationships which are built through frequent visits and elaborate courtesies. The maintenance of these relationships is often far more important than sales level of a certain product or short-term profitability, and includes the occasional provision of money to 'send the son to school,' frequent exchanges of gifts, friendly discussions, and very little direct pressure to sell. Time is, of course, the key to build such relationships.

The competitive advantage of close producer–retailer–customer ties lies in their ability to harness contextual, qualitative, delicate, and in-depth knowledge about customer preferences, product performance, and possible improvement opportunities. The overreliance on a close customer relationship, however, has also contributed to the low efficiency of the Japanese retail sector (Czinkota, 1985). Furthermore, a focus on maintaining relationships with existing customers may lock the attention of the firm into the development of products that fit the tastes of its existing customer base, with a loss of opportunities to create dramatically new products to serve new customers.

Producer–bank linkage and knowledge creation

In Japan, the dominance of connectual governance also extends to producer–bank relations. Instead of the arm's length relation that is typical between producers and banks in the USA, the relationship between Japanese firms and their major banks is cooperative and long-term oriented. Such a relationship is reinforced through cross shareholding, interlocking directorships, and other forms of connections (Gerlach, 1992). The competitive advantage of long-term producer–bank relationships lies in the firm's ability to focus on long-term investment in capabilities and in the ability of banks to base their investment decisions on the acquisition of delicate, in-depth, qualitative, and contextual knowledge about firm performance and business opportunities, rather than simply on abstract data about short-term profit and return on investment.

Notwithstanding this, the Japanese investment system also has many disadvantages. First, it lacks venture capital markets to support innovations outside the domain of large corporations and affiliated firms, impairing the independent innovative activities by individualistic entrepreneurs (Westney, 1993). Second, the cozy relationship between bankers and firms can lead to an unconstrained expansion in times of high-flight expectations, which contributed to the formation of a bubble economy and its subsequent collapse in the early 1990s. Third, because of their heavy reliance on connectual governance, Japanese banks generally do not know how to deal with strangers. At the height of the global expansion of Japanese banks and other financial institutions in the 1980s, most Japanese banks simply focused on the provision of financial services to transplanted Japanese firms within the same inter-market *keiretsu* (Sullivan, 1995). When some Japanese financial firms tried to venture into the business of providing loan and financial services to foreign companies, they tried to foster long-term relationships rather than doing business in a contractual way. Such an effort of relationship building met with great failure in the American cultural environment of individualism and contractual mentality (Sullivan, 1995).

Connectual capitalism and knowledge appropriation

The dominance of connectual governance in Japan has also pervaded inter-corporate relations to form what Gerlach (1992) called *inter-market keiretsu*, consisting of a major trading company, a major bank, an insurance company, a construction company, a real estate company, and one company from each major industrial sector. While many works have been done on the historical rise of inter-market *keiretsu* in Japan (e.g. Gerlach, 1992), few have focused on its impact on knowledge creation and appropriation. From a knowledge regime perspective, inter-market *keiretsu* can be seen as a connectual governance structure that aims at appropriating knowledge by horizontal exchange and fusion and at establishing a complete set of knowledge bases and capabilities to aid knowledge diffusion and fusion. In the American case, the dominance of contractual governance leads to the appropriation of knowledge through the contractual market and the standardization, specialization, modularization, encapsulation, and professionalization of knowledge. As stated before, the contractual governance of knowledge exchange has high transaction costs in the exchange of the types of knowledge that are tacit, contextual, firm-specific, cross-functional, and relational.

The connectual governance of inter-market *keiretsu* can overcome the failure of contractual markets in the exchange and appropriation of information and knowledge. First, the connectual logic, together with its emphasis on knowledge integration and fusion, makes it possible to apply all types of knowledge created in one area of business to all others. Second, the *completeness* of knowledge and knowledge capabilities within a given inter-market *keiretsu*, as represented by the completeness of business areas and industrial sectors, makes any forms of new combination, integration and fusion of knowledge, expertise, and capabilities possible. Third, the completeness of business areas and industrial sectors within an inter-market *keiretsu* makes it possible to completely apply, and therefore fully appropriate, knowledge and capabilities developed in one business to all other industrial sectors. The forms of appropriation include the diffusion, transformation, application, synthesis, integration, and fusion of knowledge, expertise, and capabilities over all firms within the *keiretsu*. With the support of the connectual logic, the inter-market *keiretsu* is especially good at the appropriation of tacit, subjective, relational, and contextual knowledge. This provides Japanese firms with a competitive edge in sectors where the creation and appropriation of these kinds of knowledge are crucial for competitive success.

Connectual capitalism and capability maintenance

From the knowledge regime perspective, both vertical and inter-market *keiretsu* can best be described as a tightly coupled ecosystem of business groups mastering mutually reinforcing and complementary assets of knowledge, expertise, and capabilities. What Gerlach (1992) called *alliance capitalism* is just such an ecosystem seeking capability preservation, enhancement, and symbiosis through strategic alliances and a balance between cooperation and competition (Sabel, 1987). The key to its effectiveness lies in its linkage structure that mutually reinforces the capabilities of individual firms.

A single practice of cooperation between two isolated firms in knowledge exchange and integration does not constitute a sustainable competitive advantage. A group of vertical and horizontal *keiretsu*, with each holding a system of complementary and mutually reinforcing knowledge, expertise, and capabilities, on the other hand, can be formidably competitive (Kash and Rycroft, 1999). It makes technology fusion possible across firm boundaries. It enables the quick diffusion of firm-specific knowledge across member firms. It also enhances the firms' capability in preserving and enhancing their core competencies. This is so because in such an ecosystem a loss of core competencies in one firm would mean a loss of capability for others, and therefore, other firms will have a great incentive to act cooperatively to prevent such a loss from occurring.

American students of technology policy learn a lesson from Sematech's failure to rescue GCA, an original innovator of the photolithographic stepper. Although with the aid of Sematech, GCA had successfully developed a new generation of technologically superior photolithographic steppers, few Sematech member firms were willing to risk buying its products out of fear of its financial instability, although the preservation of GCA's capability was assessed as crucial to the competitiveness of the US semiconductor industry. The result was the death of GCA (Randazzese, 1994).

To the extent that firm-specific knowledge, expertise, and capabilities die with the firm, GCA's ruin means an indispensable loss of complementary assets to US firms in the semiconductor sector. The problems that happened in other US sectors, such as consumer electronics, may be traced back to some similar events in the death of isolated firms, which led to the loss of complementary assets for the others. This in turn facilitated the demise of the whole ecosystem of consumer electronics in the USA.

In summary, in an atomic form of capitalism like the American system of mass production and contractual governance, its capability for radical innovation may be high, but the firm-specific knowledge acquired through those radical innovations may fail to grow and even die out. This is especially true when a dearth of effective inter-firm linkages deprives innovative US firms of the opportunity to synthesize with complementary knowledge across firm boundaries (Kash and Rycroft, 1999). Atomic firms in the USA also lack a defending system to come to their rescue when management makes some miscalculations in their strategic planning. As a result, even though US firms are generally competitive in radical product innovations, they may lose to their Japanese competitors when the strategic focus shifts from product to process innovation. This can happen simply because individually isolated firms fail to maintain their capabilities, in addition to their disadvantage in incremental improvement. With increasing emphasis on strategic alliances and partnerships, this situation has somehow changed during the 1990s, giving US firms competitive advantage in the fast emerging and changing sectors of information technology and e-business.

Connectual government and knowledge creation

In addition to all the advantages of *keiretsu*, Japanese firms have another powerful tool for enhancing their competitive advantage – the Japanese government, especially MITI. While the positive role of MITI in assisting the rise of certain Japanese high-tech industries is widely acknowledged (Okimoto, 1989), the nature of the assistance is not. From the knowledge regime perspective, the Japanese government can be seen as both the enabler for connectual governance and an indispensable organizer in the Japanese system of knowledge creation.

Indeed, as Okuno-Fujiwara (1997) rightly points out, in contrast to the *rule-based* US government, the post-war Japanese government is *relation based*. In observing the importance of informal relationships between government officials and business leaders, Okimoto (1989: 155) notes that: 'if its officials did not devote so much time and energy to cultivating personal relationships with key leaders in the private sector, MITI would not be nearly as effective as it is.' In describing the nature of personal relationships, he (1989: 157) further observes:

> Over the course of repeated contact, during which the boundaries between work-related interaction and personal socializing become blurred, the relationship between MITI bureaucrats and industrialists often moves beyond what is purely business into the realm of personal friendship ... The blurring together of professional and personal ties gives government-business relations their distinctively Japanese flavor. This phenomenon might be described as the 'personalization' of professional interactions, or the intrusion of affective bonds into the domain of public policy making.

The long-term personal ties between MITI officials and industrialists are forms of connectual governance that promote trust, reciprocity, and cooperation, and facilitate the sharing of information and knowledge between MITI officials and industrialists, as Okimoto (1989: 156) puts it:

> Japanese policy networks are extensive and serve as channels for the transmission of valuable information. Business executives are often willing to take MITI officials into their confidence, sharing sensitive information, even to the extent of divulging what may be proprietary in nature. This is done on the basis of reciprocal, confidential disclosure. Each side is expected to give information of roughly equivalent value to the information that is received and to keep what is received strictly confidential.

The effective exchange of sensitive information and knowledge between MITI officials and business leaders is certainly the basis for MITI's success in formulating and implementing certain industrial policies. MITI's role in connecting competing business firms together through its industrial policy is also a key factor.

MITI's efforts are, however, not without failure. First, when the boundaries of public and private interests are blurred, this often leads to cronyism and favoritism that has had consequences in the East Asian financial crisis in the period 1997–1998. Second, the cozy relationship between MITI and business leaders might have hindered the much-needed effort of restructuring and reengineering in the 1990s, which might have contributed to the prolonged Japanese recession. Third, while MITI had facilitated the catch-up of Japanese firms with the USA before the 1990s, it has shown little success in leading and directing Japanese efforts at the technological frontiers of innovation (Callon, 1995). The spontaneous, fast-changing and uncertain nature of technological change at the frontier makes the effort of planning and organizing ineffective. More importantly, as Austrian economists rightly argue, at the technological frontier, MITI bureaucrats simply do not have the knowledge and resources to dictate the emergence of new technological trajectories and new business paradigms (such as e-business). Indeed, any direct guidance by MITI can actually reduce the extent of experimentation and therefore lock the attention of Japanese firms into a losing technological trajectory such as mainframe computers (Callon, 1995).

Discussion: hybrid forms and the synergy of governance mechanisms

It is interesting to observe a dialectic learning and synergy process involved during the dynamic interaction between the US and Japanese systems of knowledge creation since the beginning of the twentieth century. As Adler and Cole (1993) and Tsutsui (1998) rightly point out, historically the emergence and dominance of the Japanese system of lean production itself has been the result of synthesizing American innovated principles of Taylorism and Fordism with Japanese ethos and ideologies. Conversely, the full articulation of the Japanese organizing principles imbedded in its lean production system and knowledge creation system has been a result of collaborative research between Japanese and American scholars. Just like the diffusion of the American system of mass production to Japan, the transplantation of the Japanese system, although traumatic, has also taken a hybrid form (Kenney and Florida, 1993; Abo, 1994). What is interesting in the process is the American superior capability in the articulation, transformation, and transcendence of the best Japanese practices such as lean production, JIT, TQM, concurrent engineering, and cross-functional teams. While many efforts of direct copying had failed, Americans have been able to create new fads that combine the Japanese principles and the

American ethos and preferences. Therefore, while JIT in Japan is relation-based, its US hybrid form is very much based on contract, electronic data interchange, and inter-organizational computing. While concurrent engineering in Japan relies on close and organic interaction among members of cross-functional teams, its US form depends on such software systems as computer-aided design (CAD) and computer-aided manufacturing (CAM) for concurrent coordination and automatic fit among design teams (Tapscott, 1996). While strategic alliance and partnership in Japan is long-term oriented and tightly coupled, its US variation is contract-based and loosely coupled. Further more, many US generated new managerial movement such as restructuring, reengineering, outsourcing, downsizing, strategic alliance, boundariless organization, competing on core competencies, supply chain management, and customer relationship management, while all indebted to a process of learning from Japan, have transcended Japanese practices by using information technology, instead of people, as the major tool for business transformation.

Indeed, with the fast advancement of information technology and e-business, many Japanese have recognized the need to learn from US practices again. As evidenced by the Japanese effort of reorganizing its R&D systems at both the government and business level in the 1990s (Hemmert and Oberlander, 1998), the Japanese system of connectual governance, including its lifetime employee systems, is in a process of dramatic transformation.

The recognition of the possibility of learning, synthesis, and transformation, however, does not mean that the US and Japanese systems of knowledge creation will converge someday in the future. Indeed, just as has happened in the past and in the USA recently, the new wave of Japanese learning from the USA will also take a hybrid form in which the technology push of imitating US practices will be dialectically interacting with the isomorphic pull of the Japanese cultural paradigm and organizing principles to form a new system of knowledge creation. In the end, rather than the convergence of governance mechanisms, the differing broad-scope isomorphism between cultural paradigms, organizing principles, governance mechanisms, technological trajectories, and knowledge regimes, although in new adaptive forms, will persist. So too will the sectoral patterns of national competitiveness.

Notes

1. For the concept of endogenous enforcement of contracts, see Bowles and Gintis (1993).
2. For the notion of the transformative potential of culture, see Tu (1996: 16).
3. For a detailed historical account, see Tsutsui (1998). Although he rightly observed the centrality of Taylorism in the emergence of the Japanese system of lean production, he failed to treat the impact from the perspective of synergy.

PART IV

Organizing for Competitiveness: Isomorphism and Sectoral Patterns

While Parts II and III have elaborated on the dominant cultural paradigms and governance mechanisms in the USA and Japan, this part will explore the relationships between dominant organizing principles of knowledge creation and the persistent sectoral patterns of US and Japanese competitiveness. Parallel to the isomorphism between cultural paradigms and governance mechanisms, there are also isomorphic relationships between cultural paradigms and organizing principles, between organizing principles and technological trajectories, and among organizing principles themselves. Indeed, as will be analyzed in this part, many organizing principles not only enable the realization of a nation's dominant cultural values, but also mutually reinforce and facilitate one another. They also act as attractors to pull the technological trajectories of a nation's sectors into a specific path that conforms to the nation's dominant cultural paradigm. It is this broad-scope isomorphism that has led to distinct, persistent sectoral patterns of US and Japanese competitiveness.

It is important to admit here that a nation's sectoral competitiveness is influenced by various historical, economic, social, institutional, organizational, and political forces. In many cases, it is shaped by historical events, individual visions, business strategies, and government policies. My purpose here is not to dismiss the influence of these forces, but rather to provide an integrative perspective that reveals the isomorphic structure underpinning these seemingly isolated forces. In so doing, I intend to identify and explain the sectoral pattern of national competitiveness that cannot be solely explained by either random historical forces or intentional business strategies and public policies.

CHAPTER SEVEN

Quantification vs. Contextualization

> In his striving for order, Western man has created chaos by denying that part of his self
> that integrates while enshrining the parts that fragment experience ... Western man uses
> only a small fraction of his mental capabilities; there are many different and legitimate
> ways of thinking; we in the West value one of these ways above all others – the one we
> call 'logic,' a linear system that has been with us since Socrates.
>
> Edward T. Hall (1976: 9)

More than twenty years ago, the American anthropologist Edward T. Hall brilliantly
observed that the USA is a *low-context* society whereas Japan is a *high-context* one.
Where the exchange of information and knowledge is concerned, he (1976: 91) notes:

> A high context communication or message is one in which *most* of the information is
> already in person, while very little is in the coded, explicit, transmitted part of the
> message. A low context communication is just the opposite; that is, the mass of the
> information is vested in the explicit code.

From the knowledge regime perspective, low-context vs. high-context communication is very much the result of the contractual vs. connectual cultural paradigm.
Under the dominance of the contractual cultural paradigm, individuals seek
autonomy and independence both in human relations and in knowing and learning,
which in turn leads to the dominance of *separate knowing* that focuses on the
creation and exchange of low-context, codified, and explicit information and
knowledge. Reciprocally, the focus on the creation and exchange of low-context,
codified, and explicit information and knowledge increases an individual's
independence and autonomy in the knowledge creation process. The exogenous
enforcement of contractual exchange through an impartial third party – the state –
further strengthens the need for low-context, codified, and explicit information and
knowledge, which is independent of knowledge holders and transactional partners.

In contrast, in Japan, under the dominance of the connectual cultural paradigm,
individuals seek long-term interdependence and mutual obligations. The *idiosyncratic* nature of connections, the trust based on relations, and the endogenous
enforcement of connectual exchange within connectual structures all require that
individuals within a connectual structure have a contextual, personalized, and
empathetic understanding of one another. This leads to the dominance of the types
of knowing that are tacit, connectual, contextual, and empathetic. Indeed, in
noticing the human relations root of the difference of low-context vs. high-context
culture, Hall (1990: 6) remarks,

> Japanese, Arab, and Mediterranean peoples, who have extensive information networks
> among family, friends, colleagues, and clients and who are involved in *close personal
> relationships*, are high context. As a result, for most normal transactions in daily life
> they do not require, nor do they expect, much in-depth, background information. This
> is because they keep themselves informed about *everything* having to do with people

who are important in their lives. Low-context people include Americans, Germans, Swiss, Scandinavians, and other northern Europeans; they *compartmentalize* their personal relationships, their work, and many aspects of day-to-day life. Consequently, each time they interact with others they need detailed background information. (*Italics added.*)

Similarly, in describing the Japanese model of knowledge creation, Nonaka (1991: 97) observes:

The centerpiece of the Japanese approach is the recognition that creating new knowledge is not simply a matter of 'processing' *objective* information. Rather, it depends on taping the *tacit* and often highly *subjective* insights, intuitions, and hunches of individual employees and making those insights available for testing and use by the company as a whole. (*Italics added.*)

The competitive implications of the two grand types of knowing, separate, explicit, and low-context vs. connectual, tacit, and high-context, are fundamental. Historically, according to Max Weber (1983), the Western drive for quantitative calculation and analysis of every aspect of an economic transaction has been the very foundation of the rise of rational capitalism that was uniquely Western. More recently, Alfred W. Crosby (1997), in his study of the history of quantification in the Western world since 1250, attributes the rise of the West to its *habit of thought* inherent in a new quantitative model of reality. This model, which developed during the Middle Ages and the Renaissance, had led to the development of universal measurement, double entry book-keeping, precise spatial representation, geographical survey, visual presentation of music through systems of notation, and above all, empirical science. According to Crosby, all these innovations in turn enhanced the ability of Western nations efficiently to harness the potential power of the material world for human well-being through the organization of a large number of people and capital for production and exchange. Indeed, as Weber (1983) rightly points out, the rational pursuits of science, of profits, of economic, legal, social, and administrative affairs were all only developed and matured in the West. By its nature, these pursuits were different from the Eastern way of knowing in the fact that the knowing process is separate, independent, empirical, systematic, specialized, and quantitative. According to Weber (1983: 26), 'the modern rational organization of capitalistic enterprise would not have been possible without ... the separation of business from household ... and, closely connected with it, rational book-keeping.' On the other hand, East Asian nations such as China failed to develop rational capitalism because 'the indispensable requisites for this independence, our rational business book-keeping and our legal separation of corporate from personal property, were entirely lacking, or had only just begun to develop.' What is important here is Weber's implicit linkage between the pursuit of independence and the system of rational book-keeping, a specific form of quantification. Not incidentally, the gradual Western adoption of a quantitative model had coincided with the rise of individualism. Indeed, such a linkage is the key for our understanding of the quantification zeal in Frederick Taylor's time-and-motion study, in Henry Ford's pursuit of standardization, in the McDonaldization of society, and in the most recent rush to digitalization and e-business. This has facilitated the American dominance not only in mass production but also in the new information and communication revolution. In the current conditions, the American drive for the systematic collection, storage, exchange, and application of explicit, objective, and quantitative information has contributed to its competitiveness in information services, consulting, fast food service, and quantitative marketing research.

In contrast, historically the cultural paradigm of connectual man had led to the dearth of quantification in both China and Japan. Although Japan has gone a long way in learning the quantitative model of the West since the mid-nineteenth century, as is particularly evidenced in its wide adoption of statistical quality control and the Taylorist principles of standardization after World War II (Tsutsui, 1998), it has affected only a handful of Japanese manufacturing sectors such as automobiles and electronics, which had the greatest international exposure. The dominant way of knowing in Japan is still connectual, tacit, and contextual. This is true even in the sectors of automobiles, opto-electronics, and mechatronics, where the synergy of quantification and connectual knowing has led to Japanese competitiveness. On the other hand, the lack of codification and quantification has contributed to the Japanese competitive disadvantage in less internationally exposed sectors such as information services where such a process of quantification is of vital importance for competitiveness.

Objectification as a means of autonomy and independence: the US advantage and disadvantage

The American emphasis on separate knowing and low-context communication, and the resultant focus on explicit, scientific, objective, quantitative, and analytic knowledge is very much the product of the American pursuit of autonomy and independence and, ultimately, the Anglo-American model of contractual man. Only when knowledge is presented in an explicit form can contractual transactions be implemented with low transaction costs. Only when outcomes can be measured objectively and quantitatively can transactions be honored without possible future disputes.

To Anglo-American minds preoccupied with the contractual mental model, a transaction based on the tacit knowledge or subjective judgment of their transacting partners is equivalent to succumbing themselves to the tyranny, or 'opportunism,' in Williamson's (1985) terms, of the latter. After all, the use of tacit, subjective, and contextual knowledge leaves individuals dependent on the judgment of others, a situation which makes them prone to opportunistic manipulation, adverse selection, and moral hazards. Conversely, the use of explicit, objective, and quantitative information enables the separation of the knowledge from its holders and gives individuals a complete control over transactional terms and their implementation in contracting with others. In other words, the use of explicit, objective, and quantitative knowledge *enables* the autonomy and independence of individuals in a world of interdependent economic exchange. The *objectification* and *quantification* of knowledge makes possible the separation of the knowledge and those holding it, of the knowers and the known, and of knowledge and its contextual environment. The result is the *depersonalization* and *decontextualization* of knowledge, making it independent of and separate from its personal link and contextual environment. In sum, both objectification and quantification are the key processes of separate, explicit, and decontextualized knowing that are predominant in the USA.

In linking the pursuit of objectivity to the Western ideal of *separateness*, Schmitt (1995: 129) observes that:

> Objectivity therefore consists of distancing oneself from all that is *personal* and *idiosyncratic* about oneself – from everything one does not share with all other members of the community of inquiry. It consists of, in the words of John Dewey, discounting 'merely *personal* factors' in the pursuit of knowledge. (*Italics added.*)

From the knowledge regime perspective, objectivity is a means of keeping one's autonomy and independence and maintaining one's separateness from others. Such a causal link has led to a penchant for explicit, objective, and quantitative knowledge in Anglo-American societies. Individual rights, including property rights, are expressed in a detailed and explicit form. Land tenures and townships are divided into uniform square miles, disregarding the natural shapes of mountains and rivers. Contracts are specific, concrete, and measured in quantifiable terms. All kinds of accounting and financial information are systematically collected, stored, assembled, and analyzed as a means of organizational control and for the provision of the tools for implementing contracts. In large and unionized firms, a contract between the labor and management can contain thousands of pages, as do the operating manual of McDonald's and the policy manuals of an American university.

According to Cohen (1982), Americans since the colonial period have shown a great zeal for quantification. Americans embraced numbers because they were hard facts, reliable, objective, and independent of personal judgment. By the mid-nineteenth century, the prestige and popularity of quantification was firmly established. Extending throughout the twentieth century up to now, the infatuation Americans have with numbers has fundamentally changed every aspect of their economic, social, and political life. Porter (1995) observes the prevalence of *trust in numbers* in modern Anglo-American society. Similarly, Innes (1990) notes the strong preference of quantitative indicators for policy-making in the USA. Such a reliance on quantitative figures can be found everywhere in modern American life. Politicians rely on polling numbers to understand the shift in public attitudes. Corporate leaders use numbers gleaned from formal marketing research for the prediction of consumer preferences. Wall Street brokers depend on numbers such as sales, profits, return on investment, return on assets, price-earning ratio, and others for their decisions about buying and selling stocks. Transnational chief executive officers (CEOs) utilize these same numbers to make strategic decisions and to manage and control their organizational divisions.

Since numbers are themselves explicit, quantitative, depersonalized, and decontextualized, in order to achieve them there must be a process of externalization, quantification, depersonalization, and decontextualization. This is exactly what has happened in the USA. The quantification tools widely used in the USA include financial accounting, information systems, statistics, formalized marketing research, standardization and Taylorism, and most recently digitalization.

Money as a tool for quantification

One of the best tools that human beings have invented to aid the process of quantification, depersonalization, and decontextualization, and therefore to maximize individual autonomy and independence, is the use of *money*, both as a commensurable measure of values and as a powerful tool for exchange. Money enables universal exchange of goods and services, overcoming the personalized and idiosyncratic nature of trade through barter. Money makes it possible for people to calculate the values of idiosyncratic goods under the same standardized and decontextualized measure, without altering the *idiosyncratic* nature of goods. Money also provides commensurability in measuring customers' preferences for goods without the need to familiarize the idiosyncrasies involved. These utilities of money enable people to engage in a contractual exchange with others without the need to have an in-depth knowledge of, or a long-term relationship with, each other. The use of money greatly reduces the complexity and therefore the transaction costs involved in the exchange of goods and services. It also maximizes the freedom, autonomy, and independence of individuals involved in the exchange relationship.

In evaluating the power of the money nexus in pure bourgeois capitalism, Karl Marx and Friederich Engels declared in their famous *Communist Manifesto*:

> The bourgeoisie has put an end to all feudal, patriarchal, idyllic relations. It has ... left remaining no other nexus than between man and man other than naked self-interest, than callous 'cash payment.' It has drowned the most heavenly ecstasies ... into the icy waters of egotistical calculation. It has resolved personal worth into exchange value... [The bourgeoisie] has converted the physician, the lawyer, the priest, the poet, the man of science, into wage-laborers. [It] has torn away from the family its sentimental veil and has reduced the family relation to a mere money relation. (Quoted in Arrow, 1996: 757)

To the extent that the USA is the purest bourgeois society (Lipset, 1996), it is understandable that the 'cash nexus,' or in our terms, the contractual transaction, is more predominant in the USA than in any other industrial societies. Through the prevalent use of money as the media of exchange, contractual transactions are *standardized, depersonalized, and decontextualized* into quantitative monetary terms. These terms in turn become the sole concern for contractual transactions, suppressing the impact of personal relations. It is in this context that we can understand that most managers in the USA have a financial background, while most of their Japanese counterparts come from technical backgrounds.

The competitive market as a tool for quantification

The mere use of money cannot transform all goods and services into monetary terms if it is not complementarily supported by the competitive market. When the value of a good is determined through a competitive bidding process, it transcends the personal and contextual influence in assessment. In other words, the competitive market process is a tool for quantification, depersonalization, and decontextualization, which in turn facilitates the autonomy and independence of individuals. It is this causal link that has led to the American persistent adherence to neoclassical economics and its model of the competitive market. The competitive bidding process is prevalent not only in business transactions but also in awards of government contracts.

Accounting as a means of separate, explicit, and decontextualized knowing

As a result of the dominance of the cash nexus and the competitive market process, both within and beyond the domain of market governance, various new practices of accounting have emerged and have become the dominant forms of information collection that assist in the governance of contractual relations. Financial accounting tries to systematically collect, record, store, and calculate monetary data to govern financial transactions between firms and monitor the performance of managers. By habitually using external accountants to audit the financial statements of public firms, these firms are able to also 'offer independent and expert assurance to shareholders and other interested parties that the books were fair and honest' (Porter, 1995: 91). Cost and managerial accounting, which have emerged, matured, and are still dominant in the USA, systematically codify information governing internal operations of a firm and its labor process. For managers, the systematic recording of accounting information frees them from their original dependency on shop-floor workers for process-based knowledge. The managers can therefore use the *separate* and *independent* record and collection of financial, cost, and managerial accounting to control the labor process and to prevent the opportunistic behavior of workers (Hopper and Armstrong, 1991). For unions, accounting information is also a powerful tool in bargaining for wage increases. Because of their emphasis on the cash nexus, US companies have a greater inclination than their Japanese counter-parts to use pure financial measures, such as return on investment (ROI) and profit, as the only criteria for measuring the performance of their divisions and whole companies (Sakurai *et al.*, 1989). The M-form organization, together with such accounting innovations as standard costs and transfer prices, further facilitates the use of ROI for management to control divisional operations (Johnson, 1992).

The use of accounting information as a major tool of governance is a double-edged sword for American competitiveness. On the positive side, first, it facilitated the rise of investor or managerial capitalism and the ascendancy and dominance of mass production (Drucker, 1990; Hopper and Armstrong, 1991). It therefore contributed significantly to the rise of the USA in the late nineteenth and the first half of the twentieth century (Bryer, 1993). With the separate collection and reporting of financial information, financial accounting enables investors and shareholders to *remotely* control the financial performance of managers without being opportunistically manipulated. The innovation of cost accounting also enabled managers to control the financial performance of divisions and workers, making possible the growth of firms far beyond the limited span of personal control.

Second, the American tendency to use accounting as the dominant tool for separate, explicit, and decontextualized knowing has facilitated the creation of a world-class sector of accounting services. The six big US accounting firms, such as Arthur Andersen and Ernst & Young, are among the ten largest in the world. They dominate the world market for accounting services. The strength of accounting services also helps US competitiveness in the banking and retailing sectors.

However, the focus on financial information as a tool of governance also creates many disadvantages for US firms. First, as financial data are always past- and present-based, an overreliance on financial measures, such as ROI, may give rise to short-term time horizons in investment decisions, which in the judgment of such authors as Dertouzos *et al.* (1989) and Porter (1992) has contributed to the US decline in competitiveness. Second, the overreliance on short-term financial performance may further hamper investment in the core capabilities and competencies that are hard to measure financially but are crucial for competitive success (Baldwin and Clark, 1994). Third, according to Johnson (1992), the overreliance on accounting information as a primary tool for governance has contributed to the dominance of what he called '*remote-control management*' in corporate America, leading to management's loss of *relevance* to shop-floor realities. Fourth, according to Drucker (1990), traditional cost accounting in the USA focuses on direct labor costs, neglecting not only indirect costs of nonproducing but also benefits of product and process improvement. Fifth and perhaps the most significant, the overreliance on separate, explicit, quantitative, and decontextualized information leads to the inability to create and appropriate tacit, connectual, qualitative, and contextual knowledge, which in turn leads to weakness in incremental improvement.

The US advantage in database and other information services

The reliance on explicit, objective, and quantitative information in the USA as a dominant tool of governance has facilitated and enabled the formation of a robust infrastructure for the systematic production, collection, diffusion, and exchange of these types of information beyond the domain of accounting. Such infrastructures include large-scale databases of retail transactions, credit history, financial transactions, and electronic data interchange (EDI), data warehouse, and data-mining. These have nurtured US competitiveness in the sectors of information processing, information services, and most recently e-business.

Standardization as a tool for quantification

The American capability to systematically quantify contractual transactions lies not only in the penchant for separate, explicit, and decontextualized knowing, but also in the standardization process that *decontextualizes* transactional situations. The standardization of costs, skills, job descriptions, tasks, parts, rules, routines, and procedures, as outlined in chapter 5, all facilitate the homogenization, deperson-alization, decontextualization, and finally codification and quantification of contractual transactions. Essentially, standardization is a process in which personal and situational idiosyncrasies are overcome, contexts are either removed or homogenized, and quality and other qualitative variations are minimized. Once this is achieved, the standardized costs, skills, jobs, tasks, parts, and procedures become identical, interchangeable, commensurable, and finally *quantifiable* and *calculable*. In sum, standardization becomes a tool for quantification.

The best example of the standardization process is McDonald's design and production of hamburgers. The pervasive standardization in McDonald's trans-formed the once idiosyncratic provision of hamburgers into a new form of service that provided efficiency, calculability, predictability, and controllability (Ritzer, 1995) that fit very well with the American penchant for autonomy and independence.

Because of this, the organizing principles of standardization, homogenization, depersonalization, decontextualization, and quantification that were imbedded in McDonald's practices have transformed every type of service sector in American society, ranging from fast food services, to soft drinks, banking, insurance, retailing, hotel services, car rental, entertainment, higher education, health care, religious services, and even funeral services (Ritzer, 1995).

In the banking and financial sector, individuals' credit is ranked numerically according to a systematic record and analysis of their financial transactions. In the retailing sector, every individual product is reduced to a standardized bar code and an attached price so that retail transactions are systematically recorded and analyzed for the management of inventory, advertisement, delivery, and production schedule (Morton, 1994). In the mail order and telemarketing sector, customers are standardized into mere phone numbers, street addresses, and zip codes so that phone calls and mail can go through. In US managed health care systems, a health policyholder becomes just a policy number whose premium and extent of reimbursed health care is determined by some abstract data about individual characteristics and standard formulae derived from statistical analysis. In higher education, the degree of knowledge acquisition is also standardized into some number of credits that are commensurable and calculable to add to a certain minimal number for a standardized degree. In the capital investment sector, individual stocks are standardized into different scales of risks and earning potentials and then become substitutable parts of a 'portfolio' that contains the best combination of stocks according to a decontextualized calculation of risks and expected earning potential.

Indeed, as a result of the diffusion of the organizing principles of standardization, combined with exports and FDI investment by US firms, there has been a process of standardization at the global level, which homogenizes both products and brands (Levitt, 1983). Empirically, according to Whitelock and Pimblett (1997), from 1973 to 1983, of the US export to the European Community, the percentage of nondurable customer goods with very substantial levels of standardization rose from 25 per cent to 42 per cent, while that of durable goods rose from 25 per cent to 38 per cent. It is clear that nondurable goods are much easier to standardize because of their simplicity in product characteristics and their production.

Statistics as a tool of depersonalization and decontextualization

The depersonalization and decontextualization process is further facilitated by the widespread use of statistics in US business. By pooling a large number of samples, random individual variations are offset by one another so that only an abstract mean and a standard variation become useful measurements. In so doing, individual persons and objects lose their identity and context and are reformulated and standardized into *average* persons and objects whose *average* characteristics are calculable.

In the automobile insurance sector, the policyholder's premium is calculated *impersonally* according to a standardized formula that takes into consideration the policyholder's points of traffic violations, years of driving experience, age, sex, driving distance, car model, and so on. Here, although personal information is used in the calculation, the formula is strictly derived from impersonal statistical estimations of the risks of accident *only* in relation to the statistical *average* and the abstract, calculable and explicit data, without considering the *contextual* information about individuals' real driving behaviors and risks. The same is true for entertainers. For them, potential viewers are not an audience with *idiosyncratic* preferences but belong to a standardized category with certain standardized tastes for certain standardized entertainment products. All these are calculated through formal marketing surveys and statistical analyses of a given sample of individuals belonging to certain categories.

Because of the American penchant for separate, explicit, and decontextualized knowledge, the application of statistical techniques to the study of consumer preferences constitutes the dominant form of marketing research in the USA. All the methods used in formalized marketing research, such as the use of third-party and external consultants in conducting research, the random sampling and abstract categorization of the population, and the standard statistical analysis of mean and variance, are powerful tools for quantification, depersonalization, and decontextualization.

Taylorism as a theory of separate knowing in management

Once we understand the causal linkage between the contractual cultural paradigm and the penchant for separate, explicit, and decontextualized knowing, we can understand why the emergence of Taylorism in the USA was not simply a lock-in of Frederick Taylor's innovation, but an expression of American disenchantment with the craft mode of production, which was transplanted from Europe, and with its reliance on tacit knowing. The whole Scientific Management movement promoted by Frederick Taylor was a process that substituted the explicit knower of mass production for the tacit knower of craft production, and replaced the tacit knowledge of craft masters with the explicit knowledge of industrial engineers. It is also a process of substituting the separate and decontextualized knower of outside consultants for the connectual and contextual knower of shop-floor craftsmen and foremen. All principles of Taylorism are the expression of the American preference for separate, explicit, and decontextualized knowing and, above all, their desire for autonomy and independence. These principles include *quantified* time-and-motion study, the separation of knowing from acting, the standardization of operating procedures, the systematic collection of performance information, and the establishment of management control systems to prevent '*soldiering*,' or in modern terms 'shirking' and 'opportunism.'

In seeking the causal link between Taylor's effort of codification and the management goals of independence and control, Jelinek (1979: 135) observes: 'Taylor sought explicitly to record and codify in order to render the organization less *dependent* on the memory, good will, or physical presence of any particular employee (*Italics added*).' The Taylorist zeal for quantification and for separate knowing permanently changed not only the industrial landscape of the USA but also the fate of all human beings through its diffusion through the world. Through Taylor's revelation of the organizing principles of separate knowing, human beings were able for the first time in world history to break out of the trap and tyranny of craft production which inherently limited our capacity for knowledge creation and for the mass production and consumption of goods.

Ironically, with the innovation and dominance of the Japanese flexible production system, Taylor's organizing principles of separate knowing, including its separation of thinking from acting, and its emphasis on functional specialization and quantification were all criticized as an impediment to further knowledge creation. Such a paradox can be solved first by Hegel's dialectics and second by the sectoral perspective used in this book. From the perspective of Hegelian dialectics, while Taylor's organizing principles and resultant mass production were the refutation and transcendence of craft production and its organizing principles, Japanese flexible production is the refutation and transcendence of the organizing principles of mass production. Mass production was not only an indispensable stage in the evolution toward flexible production, the organizing principles of the former were also absorbed, digested, and fused into the operation of the latter (Adler and Core, 1993). From the sectoral perspective, although it was transcended and therefore superseded in some sectors such as opto-electronics, Taylorism is still a very effective means of knowledge creation in some other sectors such as chemicals, and other processing sectors. Indeed, as will be analyzed later, Taylorist principles are also underpinning the very rise of the digital economy and e-businesses in the USA in the mid- and late 1990s.

Quantification as a tool for strategic planning

In the field of management, the Anglo-American drive for quantification is best revealed in its obsession with formal strategic planning. According to Mintzberg (1994), the leading scholar who vehemently criticized quantification, the 'grandest assumption' underlying such an obsession is the notion that 'analysis can provide synthesis' (p. 223). Following this is the *assumption of detachment* in which 'thought must be detached from action, strategy from operations, ostensible thinking from real doers, and therefore "strategists" from the object of their strategies' (p. 223). This principle of detachment is further supported by the *assumption of quantification* in which 'the strategic making process is driven by "hard data," comprising quantitative aggregates of the detailed "facts about the organization and its environment."' (pp. 223–224).

From the knowledge regime perspective, all these assumptions are the result and therefore evidence of the Anglo-American drive for separate, analytic, and decontextualized knowing. Without these assumptions, the autonomy and independence of top managers will be threatened. Actually, Mintzberg himself recognized such a linkage, as he (p. 234) notes:

> Having to probe into the messy world of details would force senior managers off their pedestals and, even worse, force planners to leave the comfort of the staff for the pressure of the line. Unless, of course, all the necessary data could be collected and combined, packaged conveniently and delivered regularly. Thus, enter the so called management information system (MIS), or in its latest rendition, a 'strategic information system.'

Not only are quantitative data systematically collected and separately analyzed for strategic control and planning, but according to Allaire and Firsirotu (1990), various quantitative indicators involved in strategic planning are also used as the basis of *contracts* that provide incentives for managers. Indeed, the Anglo-American model of strategic analysis has reached such a point that the Boston Consulting Group rationalizes Honda's successful inroad into the US motorcycle markets through a lens of rational analysis and quantitative justification, although the real process is messy and involved much learning by trying and improvising (Pascale, 1984).

In contrast to this obsession of analysis, detachment, and quantification, the Japanese way of strategic management pays every attention to qualitative thinking, contextual situations, and specific tasks, as Lauenstein (1993: 241–2) puts it:

> Japanese tend to guide their actions more by practical requirements of a specific situation than by abstract rationalization. They prefer to approach business situations on a case-by-case basis rather than to commit to follow predetermined principles ... The Japanese executives are more oriented to qualitative than quantitative strategic thinking. They express skepticism about anyone's ability to forecast the future in specific terms.

To the extent that they do not follow the Anglo-American model, the prominent developer of this model, Michael Porter (1996), argues that Japanese firms don't have strategies!

Notwithstanding Mintzberg's criticism, formal strategic planning is not without its advantages. First, it focuses attention on systematic collection and analysis of data and on explicit articulation of basic assumptions, and therefore forces people to think systematically and with foresight. Second, it facilitates the articulation, systemization, and integration of various factors affecting a firm's competitive advantage in various industrial sectors, as represented by Porter's work (1985). To this point, the advocates of the systematic approach to strategic management such as Jelinek (1979) are still correct. Indeed, the very capability of the US business consulting industry to analyze the future pattern of competitive advantage as well as the management willingness to seek and follow systematic advice has been one of the contributing factors for the rapid rise of mass customization and e-business. On the other hand, with the increasing advance of new information technology and the tremendously increased pace of change, the Japanese way of strategic management, which is by and large *ad hoc* and intuitive, has already shown many of its negative impacts.

The competitive advantages and disadvantages of quantification

More generally, the competitive implications of the American preference for separate, explicit, and decontextualized knowing and the resultant dominance of the organizing principles of quantification, depersonalization, and decontextualization are like a double-edged sword whose impact is sector-contingent. On the positive side, they have contributed significantly not only to the rise of mass production and managerial capitalism but also to the consistent American success in accounting services, databases, information processing, fast food, soft drinks, warehouse retailing, entertainment, banking, credit reporting, car rental, hotel, health care management, insurance, and marketing research. On the negative side, these same organizing principles are also responsible for the American decline in sectors such as automobiles and consumer electronics where the old paradigm of separate knowing and mass production alone can no longer work effectively.

As early as 1982, in their hugely successful book, *In Search of Excellence*, Peters and Waterman (1982) attribute the failure of many US firms to the penchant of their CEOs for quantification. In an influential article, Hayes and Abernathy (1980) also trace the decline of many US sectors to the 'new management orthodoxy' that places too much emphasis on quantifiable short-term financial criteria and too little on hands-on experience and non-quantifiable non-financial criteria. In his systematic critique on the Anglo-American tendency of relying on 'hard data' for strategy making, Mintzberg (1994: 259–266) offers the following points:

> Hard information is often limited in scope, lacking richness and often failing to encompass important noneconomic and non-quantitative factors.
> Much hard information is too aggregated for effective use in strategy making.
> Much hard information arrives too late to be of use in strategy making.
> Finally, a surprising amount of hard information is unreliable.

With the increasing pace of digitalization, some of the above problems can be solved. Indeed, the US penchant for codification and quantification is the very underlying force that has pulled it to the frontier of the emerging digital economy. Reciprocally, this new trend of digitalization has shifted the pendulum of competitiveness to the US side, giving many US companies a huge competitive advantage.

Notwithstanding this advantage, even in the digital age, in the drive for hard data what is missing are the opportunities for creating and applying tacit, contextual, connectual, and task-, industry- and firm-specific knowledge for both strategy-making and technological innovations. Put it another way, *at the center of the problem is the fact that quite a few forms of knowledge that are crucial for the competitiveness of many sectors are difficult to quantify, standardize, decontextualize, and objectify, nor can they easily be transformed from tacit to explicit, from connectual to separate, or from contextual to propositional.* An overemphasis on the latter forms of knowledge as the only legitimate ones, leave the former forms of knowledge, whose creation and application are of vital importance for international competitiveness in many sectors, out of the running and, therefore, cause competitive disadvantage.

Contextualization as a means of connectual knowing: the Japanese advantage and disadvantage

In contrast to the American emphasis on explicit, objective, and quantitative information and knowledge, Japanese culture has always emphasized the tacit, subjective, connectual, contextual, and qualitative parts of knowledge. A cultural penchant for interdependence and mutual obligations leads to the Japanese focus on mutual understanding through tacit, connectual, contextual, and sympathized knowing. Unlike individual rights under contractual governance in the West that can always be demarcated and self-contained, mutual obligations under connectual governance in Japan are always tacit, connectual, contextual, and empathetic. To the Japanese mind, as well as those of all other East Asian societies, an obligation that is clearly stated loses its value in connecting two persons because the very act of demarcating obligations destroys the sense of unity, identification, interdependence, trust, and loyalty that are shared by connected members.

The same is true for tacit knowledge. In the epistemology of Taoism, the Tao that is articulated is no longer a *genuine* Tao. At the center of the Taoist denial of any forms of explicit knowledge as *genuine* knowledge rests a firm assertion of oneness and unity among 'Heaven, Earth, and Human-beings.' Such oneness requires the unity of knowing and acting, of body and mind, of human beings and their environment, and of individuals and their connectual structures of families, clans, villages, communities, corporations, and societies at large. As a result of this holistic world-view, any effort to separate knowing from feeling, knowing from acting, the knower from the known, and the observed object from its environment, as dominant in Western epistemology, is not a legitimate way of acquiring *genuine* knowledge in the East in general and in Japan in particular.

Here the contrast between the Eastern and Western notion of *genuine* knowledge could not be sharper. While in the East, any decontextualized form of knowledge is seen as not *genuine* and therefore treated with great suspicion, in the West only decontextualized and propositional knowledge is seen as *genuine* and therefore valued highly. It is within this context that we can understand why the philosopher Michael Polanyi (1958/1964) took pains to legitimize tacit knowledge as late as 1958 and the organizational scientist Mintzberg (1976, 1994) had to continuously challenge the dominance of analytic and quantitative thinking in the Anglo-American management mainstream from the mid-1970s to the late 1990s.

Because of this emphasis on tacit, connectual, and contextual knowing, historically, China, Japan, and other East Asian societies failed to initiate any branch of sciences in the modern sense, even though China was ahead of the rest of the world in technological development until the sixteenth century (McNeil, 1995). After all, all sciences are the result of a pursuit of objectivity that separates the observer from the observed, mind from body, and the observed object from its environment. It is also because of a lack of emphasis on separate knowing that all East Asian societies failed to invent a system of mass production, even though countries such as China had developed mature craft production thousands years ago.

In modern times, although with a new emphasis on science and technology and mass production, the use of formal, explicit, quantitative, and decontextualized information in Japan is still far less frequent than in the USA. This is reflected in the Japanese lack of the systematic use of accounting (Hiromoto, 1988), formal credit recording, rating, reporting, and research (Dattel, 1994), formal marketing research (Johansson and Nonaka, 1993), and formal strategic planning (Porter, 1996). It is also evidenced by the Japanese reluctance to use such pure financial measures as ROI to justify investment projects (Duenyas *et al.*, 1995).

As shown in Table 7.1, US firms have a much higher propensity than their Japanese counterparts for adopting quantitative techniques in cost and managerial accounting practices. The difference is especially pronounced in the adoption of waiting lines, decision support systems, network analysis, probability/decision theory, mathematical and linear programming, in all of which the adoption rate in Japan is less than 25 per cent that of the USA.

If we dig deeper for the reasons of the lack of adoption of quantitative techniques, as shown in Table 7.2, the differences are even sharper. While Table 7.1 confirms my conjecture concerning the American penchant for quantification and the Japanese suspicion of it, Table 7.2 validates my postulate about the Japanese focus on

Table 7.1 Adoption of quantitative techniques in cost and managerial accounting practices: a US–Japan comparison

Quantitative Method	Adoption rate		Japan/USA (US = 100)
	USA	Japan	
Simulation	55.9	47.4	85
Forecasting techniques	69.9	50.6	72
Spreadsheet	94.2	63.7	68
Input/output analysis	31.4	19.9	63
Statistical analysis	61.8	36.5	59
Inventory methods	65.7	28.8	44
Linear programming	35.6	10.3	29
Probability/decision theory	38.2	9.6	25
Mathematical programming	22.5	5.1	23
Network analysis	46.8	6.4	14
Decision support systems	45.1	6.5	14
Waiting lines	2.0	0	0

Source: Adapted from Kato (1989: 456, 460).

Table 7.2 Ranks of perceived barriers to adopting quantitative methods*

	Japan	USA
Management distrust of using quantitative models	17	14
Necessary information for managers is not available from quantitative models	16	10
Required data are not available	15	7
Unrealistic assumptions of the model	14	4
Difficulties in understanding output information models	13	11
Key management personnel do not encourage use of models	12	12
Models require use of computer, and management are unwilling or unable to use computer for decision-making	11	16
Recent college graduates with quantitative training have not yet attained position of influence	10	17
Required data are difficult to quantify	9	2
Users of output information have little involvement or influence in the modeling process	8	13
Lack of proper reporting systems or channels to communicate output information to top management	7	15
High costs of acquiring the required data for the model	6	6
Management is successful without using quantitative models	5	5
Benefits of using models are not clearly understood by managers	4	1
High costs of developing and running models	3	9
Lack of knowledge of quantitative models by management and accounting personnel	2	8
Insufficient time for managers to examine the use of the model	1	3

* The higher the number, the higher the rank.
Source: Adapted from Kato (1989: 468).

connectual knowing and the American emphases on separate knowing and contractual governance. It indicates that the Japanese are reluctant to adopt quantitative techniques not because of a lack of knowledge, nor because of high costs of development and running, nor because of the management's inability to understand the benefits (these factors are ranked the lowest!). Rather, it is because managers distrust the use of quantitative models. They are interested in qualitative information that is not available from the model. They do not as often systematically record all the necessary data for quantitative analysis. And they think the abstract and decontextualized model unrealistic (these factors are ranked the highest as barriers!). In contrast, the most important barriers perceived by the USA are not the challenge to the assumptions of the model, nor the lack of data, but a contractual governance in which the well trained are not in the position of adopting quantitative techniques, of communicating to the top managers, and of using computers for decision-making. More interestingly, while the lack of knowledge of quantitative models is perceived as a moderately important barrier to adoption in the USA, it is the least important barrier in Japan!

The Japanese competitive advantage and disadvantage in banking and financing

The lack of systematic collection and application of accounting information in Japan for organizational control astonished many early Western observers. Indeed, from the Western mind of contractual man, it is really a paradox to find out that even though Japan has caught up with the USA in economic and technological development, its accounting structure has been lagging behind (Someya, 1996). In Japan formal credit research and market research were also rare until very recently. In the 1980s when Akio Mikuni tried to set up Japan's first independent credit rating firm, he faced great opposition from the Ministry of Finance, because credit rating was judged *un-Japanese* by the latter (Rohwer, 1998). With regard to Japanese financial institutions, Dattel (1994: 70) observes that 'in Japan, there was no precedent for analysis of private sector credits, as Japanese corporate issues were collaterized.' While prevalent American practices of credit recording, collecting, reporting and analyzing are very much the results of their penchant for autonomy and independence, the Japanese lack of it is due largely to their desire for connection and interdependence and their distrust of any forms of knowledge that are decontextualized. Yoshimura and Anderson (1997: 142) note vividly Japanese reluctance to use quantitative analysis in the financial sector:

> Despite being exposed to sophisticated quantitative methods, the Japanese had no intention of trying to use their newly developed financial analysis skills to help their companies. To a man, the salarymen were skeptical about quantitative forecasts. At best, they were viewed as adjuncts to the important considerations, which are qualitative. Said one respondent, 'When trouble happens, American employees often use the output from a computer to try to justify their decisions. I tell them they should doubt numbers.'

The widespread Japanese skepticism toward quantification is further evidenced by such facts as the unwillingness of investors to pay attention to quantitative analyses of stock market performance, the unused quantitative skills by American-trained

Japanese MBAs, and even the skepticism of numbers by those who produced them (Yoshimura and Anderson, 1997: 142–147).

A resort to decontextualized credit history and the system of reward and punishment based upon it enables US banks to grant credit to strangers. On the other hand, the tendency to base trusts only on personal and corporate connections makes Japanese banks focus their financial services on the interlocked and connected long-term customers. While US banks rely on explicit, objective, and quantitative information of financial transactions and the following analysis as a source to judge the trustworthiness of their customers, their Japanese counterparts rely on long-term mutual understanding and obligations as the basis for judgment and decision-making.

The competitive implications of the two systems of banking are sector-specific. In the financial sector itself, the American system enables efficient services for independent customers, whereas the Japanese system provides the best service for long-term inter-linked ones. When it comes to the spillover effect, while the American system of banking is best in providing venture capital for independent innovators, the Japanese system is most capable in providing long-term financial commitment for the building up of manufacturing capabilities whose short-term profits are difficult to calculate and justify. In regards to the globalization process, while the Japanese system of banking can best serve the worldwide expansion of affiliated firms, its globalization strategy is fraught with failure because of its inability to deal with strangers and to assess risks in a decontextualized environment (Dattel, 1994). When Japanese financial firms set up operations on Wall Street, many fail because they not only do not adopt analysis models, until very recently, but also downplay analysts' views, even though analysis is becoming increasingly important on Wall Street (Sullivan, 1995).

The Japanese competitive advantage and disadvantage in marketing research

The emphases on divergent forms of knowledge between the USA and Japan have also led to different marketing methods, strategies, and infrastructures. Because of their preference for explicit, objective, quantitative, and propositional knowledge, US firms emphasize formal, large-scale marketing research tools. On the other hand, the Japanese tendency toward connectual and contextual knowing leads to their focus on hands-on experience and direct empathetic knowing of consumer demands.

In their study of the Japanese style of marketing, Johansson and Nonaka (1993) observe that Sony's chairman Akio Morita decided to introduce the Walkman in spite of unfavorable results of a formal marketing survey. They (1993: 289) further note the widespread Japanese skepticism of formal market research tools:

> Morita's disdain for large-scale consumer surveys and scientific research tools isn't unique in Japan. Matsushita, Toyota, and other well-known Japanese consumer goods companies are just as skeptical about the Western style of market research. Occasionally, the Japanese do conduct consumer attitude surveys, but most executives don't base their marketing decisions on them or on other popular techniques. As the head of Matsushita's videocassette recorder division once said, 'Why do Americans do

so much marketing research? You can find out what you need by traveling around and visiting retailers who carry your product.'

Reflecting the general Japanese skepticism toward the American-style 'scientific market research,' the marketing director at Hitachi, Toru Nishikawa, offers the following reasons against using formal methods of consumer survey for new product development, as quoted by Czinkota and Kotabe (1998: 156):

Indifference: Careless random sampling causes mistaken judgement, since some people are indifferent toward the product in question.
Absence of responsibility: The customer is most sincere when spending, but not when talking.
Conservative attitude: Ordinary consumers are conservative and tend to react negatively to a new product.
Vanity: It is a human nature to exaggerate and put on a good appearance.
Insufficient information: The research results depend on the information about product characteristics given to survey participants.

Indeed, all the above problems are the result of the decontextualization imbedded in the formal market research process. To overcome them, Japanese firms prefer hands-on, 'down to earth,' and context-specific methods of information gathering about customer preferences (Czinkota and Kotabe, 1998). In summarizing the Japanese hands-on method of market research, Johanson and Nonaka (1987) observe that Japanese managers want both 'soft data' obtained from retailers, customers, and other channels and 'hard data' obtained from transactions about shipment, inventory, and retail sales. While 'hard data' are explicit, objective, quantitative, abstract, and context-free, 'soft data' are tacit, subjective, qualitative, concrete, and context-specific. The Japanese preference for, and trust in, 'soft data' derives not only from the Eastern epistemological emphasis on contextual and connectual knowing, but also from the Japanese infrastructure built around it. Long-term supplier–producer and producer–customer relationships enable not only an effective flow of contextual information about possible improvement opportunities, but also an accumulation of relation-specific knowledge and capabilities for the improvement of products, processes, and services.

On the other hand, the American preference for, and trust in, 'hard data' derives not only from the Anglo-American epistemological emphasis on separate knowing and objectivity, but also from the American system of accountability and the arm's length relationship between suppliers and producers and between producers and customers. When accountability is considered, while a failure based on personal judgment is the sole responsibility of the manager, a failure derived from the results of formal market research is not. Furthermore, the arm's length relationship between producers and retailers, between producers and suppliers, and between producers and consumers means that information feedback, especially 'soft data' from the latter, may not only be inaccurate, but could also be full of opportunistic manipulations. Indeed, transaction cost economists propose to use the codification of information or the design of a governance mechanism of vertical integration to overcome the problem of opportunism.

The reliance on 'soft data' creates both advantages and disadvantages for Japanese firms. To the extent that 'soft data' provides managers with context-rich knowledge that formal surveys and other quantitative research methods cannot supply, the Japanese style of market research provides rich information about possible future improvements in products, processes, and services. It will therefore offer a competitive edge for Japanese firms in the sectors where such qualitative feedback from retailers and consumers is vital for product and process improvement. In complex consumer products such as automobiles and consumer electronics, many complicated and esoteric dimensions of product characteristics exist, and contextual improvement opportunities exist everywhere in the producer–customer and supplier–producer interface. Here, the Japanese system of contextual knowledge creation and appropriation, including the production and exchange of 'soft data,' certainly provides a competitive edge.

Because of its contextual and connectual approach, the Japanese system of market research can not only reveal possible improvement opportunities, but can also enable the *articulation* of latent patterns of consumer demand. In Kodama's (1991) view, the superior Japanese capability for *demand articulation* has been one of the key elements for their competitiveness in many sectors. This is especially true in the sectors with a high degree of contextual linkages, such as automobiles and consumer electronics. Here, formal market research methods, as prevalent in the USA, can hardly reveal the *delicate* patterns of consumer behavior, nor can they articulate the *intricate* future demand pattern.

The landscape of competitiveness between US and Japanese market research reverses when we shift from complex to simple products and processes. In simple and standardized consumer products, such as soft drinks and consumer chemicals, there exist only limited product characteristics, rare contextual linkages between products and consumers, and few opportunities for contextual improvements. Consequently, large-scale formal market research can reveal the patterns of consumer behavior better than the informal method focused on soft data. The result is a competitive advantage for US firms in these sectors.

In addition, the emphasis on formal market research has led to American dominance in the sectors of marketing, advertisement, and opinion research. The focus on informal and hands-on market research has led to lackluster Japanese performance in the same sectors. As shown in Table 7.3, of the top 25 marketing research firms in 1996, the USA had 13, whereas Japan had only 3.

Moreover, no Japanese marketing firm entered the top ten list, whereas the USA had 5 in that list. More interestingly, although they had a smaller economy than Japan, the UK had 3 firms listed among the top 25, with one ranked third, while Germany also had 3. Overall, although having the same number of firms listed among the top 25, the average rank of Japanese firms was lower than that of British and German firms.

The US advantage in the digital economy

In this age of e-business and the digital economy, new tools of financial accounting such as activity-based accounting, combined with huge databases of customer information, enables US firms to conduct one-to-one marketing and mass customization. Business-to-business transactions are also increasingly taking the digital form with inter-organizational computing (US Department of Commerce, 1998). Indeed, the high propensity for systematic codification, collection, storage,

Table 7.3 Rank of top 25 global market/advertising/opinion research firms

1996	1995	Organization	Headquarters	Country
1		ACNielsen Corp.	Stamford, CT	USA
2		Cognizant Corp.	Westport, CT	USA
3	2	The Kantar Group Ltd	London	UK
4	3	Information Resources Inc.	Chicago, IL	USA
5	4	GIK AG	Nuremberg	Germany
6	5	SOFRES Group S.A.	Paris	France
7	6	Infratest Burke AG	Munich	Germany
8	8	IPSOS Group S.A.	Paris	France
9	10	The Arbitron Company	New York	USA
10	9	PMSI/Source Informatics	Phoenix, AZ	USA
11	11	Westat Inc.	Rockville, MD	USA
12	7	Video Research Ltd	Tokyo	Japan
13	12	Maritz Marketing Research, Inc.	St. Louis, MO	USA
14	13	NOP Information Group	London	UK
15	14	Taylor Nelson AGB Plc.	London	UK
16	17	NFO Research Inc.	Greenwich, CT	USA
17	16	The NPD Group Inc.	Port Washington, NY	USA
18	15	Marketing Intelligence Corp.	Tokyo	Japan
19	18	Market Facts Inc.	Arlington Heights, IL	USA
20	20	Audits & Surveys Worldwide Inc.	New York, NY	USA
21	22	Sample Institute GmbH & Co. KG	Molln	Germany
22	21	The M/A/R/C Group. Inc	Irving, TX	USA
23	19	Dentsu Research	Tokyo	Japan
24	26	The BASES Group	Covington, KY	USA
25	24	Goldfarb Consultants	Toronto	Canada

Source: Marketing News, Chicago, August 18, 1997.

and exchange of hard data about both customer transactions and business processes has given the USA a great competitive advantage in digital economy and e-business. By contrast, the suspicion concerning hard data has generated a competitive disadvantage for Japan in this new age.

The Japanese competitive advantage in tacit, contextual knowing

While Japan has competitive disadvantages in the production of 'hard data,' it has a great advantage in the production of 'soft data.' This is derived from its emphasis on tacit, connectual, and contextual knowing. According to Nonaka and Takeuchi (1995: 59): 'Tacit knowledge is personal, context-specific, and therefore hard to formalize and communicate. Explicit or "codified" knowledge, on the other hand, refers to knowledge that is transmittable in formal, systematic language.' Tacit knowledge derives from hands-on experience, empathy, intuitions, and a deep personal involvement with the known objects and their contextual environments. In Michael Polanyi's (1969: 160) words, tacit knowing 'appears as an act of *indwelling* by which we gain access to a new meaning.' Indwelling is a process in which we involve and commit both our mind and body to the known object and its contextual environment.

Here, knowing is no longer the cool observation of an external and separate object, as is the case in explicit knowing; rather, it is a passionate projection of oneself into the object to acquire the knowledge of it *empathetically* through unifying with it. Discussing the nature of tacit knowing in mastering a skill, Polanyi (1969: 160) observes that, 'when exercising a skill we literally dwell in the innumerable muscular acts which contribute to its purpose, a purpose which constitutes their joint meaning.'

Since tacit knowing requires integration between mind and body, the knower and the known, and the object and its environment, it is at odds with dominant Anglo-American epistemology which legitimates only those types of knowing that are detached, objective, quantifiable, decontextualized, and propositional (Schmitt, 1995). The need for *organic and contextual integration* and the impossibility of separation of the knower and the knowledge also render impossible individual autonomy and independence. As a result, tacit knowing is not preferred in Anglo-American societies. In contrast, as discussed previously, both Eastern holistic epistemology and the Japanese cultural paradigm of connectual man emphasize and facilitate tacit and contextual knowing.

In Japan, the emphasis on contextual knowing is facilitated by intra- and inter-firm transfer of engineers and the resultant broad on-the-job training. According to Kusunoki and Numagami (1997: 199), instead of a focus on universally defined technical skills, job transfer as training in Japan 'aimed to enhance various local skills needed for specific engineering tasks within the organization.' This contextual knowing in Japan has contributed to a much greater extent of customization and contextualization in both production technology and marketing strategies. As shown in Table 7.4, Japanese firms have a much higher tendency to use customized technology (including custom technology and small batch, job shop technology) than their US counterparts. The score of nonroutineness represents the extent of customization and contextualization.

Table 7.4 Comparison of production technology

Type of production technology	Score of nonroutineness	USA (%)	Japan (%)
Custom technology**	5	12.5	22.2
Small batch, job shop technology	4	14.8	17.7
Large batch technology***	3	35.4	24.5
Mass production technology	2	19.3	15.0
Continuous process technology	1	17.9	15.0
Average scores of nonroutineness*		2.86	3.05

*Significant at 0.05 level; ** 0.01 level; *** 0.001 level.

Japanese global expansion shows a similar tendency of customization. As indicated in Table 7.5, in the UK market, the Japanese subsidiaries have a statistically significant higher extent than their US counterparts in adapting their marketing strategies, promotions, distribution approaches, and pricing policies to

Table 7.5 Adoption of marketing strategies to the UK market: a US–Japan comparison (percentages)

	US	Japanese
Marketing strategies are modified to a great extent to suit the UK**	47	73
Products modified to a great extent to suit the UK	47	40
Promotions modified to a great extent to suit the UK**	57	80
Distribution approaches adapted to a great extent to suit the UK***	66	93
Pricing policies are adapted to suit the UK*	33	53

* Statistical significance is at the 20% level; ** 10% level; *** 5% level.
Source: Doyle *et al.* (1992: 434).

suit the UK's specific conditions.

According to Doyle *et al.* (1992), these differences in contextualization and customization have contributed to the relative success of the Japanese in the UK market. Similarly, in his study of the strategy of Japanese and US manufacturing investment in Europe, Dunning (1994: 70) finds that while US multinationals 'have a comparative advantage in the administration of *formalized* but more technical and *standardized* transactional relations,' their Japanese counterparts are 'especially successful in managing *idiosyncratic human-intensive* transnational relations.' (*Italics added*.)

In their study of the joint venture between Mitsubishi Heavy Industries Ltd of Japan and Caterpillar Inc. of the USA, Nonaka and Takeuchi (1995) also found that while Mitsubishi preferred customization, Caterpillar demanded standardization of both product and process design. In the design process, while Japanese engineers were adroit in sharing knowledge at the tacit level, their US partners were insistent on explicit articulation and documentation of accumulated knowledge.

Kaizen *and knowledge for incremental improvement: the Japanese advantage*

It is important to point out that at the individual level, entrepreneurs in the USA also rely heavily on tacit knowing, intuition, and empathy to acquire creative ideas (Leonard and Rayport, 1997). Moreover, learning by doing and by using at the individual level are also prevalent in the USA. As long as it is an individual endeavor, it remains a form of separate knowing. What makes the difference is the group and organizational level of such tacit and empathetic knowing. When individuals in Japanese firms share, transform, and integrate their tacit and connectual knowing through the socialization process, they create numerous improvement suggestions in the manufacturing processes, which in turn provide competitive advantages for Japanese firms to achieve flexibility, shrink lead-time, increase quality, and reduce costs.

Unlike the knowledge needed for technological breakthroughs, which is largely domain-specific, the knowledge required for incremental improvement is largely tacit, contextual, and relation-specific. While explicit, separate, and decontextualized knowledge can be created by heroic individuals in an isolated setting, connectual and relation-specific knowledge can only be brought about through hands-on shop-floor experience and various group processes of knowledge creation such as quality circles, job rotation, JIT, cross-functional teams, and concurrent engineering. These practices, which themselves are the results of the Japanese connectual cultural paradigm, have contributed significantly to superior Japanese capabilities in the creation, transformation, and appropriation of tacit, connectual, contextual, and relation-specific knowledge for incremental improvement. It has created a competitive advantage for Japanese firms in the sectors of automobiles, consumer electronics, opto-electronics, and mechatronics where a superior capability in incremental improvements is the key for competitive success.

In an influential book, Imai (1986) describes how the Japanese system of *Kaizen* – *'ongoing* improvement involving everyone – top management, managers, and workers' – has created a competitive edge for Japanese firms. As described in detail by Imai, knowledge about incremental improvement is not derived from formal R&D, nor is it created by industrial or manufacturing engineers: rather, it is derived from the experience and group efforts of shop-floor workers. In contrast, as a result of its neglect of shop-floor learning in the creation of the types of knowledge that are tacit, subjective, contextual, relational, and cross-functional, US firms usually perform badly in the creation of knowledge for incremental improvement. Table 7.6 shows the huge gap between the USA and Japan in their performance in incremental improvement. The number of effective improvement suggestions per employee per year is only 0.035 in the USA, as compared with 28.14 in Japan.

Table 7.6 Comparison of improvement suggestions: a US–Japan comparison, 1990

Variables	USA	Japan	Japan/USA
Ratio of participation	9%	72%	8
Numbers of improvement suggestions per employee	0.11	32.35	294.1
Adoption rate of improvement suggestions	32%	87%	2.71
Number of effective improvement suggestions per employee	0.035	28.14	799.6
Average financial reward for each improvement suggestion	$491.71	$2.50	1/197

Source: Adapted from Robinson and Schroeder (1993).

An intriguing reverse scale difference also exists in the average financial reward for each adopted improvement suggestion. The figure is $491.71 in the USA vs. $2.50 in Japan. In sum, even though the financial incentive for improvement suggestions in the USA is 197 times that of Japan, the number of effective improvement suggestions per employee in the USA is only 1/800th that of Japan! At the aggregate national level, according to the estimate by the Japan Human Relations Association (1988), in 1986 Japanese employees generated nearly 48 million improvement suggestions for their companies, while their US counterparts produced only about one million, a number much smaller than the 2.56 million generated in Toyota alone. This giant gap in the performance of incremental improvement, as Imai (1986) correctly points out, provides a powerful competitive edge for Japanese firms.

Such a powerful edge, however, can only be realized in the sectors where opportunities for continuous incremental improvement are abundant and where continuous incremental improvement is the key for competitive success. The sectors that belong to this category are generally the complex fabricating manufacturing sectors of relatively mature products such as automobiles, machine tools, electronics, and opto-electronics. Unlike simple processing manufacturing where opportunities for human intervention are relatively few once the whole process is set up, the process of complex fabricating manufacturing has numerous opportunities for human intervention. The simple products of processing manufacturing, once innovated, have a higher degree of appropriation and low opportunities for incremental improvement. In contrast, the complex products of fabricating manufacturing have a lower degree of appropriation and huge opportunities for incremental improvement.

The Japanese competitive advantage of synergy

The Japanese competitive advantage in incremental improvement, however, is not solely derived from its strength in tacit, connectual, and contextual knowing, nor is it solely derived from its organizing principles of connection, contextualization, and people-dependent integration. The advantage is the result of successful Japanese synergy between tacit and explicit knowing, between contextual and abstract knowing, and more broadly, between endogenous dominant organizing principles and exogenous ones transplanted largely from the USA.

Total quality management (TQM) as a synergy between explicit and tacit knowing

One of the best examples of the Japanese synergy between tacit and explicit knowing is the practice of TQM. By adopting the statistical quality control techniques initiated by the American pioneer W. Edwards Deming, the Japanese absorbed the American way of explicit and propositional knowing. By incorporating the endogenously innovated group process of quality circles into TQM, the Japanese successfully appropriated their own ways of connectual and contextual knowing. By directing the group process of quality circles to the transformation of tacit knowledge to explicit knowledge and explicit knowledge to tacit knowledge (Nonaka, 1994), the Japanese successfully synthesized the very best of both tacit and explicit knowing. In the process, the redundancy of information and knowledge among participants, enabled by such practices as job rotation, contributes greatly to the Japanese capability of knowledge creation. As Nonaka (1990) notes, such a redundancy enables a cross-functional and group process of socialization, internalization, externalization, and combination in which the 'spiral of knowledge creation' happens. Indeed, as Nonaka and Takeuchi (1995) rightly point out, the Japanese capability in creating tactic knowledge and transforming it into the explicit form, as well as its capacity in internalizing explicit knowledge into the tacit form, are the major reasons for Japanese competitiveness in complex fabricating manufacturing sectors.

Synergy of abstract and contextual knowledge

In the case of performance evaluation and corporate goals, the Japanese synergy of abstract and contextual knowing is realized through the recontextualization of quantification by using multiple measures and indicators to represent multiple facets of realities and contexts. Indeed, as evidenced by the empirical study by Sakurai *et al.* (1989), while 'most U.S. companies use ROI not only in performance evaluation, but also in corporate goal setting' (p. 164), their Japanese counterparts have made little use of ROI. Instead, 'Japanese managers tend to use a variety of performance measures' (p. 165). The use of multiple measures helps the Japanese to understand more accurately and in more detail and depth production processes and the various quality dimensions of products.

Toyotarism as a synergy of separate and connectual knowing

Looking at a much broader context, the very form of Japanese organizational innovation, the Japanese manufacturing system, variously called Toyotarism, lean production, or flexible production, has been the product of Japanese efforts in synthesizing tacit and explicit knowing, and separate and connectual knowing. The impact of Taylorism on the rise of the Japanese system of management and human resources is widely acknowledged (Warner, 1994; Tsutsui, 1998). In an intriguing study, the American management scientists Alder and Cole (1993) conducted a comparison of the new Japanese manufacturing system (lean production) with the old American practice of mass production and the Swedish 'human-centered model.' According to them, what makes Toyota's lean production model so distinguished is its successful integration of the seemingly contradictory practices of standardization and learning, and of specialization and integration. In conventional GM auto factories there were practices of standardization without effective shop-floor learning, and practices of specialization without cross-function integration (Alder and Cole, 1993). In the Swedish Volvo's Uddevalla plant, there were practices of integration and learning but few practices of standardization and specialization. In Uddevalla, the whole automobiles were assembled by only a group of *polyvalent* workers without strong specialization, nor was there use of a conventional assembly line.

Judged from the conventional theory of transaction costs (Williamson, 1985), standardization and specialization reduces the transaction costs of an employer's contracting with employees. Judged from Chandler's (1990) framework, the practices of standardization and specialization effectively exploit economies of scale and reduce the costs of monitoring employee effort by top managers. The problem with these two orthodox theories of economic organization lies in their neglect of learning effect and their inattention to the problem of knowledge creation, transformation, and appropriation. Chandler (1990) emphasizes the importance of persistent large-scale investment in management, production, and marketing, but fails to notice the need for harnessing dispersed, contextual, and connectual knowledge about improvement opportunities on the shop floor. By focusing on transaction costs and opportunism, Williamson (1985, 1996) fails to place capability building and knowledge creation at the center of his analysis (according to Winter, 1991). His central problems are the information asymmetry and incentive constraints and means of fighting against opportunism. Overall, the central focus of both analyses is cost and control, with Williamson focusing on transaction costs and control by contracts and hierarchies, and Chandler on production costs and administrative control.

Indeed, with their primary concern of costs and control, the theories by Williamson and Chandler can both be seen as theories of the old paradigm of mass production and as a revelation of the American cultural paradigm of contractual man. After all, when everything is standardized, from products, to processes, to skills, knowledge and other productive inputs, the only problems faced in American mass production firms are the costs of production and transaction and the control of both the labor and market processes. There are very few opportunities for incremental improvement. There is therefore also a trade-off between quality and costs. A higher quality needs more input and therefore incurs a higher cost. The focus on costs and control and the lack of scope for continuous incremental improvement due to the dominance of the standardization process has certainly contributed to the decline of the US automobile sector in the 1970s and 1980s.

In contrast to the neoclassical notion of trade-off between quality and cost, the Japanese system of connectual governance and flexible manufacturing embraces and institutionalizes the belief that improved quality also means reduced costs (Johnson, 1992). Judged from Deming's (1986) emphasis on quality and employee empowerment, and Senge's (1990) concept of learning organization, the American system of mass production greatly wasted the learning capacity and knowledge creation capability of shop-floor employees. Moreover, its sharp division among functions with centralized control as the only legitimate coordination tool, and its overemphasis on standardization without an effective method of continuously pushing forward and refining standards through shop-floor learning, had also greatly limited firms' capability of learning and knowledge creation. Using Arthur's (1990) term, *the as positive feedback* between functions was cut off in the old system of mass production, leaving an isolated R&D department as the only agent responsible for innovation and improvement.

The Japanese system of flexible manufacturing can best be described, in Florida and Kenney's (1993) words, as *innovation-mediated production*. It is a system in which every possible source of dispersed knowledge is exploited and every conceivable way of integrating functional knowledge is institutionalized. Judged by Simon's (1957) concept of *bounded rationality*, standardization and specialization are tools that aim at overcoming the bounded rationality of individual employees (Jin, 1995). Indeed, division of labor and specialization have been the most powerful organizing principles in attacking the problem of complexity (Arrow, 1979). The problem with the Swedish system of craft production (Berggren, 1992) is that its lack of standardization and specialization fails to overcome the bounded rationality of human learning and of human thinking and acting capabilities (Adler and Cole, 1993). In other words, the system relies too heavily on individual workers' skills without reducing the complexity and burdens of their work.

The Japanese system of manufacturing has tried to incorporate the best of the American system of mass production and the Swedish system of craft production. Through specialization, delicate and in-depth knowledge and skills are developed. Through standardization, the knowledge and skills acquired are made explicit and further imbedded in organizational routines. It thus overcomes the bounded rationality of individual employees. Through the practice of TQM, JIT, and concurrent engineering, sources of dispersed and interconnected knowledge are constantly discovered to improve the standard operating routines, best utilizing the learning and knowledge creation capability of individual employees (Alder and Cole, 1993). It is important to observe that, because this synergy effect is supported by the specific cultural and institutional environment, even though the Japanese system of production is transferable to other countries, the transplants are less productive than their original firms in Japan (Hagen and Choe, 1998).

Conclusion

In summary, the sectoral patterns of competitiveness among nations can be explained according to the effectiveness of contrasting forms of knowing as dominant in different nations: explicit vs. tacit, separate vs. connectual, and propositional vs. contextual. In the USA, the contractual cultural paradigm has led to the dominance of explicit, separate, and propositional knowing and the organizing principles of standardization, quantification, depersonalization, and decontextualization, which in turn have contributed to American competitiveness in databases and other information services, professional services, consulting, banking, insurance, warehouse retailing, fast food, soft drinks, hotel management, and formalized marketing research. In contrast, the cultural paradigm of connectual man has led to the dominance of tacit, connectual, and contextual knowing in Japan, which in turn has created competitive advantages in incremental improvement, synchronization, organic customization, which are of vital importance for Japan's competitive success in automobiles and consumer electronics.

The Japanese competitive advantages are, nevertheless, not solely derived from its emphasis on tacit, connectual, and contextual knowing, but also caused by its synergy between tacit and explicit knowing, between separate and connectual knowing, and between propositional and contextual knowing. More especially, the synergy of endogenous and exogenous organizing principles between standardization and customization, and between specialization and integration is behind the Japanese innovation of lean production and therefore has contributed significantly to Japanese success in automobiles and consumer electronics.

What is intriguing here is that until very recently Japan failed to extend its synergistic effort in the manufacturing sectors to the service sectors of banking, retailing, and information services. This is largely because all these sectors had been isolated from international competition and therefore were unable to move away from the isomorphic pull of connectual knowing. Once these sectors are exposed to international competition, it will be interesting to see whether Japan can generate a new synergistic effect, as it has done in the manufacturing sectors.

CHAPTER EIGHT

Spontaneous vs. Organized Fusion

> Rules which are to enable individuals to find their own places in a *spontaneous order* of the whole society must be general; they must not assign to particular individuals a status, but rather leave the individual to create his own position. The rules which assist in the running of an organization, on the other hand, operate only within a framework of specific commands which designate the particular ends which the organization aims at and the particular functions which the several members are to perform. (*Italics added.*)
>
> F. A. Hayek (1964: 463)

In his recent works, the Japanese expert in technological innovation Fumio Kodama (1991, 1992, 1995) attributed Japan's success in high-tech sectors to the superior Japanese capability of what he called '*technology fusion.*' In contrasting the Japanese approach of technology fusion to the American style of '*technology breakthrough,*' Kodama (1992: 70) observes that while the 'breakthrough approach' tries to create a totally new generation of technology to replace an old one, the 'technology fusion' approach focuses on 'combining existing technologies into hybrid technologies.' In further elaborating on the differences, he (p. 70) notes:

> [The breakthrough approach] is a linear, step-by-step strategy of technology substitution: the semiconductor replaced the vacuum tube, the CD replaced the record album. Technology fusion, on the other hand, is nonlinear, complementary, and cooperative. It blends incremental technical improvements from several previously separate fields of technology to create products that revolutionize markets. For example, marrying optics and electronics created optoelectronics, which give rise to fiber-optics communications systems; fusing mechanical and electronics technologies produced the mechatronics revolution, which has transformed the machine-tool industry.

While the notion of the US advantage in technological breakthrough and Japanese advantage in technology fusion is widely accepted (Florida and Kenney, 1990), the dichotomy is too simple to deepen our understanding of both the complex innovation process and the competitive landscape of nations. After all, if we explore the innovation process in depth, many technological breakthroughs brought about in the USA, especially those of complex products and processes, were the result of *fusing* and *synthesizing* technologies across many sectors (Kash and Rycroft, 1999). Indeed, from the Schumpeterian perspective, innovation, although a force of creative destruction, is itself a result of *new combinations* of existing factors of production to create new products, processes, and services. As Hargadon and Sutton's (1997: 716) case study indicates, many US innovations are 'built from existing but previously unconnected ideas.' Historically, the creativity and inventiveness of Thomas Edison's laboratory rested in its capability in the transformation and fusion of existing technologies across industrial boundaries (Hughes, 1989b; Millard, 1990). In the words of Hargadon and Sutton (1997: 716), 'Edison's products often reflected blends of existing but previously unconnected ideas that his engineers picked up as they worked in these disparate industries.'

As Kash and Rycroft (1999) rightly point out, in an increasingly complex world, technological innovations more often take the form of *combining, synthesizing, and fusing* existing core competencies of broad technological disciplines. The central issue in differentiating US and Japanese styles of innovation is, therefore, not so much a dichotomy between technological breakthrough and technology fusion as it is an exploration of differing social constructions of technology fusion. The best way of doing this is to examine where and how technology fusion happens. There are several very puzzling phenomena here. First, while most major innovations in Japan happened in large corporations such as Sony, NEC, and Toshiba, large established firms in the USA have not been as innovative (Hughes, 1989a; Westney, 1993). Second, while most major technological innovations in the USA were made by independent start-up entrepreneurial firms, start-up firms in Japan played a very small part in innovation (Westney, 1993). Third, while most US R&D efforts focus on product innovations, the Japanese are famous for their strength in process innovation (Mansfield, 1988a,b). The first two contrasts are best illustrated by the very existence of the Silicon Valley model of innovation in the USA and its absence in Japan, constituting the sharpest divergence in the landscapes of technological innovation between these two industrial giants.

The innovativeness and dynamism of high-tech start-up firms in the USA has produced a string of corporate giants such as Intel, Microsoft, Dell, Oracle, Cisco, and most recently America Online (AOL) and Yahoo! that dominate the world in microprocessors, computers, prepackaged software, databases, online services, and e-business. It is through these rapidly rising stars that corporate America dominates the world in these high-tech sectors. Conversely, the dearth of rising stars in the age of information technology is the very reason for the Japanese lack of competitiveness in these same sectors. Partly as a result of this, and more so because of the dominance of connectual governance, almost no Japanese start-up firms can rise to a dominant position as that which has been enjoyed by Intel and Microsoft.[1] As shown in Table 8.1, the top ten Japanese electric machine makers in 1990 were exactly the same as those in 1970. Similarly, in the Japanese sectors of machine tools and pump makers, none of the top ten firms in 1990 was established after 1955 (Whittaker, 1994).

More strikingly, existing large Japanese firms dominate the newly emerging sectors such as semiconductors, semiconductor equipment, and information processing and services. In the information service sector, eight of the top ten firms have been established by large firms, with the remaining two being established in the 1960s (Whittaker, 1994). In the computer hardware and software sectors, most of the dominant players come from established giants of electronics and telecommunications (Fransman, 1995). Even such a brand-new sector as biotechnology is mostly composed of firms that entered from related industries with established positions (Okimoto and Saxonhouse, 1987).

Using the data from the US Office of Patent and Trademarks, it can also be seen that there is a much greater weight of large Japanese established firms in total patenting activities of all sectors than that of their US counterparts. As shown in Table 8.2, the Japanese concentration ratio of top ten established firms in cumulative

Table 8.1 Top ten Japanese electric machine makers, excluding appliances, 1970–1990

	1970	Sales (¥bn)	1990	Sales (¥bn)
1	Hitachi	675.0	Hitachi	3,788.80
2	Toshiba	550.2	Toshiba	3,227.70
3	Mitsubishi Electric	376.1	NEC	2,961.10
4	NEC	195.7	Mitsubishi Electric	2,588.80
5	Matsushita Electric	119.9	Fujitsu	2,337.80
6	Fujitsu	119.4	Nippon Denso	1,379.30
7	Fuji Electric	103.3	Matsushita Electric	971.3
8	Nippon Denso	85.3	Fuji Electric	591.9
9	Oki EI	57.5	Oki EI	582.1
10	Matsushita CI	43.7	Matsushita CI	441.7

Source: Whittaker (1994: 215).

patents of all technologies and all types from 1977 and 1999 is 3.27 times that of their US counterparts. In the mechanical, electrical, and chemical classes, the numbers are respectively 4.87, 2.05, and 1.46. These contrasts reveal that in all technological sectors, Japan depends more on large established firms for major innovations than the USA does.

Table 8.2 Concentration ratio of top ten firms in patents: 1963–1999

Sectors	USA	Japan	Japan/USA
All technologies, all type, 1977–99	0.098	0.320	3.27
All technologies, utility patent, 1963–99	0.090	0.304	3.38
Utility patent: mechanical class, 1977–99	0.054	0.263	4.87
Utility patent: electrical class, 1977–99	0.266	0.545	2.05
Utility patent: chemical class, 1977–99	0.149	0.217	1.46

Source: Calculation from various reports by US Patent and Trademark Office.

From the perspective of this book, this divergence in the locus of innovation is caused by the differing modes of technology fusion. Following Hayek's (1964) distinction of spontaneous vs. organized order, we describe the dominant mode in the USA as *spontaneous technology fusion*, while that in Japan we describe as *organized technology fusion*. Spontaneous technology fusion happens when a small team of individuals with complementarity in core competencies realizes a shared vision of new products, processes, and services. Here, several characteristics of the team need to be emphasized. First, team members are attracted together through a *shared vision*. In most cases, team members come from different backgrounds and different organizations; they gather together through either spontaneous association or contractual recruitment. Second, team members hold mutually reinforcing core competencies to form an *autocatalytic set* (Waldrop, 1992) in facilitating the possible fusion of these competencies to innovate new products and processes. Third, although process innovation is possible in some specific situations, most innovations brought forth by these separately formed teams are product-oriented. Fourth, teams are formed contractually with pre-agreed shareholding plans and limited time horizons. Fifth, once the team realizes its shared vision of a new product, process, or service, it may disband. Sixth, because of the spontaneous nature of team assembly, spontaneous technology fusion mostly happens outside large corporations. In some exceptional cases, spontaneous technology fusion can also occur in some separate research labs such as Bell Lab and Xerox PARC, where researchers are free to choose their own research topic with full resource commitments and the power to freely recruit and assemble the best talents. Finally, since team members are formed from different backgrounds, without the burden of existing architectural constraints (Henderson and Clark, 1990), they may generate technological discontinuities that destroy existing dominant designs, dominant business models, and create new ones (Anderson and Tushman, 1990; Christensen, 1997).

By contrast, organized technology fusion happens when core competencies across different technological domains fuse. Whereas spontaneous technology fusion occurs primarily in start-ups, organized technology fusion is realized in large established firms. Whereas new forms of combination are stumbled upon 'unexpectedly' in the former case, the latter combines existing technologies in a predictable way. Whereas the former creates a separate domain of knowledge, the latter *blurs* the boundaries of existing technologies and brings them together *seamlessly* and *organically*. Whereas the former is often micro fusion, the latter is mostly macro-based.[2] Whereas the former usually brings about new technologies and products that make the old ones obsolete (competency-destroying), the latter finds a new way of exploiting existing knowledge bases and competencies (competency-enhancing). Consequently, while the former facilitates the emergence of brand-new technological trajectories, the latter enables the macro fusion of many existing technological paradigms such as electronics, mechanics, and optics.

The distinction between spontaneous and organized technology fusion not only explains the dilemmas and divergence that existed between the USA and Japan in their dominant modes of innovation, it also reveals the causal relations underpinning the divergent competitive landscapes of these two nations. From the point of view of national competitiveness, the superior capability for spontaneous fusion has created an American drama that almost no other nation has experienced: a flock of new-generation corporate stars are continuously superseding the giants of previous generations. This is especially true in the computer industry. IBM, the onetime mainframe monolith, was replaced by latercomers Intel and Microsoft as the top companies in computer hardware and software; Digital Equipment Corporation (DEC), the old star of minicomputers, was taken over by Compaq, the rising star of PC manufacturing (*Business Week*, February 9, 1998, cover story); and by its innovation of direct sale model, Dell Computer superseded Compaq as the Number One PC maker in 1998.

Organizing for spontaneous technology fusion: the US advantage

This US superior capability in spontaneous technology fusion is facilitated by the dominance of contractual governance mechanisms for knowledge creation and the corresponding organizing principles of separation, modularization, and encapsulation. The high levels of sociability, mobility, and spontaneous association in the USA further strengthen such a capability. In the cases of biotechnology and software, this enables the rapid *formation* and *reconfiguration* of networks of innovators that combine all the necessary and most advanced knowledge, skills, and core competencies for knowledge integration and technology fusion (Liebeskind *et al.*, 1996).

Free configuration of the very best

One great advantage of contractual governance is its ability to recruit the very best minds for knowledge creation. Indeed, the American-style technology fusion relies on the ability to bring together the best minds from around the world either by spontaneous association or through aggressive outside talent searches and recruitment. Two good examples are AT&T's Bell Lab and Xerox PARC. While Bell Lab's invention of the transistor brought about the new age of microelectronics, Xerox PARC's innovations of the computer mouse and others enabled the revolution in computers, computer operating systems, network communications, and office machines (Perry and Wallich, 1985). Two important observations about Xerox PARC's success are worthy of notice. First, all its successful innovations are simultaneously technological breakthroughs and a kind of technology fusion. They are technological breakthroughs because they have brought about new technological paradigms and trajectories. They are a kind of technology fusion since they combine existing ideas, knowledge, and core competencies in many fields. Second, all the innovations were the result of brilliant people assembled by aggressive recruitment who have a set of core capabilities that are complementary to one another.

In the case of Xerox PARC, because of aggressive talent searching and recruiting, 'in the mid-1970s, close to half of the top 100 computer scientists in the world were working at PARC, and the laboratory boasted similar strength in other fields, including solid-state physics and optics' (Perry and Wallich, 1985: 62). According to Iansiti (1998), the American competitive comeback in the semiconductor sector is also largely due to the ability of US firms to search and recruit the best minds at the cutting edge of scientific and technological disciplines to integrate the best available technologies. According to the same source, Silicon Graphic's successful development of workstations was based on its ability to simulate, validate, and synthesize possible designs and innovative concepts acquired from universities and other companies. Similarly, the successful development of software in Microsoft and Netscape resulted from their ability to rapidly and agilely gather new knowledge, recruit new talents, and fuse these newly acquired insights into project development (Iansiti, 1998). The ability to recruit the best talents also underlies American success in the sectors of information processing and financial services (Quinn *et al.*, 1996) and in Silicon Valley (Cohen and Fields, 1999).

Division and separation as enablers for spontaneous fusion

The nature of spontaneous technology fusion requires that any complex technological problems be divided and separated into independent technological domains so that a small team of specialists can have enough competencies to attack them. The American drive for autonomy and independence also requires and facilitates the delicate division and specialization of technical domains so that the process of separate knowing can be successful. The dominance of separate knowing also leads to the burgeoning of new disciplines in the USA, which in turn gives rise to thinner and more specialized scientific and technological domains.

When there is a need to solve a knowledge problem across several preexisting disciplines, instead of combining them together, the American way is to separate domains scattered across different disciplines to form a new, self-contained, and independent research domain. Many American successes in spontaneous technology fusion often rely on the superior ability of research teams to identify, separate, and isolate a relatively independent and self-contained technological domain for separate knowing. While this ability depends on the creativity and innovativeness of team members, often the extent of success or failure in effective separation depends on the types of innovation and the nature of technological sectors. First, it is always easier to separate and isolate an innovation that requires the application of simple technologies than one that requires the application of complex technologies. Therefore, as Kash and Rycroft (1999) find, the USA is good at the innovation of simple technologies but not as good as Japan in the innovation of complex technologies.[3] According to Christensen (1997), most ground-breaking technological innovations in the USA are generated by start-ups and are simpler than the existing technologies they challenge.

Second, it is usually easier to separate the technological domain for product innovation than for process innovation, since the effectiveness of the latter requires the creation of connectual knowledge that cannot be acquired from the process of separate knowing. This is why the USA has focused more on product innovation than on process innovation up to the 1980s (Mansfield, 1988a,b; Branscomb, 1992).

Third, within the same domain of process innovation, some processes are much easier to separate, sequentialize, modularize, and encapsulate, while others are more difficult. The former includes the development of software, biotechnology, drugs, and information processing and services. The latter include the innovation and improvement of complex fabricating manufacturing processes. Therefore, while the USA has a competitive advantage in the former, Japan is more competitive in the latter.

Good examples are American superior capability in specialized semiconductor chip design and Japanese exceptional capacity in semiconductor photolithographic equipment (Henderson, 1996) and semiconductor manufacturing. By separating product from process design, many start-up US 'fabless' semiconductor firms emerged. These firms specialize in semiconductor designs and outsource their production to Asian countries such as Japan, South Korea and Taiwan with most state-of-the-art foundries (Macher *et al.*, 1998). According to Macher *et al.* (1998: 119), 'the fabless firm is largely a North America phenomenon – more than 300 of the world population of roughly 500 "fabless" firms were located in North America in 1998.' The spontaneous emergence of this large number of 'fabless' design firms created a superior capability in logic chip design and partly contributed to the American revival in the semiconductor sector, especially in the design of logic chips such as microprocessors (Macher *et al.*, 1998).

Modularization and encapsulation as enablers for spontaneous fusion

A dominant way of separating and isolating one technological domain from its surroundings is by modularization and encapsulation. Modularization is a particular way of partitioning a system into a set of subsystems and then encapsulating these into relatively independent modules so that both their physical interactions and knowledge links are minimized. As Langlois and Robertson (1995: Ch. 5) note, there are modular systems and closed systems. From the knowledge regime perspective, a modular technological system is one that could be effectively divided into independent subsystems for spontaneous separate knowing without the loss of potential opportunities for knowledge creation and integration. A closed techno-logical system, on the other hand, is one in which an artificial modularization will incur a great loss of such opportunities. In the real world, a computer system with open systems architecture is a modular system, whereas automobiles and most electronic appliances are essentially non-modular systems (Langlois and Robertson, 1992).

Where a technological system can be effectively modularized, such as PCs with open system architecture, it paves the way for numerous separate knowers and individualistic entrepreneurs to *simultaneously* experiment with new ideas upon independent modules. The result is a plethora of spontaneous fusion. In discussing the nature of *autonomous* innovation – or in the terms of this book, spontaneous fusion in a modular system – Langlois and Robertson (1992: 301) observe:

> A modular system is open to innovation of certain kinds in a way a closed system – an appliance – is not. Thus a decentralized network based on modularity can have advantages in innovation to the extent that it involves the trying out of many alternate approaches simultaneously, leading to rapid trial-and-error learning.

On the other hand, when a technological system cannot be effectively modularized, as is the case with the closed systems of automobiles and electronic appliances, there is very little possibility and opportunity for spontaneous technology fusion, because the very existence of dense and tight connectivities leaves little room for autonomous innovations. When such a technological system is artificially modularized, it will still hinder spontaneous fusion because such a process severs necessary knowledge links and therefore incurs a great loss of knowledge creation opportunities.

Although various technological systems have different possibilities of effective modularization because of their different knowledge structures, the evolutionary trajectory of a given technological system in a nation is, however, not solely determined by its technological characteristics. Often such a trajectory, especially in its emergent stage, is socio-culturally constructed. As stated before, in the USA, the cultural penchant for autonomy, independence, and separate knowing leads to modularization as one of the dominant organizing principles. In such modularizable technological systems as computers and software, the possibility of modularity combined with the dominance of the organizing principle of modularization have led to the American innovation of PC systems with open systems architecture which in turn greatly facilitated successive waves of spontaneous innovations. On the other hand, in closed technology systems such as electronic appliances, where modularity cannot work effectively, American efforts at modularization have generated a competitive disadvantage.

Standardization as an enabler for spontaneous fusion

In many cases, modularization, or the process of minimizing physical interactions and knowledge links among subsystems or components, is facilitated by the standardization of the interface among subsystems or components. Such a process provides universalistic specifications for each subsystem or component so that it is compatible with all others. The standard interfaces *encapsulate* all necessary physical and knowledge links so that subsystems or components achieve great autonomy and independence for *autonomous* innovation and *spontaneous* fusion. Individual vendors can experiment with all forms of innovation for the subsystems or components they specialize in and can still expect compatibility as long as they follow the universal specifications.

In the case of the Wintel PC system, as long as they follow the universal specifications provided by the Intel Pentium III and Microsoft Windows 2000, individual vendors of hardware components and application software do not need to have an in-depth knowledge of the inner workings of Pentium III and Windows 2000. Separate entrepreneurs can simultaneously experiment with all technological alternatives using their specialized competencies without worrying about the problem of compatibility. As happened in the Wintel ecosystem, the vast improvement of one key component such as microprocessors or operating systems gives rise to a great wave of effort in the whole communities of PC hardware and software developers to upgrade the capabilities of all components and application software (Baldwin and Clark, 1997).

Once again, while each technological system has different needs for, and possibilities of, standardization and universalistic interface owing to different knowledge structures, its trajectories and extent of standardization differ among nations as a result of isomorphic pulls from different cultural paradigms and dominant organizing principles. Because of the American penchant for autonomy and independence, the business practices and technological trajectories of US industrial sectors have been dominated by the principles of standardization. From the American system of manufactures in the late nineteenth century, to the Fordist mass production system, and from the fast food sector to the PC industry, the organizing principle of standardization has been ubiquitous. As a result, US firms are competitive in those sectors where the organizing principles of standardization can effectively facilitate spontaneous technology fusion.

The linear model of innovation as a facilitator for spontaneous fusion

Another way of modularization and encapsulation is by partitioning, separating, and isolating the tasks of technological innovation and then sequentializing them into a linear relationship. Here, the linear model of technological innovation as dominant in the USA since World War II has played an important role as a facilitator for spontaneous fusion in the science-based sectors of chemistry, drugs, biotechnology, computers, and scientific instruments. By organizing the innovation process into a sequential movement of relatively independent knowledge creation tasks, the linear model transforms the chain-linked and interdependent knowledge structure of the innovation process into one-way dependency, in which generic knowledge discovered in basic research provides the basis for applied research, and knowledge created in the latter in turn provides the basis for product and process development. The sequentialization of the innovation process further solves the problem of one-way dependency in which the latter stage takes the knowledge from the earlier stage as a given input for its independent effort (Figure 8.1).

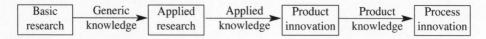

Figure 8.1. The linear model of innovation
Source: Adapted from Kline and Rosenberg (1986).

In the USA, the cultural penchant for autonomy and independence and the epistemological emphasis on separate knowing had led to the dominance of the linear model from World War II to the 1980s. This has contributed to the creation of a superior knowledge creation infrastructure for basic research. The huge base of generic knowledge generated in great American research universities and federal labs constitutes the 'primordial soup' from which spontaneous innovations emerge and thrive throughout the sectors of chemistry, biotechnology, software, information technology, aircraft, and scientific instruments, providing a competitive edge for US firms in these sectors. This is evidenced by the pivotal role Stanford University, U.C. Berkeley, and U.C. San Francisco played in stimulating innovation in Silicon Valley (Cohen and Fields, 1999), and the similar role of MIT in assisting the high-tech region of Route 128 in Boston (Bolland and Hofer, 1998).

Separate labs and R&D centers as incubators for spontaneous fusion

Just as world-class research universities and federal labs provide the 'primordial soup' for new combinations of knowledge and competencies to facilitate spontaneous technological fusion, the huge number of corporate R&D centers play the role of incubators which enable many innovative ideas to emerge. One good example is Xerox PARC. As Florida and Kenney (1990: 29) note, Xerox PARC is 'the classic case of what happens when R&D and manufacturing are physically and socially isolated from one another.' According to Pake (1985: 54), a founder of Xerox PARC, such a separation was the result of 'a conscious effort to imitate the best research in universities by providing an *intellectual* environment.' Other principles Xerox PARC adopted included: to 'recruit the best, most creative researchers you can find,' and to 'give the researchers the most supportive environment you can provide, including ample amounts of the most advanced instrumentation.' All are key elements for effective spontaneous technology fusion.

The irony here is that Xerox failed to harness the benefits of PARC's revolutionary innovations. As Florida and Kenney (1990: 29) point out, 'PARC was the source of some of the most important advances in computer technology in the past three decades – virtually none of which were exploited by Xerox.' Ironically, just as the isolation and separation of R&D activities from manufacturing was the source of Xerox PARC's successful spontaneous innovations, it was also the cause of Xerox's failure to harvest the fruit of these innovations.

The cases of Bell Lab and Xerox PARC are more exceptions than the norm in large US corporations. In general, while not lacking innovative ideas, many large US corporations have been unable to harness dramatically new ideas for spontaneous technology fusion. The existing contractual governance structure and its architectural knowledge (Henderson and Clark, 1990), and the focus on existing customers and existing businesses (Christensen, 1997) leave little room for the spontaneous fusion and implementation of totally new ideas.

Consequently, as Storper (1993) observes, major innovation in the USA usually happens as a spin-off from existing corporations. Research scientists and engineers with innovative ideas that developed during their stay in a large corporation leave to form start-up ventures to engage in new innovations. It is legendary how spin-offs from Fairchild and IBM grew up into such corporate giants as Intel, Oracle, Sun Microsystems, and SAP. While the inability of large US corporations to harvest the fruit of the research labs has been blamed for the decline of US industries (Florida and Kenney, 1990), we need to acknowledge their significant contributions in incubating spin-off innovations that have created new giants for corporate America.

The garbage can model of spontaneous fusion

The central issue here is the unit of analysis. Those scholars who blame the frequent spin-off of innovative ideas as the major reason for the trouble of corporate America in the 1980s fail to look at a larger picture as to how those ideas have contributed to the superior American capabilities in spontaneous technology fusion as a whole. It is ironic to see that even as late as 1990, the superior capability in spontaneous technology fusion, the very force behind American revival in the 1990s, was labeled in 'the breakthrough illusion' (Florida and Kenney, 1990).

In the following, I borrow and adapt the garbage can model of organizational decision-making (Cohen *et al.*, 1972) to describe the key elements and processes of spontaneous technology fusion. In our garbage can model (Figure 8.2), spontaneous technology fusion occurs when entrepreneurs, the primordial soup of innovative ideas, fusion opportunities, and the catalysts of venture capital, which are all floating randomly within the garbage can, are haphazardly connected. Such a connection is facilitated by professional associations, networks of acquaintances and old friends, the hyper-mobility of knowledge workers, and external consultants. The garbage can here in my model is not formed within an organization, as was originally meant in Cohen *et al.*'s model, but is rather region- or nation- based. The whole Silicon Valley, or to a large extent, the whole US system of innovation, can be seen as a macro garbage can for spontaneous technology fusion.

Within this super-sized macro garbage can, numerous innovative ideas simultaneously emerge and are commercialized by entrepreneurs and tested by the market. Here, while the macro garbage can plays the role of the generator, incubator, and synthesizer of innovative ideas, the market acts as the selector and gatekeeper so as to make sure that only those innovations that best fit the needs of consumers prosper.

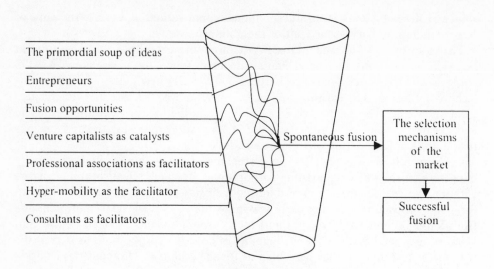

Figure 8.2 The garbage can model of spontaneous technology fusion

The spontaneous order of micro fusion

American superior capability of micro fusion rests in its spontaneous nature and the macro institutional and technological environment that facilitates it. In the terminology of Hayek (1964), the US innovation system is a *spontaneous order* in which the *generalized* rules of market competition enable those with innovative ideas, including entrepreneurs, research scientists and engineers, and venture capitalists, to freely exploit their individual insights, knowledge, and competencies in exploring new opportunities. In the process, not only can individual entrepreneurs with dispersed knowledge about innovative opportunities *simultaneously* experiment with their ideas, they are also free to configure and reconfigure innovative teams to realize their vision.

In regards to this spontaneity, what is remarkable is not the talent and creativity of individual innovators, but what Don Lavoie (1985: Ch. 3) has called '*social intelligence.*' This is achieved neither through any system of centralized planning nor through organizational hierarchies or industrial policies, but through the free-floating of ideas within the macro garbage can in which numerous innovative ideas *simultaneously* seek fusion opportunities to realize their market value and are *spontaneously* tested by the rigor of market competition.

The primordial soup of innovative ideas

The central element in the macro garbage can is the *primordial soup* of innovative ideas dispersed among individuals throughout American society. The richness of innovative ideas in the USA has been greatly enhanced by its system of knowledge creation. Contributing elements within this superior system include: (1) an educational system which emphasizes creativity rather than memorizing; (2) the unparalleled system of research universities and federal labs; (3) huge federal funding for basic research in the creation of generic knowledge; (4) a plural, decentralized, individual-oriented, and peer-review-based research funding system; and (5) the world-class corporate R&D system that emphasizes separate knowing and experimentation. All these elements have contributed significantly to the plethora of innovative ideas in the US macro garbage can, unparalleled in the world.

The entrepreneurial effort for new combinations

Without the efforts of a huge flock of entrepreneurs who try to combine, synthesize, fuse, and transform innovative ideas into real products, processes, and services that are saleable to the market, the primordial soup of innovative ideas would contribute little to American competitiveness. It is the entrepreneurial process – an indispensable part of the knowledge creation system – that discovers new combinations of existing knowledge, competencies, products, processes, and services. In the USA, entrepreneurship is very much based on individuals. They are motivated by the search for independence and the need for individual achievement. Here, the American axial principles of autonomy and independence, combined with the preference for separate knowing, has led to a plethora of individualistic entrepreneurship.

According to *Forbes* magazine (December 18, 1995, p. 268), in 1993, the USA had more than 700,000 new business openings, or approximately 2756 per million inhabitants, while Japan has just 95,000, or 766 per million inhabitants. In other words, if we simply measure the propensity of individualistic entrepreneurship by the number of new business openings per inhabitant, then the USA has 3.6 times the propensity for individualist entrepreneurship than that of Japan. According to another estimate, in 1995 the total number of new business formations amounted to 4553 million in the USA (Dennis, 1997). In Silicon Valley alone, in 1997 about 3575 new firms were formed (Cohen and Fields, 1999). In the sector of software and computer-related services, during 1975–1995, the number of establishments increased 8.77 times from 6443 to 56,480 in the USA, an impressive 11.47 per cent annual growth rate. At the same time, the Japanese number grew only 4.55 times from 1276 to 5812, only one-tenth of the US number and lower than even that of Netherlands, and a mere 7.88 per cent annual growth rate (Table 8.3). Of those establishments, the USA has 15 firms within the top 20 worldwide software companies while Japan had only 2 in 1996 (Table 2.32). Among these top 15 US firms, many have grown from start-ups during the 1970s and 1980s. Indeed, the great propensity for business formation has contributed greatly to American competitiveness in software and computer-related sectors.

Venture capitalists and business angels as catalysts

In many cases, entrepreneurship would not thrive if it were not supported by rich networks of venture capitalists. According to Zider (1998), venture capitalists not only provide financial resources, they also serve as directors and monitors, helping to recruit managers, bring in consultants, offer management advices, supply contacts, secure credibility, enforce discipline, and deliver moral support, all of which are greatly needed in the business of transforming innovative ideas into successful

Table 8.3 Number of establishments in software and computer-related services

	USA	Japan	France	Canada	Australia	Netherlands
1975	6,443	1,276				
1980	16,610	1,731				
1985	25,191	2,556			1,200	3,300
1990		7,042		10,924		5,000
1991	43,553	7,096		11,447		5,500
1992	54,431	6,977		12,001		5,800
1993		6,432	21,154	13,203	4,886	8,700
1994		5,982	21,083	13,611		9,400
1995	56,480	5,812	21,900	14,364	9,672	9,600

Source: OECD (1997b: 19).

products, processes, and services (Table 8.4). The multiple roles of venture capitalists in facilitating the growth of start-ups are further supported by the emergence of many standardized venture capital financing practices and institutions. One noted example is the venture capital limited partnership, which emerged in the 1960s.

Table 8.4 How US venture capitalists spend their time

Activity	% of time
Serving as directors and monitors	25
Recruiting management	20
Acting as consultants	15
Assisting in outside relationships	10
Soliciting business	10
Selecting opportunities	5
Analyzing business plans	5
Negotiating investments	5
Exiting	5

Source: Adapted from Zider (1998: 137).

Florida and Kenney (1990) note that through this new form:

> Venture capitalists could now raise money from outside 'limited partners' – banks, corporations, pension funds, and wealthy families. This capital will be controlled and invested by professional venture capitalists, who function as 'general partners.' (p. 93)

As a result of the 'golden rush' for start-up entrepreneurial ventures, from 1980 to 1989 the volume of formal venture capital in the USA increased nearly ten-fold, from less than $3.5 billion to more than $33 billion (Florida and Kenney, 1990: 65). According to another estimate, the total venture capital under management grew from $6.3 billion in 1983 to $37.2 billion in 1995 (Brophy, 1996; see Table 8.5). Of the $3859 millions disbursed in 1995, 20 per cent went to software and services, 19 per cent to biotechnology and medical/health care related industry, 10 per cent to telecommunications, and 5 per cent to computer hardware and systems (National Science Board, 1998: A-383).

Table 8.5 Venture capital under management in the USA and disbursements: 1983–1995 (millions of US dollars)

	New capital commitment	Total venture capital under management	Disbursement
1983	3,400	6,208	2,581
1984	3,200	9,497	2,771
1985	2,300	11,614	2,681
1986	3,300	14,693	3,242
1987	4,200	17,799	3,977
1988	2,947	20,217	3,847
1989	2,399	23,154	3,395
1990	1,847	24,139	1,922
1991	1,271	24,758	1,348
1992	2,548	25,868	2,540
1993	2,545	28,925	3,071
1994	3,765	32,670	2,741
1995	4,227	37,154	3,859

Source: Adapted from National Science Board (1998: A-381).

According to another estimate (US Department of Commerce, 1998: p. A2-5), in 1995 of the total $7.6 billion US venture capital, $3.3 billion (44.2 per cent) went to the information technology sectors of software & information, communications, computers & pereripherals, electronics & instrumentation, and semiconductor/equipment. In 1997, the number was $7.1 billion (55.8 per cent) out of a total $12.8 billion. When geography is considered, in 1997 $2.7 billion venture capital was invested into Silicon Valley alone, about 20 per cent of the national total (Cohen and Fields, 1999).

Complementary to this relatively formal form of financing, there is a plethora of informal venture capital in which industrialists, entrepreneurs, engineers, research scientists, and other wealthy individuals play as business angels to invest capital for new ventures. According to the estimate of the OECD (1996: 8), in the USA, the amount business angels invested is five times greater than that of the institutional venture capital industry. The former also covers 20–40 times the number of companies as does the latter. As a result of their early and pervasive commitment to new ventures, in the USA business angels play pivotal roles in providing capital for the early stage of new ventures whose risks are too high for institutional venture capital firms (OECD, 1996). The huge volume of venture capital has contributed greatly to the rise of such American icons as America Online, Yahoo!, Amazon.com, eBay, E*Trade, and so on.

Consultants, law firms, and professional service firms as catalysts

Accountants, financial experts, management consultants, lawyers, information system specialists, and other professionals in marketing research, advertising, logistics, and systems integration all play important roles for the success of spontaneous fusion. They hold the necessary expertise and knowledge base to serve new start-ups in specific functional areas that are of crucial importance for their successful growth. Consultants and professionals provide *standardized* knowledge, expertise, and skills in the name of *best practices* to secure the best performance of the start-up firms in every functional area and to maximize their growth potential and market values. Here, competitiveness in management consulting, information services, and other professional services contributes greatly to American prowess in spontaneous technology fusion.

In addition, according to Hargadon and Sutton (1997: 718), product design and engineering consulting firms such as IDEO at Silicon Valley play the role of a technology broker who 'recognizes, blends, and transforms existing ideas into new and innovative combinations.' This is achieved through an assembling of competent engineers who have distinctive backgrounds, experience, and expertise across various technological domains, as well as wide and deep connections with clients in various industries. These connections are achieved not through the establishment of any stable connectual structure as the case in Japan, but through a constant movement of client base from one company to another and from one industry to another. In the case of IDEO, Hargadon and Sutton (1997: 718) note:

> By having strong connections to many industries but not being central to any one, the engineers in this firm have constant opportunities to learn about technologies from a broad range of industries. The firm exploits its network position with internal routines that help its designers create products for current clients that are new combinations of existing individual technologies these designers have seen before. Many of these products reflect the transfer of ideas to industries where they have not been used before and the creation of combinations of ideas that no one in any industry has seen before.

As a result, IDEO has designed over 3000 new products, including such famed products as the Apple computer mouse and the Hewlett-Packard printer (Hargadon and Sutton, 1997).

Hyper-mobility as a facilitator

It is worth noticing the constantly emerging, configuring, and reconfiguring nature of the networks and innovating teams at IDEO, a general characteristic of American contractual governance. This propensity is further facilitated by the hyper-mobility of high-tech knowledge workers. According to Florida and Kenney (1990: 81), in high-tech companies in Silicon Valley and Route 128, the two most prominent high-tech regions, turnover rates reach an astounding level of 25 to 35 per cent or even 50 per cent per year. Cohen and Fields (1999) attribute Silicon Valley's huge success partly to the high mobility of its knowledge workers. While such a high level of mobility creates problems for existing large corporations to maintain core competencies, it greatly enhances spontaneous technology fusion in the contractual marketplace through the free movement and configuration of knowledge workers. This capability of freely recruiting the very best has been the key contributor for the success of IDEO, Microsoft (Cusumano and Selby, 1995), and Andersen Consulting (Quinn *et al.*, 1996). In addition, highly mobile knowledge engineers themselves also play the role of technology brokers who blend and fuse previously unconnected ideas and competencies into new products.

Informal networks and professional associations as facilitators

Hyper-mobility of knowledge workers further facilitates the formation of informal networks consisting of former colleagues, friends, and acquaintances. In describing the richness of informal personal networks brought about by hyper-mobility in Silicon Valley, Case (1992: 130) quotes an industrial veteran as saying, 'we all know each other. It's an industry where everybody knows everybody because at one time or another everybody worked together.'

This phenomenon of 'everybody knows everybody' provides a huge advantage for spontaneous technology fusion. First, it creates 'networks of information sharing that accelerate the diffusion of technological capabilities and know-how' (Cohen and Fields, 1999: 125). Second, numerous fusion ideas can spontaneously emerge when people exchange information, knowledge, insights, and innovative ideas across their informal networks. Third, when people have an innovative idea, they know where they can find the right persons with the right expertise to contribute to the innovation effort. Finally, such informal networks often extend into venture capitalists, consultants, and various professionals so that they can help locate necessary financial capital and professional services needed for the innovation.

In addition, participation by knowledge workers and entrepreneurs in formal networks such as industry-wide associations and professional associations provide opportunities not only for knowledge exchange but also for building up informal networks that are much needed for spontaneous technology fusion. In her comparison of Silicon Valley and Route 128 near Boston, Saxenian (1994) attributes Silicon Valley's success to the hyper-mobility of its knowledge workers, its dense informal networking, its entrepreneurial culture, and a 'more flexible business model' in which firms have networked closely with outsider suppliers, customers, and even competitors.

Contractual alliance, autocatalytic set, and symbiosis

The final contributor to the superior American capability of spontaneous technology fusion rests in its ability to align the interests of individuals with those of organizations through pre-bargained explicit contracts of stock options and profit sharing. The prospect to become a multi-millionaire greatly enhances the incentive for every team member to maximize his or her effort. Lavish pay for great talents and efforts becomes the norm for entrepreneurs and knowledge workers in the USA.

To some extent, the contractual alliances that bring together entrepreneurs, venture capitalists, teams of knowledge workers, external consultants, and other professionals in realizing their shared vision of new products, processes, or services can be seen as an *auto-catalytic set* (Waldrop, 1992) in which elements mutually reinforce one another to greatly speed up the spontaneous emergence of new products, processes, and services. More broadly, all the elements in the macro garbage can discussed above can be seen as the auto-catalytic set for accelerating spontaneous fusion.

The competitive market as the selective mechanism

While the macro garbage can of spontaneous technology fusion secures the emergence of a plethora of innovations, the competitive market process insures that only the very best innovation is selected by the market to dominate a technological sector. Although there is the possibility of a lock-in of inferior technologies due to the existence of increasing returns, the unending push of spontaneous technology fusion ensures that no technology can dominate forever. There are always opportunities to leapfrog and make the existing dominant technology obsolete. From this point of view, the locus of national competitiveness rests not in the dominance of given technologies, but in the effectiveness of a nation's macro garbage can in promoting spontaneous technology fusion.

Sectoral implications

American competitive advantage in spontaneous technology fusion is the under-pinning of the very success of the Silicon Valley model. The American system has the advantage of creating a plethora of innovative ideas and technology breakthroughs, of rapidly generating new capabilities, and of avoiding possible lock-in to existing technologies. Indeed, the prowess of spontaneous technology fusion as observed in Silicon Valley is unparalleled throughout world history.

America's superior capability in spontaneous technology fusion works especially well in the following situations. First, as we analyzed before, it works most effectively in loosely coupled and modular technological sectors in which one can effectively separate, modularize, and encapsulate the whole system into a set of modular subsystems and components without the loss of knowledge creation opportunities. Second, since product innovation in many cases is more separable, whereas most process innovations involve many contextual connections, the former has always been the focus of spontaneous innovation. Third, when the whole life cycle of product innovations is considered, spontaneous fusion is most effective in the emergent stage in which various entrants compete for the domination of their designs. Once the dominant design is formed, continuous process improvement and organic fusion within the dominant design will become the key for competitiveness. Fourth, spontaneous fusion works best in the sectors where opportunities for creating technological discontinuities are abundant, and dominant designs have often been made obsolete. Fifth, spontaneous fusion also works best in the sectors that involve great uncertainty in both new product development and the emergence of new technological trajectories. In such a case, what is important is the simultaneity and plethora of experimentation that increases the probability of success. Finally, spontaneous innovations also work best when the pace of scientific knowledge is very fast so that the ability to lead the frontier of research and the capability of swiftly configuring and reconfiguring the very best talents become the key for competitive success. The sectors of biotechnology and information technology satisfy part or all of the above situations.

Notwithstanding its advantages, in the non-modular and tightly coupled technological sectors such as opto-electronics and mechatronics where it is difficult to effectively separate, modularize, and encapsulate everything into a modular system without a loss in knowledge creation opportunities, American spontaneous technology fusion cannot work effectively. In these sectors, technological innovations tend to have resulted from the fusion of two or more macro techno-paradigms such as electronics, optics, and mechanics. They also reinforce, rather than destroy, existing competencies.

Even in modular and loosely coupled technological sectors, when the focus shifts from the endless spontaneous product innovations of various subsystems or components to process innovation and improvement for the manufacturing of innovated subsystems and components, the US system of spontaneous technology fusion may face a great challenge from Japan. As has been stated elsewhere, process innovations, especially in fabricating manufacturing, can hardly be modularized. The latter requires, rather, synchronization and organized technology fusion. Finally, as analyzed in chapter 6, when it comes to the preservation, maintenance, and enhancement of existing capabilities, in many cases the American system also performs poorly.

The Japanese deficiency in spontaneous technology fusion

In sharp contrast to the American superiority, Japan performs poorly in spontaneous technology fusion. Almost all the constituent elements in the macro garbage can model are missing in the Japanese case. The Japanese education system encourages the mastering of existing knowledge rather than the creation of totally new ideas. Japanese universities are not world-class in basic research. Its public research funding system is relatively centralized and institution-based, and there is very little room for individual initiatives. The organizing of research is also hierarchy-based, with senior research scientists having more weight in determining the direction of research than young scientists have. As a result, as Herbig (1995: 93) observes: 'many of Japan's best and brightest young scientists continue to find their creative urges stifled by a social fabric that seems to idolize seniority, loathe individualism, and muffle debate.' All of the above factors have contributed to a lack of *independently* held innovative ideas in the primordial soup of the Japanese macro garbage can. Since the 1980s, Japanese firms have tried to overcome this deficiency by investing heavily in the best US research universities in the sectors of biotechnology and information technology (Mowery and Teece, 1993), but have had little success to the present day (Forrest, 1996).

In Japan, there is also a chronic dearth of venture capitalists and individualistic entrepreneurship (Herbig, 1995; Tall, 1995). According to *The Economist* (October 16, 1993, p. 93), in 1993, while the USA had about $30 billion specialist venture capital, Japan had only about $7 billion. Of the 130 limited partnership funds in Japan, only 55 were active, and about 80 per cent were subsidiaries of or affiliated with financial institutions, and they invested most funds in established firms rather than in brand-new start-ups. About 70 per cent of the fund characterized as venture capital was actually in the form of loans that went to established firms (Hulme, 1994), largely due to the lack of technical competencies for Japanese venture capital firms to identify and assess seed-stage technological opportunities (Yasui, 1996). Since most venture capital firms are institutional investors, not independent technological entrepreneurs, they also cannot play the role of network organizer and business coordinator (Yasui, 1996). According to Yasui (1996), only 25 per cent of Japanese venture capital firms have consulting capability to assist new ventures they invest in. In summary, in addition to its much smaller size, the Japanese venture capital industry fails to carry out the important functions of identifying innovative ideas, investing in the early-stage venture businesses, providing advisors, and developing networks, all of which are pivotal for American success (Yasui, 1996).

This lack of venture capital funds and value-added services is accompanied by a shortage of individualistic entrepreneurship. Here, the low mobility of workers, the tendency to work with people of long-term relationships, and the behavior of only trusting the knowledge of interconnected people, all hamper the spontaneous emergence of contractual teams for micro fusion. As Herbig (1995: 89) puts it:

> Venture business activity is not as likely in Japan as in the West due to low labor mobility and the Japanese capital market. The supply of capital for potential entrepreneurs is limited in Japan due to an underdeveloped equity market; the bank loan market tends to lend primarily to large sister *keiretsu* firms. The cost of failure for an entrepreneur has traditionally been much higher in Japan due to a lack of mid-career entry opportunities. The cost of breaking into a market is also much higher in Japan due to *keiretsu* structures and interconnecting relationships; hence the higher likelihood of failure in Japan for entrepreneurs.

In addition, the dearth of consulting and other professional services, and an emphasis on connectual knowing, which downgrades specialists and outside consultants, all contribute to Japan's lackluster performance in spontaneous micro fusion in the fields of biotechnology, software, and information services. This deficiency has continued despite the fact that the Japanese government has made information technology and biotechnology a top national priority and supported its development through various tools of industrial policy (Callon, 1995; Forrest, 1996). In comparing US and Japanese innovation patterns in biotechnology, Okimoto and Saxonhouse (1987: 401) observe:

> Although the Japanese government has made biotechnology a national priority, and even though business surveys rank biotechnology as the industry with the most potential for the future, the industry comprises only firms that entered from *established* positions in related fields. By contrast, 111 new U.S. firms were formed between 1977 and 1983 with the explicit intention of exploiting the technological and commercial potential of biotechnology. Venture capitalists in the United States have invested $2.0 billion into these biotechnology ventures, not to mention other sources of finances. This is about 13–14 times the entire amount of venture capital available in Japan for all industries. (*Italics added.*)

In the mid-1990s, while the USA had about 1300 biotech related companies, Japan had a mere 245 (Sawinski and Mason, 1996: 141–145). In the software and computer-related sector, in 1995 the number of establishments in Japan was only 10.3 per cent of the US number (Table 8.3). All these factors have contributed to Japan's lack of competitiveness in biotechnology.

Organized technology fusion: the Japanese advantage

While the USA is superior in spontaneous technology fusion, Japan is unparalleled in organized technology fusion. The dominance of established firms in innovation in

Japan vs. new firms in the USA is widely acknowledged (Westney, 1993; Herbig, 1995: 89). In contrast to the American form of spontaneous technology fusion, the Japanese model of technology fusion is very much organized around the principle of synthesizing existing knowledge across functional and organizational boundaries. What Kodama called 'technology fusion' in Japan is, from the knowledge regime perspective, only one kind of technology fusion that is organized within the connectual governance of Japanese corporations. It is also a fusion of two or more macro technology regimes. Examples are the fusion of optics and electronics to form opto-electronics, and the fusion of mechanics and electronics to form mechatronics (Kodama, 1991). The fusion as described by Kodama, or organized fusion in the terminology of this book, is not a simple combination of existing technologies, nor is it the mere sum of complementary competencies. It is rather an *organic* synthesis of not only competencies of different technological sectors but also the connectual knowledge of how technologies from different sectors can best be synthesized. As Kodama (1995: 203) observes:

> Fusion is more than complementarities because it creates new markets and new growth opportunities for each participant in the innovation. Fusion goes beyond the cumulation of small improvements because it blends incremental improvement from several (often separate) fields to create a product with some extra ingredient not found elsewhere in the market. It goes beyond interindustry relationships because, through joint research, different innovations in different industries progress in parallel with each other.

Unlike spontaneous technology fusion, which depends on modularity and separate knowing as a major means of knowledge creation, in organized technology fusion, connectivity and connectual knowing are the primary means of knowledge creation. Through on-the-job training, job rotation, cross-functional teams, quality circles, close R&D–manufacturing–marketing interaction, and frequent knowledge exchange among producers, suppliers, and customers, Japanese firms create and maintain a knowledge base that is firm-specific, cross-functional, relation-specific, integrative, and contextual. In their comparison of the differences of product development practices between the USA and Japan, Imai *et al.* (1985: 351) observe:

> Division of labor works well in a [US style] system where tasks to be accomplished in each phase are clearly delineated and defined. Each project member knows his or her responsibility, seeks depth of knowledge in a specialized area, and is evaluated on an individual basis. [In Japan,] the norm is to reach out across functional boundaries as well as across different phases. Project members are expected to interact with each other extensively, to share everything from risks, responsibility [and] information to decision making, and to acquire breadth of knowledge and skills.

The Japanese focus on the creation of relation-specific, cross-functional, and contextual knowledge, together with the connectual governance in support of it, contributes greatly to their competitive advantage in organized technology fusion.

Connectual knowing and organized technology fusion

The essence of organized technology fusion is to synthesize various existing technologies seamlessly and organically. To do so, people not only need to have in-depth separate knowledge about each technological domain, but also a wide scope of connectual knowledge about how best to synthesize all the technologies in specific context so that the innovated products not only have the best technical functions but also the highest consumer satisfaction with the lowest costs. Organized technology fusion is, therefore, as Kodama (1995) notes, a process of creating new ways of consumer satisfaction by providing the best function, quality, and lowest costs.

There are several ways to achieve these simultaneous goals. One is by *reducing* the number of components by integrating some of their functions and by *simplifying* the architectural design. The second is through the *simplification* of the production process by combining several once-separate processes together. The third is the practice of design for manufacturing and assembling so that manufacturing costs can be minimized. The fourth is through continuous process and product improvements so as to continuously upgrade functions and reduce costs. All of these methods rely on a superior capability for connectual knowing to effectively create cross-functional, relation-specific, and contextual knowledge for seamless integration, design for manufacturing, and continuous improvement. Here, according to Nonaka (1990), redundancy of knowledge among functions and overlapping organization is the key for the Japanese approach to innovation management, which in the perspective of this book promotes organized fusion. Similarly, Kusunoki and Numagami (1997) also find that cross-functional knowledge created through frequent intra-firm transfer enabled integration of technologies at the functional level.

One good example of this is what Fruin (1997) called 'Knowledge Works' at Hitachi. By bringing together engineers from multiple functions within the firm and suppliers of various parts and subsystems, Hitachi was able to fuse and integrate core competencies across various technological domains to bring forth the world's first SuperSmart card. The Japanese ability of fusing and integrating core competencies across broad technological disciplines also underpins Canon's successful innovation of the AE-1 camera, the world's first single-lens reflex camera with a built-in microprocessor, and the Mini-Copier, the world's first copier that is small, light, inexpensive, easy to use, and maintenance-free. According to Nonaka and Takeuchi (1995: 140–150), by adopting a multi-disciplinary approach which brought nearly 200 knowledge engineers and professionals from all functional areas that were extensively cross-trained, Canon was able to fuse and synthesize its core competencies across various technical domains of product design and process engineering for the innovation of the Mini-Copier, a product of opto-electronics. In product design, the fused core competencies include the design of photoreceptor, toner, copying process, electronics, mechanics, optical system, and copier chemical products. In process engineering, they include cost-down of rubber roller, inspection w/o visual image formation, non-adjust assembly, rational main assembly line, rational unit assembly, plastic molding, foam-plastic for outer structures, roll machine line, press machine line, and photoreceptor drum product line. This process of fusion enables Canon to reduce the number of parts by one-third in the Mini-Copier and by 30–40 per cent in the AE-1 camera. Canon has also dramatically simplified the production process, reduced costs, and increased parts-process precision *ten-fold* (Nonaka and Takeuchi, 1995: 149). By continuing its effort of fusing electronics and optics and by extending the knowledge acquired through the Mini-Copier project, Canon was able to continuously push out new synthetic innovations of opto-electronics such as laser-beam printers, facsimiles, and micro-film reader-printers (Nonaka and Takeuchi, 1995). According to Henderson (1996), Canon's exceptional capability in a series of innovation in the photolithographic alignment equipment industry is also due largely to the creation of architectural knowledge crossing functional boundaries. From the knowledge regime perspective, this is very much the result of Canon's emphasis on connectual knowing and organized fusion. Indeed, Canon's superior capability of innovation and fusion in opto-electronics has earned it the second place in the top ten patenting corporations of US patents (see Table 8.6). Also among the top ten are the Japanese electronics and opto-electronics companies of NEC, Hitachi, Mitsubuchi, Fujitsu, Sony, and Matsushita. Indeed, according to the National Science Board (1998: 6–21), the Japanese strength in opto-electronics is best reflected by its superior patenting performance in photography, photocopying, and consumer electronics.

Table 8.6 Top ten patenting corporations in the USA

In 1996		1977–1996	
Company	Patents	Company	Patents
IBM	1,867	GE	16,206
Canon	1,541	IBM	15,205
Motorola	1,064	Hitachi	14,500
NEC	1,043	Canon	13,797
Hitachi	963	Toshiba	13,413
Misubishi	934	Misubishi	10,192
Toshiba	914	US Philips	9,943
Fujitsu	869	Kodak	9,729
Sony	855	AT&T	9,380
Matsushita	841	Motorola	9,143

Source: National Science Board (1998: 6–19).

Customization and contextualization as enablers for organized fusion

Underpinning the Japanese superior capability in opto-electronics is the capability for contextually linking many existing technologies for the application to a specific mission of fusion. Here, Japan's connectual governance and its dominant organizing principles of organic customization and contextualization play a significant role as the enabler for organized technology fusion. Organic customization happens when specific technologies, tools, and skills are developed from existing pools for the completion of a specific task in a specific context. According to Fruin (1997), in its effort to develop the SuperSmart card (computer-on-a-card) in the mid-1980s, Toshiba was able to realize the demanding technical requirements of reliability, miniaturization, and multi-functionality by pooling teams of multiple competencies to develop tailored display technology, integrated circuit, assembly technology, transducer, battery, software development, and system software that integrate many of its existing state-of-the-art technologies. Similarly, in its innovation of the 3.5 inch micro floppy disk drive, Sony was able to realize its mission of reduced energy use, increase storage capacity, and increased reliability and quality by pooling, synthesizing, and customizing its core capabilities in designing and processing: (1) the disk drives adapted from video recording, (2) media materials enhanced from magnetic storage; (3) the plastic shell extended from experience with cassettes; (4) the motor from its electronics components group; and (5) LSI technology derived from its semiconductor division (Kash and Rycroft, 1999: 135). Sony was also able to invent the CD Player and Playstations through the same process of fusion and customization.

In the case of the semiconductor sector, while the USA is superior in the design of separate, standardized, and general purpose logic chips, the emphasis on connectual knowing in Japan has led to its strength in the design and manufacturing of customized, imbedded, and specialized micro chips organically and seamlessly integrated into automobiles, cameras, game machines, camcorders, and other home electronics, opto-electronics, and information appliances.

Trickle-up innovation for organized technology fusion

The superior capability in organized technology fusion is also embodied in the preponderance of *trickle-up* innovation. In his study of innovation and commercialization in Japanese consumer electronics firms, Branscomb (1989) observes that, in contrast to the predominance of *spin-off* innovation in the USA, the Japanese approach to technology innovation and commercialization is a 'trickle-up' process in which:

> A new technology is introduced in a consumer item rather than a high-end or industrial product in order to gain manufacturing experience at low functional levels and at low cost. At the same time, studies are conducted on functions that are necessary for products in higher-value markets. Only after the process and the technology is mastered is the technology introduced into markets with higher margins and more specialized applications (Kodama, 1995: 54–56).

From the perspective of this book, the sharp contrast of trickle-up and spin-off innovation is precisely the result of a contrast between connectual and separate knowing and between organized and spontaneous technology fusion. Since organized fusion needs the establishment and maintenance of existing technologies, it is understandable that Japanese firms begin with the very basic production of consumer products. This enables the accumulation of cross-functional and cross-technological knowledge and expertise that is crucial for further integration and fusion to move up the ladder of technological sophistication. The needs for fusing product design with process innovation and for integrating cross-functional and relational knowledge require that a firm build its competencies from the ground up.

On the other hand, in the American case, a possibility of isolating a technological domain for product innovation and the availability of expertise and core competencies in the market enable spontaneous technology fusion to happen without the need to gradually build up competencies and accumulate connectual knowledge. The hyper-mobility of knowledge workers and professionals further facilitates spin-off innovations in the USA.

Process innovation and organized technology fusion

Such a fundamental difference is also behind the Japanese focus on process innovation vs. the American preoccupation with product innovation. According to a survey of US and Japanese firms, Mansfield (1988a) found that Japanese companies invest roughly two-thirds of their R&D in process innovation, double the one-third proportion of their US counterparts. According to another estimate by Mansfield (1988b), the percentage of total R&D costs devoted to tooling and manufacturing equipment and facilities in Japan is about twice that in the USA.

As stated above, in many cases, product innovation is much easier to be separated, modularized, and encapsulated than process innovations is. As a result, spontaneous technology fusion mainly occurs in the domains of the former whereas organized technology fusion always involves the creation of connectual knowledge between product design and process design and among various manufacturing processes. The best example of this is the emergence of 300 specialized 'fabless' semiconductor design firms in the USA and the dominance of vertically integrated electronic, semiconductor, and computer firms in Japan. While the former focus on product design, the latter stress the seamless integration of semiconductors with electronics and the manufacturing process.

In the manufacturing sectors, an artificial separation of product and process design in US firms has led to a much higher percentage of innovation costs for manufacturing start-up than is the case for their Japanese counterparts (Mansfield, 1988b). This is especially true in the sectors of machinery and rubber and metals, in which the ratio is 5 per cent vs. 20 per cent and 6 per cent vs. 15 per cent respectively between the USA and Japan (Mansfield, 1988b). This has given Japanese firms competitive advantage in these sectors.

Incremental improvement and organized technology fusion

Japan's focus on incremental improvement is, to a large extent, also related to its stress on organized technology fusion. While incremental improvements play a crucial role as a facilitator here, its impact on spontaneous technology fusion is minimal. First, incremental improvements often occur when connectual and contextual knowledge is created that links various technological processes. Second, in many cases, incremental improvements happen when people continuously change the interface among subsystems and components. Third, in many cases, incremental improvements within one task and technological domain are directed toward improvement in the execution of other tasks and other technological functions, as happens in design for manufacturing and assembling. It is clear that in many cases, organized technology fusion would not be possible without the support of the knowledge accumulated through incremental improvements.

Organized fusion of external technologies

The Japanese emphasis on connectual knowing and organized fusion also enables a fast and cost-effective absorption of external technologies. Because of extensive cross-training and a close monitoring of outside technical advancements (Lynn *et al.*, 1993), Japanese engineers are more likely to incorporate and synthesize external technologies for internal development and fusion. Indeed, according to a survey by Mansfield (1988b: 1160), 'the ratio of innovation cost or time for a new product based on external technology to that for a new product based on internal technology tends to be much lower in Japan than in the United States.' As in the case of the digital watch industry (Numagami, 1996), the emphasis on connectual knowing and fusion has enabled Japanese electronics firms to absorb liquid crystal display (LCD) technology and fuse it with its strength in electronics and mechanics to create a strong digital watch industry that beats both their US and their Swiss competitors. This episode has happened repeatedly in the sectors of automobiles, home electronics, and semiconductors.

The Japanese tendency to absorb and synthesize US technologies is best evidenced by the fact that Japan has been the largest buyers of US intellectual property rights as represented by royalties and license fees since the 1980s. As Table 8.7 indicates, in 1995 alone the USA had a trade balance of $1221 million with Japan generated from the exchange and use of patents and other proprietary inventions and technologies. Although it has declined since 1987, US exports to Japan were 5.36 times its imports from Japan in 1995.

Table 8.7 Bilateral US–Japanese trade in patents and other proprietary inventions and technology, 1987–1995 (millions of US dollars)

	Receipts	Payments	Balance	Export/import ratio
1987	723	88	635	8.22
1988	883	108	775	8.18
1989	897	109	788	8.23
1990	1028	141	887	7.29
1991	1219	138	1081	8.83
1992	1268	145	1123	8.74
1993	1434	191	1243	7.51
1994	1373	262	1111	5.24
1995	1501	280	1221	5.36

Source: Calculated from National Science Board (1998: A-369).

While this large gap in technology transfer partly reflects the US dominance in high technologies (National Science Board, 1998), it also supports the hypothesis that Japanese firms are more receptive to external technology. Such a great gap may also reflect that while many US innovations are externalized and encapsulated into saleable forms such as patents and licenses, most Japanese inovations are imbedded, fused, and customized in firm-specific and mission-specific manufacturing technologies that are difficult to sell through the contractual markets.

Fusion and the Japanese advantage in advanced manufacturing

Indeed, in addition to the advantage of opto-electronics and mechatronics, the great advantage of organized technology fusion lies in the terrain of advanced manufacturing technologies. Its closely coupled nature, its imperative for customization, its need for organic integration and shop-floor learning, and its requirement for seamless integration of various technologies and processes all generate competitive advantage for Japanese firms that focuses on connectual knowing and organized fusion.

Conclusion: the entrepreneurship debate reconsidered

The distinction between spontaneous and organized technology fusion and an analysis of their differential impact on sectoral patterns of national competitiveness can solve many dilemmas surrounding the debate about the role of individualistic entrepreneurs, venture capital, hyper-mobility, industrial *keiretsu*, and industrial policy. Often the dominance of a governance mechanism that facilitates one kind of technology fusion hampers another. Therefore, while individualist entrepreneurship, venture capital, and hyper-mobility facilitate spontaneous technology fusion, they usually inhibit organized technology fusion. Conversely, while the practices of long-term subcontracting relationships, lifetime employment, an emphasis on generalists, job rotation, and vertical and horizontal *keiretsu* facilitate organized technology fusion, they are inimical to spontaneous technology fusion.

Since the relative effectiveness of spontaneous vs. organized technology fusion is sector-specific, so are the impacts of different governance mechanisms for knowledge creation on national competitiveness. From this point of view, without differentiating sector-specific effect, it is misleading to debate the virtues of American-style 'free market' economy vs. Japanese-style 'organized market' economy. This is especially true when debating the relative merits of the values of individualistic entrepreneurship, venture capital, hyper-mobility, long-term subcontracting relationships, vertical and horizontal *keiretsu*, and industrial policy in particular. All of the mutually opposing views could be both right and wrong depending on which sector one chooses as the exemplar. In the technological sectors of opto-electronics, mechatronics, and opto-mechatronics, because of the non-modular nature of their knowledge structure, organized technology fusion is still the most important form of innovation. Consequently, when one focuses on the national competitiveness of these sectors, all the previous criticisms of individualistic entrepreneurship, venture capital, short-termism, and hyper-mobility (Kash, 1989; Florida and Kenney, 1990; Porter, 1992; Baldwin and Clark, 1994) are still valid; so are the praises of long-term supplier relationships, employment relationships, as well as cross-functional teams, and tacit learning.

However, when we shift our attention to the new economy of information technology, software, information services, and biotechnology, where one can either effectively separate, modularize, and encapsulate a whole system into modular subsystems for independent and spontaneous innovation, or explore the logical connections systematically, all of a sudden all the merits and problems as discussed through the exemplars of automobiles and home electronics *turn upside down*. The very factors that were blamed for the decline of American competitiveness in automobiles and electronic appliances become the great contributors for American competitive success in these emerging sectors.

The positive impact of individualistic entrepreneurs, venture capitalists, and hyper-mobile knowledge workers in the newly emerging sectors of information technology, software, and information services, however, does not constitute proof of the *universal* validity of the ideological advocates of neo-liberal and free-market policies. Although its importance may decline with the new economy of knowledge and of e-business, organized technology fusion and therefore all its facilitating factors are still crucial for the success of the complex technological sectors of automobiles, opto-electronics, mechatronics, and opto-mechatronics.

Indeed, with the increasing importance of software, information technology, databases, information services, and other knowledge-based professional services in the emerging new economy, we can assume that *the pendulum of national competitiveness is shifting back from Japan to the USA*. It would, however, be premature to announce the death of the Japanese mechanisms of connectual governance and connectual knowledge creation. With its superior capability in organized technology fusion, Japan is and will continue to be a powerful player in many advanced, non-modular, and complex technologies.

Moreover, it is highly possible that once the new information revolution reaches its limits and becomes a relatively mature sector, the Japanese may still take over the world markets of semiconductors and computer hardware, especially those that need to be seamlessly integrated into consumer electronics, and mechatronics, by exploiting their superior capability in manufacturing and in organized technology fusion. Indeed, as the focus of computer industry is shifting from PCs to information appliances, and consequently from universal microchips to specialized chips for specialized devices, there is already some evidence of Japanese competitiveness in the latter (Takahashi, 1998). Even in the sector of computer software, the development of technology may reach such a point, as many Japanese technologists have dreamed, that many functions of software products must be imbedded in the design of hardware so that the Japanese could regain their competitive advantage through their superior capability in the seamless and organic technology fusion of software and hardware. This scenario is much more easily achieved once specialized chips in information appliances begin to dominate the market. Notwithstanding these possible trends, the USA can still stand at the frontier of the next waves of industrial revolution: biotechnology and life sciences.

Aside from all the above postulates, indeed, what we should claim is not the end of Japanese connectual governance, as some scholars prematurely announced during the height of the East Asian financial crisis in 1997 and 1998, nor the end of history culminating in the American model of 'free-market' capitalism, but rather the end of Newtonian thinking which claims that there is only one best way of doing things and of creating knowledge for all situations. Instead, what we need is discretionary, contingent, and sector-specific thinking that can accommodate the increasing complexity of our socio-technological world.

Notes

1. One possible exception might be Softbank, a computer service and software distribution company who started in 1981 and rose rapidly in Japan.
2. I owe the concept of micro fusion vs. macro fusion to Dr. Christopher T. Hill.
3. More accurately, as will be analyzed in chapter 10, the USA is good at technological systems of large-scale complexity, while Japan is excellent at those of middle-range complexity.

CHAPTER NINE

Modularity and Connectivity

A study of underlying rules fosters insight into characteristic ways developed in the United States to organize tasks appropriate to any complex modern culture. My claim is not that everything in American life has become *modular*, but rather that the remarkable range of domains where *modular* organization is prominent justifies thinking of such rules as *distinctively* American in their flowering. (*Italics added.*)

John G. Blair (1988: 9)

Two ways of dealing with complexity: the impact of culture

With the increasing complexity of technology, the problem of how effectively to deal with it has been the key challenge of our time. As a result, the ability of a nation or a firm to attack such a challenge will largely determine its competitiveness. Technically, there are two fundamentally different methods. The first tries to *divide* and *partition* a complex system into subsystems and then *modularize* and *encapsulate* them into relatively *independent* modules for an independent investigation by specialists. The second takes the system as a whole and tries to solve the problem of complexity by exploring the *connectivity*, interdependence and interaction of subsystems and by creating synthetic knowledge about the system to simplify and streamline not only component design but also component interfaces. While the first method can be called 'modularization,' the second can be called 'connectualization.'

There are fundamental differences in these two ways of dealing with complexity. Whereas modularization is more or less mechanical and analytical, connectualization is organic and synthetic. While the former stresses specialization as an effective way of dealing with complexity, the latter emphasizes the importance of generalists and cross-functional synthesis. Whereas the former highly values separate knowing, the latter cherishes connectual knowing.

The organizing principles of modularization and connectualization can often be competing and mutually exclusive. In many cases, the more one can effectively modularize a problem or a system, the less there is the need for connection. Conversely, in many complex systems, the denser and tighter the connectivity of the subsystems, the less the possibility of effective modularization. Notwithstanding this, often the principles of modularization and connectualization can be complementary in attacking the problem of complexity, especially for the development of complex socio-technical systems. There are always limits of division and modularization, just as there are burdens of connectualization. First, both within an encapsulated module and across many modules, there are always some connections that are difficult to be completely revealed by separate knowing. Second, the effectiveness of modularization requires an in-depth knowledge of the pattern of connectivity among subsystems and components. When such knowledge does not exist, it often leads to the wrong modularization that severs important knowledge links. Third, effective modularization minimizes unnecessary connections and enables people to focus on either the much more delicate connections within the module or the much broader abstract connections in a higher level system.

Because the organizing principle of modularization makes possible the independent attack of complex problems, it is always preferred in the most individualist society – the USA. On the other hand, since it makes parts interdependent and connected with one another, the organizing principles of connectualization are better fitted into the collectivist culture such as Japan. Indeed, as the experimental study by Chow *et al.* (1991) proves, while workers with a high individualist cultural orientation have a higher manufacturing performance when work flow and/or pay are *independent*, workers with a low individualist cultural orientation have a higher manufacturing performance when work flow and/or pay are *interdependent*. Therefore, when it comes to the case of the USA, a country with extreme individualism, in addition to the cultural push for independence, it is also economically rational to follow the organizing principle of modularization to make both work flow and pay of individuals independent. Conversely, in the case of Japan, a country with a strong level of collectivism and groupism, both the cultural preference and the economic rationale lead to the dominance of the organizing principles of connectualization so that both the tasks and the incentives of individuals within a connectual structure are interdependent in attacking a complex issue. Therefore, it is clear that US firms generally have a comparative advantage in the sectors where tasks can be divided into independent modules, whereas Japanese firms have a comparative advantage in the sectors where tasks are interdependent and cannot be divided into independent modules without the loss of knowledge creation opportunities.

Modularity as a design role

According to Baldwin and Clark (1997: 84), modularity is a design rule that builds 'a complex product or process from smaller subsystems that can be designed independently yet function together as a whole.' To realize the independence of subsystems, there is a need for minimizing not only incidental interactions (Ulrich and Tung, 1991) but also knowledge links between subsystems. This is achieved through what Fodor (1983) calls *information encapsulation* in which a subsystem operates according to rules and information within its own boundaries, which is largely in isolation from the information from other subsystems and the whole system. In so doing, it eliminates the need for knowledge exchange in the development of subsystems. In other words, in a modular system, information and knowledge for each module are *self-contained* and therefore *encapsulated*. There is minimal need for the information and knowledge of other modules in order to design, produce, and operate a specific module in a system. When the internal design of one module is changed there is also no need to change the others as long as the external interface stays the same. By minimizing the interdependence of subsystems, the design rule of modularity enables *simultaneous* and *independent* innovation in all subsystems (Langlois and Robertson, 1995). It also insures that any improvement in one module will automatically be transformed into an improvement in the whole system.

Modularity as a characteristic of the knowledge structure of a system

The effective implementation of the design rule of modularity, however, depends on the nature of the products or processes under development, the type of technologies applied, and fundamentally, the knowledge structure imbedded. When the knowledge in the design of one component is crucial for the effective design and production of other components, the knowledge structure of the system is interconnected and therefore non-modular. Conversely, the knowledge structure of a system is modular when: (1) the effective design and production of any component does not require the knowledge input from other components; (2) a change in the design and production of one component does not require any change in the design and production of other components in order for the operation of the whole system to be effective; and (3) the system reaches optimum when each component is optimal in its function. Because of the sectoral differences in knowledge structure, while any technological system has both possibilities of modular and non-modular design, the knowledge creation consequences of modularity in the design and production processes are sector-contingent. In some sectors where the knowledge structure is modular, such as PCs, software packages, information services and other professional services, it is relatively easy to modularize the design of products and processes without the potential loss of knowledge links and knowledge creation opportunities. In some other sectors, such as automobiles, opto-electronics, and mechatronics, it is much more difficult to do so. Modularization in the former (where the knowledge structure is modular) leads to a plethora of spontaneous technology fusion, whereas the artificial modularization of the latter can cause failure in identifying potential knowledge links and in exploiting knowledge creation opportunities.

Modularity and connectivity as two functions of mind

Modularity and connectivity are also two fundamentally different ways of organizing information processing in the human mind. As early as the 1970s, Ornstein (1975) observed that there are two hemispheres of the human brain. In the left hemisphere, information is processed in a linear, modular, sequential, analytical, and separate way. In the right hemisphere, information is processed in a simultaneous, parallel, holistic, connectual, and relational way. Although neuro-scientists today recognize that there is no *rigid* compartmentalization of functions, they still admit the modularity of the mind and the general split between the two functional parts of modularity and connectionism (Ornstein, 1991; Pinker, 1997).

Further evidence of such a functional split can be found in the ongoing debate between the *modularity hypothesis* and the *connectionist theory* of the human cognitive process (Garfield, 1987). The modularity hypothesis (Fodor, 1983) assumes that modularity is the primary means of organizing information in the cognitive architecture of the mind as well as natural language presentation. It further assumes that all cognitive processing is domain-specific, sequential, and informationally *encapsulated*. The connectionist approach of cognition, on the other hand, argues that information processing is massively *parallel*. Bits of information *simultaneously* go through extensive networks of connections between nodes in the nerve system (Garfield, 1987). While neither side denies the relevance of the other, the real issue of the debate focuses on the relative importance of modularity vs. connectivity in human information processing.

Modularity and connectivity as cultural patterns of thinking and knowing

This debate cannot be resolved without resort to cultural differences in the dominant patterns of information processing. In proposing his theory of human information processing, Ornstein (1975, 1991) observes that Western psychology has focused almost exclusively on left-hemispheric consciousness, whereas its Eastern counterpart has concentrated on the right-hemispheric consciousness. According to him, the evolution of cultural differences in the patterns of information processing results from the fact that the nerve system of a person becomes wired up in a particular way because of experiences early in infancy. Similarly, Gardner (1999: 34) admits that human beings exhibit multiple intelligences and faculties of information processing that 'can be activated in a cultural setting to solve problems or create products that are of value in a culture.' According to Markus and Kitayama (1998: 68), while the socialization process in the West has nurtured 'the independent model of personhood,' the same process in Japan has fostered 'the interdependent model of self.' The former treats individuals as independent, self-contained, autonomous, and decontextualized, whereas the latter sees a person as 'an interdependent entity who is part of an encompassing social relationship' (p. 69). The independent model of self promotes modular thinking in which individuals separate themselves from others and their surrounding social contexts, and make decisions according to an objective calculation of self-interest and universal rules. Conversely, the interdependent model of self facilitates connectual and contextual knowing in which individuals connect themselves with others and with their surrounding social contexts and make decisions according to a specific context of relationships and situations.

From the view of linguistics, it is evident that 'language also shapes our higher order cognitive processes' (Kashima and Kashima, 1998: 462). While the abstract and linear nature of the English language has facilitated the Anglo-American tendency of modular and decontextual knowing, the relational, contextual, and synchronic nature of Chinese characters that are used both in China and Japan has certainly contributed to the dearth of abstract/analytic thinking and to the richness of connectual and contextual thinking in these two countries.[1]

In addition, the dominant philosophy in the West has facilitated the rise of modular thinking. This is reflected not only in the rise and dominance of analytic philosophy, logic positivism, and various other Western modernist thoughts, but also in the Newtonian world view. According to Chia (1995: 585), inherent in both Newtonian and Western modernist predisposition is 'a fundamental belief in the *isolatability* of different aspects of human experience.' According to Whitehead (1985) as cited by Chia (1995: 585), this is reflected in a fundamental assumption of the concept of an '*ideally isolated system*' in which things, social entities and events are able to be isolated. This world view of modular systems is also apparent in Parsons' theory of social systems, as Piore (1996: 742) comments: 'In Parsons, society is understood as one vast system divided into a series of distinct and relatively autonomous realms, or subsystems. Each realm is connected to the others at a limited number of particular points.' Similarly, in proposing the design of hierarchical organizational systems to attack the problem of complexity, Simon (1962, 1976) advocates the design of a 'nearly decomposable system' in which the interdependence of components is minimized.

By contract, as analyzed in chapter 4, the dominant philosophies in the East in general and in Japan in particular, including Confucianism, Taoism, and Buddhism, not only lack the tradition and spirit of analysis, but also promote a holistic world view that emphasizes connectivity, interdependence, and associative thinking. Indeed, there is an increasing body of work supporting this East–West division in the patterns of thinking and knowing. While the Western way of thinking is more analytic, modular, and abstract, the Eastern way is more synthetic, connectual, and contextual (de Bono, 1991, 1994; Hampden-Turner and Trompenaars, 1993; Lessem and Neubauer, 1994).

Modularization and connectualization as organizing principles: the socio-cultural construction of technological trajectories

Once we acknowledge the cultural differences in the patterns of thinking and knowing, it is understandable that the knowledge structure and therefore the possibility of modularity in a sector do not *alone* determine the technological trajectories in a nation. The evolutionary path of a technology is very much socio-culturally constructed as well as technologically shaped. In the case of modularity, its emergence and dominance in a given sector is not solely determined by technology, but rather influenced by dominant cultural paradigms and institutions. It is in this socio-cultural construction of technological trajectories that we distinguish between modularity as a design rule and modularization as a socio-cultural organizing principle. As stated elsewhere, in the USA, the penchant for autonomy and independence, together with an emphasis on separate knowing, leads to the dominance of the organizing principle of modularization, which in turn leads to the *emergence* and *preponderance* of technological trajectories that are modular. Conversely, the Japanese preference for connection and interdependence, combined with its stress on connectual knowing, leads to the organizing principles of connectualization, contextualization, and customization, which in turn have given rise to the emergence and dominance of non-modular technological development.

While an examination of concrete examples will be given below, it is important to point out here that the focus on the *emergence* and *dominance* of a given technological trajectory is crucial in our effort to link cultural paradigms and technological trajectories. It is obvious that once a given technological trajectory has proved its superiority, it is always open for imitation by other nations. The possible final convergence of technological trajectories is of interest neither to our research nor to the study of national competitiveness. The pertinent question here is why a given technological trajectory *emerged* and *predominated* in one country rather than in others. Following this is the question that once the superiority of a given technological paradigm or trajectory is recognized, how do other nations react to and learn from it? Will they simply copy what is practiced or will they synthesize their endogenous organizing principles with transplanted ones? It is in answering these questions that the knowledge regime perspective employed in this book can provide insights that the current studies of technological innovation, technology policy, and competitiveness fail to deliver.

The dominance of modularization in the American life

While many works have been written about the importance of modularity as either a design rule or a product characteristic (von Hippel, 1990; Ulrich and Tung, 1991; Langlois and Robertson, 1992; Morris and Ferguson, 1993; Ulrich, 1995; Baldwin and Clark, 1997, 2000), there is unfortunately a dearth of studies on how cultures impact on the practice and adoption of modularity – or what I call the organizing principle of modularization – in technological sectors.

As one exception, in a fascinating book *Modular America: Cross-Cultural Perspectives on the Emergence of an American Way*, the American scholar John Blair (1988) explains how various aspects of American life have been organized according to the rule of modularity. The modular systems he explored include: the American system of manufactures, American college curriculum, skyscraper architecture, American football, blues and jazz, Walt Whitman's poetry, and American rules for land tenure. The American system of manufactures as it emerged in the late nineteenth century was a modular system in which each part of a product was modularized and standardized so that it was interchangeable and therefore could be assembled without the specific need for fitting and reworking. By inventing and using precision tools, such as jigs and gauges, and specialized machines, and by the design rule of standardization, interchangeable parts could be produced and assembled by unskilled labor. In so doing, the knowledge links between parts and in their assembly were either minimized or encapsulated into the design of standards. The college curriculum developed in the USA is also a modular system in which each course is a relatively independent module that carries certain quantitative credits. Credits earned from one course are additive and interchangeable with some others. When the accumulation of credits reaches a certain number, students are eligible to earn a degree. The knowledge links among the modules of courses are imbedded in the design of prerequisites, required courses, and distribution requirements.

A careful examination of the American way of life can lead to an extension of endless modular systems that have emerged and are still dominant in the USA. These include, among others, the M-form organization; the linear model of innovation; American academic disciplines; the system of professions; the American system of jobs and employment; the American system of contractual supplier relationships; the American system of information service; the American hamburger, buffet, and canned and prepared foods; American furniture; American credit recording, rating, and reporting system; American movies and TV series; the IBM 360 mainframe; the American invention of cargo containers, and object-oriented programming languages such as C + + and java.

Taylorism as an institution for modularization

Not only was the American system of manufactures in the nineteenth century a modular system, but Taylorism, the very force that transformed corporate America from craft production to mass production, is also a mechanism for modularization. According to Littler (1978), Taylorism involves the systematic analysis of work, the division of labor, and the resultant process of decomposition. The five principles for *decomposition* in Taylorist organization as summarized by Littler (1978: 188) include: (1) a general principle of *maximal* fragmentation; (2) the divorce of planning and doing; (3) the divorce of 'direct' and 'indirect' labor; (4) minimization of skill requirements and job-learning time; and (5) minimization of material handling. From the knowledge regime perspective, all these principles serve to maximally divide, separate, modularize, and encapsulate the organizing of business functions.

First, by separating thinking from executing and by assigning the work of product and process design solely to industrial/production engineers, the Taylorist firm separates design activity from operation activity and modularizes and encapsulates both of them into relatively *independent* functions. While industrial engineers design what they consider to be the best operating procedures, the blue-collar workers need only follow the standardized routines. By separating thinking from doing, such a modularization process minimizes the knowledge exchange between industrial engineers and shop-floor workers. By partitioning and modularizing the function of knowledge creation further into independent professions of industrial engineers, design engineers, and manufacturing engineers, the modularization process also minimizes management's dependence on the skills of craftsmen, and ultimately has led to the demise of the craftsmen class in most American industrial sectors.

Second, by the use of specialized machines, the design of detailed and standardized operating routines, and the standardization of job tasks, the Taylorist firm minimizes the skill requirements of blue-collar workers and makes them interchangeable. Taylorism therefore transforms the labor into a fungible, modular, and interchangeable factor of production. Third, by proposing a further functional specialization within the role of managers into relatively independent departments of accounting, personnel, marketing, and planning, and by the resultant systematic collection of information, the Taylorist firm minimizes its dependency on the local knowledge of first, foremen and later, middle management. Davis (quoted in Littler, 1978: 192) summarizes the 'minimum interaction model' of Taylorism:

> There is a minimal connection between the individual and the organization in terms of skill, training, involvement and complexity of his contribution, in return for maximum flexibility and *independence* on the part of organization in using its manpower. In other words the organization strives for maximum *interchangeability* of personnel (with minimum training) to reduce its *dependency* on the availability, ability, or motivation of individuals. (*Italics added.*)

Jelinek (1979), Gillespie (1991), and Nelson (1995) also interpret Taylorism as a way of seeking *independence* for managers and owners in the increasingly complex world of manufacturing. Once we accept this linkage, the reason for Taylorism emerging and predominating in the USA is easily understood.

The Fordist mass production firm as an institution for modularization

While instituting most Taylorist principles, the Fordist firm – a further development of Taylorism – also adopts the organizing principles of linearization and sequentialization as facilitators for modularization. By arranging corporate design and production activities, including the innovation process, in a sequential way, and by adding *buffers* to reduce the *interdependence* between production procedures, the Fordist firm makes each process relatively modularized, encapsulated, and therefore independent.

The first way of modularization is the *decoupling* of production lines through the use of inventory as buffers, as Johnson (1992: 38) notes:

> To cope with the complexity of variety, Americans *decoupled* the [production] line, allowing different processes to operate at *independent* rates, and created inventory buffers and warehouses to absorb production surpluses and deficits between processes. (*Italics added.*)

Parallel to the decoupling of the production line is the decoupling of the design of visible parts (focusing on the creation of styles) and the design of invisible parts (delivering purely technical functions). In the case of the US automobile sector, Clark (1987: 20) quotes the findings of Bill Abernathy:

> Following the initiative of GM in creating a central styling department (in 1926–1928) the design policy became one of dealing *separately* with the visible and invisible parts of the car. The visible parts, the outer skin and the interior, were subject to creative styling skills aimed at creating a consumer image of evolvement towards high style. Changes of the outer skin were typically of a small-scale, cosmetic nature. Occasionally, say every decade, there would be a major shift. Many of the styling changes could be *readily* accommodated on the final assemble lines simply by substituting components or adding new items. Beneath the outer skin of the large US cars there was *plenty of room* for factoring in the overall processes of the corporation into *distinct subparts* each undertaken in a very large value in specialized productive units. (*Italics added.*)

Because of the modularity of parts and their design, GM, as well as other US car-makers who followed its lead, could retain the economies of scale and at the same time provide multiple car models for various market segments. Car designers could also change styles for each model every year with little cost, since they only needed to change the visible parts, while leaving most invisible parts unchanged.

The third way of modularization is through the decoupling of parts configuration by leaving many vacant rooms and spaces as buffers for independent adjustment. This makes it possible to change the design of one part, or to add new parts, with little need to change other parts and their configuration. This further reduces the costs of model changes, although it involves the cost of wasted space, increased weights, and clumsy designs. Finally, as discussed in chapter 5, the modularity of the Fordist firm is further enhanced by a sharp division of labor between design and manufacturing engineers, between engineers and blue-collar workers, and between production and marketing, and by the standardization of parts, skills, jobs, routines, and procedures.

The competitive market as a form of modularization

The competitive market as predominant in the USA can also be viewed as a mechanism for modularization. First, each firm in the USA can be seen as an independent module that can be freely sold, merged, disbanded, and spun off at the owner's will. Second, through the competitive job market, combined with the standardization of skills and job classifications, each employee becomes an independent module that can be freely substituted through recruitment. Third, the suppliers of standard components can also be treated as independent, interchangeable, and substitutable modules that can be acquired through arm's length transactions and in a competitive bidding process. In sum, the competitive bidding process transforms each firm, its employees, and its suppliers into independent modules that are interchangeable and fungible in the contractual market.

Professionalization as a form of modularization

The modularization of employees, especially knowledge workers, cannot be complete without the complementary process of professionalization. From the knowledge regime perspective, professionalization is a process of standardizing, modularizing, and encapsulating a special domain of knowledge, skills, and expertise that is sufficiently different from, and independent of, other domains and therefore saleable in the contractual market. The first step of professionalization is to separate a specific domain for independent and separate knowing. The second is to dismiss the contextual insights of laymen by establishing special jargons, well-guarded credentials, and contested methodologies. The third step is to standardize the established knowledge, skills, and expertise not only to safeguard quality but also to mark the market value. Through these steps, the contextual knowledge links are either dissolved or transformed, individual idiosyncrasies in knowledge and skills are removed, and laymen's contextual claims for knowledge dismissed. As a result, professionals within the same field become modules of capability carriers that are interchangeable and substitutable in many cases.

In the USA, the preference for separate knowing, together with its zeal for autonomy and independence, has led to the proliferation of professions far beyond the imagination of East Asians who take a more connectual view. For example, while marketing, finance, human resource management, and more generally management are seen as independent professions and highly valued in the USA, the Japanese would see these domains not as scientific professions but rather as activities whose knowledge can only be accumulated through insights and experiences (Locke, 1996; Johansson and Nonaka, 1996). The competitive implication of professionalization is sector-contingent. It is advantageous in such sectors as professional services where the whole knowledge creation process can be effectively modularized and encapsulated without the loss of potential knowledge creation opportunities. Conversely, as analyzed before, in the sectors of manufacturing, it can be disadvantageous.

Abstract connectivity and modularization

In any complex technological system, with all the possibilities of modularization, there are always irreducible connections among subsystems and components. While the extent of connectivity varies across technological sectors, its *nature* also changes not only across technological sectors, but also across nations. In the USA, the penchant for autonomy and independence has led to the dominance of *abstract connectivity* in which different modules, components, and subsystems of a socio-technical system are connected by *universalistic* rules, logistics, routines, standards, modules, and formal coordinating mechanisms. In Japan, the penchant for connection and interdependence has caused the dominance of *contextual connectivity* in which different modules, components, and subsystems of a socio-technical system are connected by organic, personal, cross-functional, seamless, and contextual links.

Of great interest here is the isomorphic link between abstract connectivity and modularization. First, by encapsulating and making self-containing the function of each subsystem, the modularization process makes possible the *abstract, universal*, and *decontextualized* connection of all subsystems. The modularity of subsystems enables the design of a system architecture that focuses on the upper-level functional connections and external interfaces among subsystems without the need for considering the inner idiosyncrasies of each subsystem. Second, the very concept of a system architecture that does not need to consider the inner-working of subsystems makes the system architecture itself an add-on and an upper-level *module* that is *independent* of the inner workings of all other subsystems. Therefore, the pursuit of abstract connectivity in the design of system architecture is itself an effort at modularization, and can therefore be attacked by specialists of systems integration. Finally, by providing universal standards, logistic maps, rules and procedures for connecting each subsystem and for imbedding all the physical, technological, and knowledge links, the abstract connectivity imbedded in the open system architecture facilitates the independence and autonomy of all subsystems as long as they follow the *universal* standards and rules.

It is this *symbiotic* and mutually reinforcing nature of modularization and abstract connectivity that makes both of them dominant organizing principles in the USA. Many mechanisms for modularization, standardization, professionalization, decontextualization, and quantification are also simultaneously mechanisms for abstract connectivity. These include, among others, the use of universal standards, universal formulas and rules, statistical models, information systems, management control systems, operating manuals, and software packages.

One good example of a system of abstract connectivity is that imbedded in such software packages as Windows 98, Peoplesoft's enterprise systems, and Oracle's database architecture. Indeed, three primary tasks of developing any software package are: (1) dividing tasks into relatively independent modules; (2) establishing a system architecture that provides explicit connectivities between modules; and (3) exploring and imbedding all possible standardized contingencies and abstract connectivities at all levels. The US competitiveness in packaged software lies partly in the possibility of making explicit and imbedding all possible abstract connectivities.

Modularization as a double-edged sword for US competitiveness

The predominance of modularization in the USA is a double-edged sword for American competitiveness. In such closed technological systems as automobiles, opto-electronics, and mechatronics, it creates a competitive disadvantage because it cuts away the contextual knowledge links and foregoes contextual and esoteric physical fits that are of crucial importance for both cost deduction and quality enhancement. Conversely, in the sectors of fast food, entertainment, computer systems, prepackaged software, information services, biotechnology, banking, and other professional services, it provides a competitive edge for US firms not only because it enables the development of modular technological trajectories in these sectors that are technologically superior to other possible trajectories, but also because it facilitates a plethora of spontaneous innovation and fusion that give rise to the vitality of the Silicon Valley model. Furthermore, in these sectors, the possibility of modularization and encapsulation both in innovation and in knowledge creation provides a huge competitive advantage for American individualistic entrepreneurship and a paramount disadvantage for Japanese firms that focus on collective entrepreneurship and connectual knowing.

Modularization in the automobile sector: the American disadvantage

Modularization in the automobile sector may cause certain disadvantages. First, it can lead to a failure in the effective *demand articulation* of future consumer needs and preferences. In such esoteric and complex technological systems as automobiles that have numerous attributes and characteristics, both objective and subjective, demand articulation cannot be made effectively by the separate knowing of independent market research professionals, nor can it be delivered by the marketing department within the firm using formal market research methods. What is needed is a connectual and empathetic knowing of the consumer's subjective and delicate preferences by long-term personal interaction with consumers not only by marketing personnel but also by design engineers who have an in-depth knowledge of the complex attributes of automobiles. In this case, the American system of separate and modular knowing suffers a disadvantage as compared to the Japanese ways of connectual and empathetic knowing. Indeed, Kodama (1991) attributes the superior Japanese capability in *demand articulation* as one of the key reasons for Japanese competitiveness.

Second, modularization, together with separate knowing, often damages the *product integrity* of automobiles. Clark and Fujimoto (1990) define product integrity as the consistency between a product's function and its structure and between its performance and customer expectations. While *internal integrity* demands that the product's concept, its components, and the structuring of these components fit together seamlessly, *external integrity* requires the product to send a consistent and coherent message to its potential customers.

According to Clark and Fujimoto, product integrity is the primary reason for the success of many Japanese automobile models. In many cases, product integrity cannot be achieved by functional specialization, or in the terms of this book, by separate and modular knowing. In such a complex, tightly coupled, and closed technological system as an automobile, a focus on functional specialization and separate knowing *artificially* cuts through and breaks away many contextual links of parts and their physical and spatial arrangement, and ultimately contextual links of knowledge interdependence that are crucial for the *seamless* fit between delicate product concepts, complex product design, and esoteric consumer preferences. Here, what we need is *connectual and contextual knowing* of all the delicate, complex, and esoteric physical, spatial, functional, technological, and above all knowledge, links, of interdependencies among the character, personality, image, and feel of a car, and of its design philosophy, consumer preferences, product architecture, component design, and manufacturing. Here, as the success of Honda and Mazda (Clark and Fujimoto, 1990) indicates, Japan's connectual and contextual knowing is much better than America's separate and modular knowing.

In the case of knowledge exchange and integration between producers and suppliers, which is of vital importance in terms of product integrity, Liker *et al.* (1995) find that while design engineers in Japanese car-making firms have had profound knowledge about the supplier's component, their US counterparts have not had this. Instead, as shown in Table 9.1, subsystem suppliers of US car-makers faced great problems in getting design information from customers. This is often caused by the fragmentation of design responsibilities, the contact's lack of component knowledge, and the large proportion of contacts who are new to the job and who know little about components. (Table 9.1 also provides empirical evidence that supports the proposition in this book concerning dominant separate knowing in the USA and dominant connectual knowing in Japan.)

Table 9.1 Problems in getting design information from customers*

	Japanese subsystem suppliers (n = 37)	US subsystem suppliers (n = 38)
Design responsibility dispersed within the car-maker	11.1%	31.6%
Contacts in the car-maker new on job	8.6%	35.1%
Contacts in the car-maker lacking knowledge	8.6%	21.6%

* Percentage of suppliers responding '4' or '5' on a 5-point scale ranging from 'Never' to 'All the time.'
Source: Adapted from Liker *et al.* (1995: 169).

Third, the emphasis on modularization has led to the pursuit of parts *commonality* both among different car models and between successive car generations in the US auto sector. According to Clark and Fujimoto (1991: 148), the percentage of auto parts newly designed for a particular model is only 62 per cent in the USA as compared to 82 per cent in Japan and 71 per cent in Europe. This high level of parts commonality is the result not only of the modularization and standardization of parts, but also of the *decoupling* of visible and invisible parts in the design process. While the latter reduces the costs of style change and promotes economies of scale, it also harms product integrity, as Clark and Fujimoto (1991: 147) state:

When parts not specifically designed for a particular model are used, parameters and functions of the components they are used in may be suboptimized from a total vehicle perspective. In other words, the use of common parts may damage total product integrity.

At issue here is the tightly coupled, non-modular, closed, and complex nature of the automobile as a technological system.[2] In such a system, a major change in the design of one part requires coherent and synchronizing changes in other parts in order to achieve the best fit among all parts and the best function of the whole vehicle. A modular design may also cause a waste of space, materials, and processing time, and therefore give rise to a clumsy design. This is more so when the pursuit of product integrity has led to the adoption of a more holistic product design and a tighter fit among parts by such techniques as unit body structure, as Clark and Fujimoto (1991: 149) observe:

> The cost impact of body-panel commonality has become particularly high with the shift to unit body structure. Because body parts are tightly integrated into chassis and other systems, major changes to the body virtually ensure major changes to the entire vehicle. The annual style change introduced by Alfred Sloan is a much more costly amenity today.

With the Japanese push for holistic product design and product integrity, it is clear that the American style of modular design in the age of mass production can no longer work effectively in the automobile sector.

Fourth, the organizing principle of sequentialization and the resultant separate knowing has led to a much longer time and higher costs for developing new car models in the USA. According to Clark and Fujimoto (1991: 178), the dominance of sequential engineering in the USA has led to an average 11.6 months of lead-time for the first engineering prototype as compared to 6.2 months in Japan, and an average US time of 34 months for product and process engineering, in contrast to 24 months in Japan. Clark and Fujimoto attribute Japan's shorter development cycle to its practice of simultaneous (concurrent) engineering, which is, in this author's view, very much the result of the stress on connectual knowing. In the auto market, where a consumer's subjective feelings about the image of cars are as important as the cost and quality of the car, such a capability in shortening the development circle has given Japanese car-makers a huge competitive edge.

Fifth, the dominance of separate knowing and the resultant organizing principles of modularization and sequentialization in the USA has led to the lag of the three big US auto companies in design for manufacturing (DFM) and design for assembly (DFA), as shown in Table 9.2. As analyzed in chapter 6, the Japanese advantage in DFM and DFA translates into a huge advantage in production cost.

Finally, the American emphasis on separate and modular knowing also leads to a great disadvantage in terms of shop-floor learning and incremental improvement. As shown in Table 7.6, the number of effective improvement suggestions per employee in Japan is 800 times that of the USA, creating an enormous disadvantage for the USA in incremental improvement and as a result in the cost and quality of vehicles. Indeed, in a tightly coupled, closed, and complex technological system such as the automobile, the largest number of opportunities for improvement rest on the shop floor, in the physical, spatial, architectural, technical, and ultimately knowledge links among various components and processes. As a result, the Japanese emphasis on

Table 9.2 Design for assembly (DFA) ranking

Company	Average rank	DFA score
1. Toyota	2.2	100
2. Honda	3.9	89.7
3. Mazda	4.8	84.4
4. Fiat	5.3	80.6
5. Nissan	5.4	80.4
6. Ford	5.6	79.2
7. Volkswagen	6.4	74.3
8. Mitsubishi	6.6	73.6
9. Suzuki	8.7	60.2
10. GM	10.2	51.4
11. Hyundai	11.3	44.6
12. Renault	12.7	35.9
13. Chrysler	13.5	31.1

Source: Adapted from Cusumano and Nobeoka (1992).

shop-floor learning and connectual and contextual knowing, as manifested through many institutionalized practices of connectual governance discussed in chapter 6, has great advantages in facilitating incremental improvement in comparison with the American focus on separate knowing and its dominant organizing principles of modularization. The neglect of shop-floor learning and the artificial separation between thinking and executing have been blamed by many as the reasons for the American decline in the automobile sector (Kenney and Florida, 1993).

Notwithstanding all the above disadvantages for US auto-makers in the past, it is important to point out that the dynamic technological capabilities will change over time. First, the diffusion and transplantation of the Japanese system to the USA has improved the competitiveness of US car-makers (Dyer, 1996). Second, with the situation of the wide dissemination of the Japanese system of lean production, in which not only US car-makers but also other countries' car-makers are gradually catching up with their Japanese competitors (Fujimoto, 1997), the opportunities for further improvement and the potential benefits obtained through applying the best Japanese practices may have diminished. Finally, once all car-makers have acquired a level of high quality, low costs, and high product integrity, the arena for future competition may have shifted to the product design of dramatically new types and new styles such as the various sports utility cars and minivans, appealing to a new generation of customers (*Business Week*, December 21, 1998, p. 56). In connection with this point, such characteristics as modularity in design and part commonality may transform themselves into a competitive advantage, rather than a liability (Baldwin and Clark, 1997; Fujimoto, 1997). On the other hand, the *overuse* of some Japanese capabilities which created competitive advantage in the past may have meant they become liabilities in the 1990s, as Fujimoto (1997: 90) comments:

> Firms tend to overshoot. They tend to overuse the capabilities that their competitive advantages once depended on. Thus, U.S. firms became competitive through mass production systems of specialization, but subsequently they suffered from 'over-specialization.' The Japanese once enjoyed competitive advantages in product variety, but now they may be suffering from over-variety. History repeats itself in this sense.

Modularization and the American advantage in prepackaged software

Overshooting and overextending also permeates the academic world, as evidenced by a wholesale embrace of Japanese 'best practices' in the 1980s and a following wholesale dismissal of them. This is due to a lack not only of a dialectical view but also of a sectoral perspective. Indeed, notwithstanding the dynamic changes in the competitive landscape, many arguments made in the 1980s about the decline of US industries are correct when their findings are confined to the automobile and home electronics sectors. Unfortunately, the drive for universalistic proposition and projection was so high that many authors overgeneralized their findings from the auto and home electronic industries into sweeping conclusions about the *universal* advantage of the Japanese system of knowledge creation (e.g., Lodge and Vogel, 1987; Florida and Kenney, 1990; Lazonick, 1990a; Dore, 1994). The great irony here is that the very factors of disadvantage that were identified by these authors, such as individualism, venture capitalism, and a division of thinking and doing, all transform themselves into factors of advantage when we turn our attention from automobiles and home electronics to software, databases, biotechnology, banking, information services, and other professional services.

As analyzed in chapter 8, the computer system with an open system architecture, like other modular systems, enables the best exploitation and appropriation of the advantages generated by the American penchant for separate knowing and the resultant predominant organizing principles of separation, division, modularization, and encapsulation. In the software industry, these have led to the software development trajectory that focuses on standardized and prepackaged software products. Conversely, the Japanese dominant organizing principles of connectivity, customization, and contextualization have given rise to the software development trajectory that concentrates on customized software products that are organically integrated with the hardware system. Table 9.3 indicates that in 1985 about 76.2 per cent of total software sales in the USA were from prepackaged software, whereas in Japan the number was a mere 9.4 per cent. Although the latter figure is an improvement as compared to a much lower 3 per cent in 1981, Japanese development of standardized packaged software products is still lagging far behind that of the USA.

Table 9.3 Packaged and customized software product as percentage of total software sales

	USA		Japan	
	Packaged (%)	Customized (%)	Packaged (%)	Customized (%)
1981	53.0		3.0	
1985	76.2		9.4	
1989	43.6	18.6		
1990			15.0	79.2

Source: Adapted from various data in Cottrell (1994).

Many factors have been singled out as the causes for US dominance in prepackaged software products. These include the large consumer base of personal computers; English as a world language; excellence in information processing and program coding; the plethora of independent developers; the availability of venture capital; unparalleled research infrastructure in computer science and software engineering; the superior education and training systems for computer programmers; and IBM's early effort of modular design that decoupled computer operating systems from their hardware (Siwek and Furchtgott-Roth, 1993; Baldwin and Clark, 1997). While all the above factors play some role, what is neglected by most researchers is the indispensable impact of the American cultural paradigm of contractual man, its emphasis on separate knowing, and its organizing principles of standardization, modularization, and professionalization. These principles have made the very possibility of modularity and standardization in the computer hardware and software sectors a reality, facilitating the emergence and dominance of the sector's technological trajectory that is standardized, modular, and encapsulated (packaged). If the world had consisted only of Japan, it is highly possible that non-modular and customized computer software might have dominated the world market.

Not only can software packages be modularized and encapsulated, but within the same package there is also a high possibility for partitioning, modularizing, and encapsulating the whole task of software development into numerous relatively independent tasks to be attacked by small teams of programmers (Cusumano, 1997). As analyzed in chapter 8, in the modular systems of computer hardware and software, individualistic entrepreneurship, specialization, professionalization, which are all characteristics of separate knowing, become the facilitators for spontaneous innovation and fusion, which in turn has contributed to US dominance in this sector.

Furthermore, there is a sharp division between the development and the reproduction of prepackaged software products. The reproduction of software involves the copying of bits and resembles nothing in the conventional manufacturing processes of automobiles and electronic appliances. There is not only little 'shop-floor' learning involved, but also few improvement opportunities. As a result, the US disadvantage and the Japanese advantage in shop-floor learning and manufacturing process improvements dissolve into irrelevance in terms of software reproduction. On the other hand, in the design and development stage of software products, the possibility of effective modularization makes the American system of separate knowing and the organizing principles of division, standardization, modularization, and professionalization a competitive advantage. Conversely, the Japanese emphasis on generalists, on-the-job training, the organizing principles of customization and *seamless* cross-functional integration become a handicap for Japanese firms in prepackaged software development.

Modularization and object-oriented information technology

The predominance of the organizing principles of modularization in the USA has also led to its innovation of object-oriented information technologies such as computer languages C++ and java. Although their emergence has specific historical paths, it is worth pointing out that object-oriented information technology can be seen as a logical expression of the American organizing principles of separation, standardization, modularization, and encapsulation. Following the design rules of modularity, object-oriented information technology tries to *decompose* a large program into an assembly of loosely coupled, minimally interdependent, and self-contained modules so that a modification in one module does not cause the need to change others. It further applies the principles of *encapsulation* and *information hiding* to achieve modularity in design. According to Fichman and Kemerer (1993), the principle of encapsulation requires the enclosure of both the data structure and all their operations so that access to the structure in a software program inside a *capsule* or *object* is independent of, and separate from, other data structures and operations. Similarly, the principle of *information hiding* requires that:

> The internal structure of a given module should be a black box that stays hidden from other modules. Information hiding insulates other modules from changes that affect a given module's internal representation but not its external interface. (p. 16)

All these principles aim to minimize knowledge interdependencies and information exchange among modules so that the operation of each module is self-contained and independent of others.

Second, object-oriented information technology uses the design principle of *abstraction* as a tool for managing complexity. It is a 'simplified description or specification of a system that emphasizes some of the systems details or properties while suppressing others' (Fichman and Kemerer, 1993: 17). From the perspective of this book, abstraction is a process that sorts out the commonality and universal characteristics of a category of objects and suppresses their *idiosyncrasies*.

Third, object-oriented information technology tries to standardize some special pieces of program codes into *classes* and *objects* so that they are *reusable* and *inheritable*. According to Fichman and Kemerer (1993: 16), an object is 'an abstraction of a real-world object that encapsulates a set of variables and methods corresponding to a real-world object's attributes and behaviors,' whereas class is 'an abstract definition or template for a collection of objects that share identical structure and behavior.' From the perspective used here, both *classes* and *objects* can be seen as the *standardization* of tasks and objects so that they can be reused any time similar tasks arise.

What is interesting to observe here are the close similarities between the design rules of object-oriented technology and the American dominant organizing principles. Such similarities cast light on the in-depth causes for the emergence, increasing popularity, and predominance of object-oriented information technology in the USA. While the technological possibilities and the USA's superior knowledge creation capability in information technology have certainly played an important role, the fact that so many of its design rules are identical with the dominant American organizing principles of separation, standardization, modularization, and encapsulation implies that there must be causal links. It is likely that the latter should have played an important role in facilitating the emergence and dominance of object-oriented technology in the USA.

Modularization in the fast food and service sectors: McDonaldization

Outside the sectors of information technology, in the fast food and service sectors, the USA's predominance in the organizing principles of separation, standardization, modularization, and encapsulation also provide a competitive advantage for US firms. The best illustration of the application of these organizing principles and the resultant competitive advantage is the worldwide success of McDonald's, as well as its other followers in the fast food industry. Not only is McDonald's hamburger a standardized and modularized product, but so also is the operation of the McDonald's empire. The modularization of a McDonald's hamburger enables customers to freely choose whatever combinations they want among the predesigned modules. The standardization process also gives the customer a sense of certainty, predictability, and controllability not only of the quantity and quality of the food, but also of the quantity and quality of service (Ritzer, 1995). The service in McDonald's is also organized in such a way that interaction between customers and service providers is *minimized* into pure and impersonal transaction. The sense of controllability and the minimization of human interaction enable the maximal freedom, autonomy, and independence of individual customers.

It is for this reason, that the principles of organizing in the operation of McDonald's have pervaded American society to such a degree that they have led to the '*McDonaldization*' of American society (Ritzer, 1995). In Wal-Mart, customers are offered maximal choices but minimal interaction. In entertainment, TV series such as *Seinfeld* are also modularized and encapsulated in such a way that episodes are independent of one another so that viewers can turn the show on and off whenever they want without affecting their understanding of the show. Indeed, the whole American competitive advantages in fast food, entertainment, and other services are primarily derived from the organizing principles of separation, standardization, modularization, and encapsulation, as well as the American superiority in spontaneous innovation and fusion.

Contextual connectivity: the Japanese advantage and disadvantage

In contrast, the Japanese cultural paradigm of connectual man facilitates the dominance of the organizing principles of customization, contextualization, and organic integration, which lead to the preponderance of what I call *contextual connectivity*, in which connections among subsystems or components are made according to their idiosyncratic needs and their contextual environment. This is in sharp contract to the American focus on *abstract connectivity*, in which universal and standardized connections are made among components without regard to their idiosyncrasies. The principle of contextual connectivity has led to the development of the technological trajectories of the Japanese industrial sectors that stress *organic* and *seamless* integration. Indeed, all practices that have emerged and are predominant in Japan such as concurrent engineering, design for manufacturing and assembling, JIT, and cross-functional teams are essentially strategies and tools to tighten the *coupling* of components, subsystems, and design and production processes so that they are seamlessly integrated.

The competitive implications of contextual connectivity are sector-contingent, but in a sharply opposite direction to the impact of abstract connectivity. In the technological systems where the knowledge links among subsystems are tightly coupled, contextual and non-modular, such as the case of automobiles and electronic appliances, contextual connectivity creates a competitive edge for Japanese firms. Conversely, in the technological systems with a knowledge structure that can be loosely coupled, decontextualized, and modular, such as the case in prepackaged software, entertainment, fast food, and other service sectors, contextual connectivity usually generates a competitive disadvantage.

Customization as a form of connectivity: the case of Japanese software

One good example is the Japanese lock-in to the *customized* software development trajectory (Cottrell, 1994; Duvall, 1995; Baba, *et al.*, 1995, 1996; Mowery, 1996). Because of the connectual world view, in Japan software is considered either a service that comes with the hardware, and is not separately priced, or a function that has to be custom-made to the specific needs of users (Duvall, 1995). As the result of the Japanese preference for custom-made goods, packaged software accounts for only 20 per cent of total software costs in Japan as compared to 75 per cent in the USA (Pollack, 1992). According to another estimate, the figures are 6 per cent in Japan vs. 65 per cent in the USA (Cusumano, 1989).

The notion of software as either an *inseparable* part of computer hardware, or a function that has to be *seamlessly* integrated with the business of the users, has given rise to the dominance of large computer makers and users as the major developers of software products in Japan. According to Baba *et al.* (1995), in 1990, the top 100 software developers accounted for more than half of total sales in Japan, of which 53 were from user spin-off firms and 17 from maker spin-off firms. The number of *independent* software firms that reached the top 100 actually declined from 35 in 1988 to 30 in 1990. When the market share of the top Japanese 100 software firms is considered, the contrast is even sharper: the user spin-off software firms had 45.4 per cent of the total sales of the top 100 firms in 1990, the maker spin-off firms had 30.3 per cent, and independent firms only had 24.3 per cent.

This lackluster performance of independent software vendors is very much the result of the preponderance of connectual knowing and the lack of separate knowing in Japan. The dearth of venture capital for software development is also a problem. According to Baba *et al.* (1995), in 1989 about 11.0 per cent of US venture capital went to the software sector, as compared to a mere 0.04 per cent in Japan. If we add the factor of a much smaller base of total venture capital in Japan, the absolute gap would be much larger.

The comparison of software development between Japan and the USA is so fascinating because it proves how different national cultural paradigms and dominant organizing principles have facilitated the emergence of divergent technological trajectories for the same technological sectors in various nations. While many students of technological innovation have noticed such a divergence (Cottrell, 1994; Baba *et al.*, 1995; Duvall, 1995; Mowery, 1996), almost none is able to make the link between cultural paradigms and the technological trajectories of software development. Most of them attribute the dominance of customized software and the lack of packaged software development in Japan to such idiosyncratic factors as the dominance of mainframe makers, the dearth of new entries in microcomputer industry, the lack of a PC user base, customers' preference for customized software products, the absence of venture capital, the difficulty of the Japanese language for use in computers, the shortage of skilled programmers, and so on. From the knowledge regime perspective, as discussed above, other than the Japanese language, all other factors are more or less the results of the Japanese cultural paradigm of connectual man and the Japanese institutions of connectual governance and connectual knowing.

It is interesting to note that, although computer software and hardware are essentially modular, or at least potentially modularizable, technological systems, whose effective development requires separate knowing, spontaneous fusion, and the facilitating organizing principles of separation, specialization, standardization, and modularization, the Japanese still adhere to their dominant cultural paradigm of connectual man and the institutions of connectual governance. They operate in the computer software and hardware sectors in a similar way to the automobile and consumer electronics sectors.

The belief in the *universal* superiority of the Japanese ways of doing business and of organizing knowledge creation had once led to a false prediction of the imminent Japanese conquest of the computer software industry. When Cusumano (1985) shifted his attention from the successful innovation and production systems in the Japanese auto industry to the ambitious Japanese efforts in software development, he was astonished by the similarity and therefore predicted the same outcome of upcoming Japanese conquest (Cusumano, 1991, 1992). Indeed, although sometimes to a lesser extent, almost all aspects of Japanese connectual governance have been present in the Japanese software sector. These include recruiting from new graduates; the emphasis on generalists; long-term employment; on-the-job training; the lack of market for software professionals; broader job descriptions; flexible design and production; quality control; and long-term cooperative relationships with customers and subcontractors (Nakahara, 1993; Duvall, 1995: Baba *et al.*, 1996).

While many of the above practices work well in the automobile and consumer electronic sectors, they do not succeed in the software sector. While Japan is still very good in customized software, the underlying logic for its very success in the automobile and consumer electronics sectors prevents it from succeeding in packaged software. One good example is the Japanese emphasis about generalists and on-the-job training. According to Baba *et al.* (1996: 112), among employees in the Japanese software industry in 1991, only less than 1.5 per cent have a masters degree, and fewer than 36 per cent hold bachelor degrees. Of the rest more than 60 per cent were special school or high school graduates. According to Nakahara (1993), not all the college graduates who entered the software industry were trained software engineers. Rather, they were composed of graduates from all kinds of majors. Following the predominant connectual logic, Japanese software firms rely heavily on generalists and on on-the-job training in creating the knowledge base for software development. While such practices have performed well in the automobile and home electronics sectors, they failed badly in software development. Indeed, this astonishing lack of specialization and professionalization in software development, as represented by the dearth of qualified software engineers, is the major reason cited by many scholars (Nakahara, 1993; Duvall, 1995) for Japan's lackluster performance in the prepackaged software sector.

Customization and flexible manufacturing systems: the Japanese advantage

Notwithstanding its failure in prepackaged software, the Japanese penchant for *seamless* integration between software and hardware and the resultant strategy of customization do provide Japanese firms with a competitive edge in numerical control machine tools (CNC) and flexible manufacturing systems (FMS). While prepackaged software products work well in performing many *independent* tasks of information processing that can be standardized and modularized into the processing of bits, the effective computer-aided processing of various metals into various idiosyncratic parts requires customized software products that take into consideration the idiosyncratic and contextual requirements of concrete product design, process design, the nature of the materials used, and the process of material handling. In such a case, what is required is not standardized software that can be *detached* from hardware, but customized software products that can be seamlessly integrated with the hardware system. Here, the American organizing principles of standardization and modularization render a competitive disadvantage and the Japanese organizing principles of connection and customization provide a competitive edge.

One good example of such a Japanese advantage is the customized software *imbedded* in machine tools, electronic appliances, and automobiles (Nakahara, 1993). The design of *imbedded software* for such closed technological systems as electronic appliances requires taking into consideration the idiosyncratic needs of operating and controlling such systems. In other words, there is a need to *seamlessly* integrate software and hardware for the best operation of electronic appliances. There are few opportunities to use a universal software product for all electronic appliances.

Another example of the Japanese advantage is in the design of software applications controlling the manufacturing processes in the relatively mature fabricating sectors. Such manufacturing processes are by nature *idiosyncratic, context-rich, and complex*. Predesigned standardized software packages cannot work well, not only because they fail to incorporate the idiosyncratic nature of the processes, but also because they are not able to *learn and evolve* on the shop floor and incorporate the local and contextual knowledge of shop-floor workers. On the other hand, the Japanese mode of connectual knowing and customization in software design and development works well not only because developers in Japanese manufacturing firms tailor-design software products for specific purposes and take the idiosyncratic nature of the complex tasks into consideration (Bensaou and Earl, 1998), but also because managers allow shop-floor operators flexibly to change the programming of the software to fit changing needs on the shop floor and to facilitate shop-floor learning.

One illuminating example is the design, development, and application of software in FMS. An FMS is a computer-controlled assembly of semi-independent workstations linked by material handling systems. In comparing the performance of FMS in Japan and the USA, Jaikumar (1986) finds that FMS in the USA produced an average number of 10 parts, about nine times less than the Japanese number of 93. He further observes that installed FMS in the USA showed 'an astonishing lack of flexibility,' 'cannot run untended for a whole shift,' and 'are not integrated with the rest of their factories.' According to him, the central cause for such a drastic disparity rests in the sharply different management styles. In US firms, designers and developers, who are usually external consultants, develop and instal FMS using very broad but *standardized* specifications that are very flexible but not tailored to the special needs of various tasks. The engineers who are assigned to maintain an FMS are not developers and are reluctant to change any specifications and programming codes. The operators are not skilled and not allowed to change the programming of an FMS. This is a typical example of failure of separate knowing, modularization, and sequentialization. Conversely, in Japan, not only is an FMS tailor-made, it is also continually adapted and improved by the project team through a learning process long after its installation. Shop-floor operators are allowed, required, and trained to make program changes for flexible needs. As a tightly coupled, closed, and complex technological system, an FMS requires *seamless* organic integration, customization, and connectual knowing in order for it to perform optimally. This is where the Japanese system of connectual governance and connectual knowing works the best.

The Japanese failed effort in integrating electronics with entertainment

While the Japanese effort of seamless integration of FMS has worked well, its effort of seamlessly integrating electronics with entertainment has not. Triggered by its ideal of integrating electronics with entertainment, the prominent Japanese electronics company Sony bought Columbia Pictures. However, its entry into the US entertainment sector failed (*Time*, December 18, 1995, p. 58).

The cause for such a failure lies in the fact that unlike electronic appliances which are tightly coupled, closed, non-modular, and require seamless integration among subsystems, many entertainment products are loosely coupled and do not require seamless integration. Other than some universal standards, electronic appliances for entertainment and entertainment products such as movies, TV shows, and music, are two totally different, independent, modularized, and encapsulated technological and knowledge domains. There is little interdependence, connection, knowledge spillover, or knowledge linkage, and therefore little need for integration between electronics and entertainment. Not only does the Japanese knowledge creation capability in electronics not translate into any applicable competencies in the entertainment sector, the organizing principles that work exceedingly well in electronics can be a hindrance when applied to the entertainment sector. As a modular system, the entertainment sector needs individualistic creativity and entrepreneurship. It requires spontaneous innovations, and its success demands separate and modular knowing and contractual governance, which are predominant in the USA, not in Japan.

Japanese success in games software and playstations

Two exceptional cases are the Japanese success in games software products and the electronic appliances such as Sony's Playstation that play them. These cases are, however, consistent with the central proposition of this book. Isomorphic to their contrasting trajectories in the computer software industry, the USA and Japan have also followed distinctly divergent trajectories in the computer games sector. While the USA has focused on the design of generic computer games that can play on the PC platform, Japan has centered its attention on the development of text-rich, customized games software that can only play on specially tailored electronic appliances such as Playstations by Sony.

The design of generic computer games software packages, such as Microsoft's Freecell, requires the separation, standardization, abstraction, generalization, and specification of all possible options, logic links, operations, and contingencies. Conversely, the design of customized games software requires the creation of specific scenarios of actions and their contextualization and seamless integration, which is highly linked to contextual knowing, in which Japan has a competitive advantage. Similarly, Japan is also good at design of customized software and microprocessors for electronic appliances (Takahashi, 1998).

Flexible modularization: the Japanese way of synergy

If we look much deeper into Japanese learning efforts, we can find that their competitive advantage in automobiles, electronic appliances, opto-electronics, and mechatronics lies not *solely* in their organizing principles of connection, customization, and contextualization. Rather, it is their willingness and superior capability in *synergizing* modularization with connectivity, and standardization with customization, that provides them with a competitive advantage in these sectors. I will call such a synergy '*flexible modularization*,' as compared to the '*rigid modularization*' dominant in the USA.

Unlike the rigid modularization process in which the standard external interfaces between modules seldom change, flexible modularization takes both standards and modules as constantly evolving and learning objects that are subject to change according to increasing acquisition of knowledge through connectual knowing and shop-floor learning. Standards are continuously improved, modules are frequently redesigned and reconfigured, and connections among modules are constantly streamlined (Adler and Cole, 1993). Because of this synergistic nature, Adler (1992) calls the Japanese system of production 'learning bureaucracy,' while Klein (1994) terms it 'dynamic Taylorism.' According to Adler and Cole (1993), the Japanese competitive advantage in the automobile sector lies in its ability to incorporate the seemingly two opposite principles of standardization and continuous improvement, and of specialization and cross-functional integration.

From the knowledge regime perspective, flexible modularization combines the very best of craft production and Taylorism. First, existing modules and standards can be used as a basis for further learning about their possible improvement (Adler and Cole, 1993). Flexibility in modularity promotes continuous improvement through the redesign of both standard interfaces and modules. Second, by the standardization and encapsulation of what has been learned through connectual knowing, it 'locks-in' improvement and prevents unlearning (Klein, 1994). Third, flexible modularization secures *product integrity* by exploiting architectural knowledge generated through connectual knowing across modules. Finally, flexible modularization also facilitates both the separate knowing of *in-depth* causal-effect relationships and connectual knowing of broad and system-wide knowledge links. Notwithstanding this synergistic advantage, the Japanese practice of flexible modularization can only be very effective in tightly coupled, non-modular technological systems. In completely modular technology systems, there is little need to change standard interfaces or reconfigure the design of modules. Therefore, the Japanese competitive advantage of flexible modularization is nullified and the Japanese competitive disadvantage in spontaneous innovation magnified.

Two types of modularization and connectivity: learning and cultural synergy between the USA and Japan

In conclusion, when we dig deeper into the original dichotomy between modularization and connectivity and their different links to American and Japanese cultural paradigms, we find a further dichotomy within the categories of both modularization and connectivity. While the American penchant for independence and autonomy has given rise to the US focus on rigid modularization and abstract connectivity, the Japanese emphasis on connection and interdependence has led to Japanese preoccupation with contextual connectivity. The Japanese effort of learning from the USA has contributed to its practice of flexible modularization.

In the 1980s, US firms put a great effort into learning the Japanese methods of flexible production, continuous improvement, quality circles, JIT, and DFM. This has contributed to the revival of US firms in the automobile and semiconductor industries (Petersen and Hillkirk, 1991; Smith, 1995). With the shifting nature of the world economy from being primarily composed of tightly coupled and non-modular technological systems such as automobiles and electronic appliances to loosely coupled modular technological systems such as software, information services, and e-businesses, it is once again high time for Japan to learn the American way.

Notes

1. For a more detailed discussion of the impact of language on ways of thinking, see Bloom (1981), and Li *et al.* (1999).
2. For the distinction of tightly coupled vs. loosely coupled technological systems, see Perrow (1986).

CHAPTER TEN

Systems Integration: People-independence vs. People-dependence

In the past, the man has been the first, in the future the system must be first.

Frederick Taylor

Two ways of systems integration: the impact of cultural paradigms

With the increasing complexity of technological tasks and knowledge links, how to systematically integrate various components and subsystems into a well-functioning and cost-effective system becomes a paramount task for knowledge workers and system integrators. This is especially true for the innovation, production, maintenance, and improvement of technological systems with large-scale complexity, such as large commercial airplanes, nuclear technology, and large-scale telecommunication systems. Just as there are two fundamentally different ways of dealing with complexity, so there are two drastically divergent paradigms of systems integration, especially with regard to the treatment of people in the system.

In the first paradigm, subsystems are designed by independent organizational units, integrated by separate divisions and/or external consultants, and operated in such a way that the function of the whole system follows its own logic, requires minimum human intervention and knowledge feedback, and maximizes worker-proofing. In the second paradigm, subsystems are co-designed by cross-functional teams, integrated by the creation of relation-specific knowledge, and operated with maximum knowledge feedback from operators. While the former treats a technological system as autonomous, separate, and independent of the people who create, maintain, and operate it, the latter puts people at the center of it with indispensable roles. While the former embodies physical and knowledge links among subsystems into an *independent system logic* so that people under individual functions can work as though they are autonomous and independent of one another, the latter relies on people to discover and provide knowledge links among subsystems and integrate them into the whole system through horizontal coordination and knowledge exchange. While the former tries to minimize human error, the latter uses people as connectors of various subsystems and therefore maximizes utilization of human talents. In essence, the former intends to create a systemic logic with minimum human intervention, whereas the latter integrates people into the system as the most important and active part. Because of this, I call the former *people-independent systems integration*, and the latter *people-dependent systems integration*.

In the USA, the cultural penchant for autonomy and independence, the management drive for control, the epistemological emphasis on separate knowing, combined with the high mobility of knowledge workers, have led to the predominance of people-independent systems integration, in which the dependence on individual knowledge workers in the design, maintenance, and operation of technological systems is minimized through various organizing principles and contractual governance mechanisms. Conversely, in Japan, the cultural penchant for interdependence and mutual obligation, the epistemological drive for connectual knowing, combined with the low mobility of knowledge workers, have given rise to the preponderance of people-dependent systems integration, in which the reliance on individual knowledge workers in the design, maintenance, and operation of technological systems is maximized.

This sharp difference in the dominant ways of systems integration exists in almost every technological sector. In the manufacturing sector, while US firms use numerical control machine tools (CNCs) and robots as a means to control labor process and minimize human intervention (Noble, 1989), their Japanese counterparts apply these tools only to do dirty and unhealthy jobs, reducing physical and mental burdens of shop-floor workers and, therefore, empowering them for shop-floor learning and knowledge creation (Rush and Bessant, 1992; Suzuki, 1997). Similarly, while the Japanese rely heavily on shop-floor operators flexibly to change the programming of a flexible manufacturing system (FMS), US firms use the same systems to replace people and do not allow shop-floor workers to make any changes (Jaikumar, 1986). In the aircraft industry, while in the USA separate knowing through fundamental research and experimentation on individual modules is the norm, in Japan the level of basic research and the number of experimentation and test facilities are much lower (Mowery, 1990). Similarly, in the semiconductor sector, while US firms rely on extensive experimentation on all technological options to find the best way of systems integration, their Japanese counterparts depend on engineers' design experiences and resultant tacit knowledge to do so (Iansiti, 1998). Finally and most importantly, as observed by Bensaou and Earl (1998: 121), while US firms manage information technology by focusing on 'system design' which adopts the most technically elegant systems and requires employees to adapt to it, Japanese firms emphasize 'human design' 'to make use of the tacit and explicit knowledge that employees already possess.'

Historically, this US focus on system design can be traced back to the pervasive nation-wide endeavor in systemization in the early twentieth century (Shenhav, 1995). Indeed, according to Marcus and Segal's (1989) detailed account, the notion of 'system' had already become the touchstone of technological development at that time that influenced virtually every aspect of American life. When this principle of systemization was applied to the management and organization of firms, it caused the rise of systematic management, Taylorism, Fordism, and big business (Litterer, 1963; Chandler, 1977; Jelinek, 1979; Hughes, 1989b).

In the governance of both employee relations and the decision-making process, US firms try to achieve worker-proofing and to minimize opportunism, as Noble (1989: 71) notes:

> Above all, engineers [in the USA] want to eliminate not particular human beings but the more abstract possibility of 'human error.' So, they design systems that preclude as much as possible any human intervention. This is called '*idiot proofing.*' This

engineering equivalent to management's *worker-proofing* betrays a cynical view of human beings. Any chance of human intervention (by workers) is *negatively* assumed to be a chance for error rather than more positively, a chance for creativity, judgement, enhancement. (*Italics added.*)

This is achieved through a pervasive use of standardized rules, explicit routines, quantitative measures, formal control systems, information systems, and the substitution of machines for workers, which can also be traced back to late-nineteenth-century America (Marcus and Segal, 1989). The Japanese, by contrast, depend on organic human interaction, consensus building, and subjective judgment for both decision-making and systems integration. This is evidenced not only in the much higher rank of control and financial departments in US firms (Kagono, *et al.*, 1984: 48), but also in the much lower adoption ratios of various *formalized* and *standardized* control and managerial systems in Japanese firms, a situation that is especially pronounced in formalized information systems and long-range forecast-ing, planning, and control systems with regard to strategies, investment, budget, competitors, and sales (Table 10.1). The Japanese lack of using information systems is also reflected in the fact that while the USA invests 4 per cent of its GDP in information technology, Japan invests only 2 per cent, smaller than 3 per cent in the UK and Australia (*Business Week*, August 31, 1998, p. 124).

In the USA the pervasive use of information systems (IS) enables managers to control the labor process without a dependence on shop-floor workers for knowledge feedback. In pointing out implicitly the people-independent nature of IS, Mintzberg (1994: 258) notes:

> For data to be 'hard' means that they can be documented unambiguously, which usually means that they have already been quantified. That way, planners and managers can sit in their offices and be informed. No need to go out and meet the troops, or the customers, to find out how the products get bought or the wars get fought or what connects those strategies to that stock price; all that just wastes valuable time. This is, after all, the age of the computer. Systems will do it, whether they go by the names of 'information technology,' 'strategic information systems,' 'expert systems,' 'total systems,' or just plain so-called 'management information systems.'

On the other hand, the Japanese lack of enthusiasm in IS adoption lies partly in their preference for people-centered face-to-face communications, especially those of a nonverbal and intuitive nature (Goldman, 1994). Although such an idiosyncratic factor as the difficulty to process more than 1000 Chinese characters for computer processing has negatively affected the diffusion of PCs in Japanese society (Fransman, 1995), this alone cannot explain the lack of use of IS at the corporate level. After all, many Japanese are well trained in English, and as compared with their US counterparts, Japanese firms do adopt more FMS that require shop-floor programming (Mansfield, 1993).

Two types of technological systems: stand-alone machine vs. people-centered socio-technical system

Indeed, beyond the seemingly plausible effect of Chinese characters, a more fundamental cause for the contrasting paths between Japan and the USA in the diffusion of management information systems (MIS) and FMS rests in the

Table 10.1 Adoption ratio of formalized and standardized managerial systems: US–Japan differences in descending order, 1980 (percentages)

Forms of formal management and control systems	USA	Japan	USA/Japan
Planning–programming–budgeting system***	30.7	3.4	903
Contingency planning system***	42.7	5.9	724
Competition analysis system***	49.8	11.0	453
Management information system***	75.6	21.0	360
Capital budgeting system**	94.2	33.1	285
Financial investment analysis system***	64.4	24.5	263
Sales force performance appraisal system***	68.4	26.9	254
Strategic planning system***	78.7	34.8	226
Sales review and analysis system***	80.0	41.0	195
Sales forecasting systems***	90.2	47.2	191
Fixed assets investment analysis system***	68.9	42.8	161
Performance evaluation system***	85.8	65.2	132
Planning system for PR and advertisements	34.7	27.6	126
Management by objectives**	68.0	55.0	124
Flexible budget control system*	63.1	51.7	122
Objective formula for wage/salary determination	72.2	62.6	115
Monthly operating reporting systems***	97.3	87.9	111
Standard cost accounting system***	92.0	73.8	108
Formalized job description	88.4	85.2	104
Short-range planning system	86.7	87.7	99
Cash-flow planning system*	86.2	93.8	92
Internal training program for managers	68.9	75.5	91
Mid-range planning system	72.4	80.0	91
Objective promotion criteria***	35.1	54.8	64
(Structural forms adopted)			
Product or brand manager system***	55.1	11.7	471
Strategic business unit system***	50.2	12.8	392
Matrix organization***	30.7	13.4	229
Project management system***	53.8	34.5	156

* Significant at 0.05 level; ** at 0.01 level; *** at 0.001 level.
Source: Kagono *et al.* (1984: 46).

fundamentally different attitudes toward technology in these two societies. While MIS in the USA is designed to get rid of the influence of people, FMS as used in Japan is centered on people. More broadly, parallel to the two ways of systems integration are two resultant types of socially constructed technological systems. While the first is designed as a stand-alone machine that is autonomous with a systemic logic that requires people to conform to it, the second is perceived as only part of a larger socio-technical system with people as connectors for subsystems. While the former is separate from the impact of the contextual and idiosyncratic environment, the latter seamlessly integrates with it. While the former standardizes the tasks it performs and requires organizations to fit in with it, the latter customizes the function of the technological system to fit the idiosyncratic needs of a firm.

In comparing the typical Anglo-American attitude toward technology with that of typical Japanese and European manufacturers, Gertler (1995: 5) notes:

> American, British, or Canadian firm regards technology as something embodied entirely within the physical properties and design of machinery and production systems themselves. This stands in sharp contrast to the approach more typical of European and Japanese manufacturers, who not only appreciate the necessity of social interaction for effective machine production and use, but also regard the technological capabilities of a production process as being produced through the interaction between machines and skilled workers who have built up a wealth of knowledge and problem solving abilities through many years of training and learning by doing ... [In contrast,] Anglo-American users of advanced machinery ... typically expect to be able to extract the full capabilities of such technologies merely by installing them correctly and 'flipping the switch.'

In describing the historical American drive for the building of technological systems that are stand-alone machines and independent of people, Hughes (1989b: 187) notes:

> Taylor tried to systematize workers as if they were components of machines. Ford's image was a factory functioning as a machine; Insull envisaged a network or circuit of interacting electrical and organizational components; and Taylor imagined a machine in which the mechanical and human parts were virtually indistinguishable.

By contrast, instead of treating employees as an adjunct to machines, Japanese firms regard the body of employees as the primary stakeholder and 'controlling group' that set the basic premises and value criteria in both corporate governance and the operation of machines (Miwa, 1996).

Such a fundamentally different attitude toward people and machines is best reflected in the sharp contrasts in the patterns of R&D expenditure and employee involvement in R&D between Japanese and US-based small and medium enterprises (SMEs) in the manufacturing sector. According to their 1994 survey of 1500 SMEs in Japan and 2700 SMEs in the USA with less than 500 employees, LeBlanc *et al.* (1997) found that while an average of 8.6 employees was engaged in R&D in Japanese SMEs, the number for their US counterparts was only 3.3. Conversely, while 55.7 per cent of US SMEs used more than $500,000 to purchase equipment for R&D, only 20.9 per cent Japanese SMEs did so. They further found that 'Japanese SMEs tend to use people and flexible manufacturing techniques for improving processes, while U.S. firms tend to use computer equipment as a solution to their technical needs' (p. 613).

This dichotomy between people-centered and machine-centered technological development is evidenced in the predominance of prepackaged software in the USA and customized software in Japan, as discussed in the previous chapter. It is especially reflected in the divergent ways of dealing with enterprise-level information systems (Bensaou and Earl, 1998). In the USA not only has the cultural drive for autonomy and independence led to the dominance of stand-alone technological systems, but the dominant Western epistemology also embraces the separation between human beings and their environment (Lakoff and Johnson, 1999). By contrast, both the cultural penchant for interdependence and the organic epistemology of East Asia promote the seamless unity of human beings with tools and environments. In comparing the relationship of self and environment in the West and Japan, Berque (1992: 93) observes:

Whereas in the modern Western view self and environment are opposing terms, in Japan they are seen as interactive; the self melds with the environment by identifying with patterns of nature which are, nonetheless, culturally constructed.

It is the Western concept of self that had led to the dominant Western notion of autonomous technology that follows its own logic, and is therefore independent of human intention, direction, and control (Winner, 1977). Contrarily, the notion of interconnectedness between persons and the material world has given rise to an artisanal tradition in Japan that tries to *humanize* and *spiritualize* the machine so that a close relationship exists between an artisan and his machine. Kondo (1992: 53) quotes from the field notes of the Japanese anthropologist Matthews Hamabata who studied large Japanese family enterprises:

> The odd thing is: all three managers felt that there was a special presence in all of their machines; ... But it wasn't a love of machinery as machinery, but of machinery as some kind of spiritual extension of themselves ... For them, machines were extensions of themselves as spiritual beings, as creators of things, things of high quality ... At any rate, there is a connectedness between men and machines, not only between men and men; there is a constant transcending of the self to create a beautiful product, a community product.

Conversely, Americans have tended to maximally use machinery to substitute for labor, as Litterer (1961: 465) puts it:

> The essential idea followed by the Americans was that the more machine work could replace human labor the better, regardless of whether the substitution meant replacing hand labor by machinery or reducing the amount of labor involved in operating a machine.

It is because of this sharp divergence of relationship between men and machines that while Americans treat NC, FMS, CIM, software packages, and IS as stand-alone machines whose systemic logic of operation is preprogrammed and people-independent, the Japanese want to customize and contextualize these technological systems to fit the specific purpose of idiosyncratic tasks and to maximize knowledge feedback from the people who operate them. This is best evidenced by the sharp contrast in developing and deploying new technologies in Japanese and US SMEs in the manufacturing sector. As shown in Table 10.2, in 1994 while 38 per cent of Japanese SMEs chose to develop their own customized technologies, only 20 per cent of US SMEs did so. Conversely, while only 8 per cent of Japanese SMEs chose

Table 10.2 Methods of deploying improved technology: a comparison of US and Japanese SMEs in the manufacturing sector, 1994, percentage of firms

	Japanese SMEs	US SMEs
Technology primarily developed at your firm	38%	20%
Adoptions and improvements to commercially available technology done by your firm	50%	59%
Only use of commercially available technology with no adaptation or improvement done by your firm	8%	18%
Other ... describe	5%	4%

Source: Adapted from LeBlanc *et al.* (1997: 606).

commercially available technologies without any adaptations or improvement, 18 per cent of US SMEs did so. The contrast of machine-centered vs. people-centered technological development between the USA and Japan is also evidenced by their almost reverse ranking of the biggest problems facing product and process development (see Table 10.3).

Table 10.3 Biggest problems facing product and process development: a comparison of US and Japanese SMEs in the manufacturing sector, 1994, percentage of firms

Problems	Japanese SMEs	US SMEs
Difficulty in hiring qualified engineers	54%	14%
Lack of motivation	20%	17%
Poor communication	10%	6%
Difficulty getting information	9%	19%
Shortage of finance	7%	43%

Source: Adapted from LeBlanc *et al.* (1997: 607).

When technological development is people-centered, the biggest problem is the hiring of qualified engineers. On the other hand, when technological development is machine-centered, the primary problem lies in the shortage of capital in financing the purchase of equipment and the hiring of external consultants in installing them.

In the case of computer-aided design (CAD) system, Whitney (1992) notes that despite the wide availability of stand-alone commercial CAD systems, large Japanese companies such as Toyota, Nissan, and Sony have all developed their own CAD systems that were a customized modification of existing commercial software packages developed in the USA. In his further case studies, Whitney (1995) observes a similar trend of customization in the use of robots to fit the idiosyncratic needs of Honda, Matsushita, and Nippondenso. Similarly, Japanese electronics companies customize their simulation and production-scheduling software to fit specific needs in house (Liker *et al.*, 1995). In their development of scheduling methods for manufacturing semiconductors, instead of adopting commercially available software as most US firms do, Japanese companies usually create their own tools and software (Duenyas *et al.*, 1995).

In his ethnographic study of a US software consulting firm, Orlikowski (1992) observes a pervasive standardization of software development tools such as 'Computer-Aided Software Engineering' (CASE) to establish the 'technological imperative' that enforces 'the only way the tools will work.' In stating the benefits of adopting standardized tools for software development, Orlikowski (1992: 417) cites the reasoning of a senior manager:

> By building standards into tools we can control what people do and how they do it. We are no longer dependent on the knowledge in people's heads. So if people leave, we aren't sunk. Tools allow us to put knowledge into a structure and embed it in technology.

Indeed, as a result of its zeal for people-independence, the USA has the highest tendency to use such standardized tools as CAD and CASE. As shown in Table 10.4, the density of CAD tools in the USA in 1986 was twice that of its major competitors in Western Europe, while the density in Japan was only about 11 per cent of the US level. In the case of SMEs in the manufacturing sector, Table 10.5 provides similar sharp contrasts in the adoption of various computer systems.

Table 10.4 Density of various technology systems and tools, by number of units per thousand employees in manufacturing

Country	CAD, 1986		Robots, 1984–1985		NC*, c. 1980		FMS**, 1987	
	Number	Index	Number	Index	Number	Index	Number	Index
USA	6.33	100	1.04	100	11.73	100	0.38	100
Japan	0.72	11	7.53	724	22.4	191	5.59	1471
West Europe							2.61	687
W. Germany	2.62	41	1.16	112	11.38	97		
France	2.89	46	0.58	56				
UK	3.17	50	0.55	53	10.5	90		
Italy	0.31	5	0.62	60				

* Per 1,000 employees in engineering industries.
** Per 10,000 employees.
Source: FMS data adapted from Mansfield (1993), the rest adapted from Carlsson and Jacobsson (1993).

Table 10.5 The use of computer systems in Japanese and US SMEs in the manufacturing sector during the past ten years, 1994, percentage of firms

Computer systems	Japan	USA	Index, USA = 100
CAD	46%	62%	74
CAM	23%	34%	68
Others (often PCs)	13%	17%	76
CIM	6%	14%	43
FMS	13%	8%	163
FMC	42%	7%	600

Source: Adapted from LeBlanc *et al.* (1997: 608).

Two systems of automation: inflexible vs. flexible

The fundamental difference between the USA and Japan in the relationship of human beings with machines is best illustrated by the vastly different purposes of automation in these two countries. While US managers have enthusiastically embraced automation as a means to control the labor process and to substitute for labor (Noble, 1989), the Japanese use automation as a means to increase productivity, flexibility, and skill utilization for shop-floor workers (Alic, 1993). This is evidenced by the astonishing gaps between Japan and the USA in adopting various flexible automation technologies such as CNC, industrial robots, FMS, and FMC (flexible manufacturing cell) (see Tables 10.4, 10.5).

In discerning the vastly different attitude of Japanese and US managers toward automation in manufacturing, Alic (1993: 360–361) notes:

> By and large, Japanese and European managers have paid more attention than Americans to the human and organizational elements in production. In their approaches to automation, too many U.S.-based companies have tried to *integrate people out of the system*, rather than into it. In too many plants, high-technology islands of automation can be found imbedded in manufacturing systems that perform poorly as systems. In such plants, shop-floor employees, even highly skilled troubleshooters, tend to be viewed simply as *adjuncts* to the rest of the system. (*Italics added.*)

In explaining the American mentality to minimizing human intervention, Alic (1993: 361) further observes:

> In the United States, the scientific management tradition still exercises dominant influences over design of production. In this view, people are unpredictable – the sources of errors, mistakes, and uncertainty, rather than solvers of problems.

In addition to this mentality of human-proofing, as Noble (1989) notes, the major impulse behind the advance of industrial automation in the USA was management's obsession with and struggle for control over workers. Automation was perceived as a substitute for labor and therefore management's emancipation from human workers.

As a result of this mentality of control and human-proofing, although the USA has invested heavily in automation in the 1980s, automation has led neither to expected recovery of competitiveness nor to increases in flexibility. This is evidenced by GM's failed effort at automation in the 1980s, and by the fact that US firms lag behind their Japanese counterparts in the effective implementation of FMS (Jaikumar, 1986).

Two types of systems architecture: modular vs. connectual

Just as a system's relationship with its environment and people's relationship with machines is different between US and Japanese ways of systems integration, so too is the relationship of subsystems and components within a technological system. As analyzed in the previous chapter, while Americans tend to modularize and encapsulate subsystems and components so that they are independent of one another both in operation and in information need, the Japanese prefer non-modular and organic links so that the function of the whole system is greater than the sum of its subsystems.

Modular systems architecture enables specialists to isolate and attack a technological problem without the in-depth knowledge of other related issues. By minimizing knowledge links among subsystems, the modularity of subsystems also enables modularization and specialization of the task of system integration. Because of the encapsulation of knowledge within each module, systems integrators only need to consider interface parameters in designing systems architecture without the need to have an in-depth knowledge of the inner function of each module. Here, American emphasis on specialists and separate knowing gives rise to a superior capability in modular systems design. Examples of modular systems architecture include aircraft, software packages, computers, as well as automobiles before the Japanese challenge in the 1980s.

In sharp contract, specialists and separate knowing alone cannot work effectively in non-modular systems architecture. Since each subsystem is interdependent of and nonlinearly linked with other subsystems through various physical, spatial, parametrical, and ultimately knowledge, links, not only the design of the subsystem is dependent on one another in functionality, but the effective integration of subsystems also requires connectual knowing of all intricate relation-specific knowledge links among subsystems. In such a case, the Japanese emphasis on generalists and connectual knowing facilitates non-modular systems design. Examples of non-modular design in Japan include the design of automobiles, electronics, and opto-electronics.

Two types of architectural knowledge: abstract vs. contextual

Parallel to the two types of systems architecture are two types of architectural knowledge. Henderson and Clark (1990) differentiate architectural knowledge from component knowledge. However, what they refer to when they talk about architectural knowledge concerns the ways in which *existing* 'components are integrated and linked into a complex whole.' They fail to acknowledge the type of architectural knowledge that aims at refining and remodeling component design so that integration among components can be seamless and therefore the whole system can function much more effectively. I call the former *abstract architectural knowledge* and the latter *contextual architectural knowledge*. While the former takes the design of components and therefore their interface parameters as given and focuses on the abstract linkages among components, the latter tries to change the design of components and their interface parameters in order to enhance the performance of *other* components, maximize the function of the whole system, and reduce the costs in manufacturing and assembling. Because of the modular nature, other than interface parameters, component knowledge plays little role for the creation of abstract architectural knowledge. Therefore in the modular systems, designers and system integrators do not need in-depth relation-specific knowledge about each component. All they need to do is to take interface parameters as abstract variables and design the interface architecture that maximizes the function of the whole system.

In contrast, in the design of non-modular system architecture, systems integrators and other knowledge workers not only need to investigate how each existing component can best be linked, but also how to change the design parameters of each component so that the function of *other* components can be improved, all components can be seamlessly integrated, and the production costs minimized. The latter needs connectual knowledge about the functional, technical, spatial, parametrical, and knowledge interdependence among components in their function and production, and more specifically, about how a change in the design of one component may affect the function of others and the system as a whole, and the manufacturability and assembility of both components and the whole system.

Because of their failure to differentiate these two types of architectural knowledge, Henderson and Clark (1990) define incremental innovation only as that which changes the design and production of components. They neglect the incremental innovations that aim at changing the design and production of one component to improve the function of *other* components, and the incremental improvement in the design of interfaces among components through a change of component design either to enhance the function of the whole system or to reduce the cost of manufacturing. These sorts of continuous innovations and improvements provide a tremendous source of competitive edge in the Japanese knowledge creation systems as identified by Imai (1986) and others. The relation-specific knowledge emphasized by Asanuma (1989) and others is exactly this type of contextual architectural knowledge that aims at incremental improvement across functional lines and firm boundaries.

The competitiveness implications

The competitiveness implications for the sharp differences in the nature of systems integration are profound and sector-contingent. In the sectors of large-scale complexity such as aircraft, nuclear technology, telecommunication systems, micro processors, packaged computer software and information systems, database management systems, and integrated application software systems, the US emphasis on people-independent systems integration gives US firms a competitive edge. On the other hand, in the sectors of automobiles, opto-electronics, mechatronics, CIM, and FMS, Japanese firms are unparalleled because of their superior capability in people-dependent systems integration.

The effectiveness of systems integration is affected by five sector-contingent variables. The first is the technical possibility of modularity in component and system design: the higher the possibility, the more effective the people-independent systems integration; conversely, the lower the possibility, the higher the effectiveness of people-dependent systems integration. Where the scale of complexity is concerned, people-independent systems integration works best at the two extremes of complexity – in either simple or extremely complex technological systems – whereas people-dependent systems integration is most effective in the technological systems of middle-scale complexity. The effectiveness of systems integration also depends on the *explicitness* and *ease* of articulating knowledge links among components and subsystems. The higher the *explicitness* of architectural knowledge and the easier the articulation and codification of knowledge links, the more effective the people-independent systems integration. Conversely, the higher the tacitness of architectural knowledge and the more difficulty in the articulation and codification of knowledge links among components, the more effective the people-dependent systems integration. Fourth, people-independent systems integration works best where knowledge links among components are mechanical and linear, whereas people-dependent systems integration is most effective where such links are organic and nonlinear. Finally, when other conditions are equal, people-dependent systems integration works best in the sectors where there are stable dominant designs, whereas people-independent systems integration is more effective in the sectors with a high degree of technological discontinuity. In the former case, contextual architectural knowledge is of great importance for continuous improvement of both products and processes, whereas in the latter case, technological discontinuity makes contextual knowledge obsolete.

People-independent systems integration: the US way of systemization

Contractual paradigm and people-independent systems integration

The US competitive advantage in so-called systems integration is widely acknowledged (Spencer, 1990). However, from the perspective of this book, the USA is only good at the type of systems integration that is people-independent, while relatively poor in people-dependent systems integration. The US strength in the former is largely derived from the predominance of the contractual cultural paradigm, contractual governance mechanisms, separate knowing, and the corresponding organizing principles of knowledge creation. Reciprocally, people-independent systems integration facilitates individual autonomy and independence. First, only when the operation of the integrated system is proof against human errors and independent of idiosyncratic skills of individual operators can managers maintain maximum autonomy and independence. Second, the dominance of contractual governance requires that both designers and operators of a system are dispensable and interchangeable. The skill requirement for each knowledge worker must be standardized so that their high mobility should not harm the operation of the system. More broadly, the system should follow its own logic and the human factor must be just an add-on to the system, an adjunct that can readily plug into the system without any interruptions when it is changed or replaced. Third, the dominance of separate knowing also requires that the knowledge for systems integration be created through objective inquiry, investigation, and experimentation. It should be independent of not only individual knowers but also their tacit knowledge and experiences. Finally, the dominant organizing principles of division, separation, standardization, modularization, and encapsulation facilitate the achievement of the above objectives.

Division and separation as a tool for people-independent systems integration

The first method to make a system independent of people, both in the design and operation phases, is through a delicate and thorough division of functions and tasks. In stating the causal link between management autonomy and the division of labor, Pfeffer (1994: 126) observes:

> Management could control the labor process only if a transfer of skills – from craft to manager – about production techniques occurred. The best and perhaps only way to transfer skill was to analyze the work process and divide the work into small component parts, each done by a separate worker. This permitted one to hire workers for each task with requisite skills for that task and economize on labor rates. Second, once the work process was decomposed, it could be studied, analyzed, and most important, the precise way in which the work was performed could be specified so that employees or machines could be instructed in how to do the work.

Management can be autonomous and independent of people only when separate knowing is the dominant form. On the other hand, separate knowing can be effective only when tasks are divided in such a way that individual knowers can attack them *independently* with effectiveness.

One of the most important ways of doing this is by separating thinking from executing. By separating the design task of a system from its operation and maintenance, and by designing a system logic that is well articulated, routinized, and preprogrammed, operators become just an *adjunct* to the system and therefore dispensable, leading to the management control of the labor process. Within the design and thinking tasks themselves, tasks are also subdivided and specialized to enable individual engineers from each distinctive profession to independently attack each task. When it comes to the operation and maintenance of a system, the logic of separation and division has also led to the dominance of what Koike (1990) calls 'the separate system' in the USA. In such a system, the tasks of *unusual operations* are assigned to specialists while shop-floor workers are left with only the *usual operations* that involve little skill. By so doing, the management reliance on shop-floor workers in the operation of the firm is greatly reduced.

A specific form of division and separation that is of importance to people-independent systems integration is the setup of separate function of systems integrators (Iansiti, 1998). By so doing, systems integrators can focus on the design and experimentation of the *abstract* systemic logic without being overburdened by the detailed, contextual, and in-depth knowledge of each subsystem. Once such a system and its operating logic are in place, there is also a division of labor among management professions in which each controls the operation of a relatively independent module.

Taylorism as a facilitator for people-independent systems integration

Judged from the above analysis, Taylorism, which emphasizes systematic management, explicit knowing, division of labor, and separation of thinking and executing, has played a significant role in the persistent American trajectory of people-independent systems integration. Ayres (1992: 31) quotes the following core assumptions of Taylorism articulated by Brooks and Maccoby (1987):

(i) The most complex manufacturing enterprise can be organized and structured hierarchically into *independent* functions, tasks and subtasks.

(ii) The most efficient method of management is to subdivide labor as indicated above and train workers to specialize in one and only one task or task element. Labor is a *fungible* commodity, insofar as virtually any worker can be trained to do non-managerial tasks. Tasks should be simplified sufficiently to minimize the training necessary.

(iii) There exists one unique 'best' way to accomplish each task, which can be discovered *once-for-all* by *experimentation* and *analysis* (time-and-motion studies). These studies, themselves, can best be accomplished by trained specialists.

(iv) 'Rule of law, not men.' Boundaries between management levels and functions must be sharply differentiated. Tasks must be *codified* and reduced to 'work *rules*.'

(v) Management is also a specialty. Managers must have absolute control over all aspects of work organization, including technology choice, investment and location. (*Italics added.*)

All these principles aim at minimizing management dependency on any knowledge workers in the design, maintenance, and operation of technological systems by transforming knowledge holders from craftsmen and foremen to either management or the system itself through the processes of standardization, articulation, codification, and routinization. According to Jelinek (1979: 5), this has led to a visible trend in the development of a US management system that persistently 'attempt[s] to transcend dependence upon the skills, memory, or capacity of any single individual.' As she (1979: 5) puts it,

> By recording the specifics of a task, a given outcome could be *replicated* by others; it could be built into a formal system, institutionalized and *independent* of the individual. Instead of depending on each individual to discover anew the steps to be carried out, instructions could be specified. (*Italics added.*)

Describing Taylor's effort of transcending the people-dependent system of craft production throughout human history, Jelinek (1979: 10) further notes:

> Until Taylor, the operation of the metal-working shop was dependent upon particular workers, on individuals and their private knowledge of the job. There could be no control where management lacked detailed knowledge about jobs. The system or method Taylor proposed rested upon 'scientific observation' through time study, and elaborate records-keeping paraphernalia. The aim was *replicability*: getting the worker to duplicate what observation had uncovered as 'the one best way.' To achieve control over throughput, procedures and the precise times in which they were to be carried out had to be specified. So, too, did information flows, to facilitate administrative control. Only thus could management reintegrate diverse, specialized, and highly subdivided tasks into a controlled, predictable whole.

Indeed, in the words of Hughes (1989b; 188):

> Taylor's fundamental concept and guiding principle was to design a system of production involving both men and machines that would be as efficient as a well-designed, well-oiled machine. He said, 'in the past, the man has been first; in the future the system must be first.'

This vision had been realized in the past through the American system of mass production. It is also underpins the great American penchant for information technology in general and computer enterprise systems in particular.

Professionalization as a tool for people-independent systems integration

Inherent in the logic of Taylorist emphasis on separation and subdivision is the standardization of skills for each independent task. By the standardization of knowledge, expertise, and skills for separately defined and self-contained technological domains and tasks, professionalization makes knowledge workers for each independent function interchangeable and therefore facilitates people-independence in the design, production, and operation of a system. Unlike the emphasis on the accumulation of tacit and relation-specific knowledge through on-the-job-training, job-rotation, and other shop-floor experiences, which is typical in Japanese firms, professionalization in the USA stresses formal education and specialized research experiences in the frontier of a specific technological domain. This is reflected in the fact that US firms have a much higher percentage of researchers, engineers, and systems integrators with doctorate and master degrees than their Japanese counterparts, especially in the software (Baba *et al.*, 1996) and semiconductor sectors (Iansiti, 1998).

Table 10.6 Knowledge structure of R&D integrators in the semiconductor sector

	USA	Japan	Korea
Percentage with explicit or *de facto* long-term employment guarantee	14	100	100
Percentage with research experience in Ph.D. programs	59	7	24
Percentage with no previous R&D project experience	34	14	14
Percentage with experience in one project	28	34	22
Percentage with experience in two projects	23	30	23
Percentage with experience in more than two projects	15	23	41

Source: Iansiti and West (1997: 77).

In the case of systems integration teams in the semiconductor sector, as shown in Table 10.6, only 7 per cent of Japan's R&D integration team members have research experience in Ph.D. programs, as compared to an overwhelming 59 per cent for their US counterparts. On the other hand, the plug-in nature of US specialists vs. the emphasis on on-the-job-training and connectual knowing in Japan is evidenced by the stark differences in the percentage of integration team members without previous R&D experience: 34 per cent in USA vs. only 14 per cent in Japan. The plug-in nature of the US systems integrators is also reflected in the fact that a very low percentage (14 per cent as compared to Japan's 100 per cent) of them are guaranteed long-term employment.

Experimentation, simulation, and people-independent systems integration

The plug-in nature of professionals (systems integrators) and its effect on promoting people-independence is further enhanced by the pervasive use of experimentation as a means of knowledge creation. Indeed, objective, and replicable experimentation is a major form of separate knowing that is transcendent of individual knowers. Experimentation makes it possible to make the research results independent of knowers and their experiences. The required objectivity, operationalibility, combined with the formalized procedures enforced, insures that the knowledge acquired from experimentation can be codified, replicable and, therefore, independent of the idiosyncrasies of investigators. This is especially true for the creation of knowledge for systems integration. Extensive experimentation can also be a substitute for firm-specific experiences and tacit knowledge in exploring the effectiveness of various technical options in systems configurations (Iansiti, 1998: 168). By making the knowledge creation process independent not only of individual knowers but also partly of their experiences, experimentation facilitates people-independent systems integration.

As a form of separate knowing, and also because of the Taylorist heritage that emphasized 'scientific observation' and time-and-motion studies, experimentation has been a prevalent mode of knowing in US firms. In contrast, an emphasis on hands-on experience, the dominance of connectual knowing, and the artisanal tradition (Kondo, 1992) in Japan have all led to much less use of experimentation as a form of knowing. In the aircraft sector, Mowery (1990: 425) observes an almost complete absence of large-scale sophisticated test apparatus and facilities in Japan, whereas US craft makers such as Boeing use extensive experimentation and simulation in the design process. Similarly, in the semiconductor sector, Iansiti (1998) notes a vast disparity between Japanese and US firms in the extent of experimentation (Table 10.7).

Table 10.7 The experimentation capability in the semiconductor sector: a US–Japan–Korea comparison

	USA	Japan	Korea
Experimentation capacity (wafers/week)	917	457	417
Average experimental iteration time	16	13	6
Minimum experimental iteration time	5	7	5

Source: Iansiti (1998: 169).

In the part and process designs of automobiles, Hammett *et al.* (1995: 249) observe that Japanese firms use much less computer simulation (virtual experimentation through a computer model), and other analytical techniques than their US counterparts.

The effectiveness of experimentation as a form of knowledge creation for systems integration depends on the possibilities of standardization and modularization and the extent of complexity, which are both sector-contingent. In the aircraft and logic microchip sectors, while the possibility of effective standardization of parts and processes makes the results of experimentation commensurable, the possibility of modularization makes it possible to independently experiment with each part and each process without the worry that the result may not add up to the functionality of the whole system. On the other hand, in the automobile sector, experimentation and simulation is less effective because it is impossible to effectively standardize and modularize all parts and processes without a loss of knowledge creation opportunities. In this case, experimentation cannot exhaust all variations and contextual situations, nor can its results add up to a meaningful whole. This sector-contingent view can explain why the absence of experimentation in Japan was blamed for its weakness in the aircraft (Mowery, 1990) and semiconductor sectors (Iansiti, 1998), while the US emphasis on experimentation in the automobile sector was also seen as a weakness (Hammett *et al.*, 1995).

Quantification, externalization, formal routines and procedures as a tool for people-independent systems integration

The knowledge for systems integration that is created through experimentation would still be dependent on systems integrators if it were not made explicit through a process of articulation and externalization that transforms knowledge into its explicit form. The application of even explicit (externalized) knowledge would also be prone to human error and dependent on people on the shop floor if it were not transformed into formal rules, standard procedures, and organizational routines. On the other hand, once such transformations from tacit to explicit knowledge and from explicit to imbodied/systemic knowledge are realized, a system's dependence on individual operators is minimized. Because of this, since Frederick Taylor and Alexander Hamilton Church, the two most prominent pioneers of the Scientific and Systematic Management movements, Americans have always focused on the systematic articulation, externalization, standardization, and routinization of knowledge discovered through experimentation (Litterer, 1961, 1963; Jelinek, 1979; Gillespie, 1991).

In the case of micro processor development, according to Iansiti (1998), Intel uses various process monitors to provide solid, quantitative indication of product quality, performance, reliability, and yield; it also tries to fully characterize, specify, and document all process technologies and equipment specifications. In so doing, Intel intends to copy exactly the best processes experimented in the development lab, as Iansiti (1998: 160) describes:

> The newly proven technology was more than transferred; rather, it was meticulously copied from the Santa Clara development fab. Identical equipment was implemented – and in a manner strictly consistent with guidelines set by the developers. An effort was made to copy every detail of the manufacturing process. Differences were explicitly documented and nothing was taken for granted.

Indeed, the 'copy exactly' philosophy is very much a derivative of Taylorism and its separation of thinking from executing. It is a denial of either the possibility of further incremental improvement on the shop floor or the capability of shop-floor workers in achieving such improvement. In the reproduction of prepackaged software and the manufacturing of soft drinks, fast foods, and perhaps micro processors, where there are few opportunities for incremental improvement on the shop floor, such a 'copy exactly' philosophy can work well. In the automobiles and home electronics sectors, where there are huge opportunities for incremental improvements on the shop floor, such a method works poorly.

Complexity, modularization, and people-independent systems integration

The central issue here is the possibility of effective division, standardization, and modularization without a potential loss of knowledge creation opportunities. In the loosely coupled and modular technological systems, it is possible to modularize each component and its design and production without potential loss of knowledge creation opportunities. Conversely, in the tightly coupled and non-modular technological systems, modularization, separate knowing, and people-independent systems integration work less effectively.

More importantly, in addition to the nature of technology itself, the effectiveness of modularization, separate knowing, and people-independent systems integration also depends on the level of complexity involved in the design, production, maintenance, and operation of a technological system. When the level of complexity involved is low, individual knowers can effectively attack a problem without the need for a group process of knowing. Conversely, when the level of complexity is in a middle scale, as in the case of automobile and opto-electronics, individuals still have the cognitive capabilities to master cross-functional, relational, and architectural knowledge, expertise, and skills to facilitate a group process of systems integration that is seamless and organic. On the other hand, separate knowing by individuals on isolated modules incurs a great loss in the creation of cross-functional, relational, and architectural knowledge for incremental improvement, organized fusion, and technology integrity. Indeed, in the automobile sector, which is of middle-scale complexity, Clark and Fujimoto (1991) and Fujimoto (1997) found a negative relationship between the degree of specialization (separate knowing) and firm performances such as product lead-times and engineering hours for new model development.

In the large-scale complex technological systems of aircraft, nuclear technology, telecommunications, semiconductors, and packaged computer software, both individuals and small groups face great limitations on cognitive capability and learning capacity. In this case, modularization, specialization, and separating knowing through division and experimentation can be effective tools to overcome the bounded rationality of knowledge workers and therefore achieve effective systems integration.

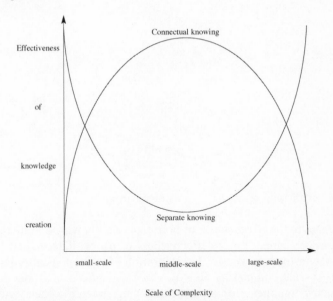

Figure 10.1 The relationship of complexity and knowledge creation

Other conditions being equal, the relationship between the scale of complexity and the effectiveness of separate vs. connectual knowing can be shown in Figure 10.1. Connectual knowing is only effective in the technological systems of middle-scale complexity, whereas separate knowing is effective at both extremes of complexity, in either simple technological systems, or large-scale complex technological systems. The similar logic applies to the effect of inflexible vs. flexible modularization and standardization on knowledge creation and systems integration. In the innovation of simple technology, there are less intricate and complex links among components, therefore, it is possible to effectively separate, modularize, and encapsulate each component for separate knowing, and standardize the interfaces among components.

At the opposite extreme case of large-scale complexity, where many technological frontiers exists within each modules and where individual teams cannot have the connectual knowledge of all components because of bounded rationality, inflexible modularization and separate knowing within each of the modules is the best way for knowledge creation and systems integration. Flexible modularization is only effective in the middle range of complexity, where individuals or teams can have enough cognitive capacity to acquire rich connectual knowledge to facilitate seamless and organic integration of all components (Figure 10.2).

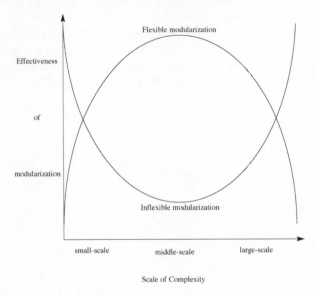

Figure 10.2 The relationship of complexity and modularization

Such differences in the effectiveness of both separate knowing and modularization have an isomorphic impact on the effectiveness of people-independent vs. people-independent systems integration. In the integration of technological systems of both small- and large-scale complexity, it is possible and effective to standardize and modularize each component for separate knowing, integrate them with abstract system logic and system architecture, and make their operation independent of people. On the other hand, in the innovation, production, and maintenance of middle-scale technological systems, an effort of standardization, modularization, and separate knowing may incur the loss of connectual knowledge that is of crucial importance for seamless and organic systems integration (see Figure 10.3). Once again, the key issue here is how the limitations of bounded rationality on knowledge creation and systems integration can be overcome by connectual knowing in a technology of middle-scale complexity, while it can only be overcome by separate knowing in a technology system of large-scale complexity.

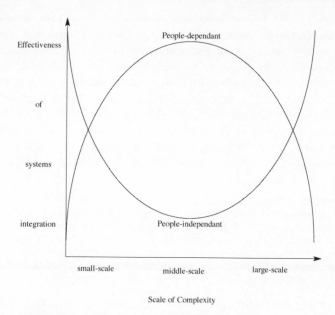

Figure 10.3 The relationship of complexity and systems integration

Such a distinction between three levels of complexity overcomes the dilemma of the complexity approach proposed by Kash and Rycroft (1999). From their perspective, the individualist American society is competitive in the innovation of simple products and processes, while the groupist culture makes Japanese firms preeminent in the innovation of complex products and processes. While such a framework is powerful to explain Japanese competitiveness in the technological sectors of middle-range complexity, such as automobiles and opto-electronics, and the American strength in such simple products as chemicals, fast foods, and soft drinks, it fails to explain the American competitiveness in the large-scale technological sectors of aircraft, nuclear technology, and telecommunication systems.

Systems integration in large-scale complex technological systems

From the perspective used in this book, the US competitiveness in large-scale complex technological systems derives from its organizing principles of modularization and its superior capability in separate knowing and people-independent systems integration. The aircraft sector is of special interest here. According to my regression analysis elsewhere (Jin, 1998), the higher level of R&D intensity in the USA cannot alone explain US strength and Japanese weakness in this sector. When such an advantage is removed, the USA still enjoys an unexplained source of competitive advantage. Mowery and Rosenberg (1985) and Mowery (1990) attribute the Japanese disadvantages in the aircraft sector largely to such factors as a lack of a domestic market, the dominance of military sales, the post-World War II prohibition on military aircraft exports, a weakness in basic aeronautical research, a lack of design capability, an almost complete absence of large-scale sophisticated test apparatus and facilities, and a dearth of inter-firm competition. Roehl and Truitt (1987) believe that the importance of economics of experience in the aircraft sector makes it difficult for the Japanese to challenge the US dominance. The high costs and high risks involved in aircraft design, the large-scale volumes required for breakeven (Mowery and Rosenberg, 1985), and the extreme need for engineering service and for safety and reliability (Roehl and Truitt, 1987) add significant entry barriers for the Japanese. In addition to these contextual factors, Hedlund (1994) and Odagiri and Goto (1996) point to Japanese weakness in complex systems design and systems integration as the most important contributing factor, as Odagiri and Goto (1996: 230) observe:

> Perhaps the gap between Japan and the USA regarding process technology and product embodied technology has been narrowing. However, Japan still lags behind the USA in management technology and design technology, which are now regarded as the most important factors for the past and present dominance of US commercial aircraft producers. The Japanese manufacturers are now finding it extremely difficult to acquire the design technology necessary for developing large aircraft, either through accumulation of their own experiences or through technology transfer from abroad.

From the knowledge regime perspective, the persistent Japanese weakness in the design and systems integration of large commercial aircraft is largely due to the dominance of connectual knowing. Many mechanisms of connectual knowing, such as an emphasis on generalists, on-the-job-training, shop-floor learning, TQM, integration of design, manufacturing, and marketing, and concurrent engineering work less well in the design and integration of large-scale complex technological systems such as large commercial airplanes. In explaining the Japanese weakness in complex systems design of aircraft and large-scale telecommunication systems, Hedlund (1994: 81) notes:

> A reason for the weakness in this area is instead that reliance on internal dialogue, largely at the *tacit* level, is less effective when very complex tasks have to be coordinated. Articulation, systemization, written information, impersonal control become necessary, although not sufficient. The Japanese model of throughput is simply too time consuming in these fields.

Unlike automobiles whose scale of complexity is at the middle range, a large commercial airplane is huge in terms of scale of complexity. In the case of the design and development of the Boeing 747, Serling (1992: 296) observes the complex work of the Boeing system designers and integrators:

> What they were putting together was an airplane with 4.5 million parts, designed from some 75,000 engineering drawings, and so huge that just to park it at an airport took up an acre of ground.

When it comes to the involvement of workers and organizations in the design and production of the Boeing 747, he (p. 291) further notes:

> Some 50,000 people were involved in the 747 programs, including construction workers and subcontractors in virtually every state and 17 foreign countries bringing in 827,000 parts, some of them still under development while the airplane was being built.

At such a level of large-scale complexity, with some 4500 engineers (Sterling, 1992: 306) and nearly $1 billion involved (Mowery and Rosenberg, 1985), the development of the Boeing 747 'was too sophisticated to be run on a gut feeling' (Serling, 1992: 297). With increases in the number of parts and their interactions, connectual knowing faces increasing constraints of both bounded cognitive capability and scarcity of attention (Simon, 1957; March, 1988). Conversely, specialization and separate knowing acquires a great advantage through overcoming the bounded rationality of designers in large-scale systems integration.

Modularity, redundancy, and spontaneous fusion in large-scale technological systems

In addition to specialization and experimentation, separate knowing in aircraft design and integration also takes the form of modularization, spontaneous innovation, abstract connectivity, sequentialization, and systems analysis. Although a large commercial airplane was considered a *tightly coupled* technological system by Perrow (1986) in his theory of complex organization and complex technological systems, it is true only when we confine our attention to its *operational* interconnectedness. It is false when we look into how its subsystems are designed and produced. First, as Hughes (1989b: 33) rightly points out, 'in a large technological system there are countless opportunities for *isolating* subsystems and calling them system for the purpose of comprehensibility and analysis.' Second, because large-scale technological systems such as commercial airplanes have many built-in *redundancies* such as buffers (multiple engines) and multiple loops to safeguard against possible component failure (Simon, 1962; Perrow, 1986; Serling, 1992: 295), they are actually less coupled than middle-scale complex technological systems such as automobiles. As a result of built-in redundancy, a failure in one component of a large-scale technological system in many cases would not cause a catastrophe of the whole system. Indeed, Perrow (1984) himself acknowledges that it takes simultaneous failures in multiple components to cause a breakdown in the operation of a large-scale complex system. The priority of safety and a smaller concern for costs and efficiency in the design and production of large-scale technological systems further strengthens redundancies in design. Conversely, because of its pursuit of economy and efficiency, middle-scale technological systems such as automobiles require minimization of redundancies and therefore maximally tighten the couplings of components.

Finally, where the design, development, and production of large commercial aircraft are concerned, their processes in the USA have been highly sequentialized (Spencer, 1990) and modularized. This is very much the combined impact of the complexity challenge, the American dominant organizing principle of modularization, and the safety imperative. Modularity as a dominant principle in organizing the design and production of large commercial airplanes and their subsystems in the USA is best reflected in the fact that about 15,000 'small vendor and subcontractor firms engaged in the production of assemblies and components for a much smaller group of contractors' (Mowery and Rosenberg, 1985: 72). This has led to a vast garbage can for spontaneous technological breakthroughs and technology fusion in which each small vendor experiments with new ideas, materials, processes, and product designs. The huge federal support for aircraft R&D both in the industry and in universities has further contributed to the creation of a giant primordial soup of innovative ideas for spontaneous fusion in the US aircraft sector (Mowery and Rosenberg, 1998: 66).

Sequentialization and passive coupling as facilitators for integration of large-scale technological systems

Once such a huge capability in component innovation is achieved, modularity in design and standardization of interfaces makes the system integration of parts a relatively easy task. Not only can it be sequentialized in the design and production process with little trade-off; it can also *passively* couple various parts together with minor design changes. In summarizing advantages and disadvantages of the sequential (serial) model of large-scale complex product development in the USA, Spencer (1990: 49) notes:

> The serial model has been the mainstream of product development for many large corporations in the U.S. and abroad for many years ... Examples of products which have been developed in this way are the 7×7 series of Boeing Aircraft, the massive development of space program, many of the large DOD [Department of Defense] programs, the IBM 360, and the Xerox development of the 9000 family of high speed copiers. Whenever it is necessary to make large investment in a *complex* program, this method of product development has many advantages. These advantages include clear responsibilities for each part of the delivery process. It is the method of product development in which U.S. corporations have become comfortable. U.S. business schools have taught many courses on management of each of these parts of product development and the interfaces between them. This type of product development is generally quite expensive, which helps to eliminate much of the competition. This type of development also takes a relatively long time and requires a stable organization.

As stated before, sequentialization reduces non-linear interaction among subsystems and their production, and therefore makes them relatively independent of one another. By so doing, each designer and producer can focus on one component and process and overcome the barriers of bounded rationality.

Inherent in both the processes of modularization and sequentialization is the act of *passive coupling*. While the effort of *active coupling* tries to change the design of one component to maximize the functionality and cost-effectiveness of other components and the system as a whole, *passive* coupling only intends to put all the components together with minimal changes in component design and systems architecture. Therefore, while active coupling requires connectual knowledge about other components, passive coupling only needs to change interface parameters for a *static* and *passive* fit. Example of active coupling include design for manufacturing (DFM), design for assembling (DFA), or concurrent engineering in general. Another example is the effort of Japanese firms of *simplifying* product design for cost-effectiveness by fusing and merging functions of components (Sarathy, 1989). While in the design and production of middle-scale complex technological systems, the effort of active coupling provides sources of competitive advantage for Japanese firms, it is less effective in the design of large-scale complex technological systems because of the priority of safety concerns and of limitations of human cognitive capacity. In such a case, passive coupling removes some of the burdens of connectual knowing and facilitates a focus on specialization.

Abstract connectivity and systems analysis for integration

Most importantly, because of modularization and passive coupling, systems designers and integrators do not need to have a fundamental knowledge about all the components, nor do they need to have detailed knowledge about production on the shop floor. What they need is to take interface parameters as abstract variables and explore the system logic at a higher level of abstraction and experiment with all possibilities of integrating various technological options (Iansiti, 1998). In such a case, there are many levels of systems integrators that take the tasks of designing systems and subsystems as relatively *independent* professions and specialize in the development of design tools and skills for a specific level of abstraction. One good example of such tools for systems design and integration is 'fault tree analysis' in aircraft design in which all possibilities of malfunctions are systematically traced and analyzed and all perceived safeguards such as the addition of redundancies are taken (Serling, 1992: 295).

In sharp contrast to the American trajectory of modularization, standardization, systemization, Baba *et al.* (1996) observe that Japan was slow in adopting 'the systemic approach' developed in the USA. In the Japanese aircraft sector, the extent of standardization and therefore modularization of components was low, and there had been a heavy reliance on craftsmanship and hands-on experience rather than scientific inquiry and formal management control, as Baba *et al.* (1996: 53) summarize their findings:

> Historically, Japanese manufacturing advancement is derived from learning-by-doing based on shared information on the shop floor with resultant dexterity and flexibility. On the other hand, Japanese tradition is relative weak in the systemic approach, that is, where the production process is scientifically analyzed and the parts of manufacturing are systematized based on analytical reasoning.

This lack of analytical reasoning and systemic approach has certainly impaired the Japanese capability in the design and production of large-scale complex technological systems. Indeed, as Odagiri and Goto (1996: 220) note, because of the lack of the scientific and systemic approach, Japan has failed to develop competitive large aircraft and aircraft engines, despite its success in developing *small* aircraft and *small* engines. This sharp contrast can best be illustrated by the contrasting effectiveness of connectual knowing and people-dependent systems integration in large-scale vs. middle-scale technological systems.

Explicit connectivity and shared database: software and information systems as integrators

Other than the scale of complexity, the explicitness of connectivity among subsystems also affects the effectiveness of different ways of knowledge creation and systems integration. When the connectivity of subsystems and components can be expressed explicitly through data and abstract logic, software systems can be used to *embody* the connectivity of various subsystems. By embodying connectivity into the systems architecture and therefore enabling systematic collection, storage, processing, analysis, and communication of information, software systems such as supply-chain management (SCM), enterprise resource planning (ERP), and customer relations management (CRM) enable the seamless and virtual integration of business processes and, at the same time, maximize the autonomy and independence of operators at each functional area. Because of its facilitation of people-independent systems integration, information technology (IT) is most pervasively adopted in American industrial sectors, especially in the service sectors. The cultural penchant for people-independence is also the driving force under-pinning the American innovation and pervasive adoption of a cohort of IT such as Universal Product Code (UPC) (Morton, 1994), electronic data interchange (EDI), Wal-Mart's inventory-replenishment system (Stalk *et al.*, 1992), Citibank's Auto-matic Teller Machines (ATM) (Rackoff *et al.*, 1985), American and United Airlines' ticket reservation systems, Merrill Lynch's Cash Management System, Federal Express's real time package tracking system, and American Hospital Supply's system of online order entry terminals (Morone and Berg, 1993).

Of special interest here is the systematic nature of innovations *spontaneously* emerged and diffused across a wide spectrum of firms, geographical locations, and industries. They are not only complementary with one another, but also serve the same cultural drive for individual autonomy and people-independence. While such a drive provides incentives for the supply push and demand pull of the innovation of technologies that minimizes human intervention, human errors, and human interdependence, the systemic nature of innovations provides not only catalysts and facilitators for new innovations but also *salients* and *critical problems* for complementary breakthroughs, as conceptualized by Hughes (1989a, 1992). In the case of UPC, its innovation reflected not only the American organizing principles of standardization, modularization, codification, and quantification, but also the managerial need to cut labor costs by substituting machine for labor and to make retail transactions independent of people at the checking-out desk, both cashiers and customers (Morton, 1994). At the same time, the innovations of laser scanners, electronic cash registers, printers, computers, packaging technology, and the emergence of the supermarket as a new dominant form of retailing all facilitated the innovation and adoption of UPC (Morton, 1994). The pervasive adoption of UPC and the advancement in communication technology in turn facilitated the innovation of such technologies as EDI, and the pervasive use of credit cards and debt cards in financial transactions.

The backbone of all these innovations is IT and more specifically information systems (IS) that systematically codify, store, and exchange data on economic transactions. They provide *explicit and automatic connectivity* of information and therefore automatic coordination for discrete movements of customer goods from production, to distribution, marketing, and retailing, and to monetary transactions, activities that were previously dispersed among separate vendors and players.

It is clear that without the American drive for people-independence both in its own cultural values and as a way of management control and of reducing labor costs, the practices of many service sectors might still have been locked into the conventional people-dependent models that are still prevalent in countries such as Japan, China, and Italy. By creating people-independent systems of fast food services, banking, retailing, renting, and entertainment, US firms contributed greatly to the technological advancement of these sectors and at the same time have rewarded themselves by their worldwide dominance in these sectors.

IT and IS as enablers for people-independence in the retailing and package-delivery sectors

While the innovation and adoption of ATM – the automatic telephone response system – and automatic package tracking systems make individual functions of a firm people-independent, what underpins their effective operation are the enterprise-wide and inter-organizational information systems that provide shared databases and much needed coordination, integration, and knowledge support.

Good examples of the American advantage in people-independent systems integration through IT include the warehouse retailing and package delivery sectors as represented by Wal-Mart and Federal Express. In the case of Wal-Mart, its huge information infrastructure systematically records and stores transactions at checking-out desks. This huge database of detailed transactions not only enables just-in-time delivery and replenishment, but also provides precious information to reveal patterns of customer tastes and preferences and to trace their dynamic change. This in turn facilitates an agile formulation of effective strategies for advertisement, shelf arrangement, and bargaining with producers (Stalk *et al.*, 1992). In Federal Express and UPS, sophisticated information and communication systems were installed so that customers could track their mails and packages on a real time base (Tapscott, 1996).

IT and IS as enablers for people-independence in the financial sectors

The American penchant for people-independent systems integration has led to its dominance in the business of credit reporting and credit card services. In credit card services, efficient integration and coordination is achieved through a vast integrated IS that *automatically* record, report, share, transmit, and implement financial transactions. In the banking sector, IT has been widely used to cope with a high turnover ratio and to facilitate the employment of unstable, low skill, and part-time labor as a means of both reducing costs and making the operation of banks independent of workers (Keltner, 1995). The deployment of IT and IS also decouples bankers' traditional close ties with customers. It transforms both current and potential customers into a set of abstract attributes and credit histories in huge databases. At the same time, bankers deal with customers based on formulas derived from statistical analyses. By transcending the limitations of *relationship banking* that is prevalent in both Germany (Keltner, 1995) and Japan (Dattel, 1994), the use of abstract formulas and explicit databases in dealing with customers enables US bankers and other related firms to extend their financial services far beyond the reach of traditional relational banking to virtually every corner of the world and every segment of the population. This is the reason for US companies such as VISA, MasterCard, and American Express dominating the world in the credit card business.

The use of software systems in the financial sector enables the best financial specialists at headquarters to systematically analyze enormous pools of data and provide investment suggestions to brokers dispersed all over the organization (Quinn *et al.*, 1996). These systems also capture and encapsulate knowledge about regulations, taxes, policies, formulas, and other rich on-line information to assist brokers in providing professional services to their clients.

Interorganizational IS as a tool for virtual integration

Where business logistics and value chains are considered, it must be said that the IS at Wal-Mart would not work effectively if they were not automatically linked to a suppliers' database. Similarly, the effectiveness of Federal Express and UPS resides in the interorganizational IS that automatically link them with customers' IS so that they know automatically customers' exact needs for package delivery (Topscott, 1996). Through establishing explicit connectivity and automatic data sharing, interorganizational IS provide automatic coordination between producers, suppliers, distributors, retailers, and customers, without the need for face-to-face communication and other forms of human interaction. These systems include EDI, on-line data sharing through the Internet, and more specifically supply-chain management (SCM) software packages. Since they automatically coordinate activities across the supply chain of a company and at the same time minimize the need for interorganizational human interaction, they fit perfectly well with the American penchant for autonomy and independence. As a result, interorganizational IS emerged and are gradually dominating the supply-chain relationship in the USA. In the case of EDI, not only do such US firms as EDS dominate its provision and service, but US firms also have a much higher propensity to use EDI than their Japanese counterparts. In the machine tool sector, in the late 1980s, 22 per cent of US firms had already used EDI to transmit purchase orders to suppliers, while none of their Japanese counterparts had done so. In the textile sector the number is 6 per cent of US vs. 0 per cent of Japanese (Table 10.8).

Table 10.8 The adoption of a specific tool to transmit purchase orders to suppliers: 1987–1990 (percentages)

	USA	Japan	Europe	China	Korea
Machine tools					
Orally	38	22	6	11	13
Written	80	89	85	98	78
Computer/EDI	22	0	26	0	0
Other	11	22	6	9	0
Textiles					
Orally	46	50	25	27	9
Written	74	56	67	89	79
Computer/EDI	6	0	17	0	0
Other	14	11	5	25	0

Source: Young *et al.* (1992: 10).

In their comparison of the US and Japanese attitudes toward adopting EDI, Bensaou and Earl (1998: 119) note:

U.S. companies used electronic data interchange (EDI) extensively, whereas most

Japanese companies still rely on tapes, disks, and courier mail. The Japanese companies had judged the use of EDI to be premature. They wanted to construct effective partnerships first, and then consider how IT could help. In other words, they didn't assume that advanced forms of electronic communication were advantageous.

EDI is advantageous to the US firms because it automatically secures explicit connectivity and at the same time secures the independence of each player. On the other hand, the Japanese treat EDI as not being advantageous because they put relationships first.

Beginning in the mid-1990s, with the astonishing diffusion of Internet technology, it is increasingly advantageous to use on-line database connections to enable a virtual integration with suppliers, distributors, and customers. For example, through the establishment of a supplier chain software system, which is linked to an integrated enterprise system, Dell Computer is able to assemble customized computers for customers, and require just-in-time delivery of components from suppliers. By embodying the interdependence within the supply chain into a systemic logic of explicit connectivity of shared database and coordinated logistics, the use of supply-chain software systems enables the automatic and virtual integration between suppliers, producers, deliverers, and customers without compromising and impairing the autonomy and independence of each player. The explicit and codified nature of transactions and data transfer also greatly reduces transaction costs involved. As a result, interorganizational IS becomes a primary enabler for contractual strategic alliance and integration among players in many US supply chains (Tapscott, 1996).

Information systems as a tool for enterprise integration

Virtual integration in the supply chain of a firm would not work effectively without the support of integrated intra-organizational information systems – i.e. enterprise systems, or enterprise resource planning (ERP). On the other hand, without the cultural drive for autonomy and independence, the operation of firms and the interaction among firms would be less IT- and IS-based. Just as the American drive for people-independent systems integration has led to the emergence and wide diffusion of inter-organizational information systems, the same drive has led to the American rush for business process reengineering and enterprise integration through installing commercially available enterprise-wide software systems such as those provided by SAP and PeopleSoft (Davenport, 1998). By designing and implementing a *generic* system architecture, system logic, and shared database, commercial software packages of enterprise systems provide automatic, coordinated, and explicit connectivities for activities among various functions and value chains of an enterprise. In so doing, dispersed activities within a firm are integrated and coordinated not through face-to-face interaction among people, but through a people-independent architecture of integrated information systems. Just as in the case of the Taylorist system, in the operation and implementation of enterprise systems operators are an adjunct to the system. Rather than focusing on knowledge creation, people are required to strictly follow the system logic (Bensaou and Earl, 1998).

Because of their emphasis on using IT as a tool for systems integration, US firms have a much higher tendency to use computers in their business processes. On the other hand, the focus on people in Japan leads to a lower level of computer usage in business process integration. In the machine tool sector, 44 per cent of US firms had extensive use of computers for production planning and scheduling in the late 1980s, as compared to a mere 17 per cent of their Japanese counterparts. In the textile sector, the US number is 14 per cent vs. a mere 3 per cent in Japan (Table 10.9)

Table 10.9 Use of computers for production planning and scheduling: 1987–1990 (percentages)

	USA	Japan	Europe	Korea	China
Machine tools					
Not at all	9	17	6	82	68
Occasionally	9	22	21	11	20
Moderate	38	39	21	0	9
Extensive	44	17	41	0	0
No response	0	5	11	7	3
Textiles					
Not at all	34	50	12	79	89
Occasionally	18	25	21	9	7
Moderate	34	19	42	0	2
Extensive	14	3	17	0	0
No response	0	3	8	12	2

Source: Young *et al.* (1992: 10).

Table 10.10 Number of PCs per 100 persons, 1994

Ranking	Nations	Computers per 100 persons	Ranking	Nations	Computers per 100 persons
1	USA	31.9	10	New Zealand	17.0
2	Australia	22.1	11	Switzerland	16.2
3	Canada	22.1	12	Ireland	15.9
4	Norway	22.0	13	Germany	15.2
5	Finland	20.3	14	Singapore	15.1
6	Denmark	19.5	15	France	14.7
7	Sweden	18.2	16	Belgium/Lux.	13.3
8	UK	18.2	17	Hong Kong	12.0
9	Netherlands	17.0	18	Japan	11.8

Source: Adapted from Forbes ASAS December 4, 1995, p. 54.

At the national level, Table 10.10 provides an even starker contrast. In 1994, the number of computers per person in Japan was only 37 per cent of that in the USA: The lowest among the 18 advanced economies surveyed. At the workplace, especially with regard to managerial and business processes, the contrast is even sharper. As shown in Table 10.11, in 1994 the number of PCs per 100 white-collar workers in the USA was 104, 4.33 times that of the Japanese number of a mere 24, the lowest among 13 OECD nations.

When the use of company-wide enterprise systems is considered, according to one estimate (Ogden, 1997: 50), 'at least 80% of the largest 500 companies in the United

Table 10.11 Number of PCs per 100 white-collar workers, 1994

Ranking	Nations	Computers per 100 persons	Ranking	Nations	Computers per 100 persons
1	Norway	112	8	UK	74
2	Switzerland	111	9	Spain	68
3	USA	104	10	France	62
4	Netherlands	80	11	Finland	62
5	Denmark	79	12	Italy	57
6	Germany	76	13	Japan	24
7	Sweden	75			

Source: Adapted from OECD (1997b: 35).

States are addressing the need for enterprise-wide systems, compared with 40% in Europe and fewer than 10% in Asia.'

IS as a tool for systemized mass customization

The widespread use of software systems for integrating both value chains and supply chains enables US companies such as Dell Computer to provide mass customization solutions to its customers (Pine II, 1993). In the sectors of micro computers and financial services, the possibilities of modularization and open systems architecture make it possible for US firms to exploit economies of scale in the production of modular components and at the same time exploit economies of scope in the mass customization of assembly.

Software packages as integrators for product development

The American penchant for people-independent systems integration is also pervasive in its effort to integrate various activities of product design and development. This is indicative of the American persistent pursuit of computer-aided design (CAD), and more broadly, computer-assisted everything (Alic, 1993). When it is properly used and where no tacit, non-linear, and constantly changing interfaces are involved, CAD enables automation of many routine design tasks, and automatic fits between various design tasks through embodying explicit connectivities. Automatic fitting also makes it possible for such companies as Boeing to implement concurrent engineering in its design of the Boeing 777 (Tapscott, 1996). Here, simultaneous design of various parts of an airplane is possible because the CAD software package adopted provides the much needed connectivities of design interfaces so that individual designers can make sure that their design parameters automatically fit into those of parts designed by others.

Comparative advantage and disadvantage of explicit connectivity as tool for systems integration

While the American penchant for people-independent systems integration has led to pervasive adoption of IT and IS as tools for integrating business processes, supply chains, and value chains, its competitive implications are, however, mixed. On the positive side, this penchant has contributed to US dominance in IT and e-businesses. The pervasive use of IT and IS also enables systematic collection and automatic transfer of information necessary for integrating business processes and for coordinating transactions within supply chains and value chains. In so doing, IT and IS vastly reduce transaction costs and coordination costs, greatly transcend the limitations of people-oriented interaction, enable a greater leverage of intellectual capital, and make it possible for mass customization. On the negative side, an overreliance on IT as tools for integration sometimes underutilizes the local knowledge of people, and makes them passive processors of information, rather than active creators of knowledge. In the sectors where tacit knowledge, non-linear feedback, non-modular connectivity, and constant change of interfaces and standards are important for competitive success, people-independent IT may produce unexpected failure owing to its underutilization of tacit knowledge, its rigidity in connectivity, and its inability to adapt to the need for fast changes.

In the case of financial services, although the use of software systems enables US such firms as Merrill Lynch to leverage the intellectual assets of its top analysts (Quinn *et al.*, 1996), the overreliance on explicit data and statistical analyses may cause unexpected failure in cases of unforeseen events such as the financial crises in Russia and Latin America, and volatile changes in the exchange rate of the Japanese Yen. In these cases, no software packages and sophisticated analytical models can substitute the tacit knowledge, intuition, and long-term experience of a good broker. As indicated by the widely publicized 1998 failure of Long-Term Capital Management, a renowned US hedge fund, neither 'rocket scientists,' nor Nobel laureates in economics could avoid miscalculation in their use of sophisticated models. Software packages and the analytical models imbedded can only be as good as the assumptions underlying them, while volatile and dynamic economic realities can escape the precise delineation of these assumptions. The very failure of prominent investment bankers such as Merrill Lynch, Lehman Brothers, and Citicorp in their investment in Russia and Latin America in the face of global crisis reflects a fundamental problem of the US financial system.

Similarly, in the areas of enterprise software systems, CIM, and CAD, the American emphasis on the system rather than on people may also backfire by producing a system that is poorly integrated with people, organizations, and corporate strategies (Liker *et al.*, 1992; Bensaou and Earl, 1998; Davenport, 1998). The overreliance on external consultants, the sharp division between thinking and implementing, and the resultant fragmentation in the US workplace all contribute to the lack of organic integration in IT implementation. As a result, while the American way of people-independent systems integration may contribute to American dominance in commercial software systems, financial services, Internet commerce, and large-scale technological systems such as aircraft and logic chips, it may greatly underutilize the tacit and firm- and location-specific knowledge of shop-floor employees, which is of vital importance to the success of CNC, CIM, and FMS, to which we will return later.

People-dependent systems integration: the dominant Japanese way of systemization

In contrast to the American effort of using system logic to integrate people out of technological systems, the Japanese put people at the center. This is reflected in almost all aspects of the Japanese governance mechanisms of knowledge creation, ranging from long-term employment focusing on skill formation, TQM, JIT, broad on-the-job training, continuous improvement, to cross-functional teams, long-term supplier relationships, DFM/DFA, and current engineering. Indeed, while high mobility of employees leads to the American focus on the design and implementation of a systemic logic that is independent of people, the long-term employment nature of core workers in Japanese firms enables the latter to rely on people and their broad skills to organically integrate technological systems with human wares.

This difference is especially pronounced in the divergent ways of dealing with IT, CNC, FMS, and CIM between US and Japanese firms. In the case of IT implementation, while Americans treat IT as a stand-alone system, the Japanese intend to integrate IT and people seamlessly so that the knowledge and skills of shop-floor employees can be maximally appropriated. Consequently, as Bensaou and Earl (1998) discovered, Japanese companies rarely experienced the lack of organic integration and seamless fit in IT implementation both US and European firms are plagued with. In fact, they (1998: 120) were surprised to find that Japanese senior executives did not even recognize the problems that were being described to them.

The central cause of such an astonishing divergence rests in what Bensaou and Earl (1998) describe as the American focus on 'systems design,' and the Japanese emphasis on 'human design.' While the former 'design the most technically elegant systems possible and ask employees to adapt to it,' the latter 'design the system to make use of the tacit and explicit knowledge that employees already possess' (Bensaou and Earl, 1998: 121). In contrasting the West with the Japanese way of managing IT, Bensaou and Earl (1998: 126) note:

> In the West, systems development tends to focus more on the business process being supported or redesigned than on the people who will use the product ... IT systems have de-skilled and routinized far more work than they have enriched ... Specialists often leave no room in their systems for human judgement or understanding when they become overly focused on technological 'solutions.'

In sharp contrast,

> In Japan, building systems is not an end in itself; enhancing the contribution of people is the higher goal. That is why the principle of 'human design' is central to the way the Japanese use IT. If a system automates work that people can do better, it is considered not a good system – and the potential for the result is raised explicitly when an IT project is under consideration.

This is the evidence in support of my distinction between people-independent and people-dependent systems integration. The divergence between the USA and Japan in their ways of systems integration has huge implications for the sectoral competitiveness of US and Japanese firms that we will analyze in detail.

Usual and unusual operations: the separate vs. integrated systems

According to Koike (1990, 1994), the effective operations of any technological systems require usual and unusual operations. While the former deals with 'routine, repetitive and monotonous work,' the latter deals with changes and problems. In US firms, usual operations are assigned to shop-floor workers, whereas unusual operations are reserved for specialists, forming what Koike (1990) calls 'the separate system.' Conversely, in Japanese firms, both usual and unusual operations are dealt with by shop-floor workers, forming what Koike (1990) calls 'the integrated system.' The separate system is people-independent to the extent that shop-floor workers are required to strictly follow operating routines predesigned by separate specialists. On the other hand, 'the integrated system' is people-dependent since shop-floor workers are at the core for the effective implementation of all operations. Dealing with unusual operations on the shop floor requires not only the formation of broad intellectual skills but also the commitment and identification of employees to the firm. To this point, the whole Japanese system of connectual governance mechanisms are Japanese innovations to nurture and tap intellectual skills of shop-floor employees for the effective solving of unusual operations of a production system. Indeed, as Koike (1990, 1994) rightly points out, the effectiveness of skill formation and application on the shop floor provides the very foundation for the manufacturing competitiveness of large Japanese firms. This advantage is especially pronounced in the manufacturing sectors of middle-scale complexity in both products and processes such as automobiles, CNC, and FMS, and CIM.

Unlike the cases of retailing, financial services, data transfer, and other information processing sectors, where most problems and contingencies can be systematically codified, standardized, routinized, and preprogrammed, in the manufacturing sectors, especially those of middle-scale complexity, it is almost impossible to standardize all unusual operations and preprogram all contingencies (Koike, 1990). As a result, the integration of shop-floor learning into the operation of the whole system becomes paramount for the competitiveness of firms.

Indeed, because of the dominance of the separate system, the lack of shop-floor learning has been the primary source for the dearth of flexibility and effectiveness in the US sectors of automobiles (Clark and Fujimoto, 1991), machine tools (Finegold *et al.*, 1994), FMS (Jaikumar, 1986), and CIM (Sobol and Lei, 1994; Upton, 1995). On the other hand, the same authors have found that the emphasis on skill formation and knowledge creation on the shop floor through such activities as broad on-the-job training, continuous improvement, TQM, and just-in-time (JIT) has provided Japanese firms competitive advantages in these same sectors. In the case of CNC, FMS, and CIM, shop-floor workers are able to make agile changes in the programming to make their operation flexible.

In addition, the separate system in the USA also leads to a lack of knowledge sharing among divisions and between suppliers and users. In the case of managing IT, the overemphasis on specialization and the mentality of separation between thinking and executing in the USA leads to a lack of understanding and knowledge sharing between IT specialists and users, the fragmentation of IT implementation, and the blind adoption of technology for technology's sake without effective integration with business strategy, organization, and culture (Bensaou and Earl, 1998). On the other hand, the emphasis on connectual knowing and generalists helps Japanese firms to develop appropriate IT that can fit seamlessly and organically within firm strategy, organization, and culture. In the process, IT specialists and users share a great deal of knowledge through such mechanisms as job rotation and organizational bonding (Bensaou and Earl, 1998).

Tacit knowing, flexible standardization, and people-dependent systems integration

One great advantage of people-centered shop-floor learning and knowledge creation is its ability to facilitate flexible standardization. In contrast, people-independent systems integration might lead to inflexible standardization that fails to take idiosyncratic conditions and strategic intents into consideration. In comparing the US systemic approach with the Japanese method of organization, Baba *et al.* (1996: 53) rightly observe:

> The Japanese method of organization made it possible to improve efficiency by allowing flexibility in the system to reflect individual situations on the shop floor; the systemic approach [of the USA], on the other hand, is rather rigid, as it ignores unique circumstances on the shop floor.

In many cases, the American penchant for people-independence in systems integration, together with its Taylorist tradition, has led to its effort to *standardize* and codify every contingency and every option of a technological system. By designing a preprogrammed systemic logic that integrates the operation of all contingencies and options, and by requiring operators to follow strictly these standardized operating procedures, US firms make it possible that the system will operate in an integrated way. This systemic approach has contributed to the development of integrated commercial software packages in the USA to deal with such purposes as word processing, database management, financial management, supply-chain management, customer relationship management, and enterprise systems (Davenport, 1998). As analyzed before, this approach works well when all contingencies, options, and connections can be *explicitly* articulated, standardized, and therefore preprogrammed. In the sectors of financial services, insurance, logistics, database management, information processing and other services, this is the case. In the manufacturing sectors of middle-range complexity both in products and processes, however, an effort of full standardization and preprogramming will not only lead to a vast waste of continuous improvement opportunities, but will also lead to a high level of inflexibility owing to both the existence of numerous unusual operations and the need for tacit knowledge on the shop floor. By imposing its own *generic* logic, the systemic and people-independent approach to systems integration fails to adapt to the local conditions, strategies, governance structures, and cultures of specific firms. It also fails to utilize, incorporate, and imbed tacit knowledge accumulated on the shop floor. In his 1998 article, Davenport rightly points out the danger of blindly implementing the enterprise systems of integrated commercial software packages without carefully adapting to local conditions (pp. 121–122):

> An enterprise system, by its vary nature, imposes its own logic on a company's strategy,

organization, and culture. It pushes a company toward full integration even when a degree of business-unit segregation may be in its best interests. And it pushes a company toward generic processes even when customized processes may be a source of competitive advantage. If a company rushes to install an enterprise system without first having a clear understanding of the business implications, the dreams of integration can quickly turn into a nightmare. The logic of the system may conflict with the logic of the business, and either the implementation will fail, wasting vast sums of money and causing a great deal of disruption, or the system will weaken important sources of competitive advantage, hobbling the company.

Indeed, while the US heavy investment in IT has been acclaimed by many as a sign of revived US competitiveness, the overreliance on generic solutions and the mentality of technology for technology's sake in its strategy of adopting and implementing IT might create many liabilities and weaknesses for US firms.

Conversely, as Bensaou and Earl (1998) note, the Japanese mind-set for managing IT has some advantages that many Americans tend to neglect in this new age of acclaiming the USA's superiority. First, the Japanese emphasis on contextual knowing enables Japan to develop customized solutions from the bottom up. It enables an organic fit between IT and business, organization, and culture (Bensaou and Earl, 1998). Second, the Japanese stress on shop-floor skill formation enables shop-floor workers flexibly to change the programming of machines to achieve flexible production. Third, the Japanese focus on tacit knowledge and its articulation enables an accumulation, articulation, externalization, and embodiment of the tacit and firm-specific knowledge on the shop floor for the continuous improvement of operating procedures, standards, and for the flexible and effective operation of IT systems. Here, flexible standardization is achieved through a dynamic process of knowledge creation and a transformation from tacit to explicit knowledge as described by Nonaka (1994). This is a process in which accumulated tacit knowledge is shared among co-workers through a socialization process and is continuously transformed into explicit knowledge through an articulation and externalization process. The articulated knowledge is further embodied into standard procedures and software programming so that it becomes a basis for further tacit and explicit knowing and learning.

Connectual/contextual knowing, flexible connectivity, and people-dependent systems integration

Another great advantage of people-dependent systems integration resides in its ability to make contextual links and organic integration between the system and its environment and among the subsystems. While in the USA the integration of subsystems is realized through the detailed specification of *explicit* connectivity and a subsequent construction of a top-down, generic systemic architecture, as discussed in previous chapters, integration in Japan takes an organic form through the development of relational and contextual knowledge that brings different parts together seamlessly. Organic and contextual integration is possible not only because various forms of knowledge and expertise from various functions and divisions are pooled and integrated, but also because knowledge workers and system integrators hold common knowledge base that is broad, cross-functional, and connectual, accumulated through long years of broad on-the-job training and broad socialization. In the case of heavyweight project management, as systematically explored by Clark and Fujimoto (1991), the design teams of Japanese car-makers such as Toyota rely on the broad and rich experience, the connectual knowledge, and the tacit insights of its heavyweight project managers to synthesize, integrate, and coordinate the dynamic knowledge inputs from team members coming from all the spectrum of functions. This has provided immense competitive advantages for the Japanese car-makers to achieve product integrity, high quality, and low manufacturing costs (Clark and Fujimoto, 1991). In addition, according to Kusunoki and Numagami (1997: 199), Japanese firms have used frequent intra-firm transfer of engineers to share specialized insights and create cross-functional knowledge, which resulted in 'a rapid use of cross-functional knowledge within each functional group' to achieve 'efficient engineering integration.'

In the case of IT systems development, while the American penchant for people-independent integration has led to the widespread adoption of off-the-shelf software packages, as so many researchers and practitioners have observed, Japanese companies prefers customized software systems developed in house, tailor-made through closely working with vendors in the long term (Mowery, 1996; Bensaou and Earl, 1998). As Bensaou and Earl (1998: 126) rightly point out, while such a system of IT development may hinder 'experimentation and the adoption of radically new and diverse technologies,' it ensures seamless fits between IT and business that is often missing in the American way of managing IT development.

Technology fusion as a form of technology integration

The Japanese emphasis on connectual knowing across technological disciplines has led to the dominance of technology fusion as a major form of technology integration. By seamlessly blending, fusing, and synthesizing two or more disciplines of technologies through connectual and contextual knowing, Japanese firms were able to bring to the markets generation after generation of new products with new functionality, high quality, and low costs that articulated customers' latent demands (Kodama, 1991, 1995). In so doing, once separated technological systems are seamlessly fused and integrated into totally new ones.

Flexible modularization and people-dependent systems integration

The Japanese emphasis on connectual and contextual knowing also enables the flexible modularization analyzed in chapter 9. People-independent systems integration works best when there is a possibility of complete and effective modularization. Indeed, many software packages are designed into a modular form so that each part can be plugged into the existing open architecture. In many other cases such as the design and production of technological systems with middle-range complexity, however, complete and rigid modularization may be harmful to product integrity, product functionality, manufacturing costs, and the future evolution and improvement of product families. In such technological systems as CNC, FMS, and CIM, rigid modularization makes it impossible to continually alter and improve interfaces between subsystems to enhance functionality and reduce costs. It may also cause technical fragmentation and lack of integration in US firms owing to organizational fragmentation and the resultant lack of knowledge sharing among organizational divisions.

Conversely, connectual knowing and the consequent people-centered systems integration make it possible to continually change the modular designs and interfaces so that not only subsystems can be integrated in an increasingly seamless and organic way but also their production and assembly can be more cost-effective and of higher quality. However, in order for it to be effective, flexible modularization requires effective connectual knowing, that can only be achieved through the connectual governance mechanisms that are dominant in Japan. In the machine tool sector, as a result of connectual knowing and the resultant capability of changing interface design, Japanese firms were able to aim at 'simplifying product, with design changes planned so as to lower the costs of manufacturing and allow for the assembly line production of the machine tools' (Sarathy, 1989).

Technology-centered vs. people-centered knowing: low-tech vs. high-tech integration

The divergent emphasis on system vs. people between the USA and Japan also leads to a vastly different attitude toward the use of most advanced technology. In the USA, the penchant for people-independence has contributed to a mind-set to use technology to substitute for people. As a result, managers have developed the mentality of technology for technology's sake in which most advanced technologies are eagerly sought as an easy fix for the problems in the firm (Bensaou and Earl, 1998) and as a means to maximize human-proofing.

In contrast, because the Japanese system is people-centered, technologies are chosen not by their own merits but because of their usefulness in maximally assisting people's knowledge creation capability. In the case of manufacturing, US firms use CAD/CAM to achieve concurrent engineering, implement complete automation to achieve quality control, install enterprise-wide software systems to achieve mass customization, establish inter-organizational IS to manage supply chain, apply groupware software packages to facilitate teamwork, and implement CIM to acquire flexible manufacturing (Tapscott, 1996). Conversely, although not rejecting the use of advanced technologies, the Japanese counterpart tend to use such people-centered approaches as JIT, TQM, and heavyweight project managers to achieve the same objectives (Bensaou and Earl, 1998). Indeed, not only do Japanese firms tend to use fewer computers than their US counterparts in manufacturing (Parker, 1992), they also rely on such low-tech means as the *kanban* system and JIT to achieve flexibility rather than adopting CIM (Duimering *et al.*, 1993).

Interestingly, Duimering *et al.* (1993), among others, found that while such people-centered approaches as JIT were systematically related to higher productivity levels, overall factory performance, and individual manufacturing performances such as reducing throughput time and simplifying production systems, the technology-driven approaches such as investment in advanced technologies of CIM showed no systematic relationship with performance improvement. Indeed, in the case of the US paper industry, Upton (1995) actually found a general decline of factory flexibility with the installment of CIM.

As Duimering *et al.* (1993) and Sobol and Lei (1994) rightly point out, the key for the failure of the technology-driven approach resides in the inability of advanced technologies such as CIM to generate and adapt to 'soft' data and tacit learning that are of primary importance to flexibility in manufacturing. The inability of the technology-driven approach to handle unpredictable circumstances and to organically integrate various subsystems including human subsystems further hampers its flexibility.

In contrast, the people-centered approach acquires great flexibility because of the human agility and adaptability in tacit learning, in capturing soft data, in handling unpredictable circumstances, and in organically integrating various subsystems. Indeed, evolutionary psychologists such as Pinker (1997) would argue that in cases of dealing with these issues, neither computers nor other advanced technologies can even remotely parallel the intelligence of human minds.

Flexible automation as a mechanism for people-dependent systems integration

The recognition of the superiority of human minds over machines does not mean that human beings do not need machines to assist their work and their knowledge creation processes. Indeed, when it is possible and when it is good in assisting shop-floor efficiency, the Japanese are always willing to adopt sophisticated technologies in manufacturing. As Bensaou and Earl (1998) note, scholars and managers visiting large Japanese manufacturing multinationals were impressed by their legendary use of robotics, FMS, CIM, and other advanced manufacturing technologies. In comparison with their US counterparts, Japanese firms actually used far more robotics (Mansfield, 1989), FMS (Mansfield, 1993), CIM (Shani *et al.*, 1992), and advanced manufacturing technologies (ATM) in general (Lei *et al.*, 1996).

The real issue is not so much the adoption of ATM as the attitude toward them. While the people-centered approach in Japan can maximally achieve both productivity and flexibility in the design, implementation, and operation of ATM, the technology-centered approach in the USA reduced ATM to inflexible machines with far less intelligence than the former. Indeed, as Lei *et al.* (1996) rightly point out, the effective implementation and operation of ATM requires the generation of tacit knowledge and firm-specific routines whose creation is dependent on shop-floor learning. In struggling for cross-functional integration, which is of great importance to ATM's effective implementation and operation, cross-functional knowledge and expertise that is generated through broad skill formation and connectual knowing is indispensable. Such a process of connectual knowing will also enable smooth synchronization among various processes within the ATM system. It is also because of the need for connectual learning, compared with their European (Hardaker and Ahmed, 1995) and US (Bensaou and Earl, 1998) counterparts, that the development and implementation of such ATM as CIM in Japanese firms is more decentralized, more likely to take a bottom-up and gradual approach, and involves more generalists on the shop floor.

Japanese competitive advantage in CNC, FMS, and CIM

Indeed, it is the people-centered approach that has greatly enhanced the Japanese competitiveness in such ATM systems as CNC, FMS, and CIM. In the design, production, and implementation of these technological systems, tacit and connectual knowing is at least as pivotal as the systematic collection of hard data, and the capability in flexible programming is more important than generic systemic design.

The Japanese competitive advantages in CNC

In its report prepared for the Presidential Office of Science and Technology Policy, the Critical Technology Institute (Finegold *et al.*, 1994) attributes the decline of the US machine-tool industry in general, and computer numerical control machine tools (CNC) in particular, to such factors as poor technology links to customers, arm's length relationship with suppliers, poor links with government-sponsored research, poor workforce skills, a low level of general education, a lack of in-company training, a lack of capital investment in new technologies, and a low-skill use of new technologies. Conversely, the opposite attributes are attributed to the competitive success of the Japanese counterparts. From the perspective employed in this book, many of these symptoms in the USA are the results of the dominance of separate knowing and contractual governance mechanisms for knowledge creation. They are also closely linked to the American mentality of control and human-proofing. On the other hand, the Japanese emphasis on tacit, connectual, and contextual knowing and the embodying connectual governance mechanisms underlie such Japanese advantages as the high level of skill formation, the close and long-term knowledge links between producers and users, technology fusion, and flexible and high-skill use of new technologies.

Unlike the American case in which low-skilled workers are treated as an adjunct to the machine, the Japanese require shop-floor workers flexibly to program CNC (Finegold *et al.*, 1994; Mazzoleni, 1997). The emphasis on connectual knowing and flexible modularization also enable Japanese firms to *simplify* product and process designs so that CNC can be mass produced with low costs (Sarathy, 1989; Finegold *et al.*, 1994). Indeed, this has contributed to Japanese competitiveness in the low-end spectrum of low cost and standardized CNC, while US firms are still competitive in the high end of specialized CNC (Finegold *et al.*, 1994). The latter is very much the result of the American emphasis on specialization and separate knowing.

In addition to this difference at the spectrum of market fragmentation, perhaps the most pronounced difference between US and Japanese CNC industry is the divergent technological paths involved. According to Mazzoleni (1997), while US firms followed the path of the closed-loop system design, the Japanese adopted the open-loop system architecture. In the closed-loop system configuration, CNC provides feedback information to automatically secure the accuracy of operation. On the other hand, in the open-loop system design, there is no such automatic feedback. In the latter case, not only is there a much tougher accuracy requirement for the design and production of CNC, operators also need to provide feedback both in terms of operation and in terms of constant and proper maintenance. Indeed, while the system itself provides necessary feedback in the closed-loop system, designers, producers, and operators offer the missing linkages in the open-loop system. It is clear that the closed-loop system requires less shop-floor learning and therefore is less dependent on operators than is the open-loop system. Mazzoleni (1997) attributes such a divergence solely to the path-dependent nature of learning in the diffusion of innovations in the CNC sector. From the perspective of knowledge regimes, the closed-loop system architecture is a form of people-independent systems integration, while the open-loop system configuration is a type of people-dependent systems integration. It is therefore highly possible that the national difference in systems integration played a more important role in the lock-in of the divergent path than the generic impact of historical path dependence did.

The Japanese competitive advantages in CIM

Just as the case of CNC and FMS, the Japanese competitive advantage in CIM is based on its emphasis on tacit learning on the shop floor. Conversely, the US lag behind in CIM (Shani *et al.*, 1992) is largely due to its same mentality of control and human-proofing. Like its treatment to CNC and FMS, in the USA CIM is thought to substitute capital for labor. The adoption of CIM is, therefore, justified not by factory flexibility, but by cost reduction and productivity improvement. As a result, not only is the promise of CIM not fully realized (Johansen *et al.*, 1995), in many cases its implementation actually reduced factory flexibility, as has been empirically evidenced in the paper industry (Upton, 1995). As a result, Rasmus (1994: 62) notes:

> Now, in the frugal 90's, many corporate boards despise the acronym CIM. Despite the hype, despite the glowing case studies, they know the dirty secret. CIM didn't work everywhere ... What went wrong was the reliance on technology. CIM offered a vision of white-collar automation through tools like manufacturing resources planning (MRPII). It then promised to link those tools to the blue-collar world of punch presses, milling machines and paint booths. For many businesses, CIM distracted them from their real concern: the customer and the product.

In pointing out the wrong reliance on automatic data collection and transfer as the only form of communication and coordination, Rasmus (1994: 63) argues that:

> CIM's success, however, depended not on computer communications, but on human communications. In too many cases the people responsible for CIM thought of it as the product, rather than that which was delivered to the customer. The people building the products sometimes rebelled against 'The System,' even to the point of sabotaging data. The people on the production and in the stockroom knew there was more to CIM than computers and software.

Indeed, many authors have pointed out the need for tacit learning and flexible programming on the shop floor for the effective implementation of CIM (Sobol and Lei, 1994; Lei *et al.*, 1996). With its emphasis on tacit, connectual, and contextual knowing, the Japanese system of organizing knowledge creation is better suited for the implementation of CIM. Hardaker and Ahmed (1995: 37) note the incremental and people-dependent nature in the Japanese way of implementing CIM:

> The Japanese way of implementing CIM and building manufacturing advantages is through an incremental process. Almost part by part, and functional area by functional area, the Japanese install CIM systems and then build interlinkages which dovetail between operations, functions and departments. Once each installation is complete and

fully integrated into the existing systems, not only in physical terms and structural terms but also managerially and in a human sense, another part of CIM is added. The importance of human and managerial integration alongside computer integration is fully appreciated by the Japanese and substantial effort is directed to this end. Full and proper integration requires not only that individuals are trained in the use of CIM technologies, but also that training is provided in an applied context. The Japanese practice of internal on-the-job training provides just this type of experience; operators *contextually* taught the 'job' within an organization attendant with its particular procedures, cultural norms and standards. (*Italics added.*)

Not surprisingly, Japan achieved greater success in implementing CIM (Shani *et al.*, 1992). Interestingly, in the CIM sector from 1990 to 1994, even though the USA had maintained a negative trade balance with Japan, the USA had maintained a trade surplus with the rest of the world and the industrial nations of France, Italy, the UK, and Germany (Jin, 1998). It is clear that even though the American mentality of control and human-proofing has harmed the effective implementation of CIM, the same effort of people-independent systems integration and separate knowing has facilitated the development and dominance of generic commercial software packages for CIM.

Discussion: Taylorism reassessed

In summary, it is clear that the divergent paths of people-independent vs. people-dependent systems integration in the USA and Japan have both positive and negative consequences, each contributing to their persistent sectoral patterns of competitiveness. While the penchant for people-independent systems integration has given rise to the American technological prowess in the sectors of information processing and services and the technological sectors of either low- or large-scale complexity, the Japanese emphasis on tacit, connectual knowing and people-dependent systems integration has brought about their strength in the technological sectors of middle-range complexity both in products and in processes, including automobiles, opto-electronics, mechatronics, CNC, FMS, CIM, and ATM in general.

With the increasing importance of the information and communication sectors, it is clear that the pendulum of overall national competitiveness has shifted to the side favoring the US systems of knowledge creation and integration. It is clear that once again Japan needs to catch up and learn from the USA, not only in the areas of advanced information technologies, but also in the American ways of organizing, integrating, and knowledge creating.

This does not mean that US firms can be complacent about their own prowess. Not only has Japan's competitiveness in manufacturing and in the technological sectors of automobile, opto-electronics, mechatronics, CNC, FMS, and CIM not diminished in any discernible way, but the possible future development and dominance of information appliances may once again give Japanese firms competitive leverage.

While in the 1980s and early 1990s, people had been so eager to dismiss Taylorism as a barrier for competitiveness, its potential contribution to the information revolution and to the rise and dominance of people-independent systems integration has been grossly neglected. While the American efforts to learn from the Japanese ways of organizing, including TQM, JIT, and cross-functional teams, have certainly contributed to the American revival in the 1990s. Ironically, it has been the Taylorist heritage and the organizing principles embodied therein that have helped to create a new American competitive edge in the new information economy. Perhaps it is time for not only Japan, but the rest of Asia, to learn the American ways of knowing, organizing, and governing from the most fundamental up.

CHAPTER ELEVEN

The Great Synergy of Civilizations

> Contrary to the belief that the decline of the United States derives from a fall in the *appropriability* of American technologies, we would suggest that this decline is linked to the diffusion of American organizing practices to other countries; at the same time new and better practices are being introduced and worked out in other countries.
>
> Dosi and Kogut (1993, p. 258)

Of the two most influential perspectives on the post-Cold War world order, 'the clash of civilizations' view by Huntington (1996) projects that the end of the ideological battle will inevitably trigger a war of civilizations between the West and the Confucian–Islamic world because of their incompatible value systems and their struggle for dominance. On the other hand, the 'end of history' proposition by Fukuyama (1992) asserts that the triumph of liberal democracy over communism symbolizes *the end of history* in the Hegelian sense that no ideology other than liberal democracy is accepted as the *only* viable and desirable route for the rest of human history.

While not arguing against the possibility of civilizational clash and the triumph of liberal democracy, this book indicates that it is the *cultural synergies* among civilizations that have contributed to the rise of Japan after World War II and the revival of the USA since the 1980s. As the pace of cultural synergy speeds up owing to the fast pace of globalization, what we observe is neither the end of history nor the clash of civilizations, but rather the *beginning* of a new *era of great synergy* among cultures which will enable human beings to enjoy a much greater level of diversity and richness in organizing principles far beyond the limits of any single nation.

My synergetic view of cultural interaction rests in my definition of culture as being composed of many '*genes*' of organizing principles from which other civilizations can borrow, assimilate, and recombine with endogenous ones. Any organizing principles have both advantages and disadvantages. None can generate a competitive edge for firms in all sectors. While a set of organizing principles generates a competitive advantage in some sectors, it creates competitive disadvantage in others. There are two ways to deal with this dilemma. The first is by combining and synergizing organizing principles across cultures, as has happened in Japan and the USA. The second is by furthering the reduction of trade barriers and therefore promoting an international division of labor across nations, based on different endowments not in resources but rather in organizing principles.

The sectoral perspective as a solution to linear thinking

Our knowledge regime perspective tries to provide a framework for analyzing the sectoral, technological, and ultimately knowledge-creating *contingencies* for predicting the competitive advantages and disadvantages of cultural paradigms, organizing principles, patterns of knowing, governance mechanisms, and technological regimes. At the center of such a framework rests the *sectoral perspective* that emphasizes the importance of the sectoral structure of knowledge creation in determining the effectiveness of different organizing principles and governance mechanisms.

By focusing on the *meso* level of sectoral analysis, the knowledge regime perspective is able to bridge the gap between the macro-level analysis of culture and micro-level studies of firm behavior. It not only overcomes the overgeneralization of the macro-level analysis of country competitiveness, but also prevents the myopic scope of firm-level analysis that neglects how macro- and meso-level factors such as cultural paradigms, organizing principles, governance mechanisms, and technological regimes have conditioned behaviors at the firm level. While the impact of these factors is pervasive at the firm level, it is at the sectoral level that their patterns of influences can best be revealed. Sectoral level analysis also prevents an over-generalization of research at the macro level, as well as the undergeneralization of research at the micro level.

When research is focused at the micro level, as often happened in business schools, too many casual, contextual, and idiosyncratic factors are picked up as the causes for the emergence and dominance of specific technological trajectories and practices, neglecting the sweeping and sometimes delicate impact of national cultures. On the other hand, when the scope of research is focused at national level (see, e.g., Lodge and Vogel, 1987), they often overgeneralize the research findings without considering sectoral contingencies so as to wrongly predict the future of nations.

Even *isolated* meso-level analyses, such as the studies of technological sectors by many scholars of technological innovation, also lead to either overgeneralization or undergeneralization. Overgeneralization occurs when scholars take the research findings of the technological paradigm in one specific sector such as automobiles as universal and extend them to formulate technology policies toward all other sectors such as software and information technology. Here, they forget that the sector of information technology in general, and software in particular, belongs to a drastically different technological paradigm that requires distinct governance mechanisms and organizing principles. When Ferguson (1990) proposed the *keiretsu* governance structure for the computer industry, or when Cusumano (1991) predicted the coming Japanese conquest of global computer software markets through its flexible manufacturing paradigm, they committed the fallacy of overgeneralization. False predictions of the impending Japanese worldwide dominance in banking, biotechnology, and aircraft are also caused by overgeneralization.

On the other hand, many students of technological studies also undergeneralize their research findings. They are so much imbrued in the technical details of an isolated case of technological innovation that they lose sight of underlying forces at the macro and meso level that have either facilitated or hampered the existence or nonexistence of so many micro-level factors. The focus at the sectoral level and the resultant integration of macro-and micro-level analyses enables us to overcome the problems of both overgeneralization and undergeneralization that are prevalent in macro-level analyses, technological case studies, and micro-level organization studies.

Coevolution and the problem of overdetermination

The knowledge regime perspective acknowledges the mutually reinforcing nature of cultural paradigms, organizing principles, governance mechanisms, and technology regimes. Such a coevolution process has shaped the formation of a specific isomorphic structure in each nation. When interacted with the sectoral structure of knowledge, it has caused the *persistent* sectoral patterns of competitiveness in different nations.

It is interesting to observe that such a process of coevolution produces the problem of overdetermination not only in the persistent sectoral patterns of national competitiveness, but also in all elements involved, ranging from cultural paradigms, governance mechanisms, organizing principles, patterns of knowing, and technological paradigms. In such a coevolution structure, components mutually reinforce one another to form an auto-catalytic set and an iron cage of isomorphism. As a result, there is no longer a simple, one-dimensional, and linear cause–effect relation. Instead, each component is simultaneously a cause for the persistence of other elements and an effect being facilitated by all others.

It is because of this overdetermination that a single variable such as industrial policy and R&D investment cannot explain the persistent sectoral patterns of national competitiveness. It also explains the once puzzling dilemma that while the powerful MITI successfully promoted the sectors of steels, chemicals, semiconductors, and electronics, it has failed miserably to enhance Japanese competitiveness in biotechnology, aircraft, and software packages. It further explains why the business strategies of increasing R&D and of joint venture with the US firms failed to change the Japanese lackluster performance in these sectors.

It is because of this overdetermination that I have avoided linear cause–effect analysis. Instead, I have adopted an approach that tries to identify systematic patterns, study the structure and process of elements within the pattern, and reveal their dynamic interactions.

Organizing principles and the synergy of civilizations

The phenomenon of coevolution, isomorphism, and overdetermination does not mean that there is no possibility to induce a systematic change within the pattern, nor does it indicate the impossibility of synergy between different patterns. Indeed, as analyzed in this book, the Japanese system of knowledge creation in general, and Japanese success in the automobile and home electronics sectors in particular, is not solely the result of its endogenous organizing principles and connectual governance, but rather the consequence of the Japanese synergy between its endogenous organizing principles and those borrowed from the USA. To some extent, we can also say that the revived competitiveness of some US sectors, such as semiconductors and to a lesser extent automobiles, has also been the result of the great American effort to learn the Japanese principles of lean production throughout the 1980s and 1990s.

The biological metaphor: organizing principles as genes

Although the existence of isomorphic structures does create difficulties in transplanting, incorporating, and reconfiguring the governance mechanisms and organizing principles originated from other nations, it does not preclude the possibility of synergy among civilizations. Nor does it mean each nation can claim its endogenously originated governance mechanisms and organizing principles as its own property. Contractual governance mechanisms are not the birthright of the West, nor are connectual governance mechanisms the exclusive possession of the East. Just as Eastern nations have benefited enormously from learning the Western ways of organizing during the last century, Western nations can also learn greatly from the East, as evidenced by certain Japanization of British and American business.

Using the biological metaphor, we can treat organizing principles originated from particular nations as the *genes* that can be combined, reconfigured, and synergized to form specific advantages for a nation. These *genes* are the common wealth of human beings, not of an individual nation. If we look back on human history, we can find that the great civilizations have been those that have successfully synergized governance mechanisms and organizing principles originated from other civilizations. They tried hard to break through the *isomorphic trap* and *lock-in* of their endogenous cultural paradigms, governance mechanisms, and dominant organizing principles. It is only those nations that have painstakingly tried to borrow, assimilate, and synthesize foreign practices that have *persistently* succeeded in the past.

Japan is an ideal example to illustrate how the penchant for learning from the strongest civilizations has paid off consistently. Japan has always tried to learn from the most advanced and most powerful nations at each specific historical period. Beginning in the imperial Chinese Tang Dynasty, for more than 1000 years, Japan learned and borrowed so intensively from China that almost all aspects of its civilization have been impacted by the Chinese. Then, beginning in the mid-nineteenth century, Japan took turns to learn from the most powerful nation at a given time: Great Britain in the mid-nineteenth century, Germany in the late nineteenth century, and the USA at the beginning of the twentieth century and especially after World War II. It is not an exaggeration to say that the post-World War II success of Japan has been largely due to its successful synergy between endogenous organizing principles and the transplanted ones from the USA. As this book and the work of Adler and Cole (1993) indicate, the Japanese system of flexible production is in essence the result of a synergy between standardization and customization, between separate knowing and connectual knowing, and between specialization and contextual integration.

We can similarly use our synergy hypothesis to explain the rise of Germany in the nineteenth and twentieth centuries. Like Japan, Germany first enthusiastically tried to learn from Great Britain, and then from the USA. Both Japan and Germany tried to learn from Taylorism and Fordism and successfully synergized them into their own systems of manufacturing and knowledge creation. In the 1980s and 1990s, both British and American manufacturing sectors had also put great efforts into learning from the Japanese system of lean production. The fact that the concepts of total quality management, just-in-time, teamwork, design for manufacturing, concurrent engineering, and others have been so enthusiastically embraced by Americans reveals their strong willingness to learn from the best Japanese practice, which in turn contributed to its revival in the mid-1990s.

The process of synergy between the East and the West also occurred in Taiwan, Hong Kong, Singapore, and South Korea. As analyzed elsewhere (Jin, 1995), the very success of the East Asian tiger economies can be explained by the synergic advantage of Confucian societies when they tried to introduce universalized rules and extended spontaneous order into their bounded governance of connections. The synergy of the Western emphasis on separate knowing and the existing East Asian strength in connectual knowing, and the introduction of individualist entrepreneurship will certainly be the next step that China, Japan, and the East Asian tigers have to take in order for them to be competitive in the new age of information technology.

The synergy process in the USA and Japan

The path of synergy in the US and Japan with regard to organizing principles of modularization and connectivity is shown in Figures 11.1 and 11.2. After World War II, Japan synergized modularization with contextual connectivity and standardization with continuous improvement in the innovation of the Japanese system of flexible production (Figure 11.1).

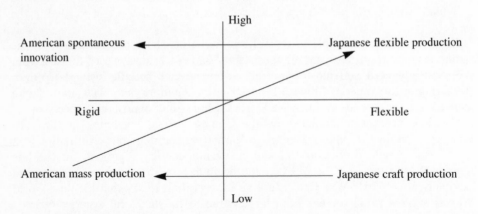

Figure 11.1 The Japanese dynamic learning path in modularity

In other words, the principles imbedded in Taylorism, Fordism, or mass production are recombined with the endogenous Japanese dominant organizing principles to form Toyotarism. In the process, the American organizing principles were neither totally dismissed nor completely adopted, but rather, conditioned for use in specific situations, redesigned for other purposes, and used to assist with other organizing principles.

The same is true for Americans learning the Japanese way (Figure 11.2). Facilitated by the America cultural paradigm of contractual man and its dominant modes of separate knowing, Taylorism, Fordism, and mass production emerged and

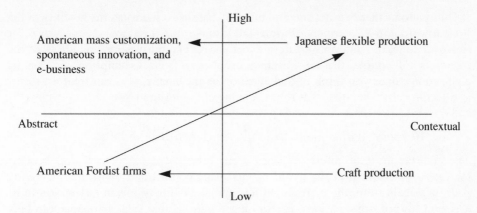

Figure 11.2 The US dynamic learning path in connectivity

predominated in the USA. It is also the place that gave birth to the Silicon Valley model of spontaneous innovation. With all its advantages in spontaneous innovation and fusion, the USA has tried to learn the Japanese way of flexible production throughout the 1980s and 1990s, creating its own style of people-independent mass customization and e-business.

With the increasing importance of mass customization and e-businesses in the new age of information technology, it is high time for Japan to learn the American way of individualistic entrepreneurship, quantification, systemization, and spontaneous innovation.

The synergy of civilizations as the theme for the twenty-first century

International competition as a positive-sum game

Once we admit the beneficial possibilities of synergy and the imperative of learning in the new age of globalization, we can realize that the real enemies of the West are neither proponents of multiculturalism nor those foreign values and organizing principles, but rather those cultural fundamentalists who reject anything that is foreign and who refuse to learn from other nations, *severing* the much-needed synergetic process for the revival of civilizations. It is the people like the managers and employees in Xerox, Ford, Saturn, and Motorola, who took pains to learn and synthesize the Japanese style of management and systems of production and knowledge creation who are the heroes of Western civilization.

Just when students, managers, and policy-makers in China, Japan, and India take pains to learn the advantage of American system of governance, American studies of other civilizations are still limited to academics. Cultural ignorance and insensitivity still exists. The assumption of one best way and the belief in universalism further undermine the willingness to learn. Historically, for more than one and a half centuries since the mid-1840s, the unwillingness to learn from other civilizations had led to the decline of China. It is the willingness to learn from the West since 1978 that has put China back on the right track toward revival.

Huntington's theory is detrimental not only because it increases the hostility of the West toward non-Western civilizations but also because it reduces the incentives for the West to learn from non-Western experiences. The most damaging effect of the theory is, of course, the self-fulfilling prophecy of the assumption of clashing civilizations: once you think of a civilization as the enemy, you will treat it as one, and reciprocally, the other will return the hostility and treat you like an enemy.

Respect, willingness to learn, and cultural sensitivity

The civilizations that refuse to learn from others will lag behind and become increasingly irrelevant in the world of increasing competition. With the increasing pace of globalization, there are no buffers and slacks for people in any nation to be arrogant toward other nations. History has taught us that such arrogance can be a lethal dose for the certain decline of nations. It blinds people and reduces their willingness to learn from other nations and to experiment with new organizing principles. It also leads to overconfidence and a consequent overextension of the limited organizing principles of a nation to all places, all situations, and all technological sectors.

Historically, arrogance combined with overconfidence has created overextended military regimes in the Roman Empire, Imperial Spain, and Great Britain, and an overextended familistic/clan model of governance in Imperial China. From the knowledge regime perspective, the unwillingness to learn from other civilizations and the overextension of domestically emerged organizing principles and governance mechanisms were among the major factors for the decline of the Roman Empire, Imperial Spain, Great Britain, and Imperial China.

In modern times, there are many examples of the rise and decline of nations due to overextension of domestically originated organizing principles and governance mechanisms. In the UK, the overextension of personal and financial capitalism had contributed to its decline in the late nineteenth and early twentieth centuries. In the USA, while the domestically innovated mass production paradigm had once facilitated USA, its dominance of the world economy in the twentieth century, its overextension contributed to its crisis in the late 1970s and early 1980s.

In Japan, the very success of its flexible manufacturing system has led not only to its overextension to all industrial sectors but also to the *illusion* of Japanese superiority in everything over all other nations. At the height of Japanese success, not only many Japanese genuinely believed that they could conquer the world economically and technologically in all industrial sectors, but many serious Western scholars thought so too. As a result, the assets of Japanese firms skyrocketed and Japanese businessmen rushed to buy assets and extend investment into such sectors as banking, entertainment, biotechnology, aircraft, and software all over the world. This unrealistic overconfidence busted in the late 1980s. Domestically, the bloated stock market, and the skyrocketed real estate markets, and together with them, the bubble economy, collapsed, leaving many Japanese firms and bankers trapped with an unsustainable debt burden. This in turn has pulled the Japanese economy into its longest recession in modern times. Internationally, while Japanese direct investment in its traditionally competitive sectors of automobiles and home electronics has been successful, its foreign direct investment in real estate, banking, entertainment, and other service sectors has met with unexpected failure. Similarly, the Japanese ambition of conquering the world in biotechnology, aircraft, software, computer systems, banking, and services has never materialized.

The central forces for the seemingly 'unexpected' Japanese failures rest in the fact that while the Japanese cultural paradigm of connectual man, its dominant connectual governance mechanisms for knowledge creation, and its preponderant organizing principles of connection, fusion, customization, contextualization, and people-dependent systems integration are superior for knowledge creation in the tightly coupled and non-modular technological sectors of automobiles, home electronics, opto-electronics, and mechatronics, they hinder effective knowledge creation in the loosely coupled and modular technological sectors of biotechnology, prepackaged software, financial services, information processing, and other professional services.

What is more important for the evolving landscape of national competitiveness is the changing nature of technology in the emerging new economy. As the loosely coupled and modular technological systems, such as information services and e-business, play an expanding role in the new economy, *increasingly the pendulum of national competitiveness is shifting from favoring Japan back to favoring the USA*. As analyzed in this book, in the loosely coupled and modular technological systems, American systems of knowledge creation have great advantages over the Japanese ones. The American cultural paradigm of contractual man, its contractual governance, its penchant for individualistic entrepreneurship, its emphasis on separate knowing, and its organizing principles of division, separation, standardization, modularization, quantification, decontextualization, and people-independent systems integration all have competitive advantages in facilitating the creation of knowledge in these loosely coupled and modular technological sectors.

From this perspective, this book further concludes that it is high time for not only Japan but also all East Asian nations and the rest of the world to learn the American way of organizing the knowledge creation process. For East Asian nations, this advice is especially pertinent and timely. While many scholars, and business leaders as well, blamed 'crony capitalism' and the resultant lack of accountability and financial prudence as the major causes of the East Asian crisis in 1997 and 1998, from the knowledge regime perspective, the roots of the crisis run deeper than these surface problems.

For the past twenty to thirty years, East Asian nations and economies performed a miracle of continuous high growth basically by imitating the Japanese success. There are two basic elements of the post-World War II Japanese ascendancy: export-orientation and investment in the manufacturing sectors of electronics, opto-electronics, and mechatronics. Like Japan, *what is missing in the East Asian system of knowledge creation is the capability for spontaneous innovation and fusion*. What is needed for East Asian revival is for these nations to learn the American way of knowledge creation, and especially its emphasis on individualistic entrepreneurship, its penchant and respect for universal rules, its emphasis on separate knowing, specialization, and professionalization, its superior capability in spontaneous technology innovation, and its organizing principles of quantification, systemization, and people-independent systems integration.

The need for East Asian nations to learn from the USA does not mean that

Americans can be complacent about themselves, nor does it mean that one can simply dismiss the whole East Asian economy and its organizing principles with such labels as 'crony capitalism,' 'socialism' or 'authoritarian.' First, Japan and other East Asian nations are, and still will be, very competitive in the tightly coupled and non-modular technological sectors, such as consumer electronics and opto-electronics. Second, as East Asian nations learn the American ways of organizing knowledge creation and synthesize them with their endogenous ways, they will revive their competitiveness. Third, it is highly possible that when the new digital economy turns to a mature stage or when some other new technology of a non-modular nature emerges as the new growth engine, the American competitive advantage in loosely coupled and modular technology may be neutralized and offset. One good example of this is the emergent fusion between microchips, imbedded software, and electronics in the digital revolution of information appliances, including digital TV, digital phones, and hand-held computers, and intelligent automobiles imbedded with microchips. Unlike the modular and standardized design of the PC, all these electronic devices require customized design of chips and software and their seamless integration with the specific functional needs of the devices. In the burgeoning and increasingly important markets for digital and intelligent consumer electronic devices imbedded with chips, there is already evidence that the Japanese electronic giants such as NEC and Hitachi are gaining a competitive edge over Intel (Takahashi, 1998). Americans cannot afford to be complacent if they wish to remain the sole superpower. It is quite possible that, after painstakingly learning and synthesizing processes, East Asian nations, especially Japan and China, will become America's largest trade partners as well as its competitors in the twenty-first century.

Free trade as a catalyst for synergy

This book concludes that each national culture has sector-contingent comparative advantages and disadvantages in organizing the knowledge creation process. If we accept this, it is clear that a free trade regime based on the national endowment not of natural resources but rather of organizing principles will greatly benefit all trade partners. There are two processes involved here. First, free trade can be the facilitator for exploiting the comparative cultural advantages of all participating nations. For example, when the trade and FDI barriers for service in Japan and China are removed, free trade can generate great revenue for the American service sectors of banking, accounting, insurance, information services, consulting, fast food, and other professional services, and it can also provide valued services to customers in China and Japan.

Second and foremost, trade can be the catalyst for assimilating and synthesizing organizing principles among nations. By reducing trade barriers among nations, organizing principles and practices originated in foreign countries can more easily be transplanted to other countries. In the case of Japan and other East Asian nations, the opening of their service sectors will not only bring in the best foreign practices and organizing principles for domestic business to learn from, it will also force them to learn, assimilate, and finally synthesize them with domestic ones to form an efficient East Asian system of services. Just as Japanese transplants in the USA have drastically changed the American industrial landscape and facilitated the assimilation of Japanese practices, American investment in the service sectors of East Asia will also change the industrial landscape there and make their service sectors more competitive and efficient.

Sector-specific policies for learning and synergy

The acceptance of the beneficial effect of trade for the exploitation of comparative cultural advantages and for the synergy of organizing principles does not mean that there is no role for the state to play. This book suggests that government policy should focus on the best utilization and exploitation of a nation's comparative cultural advantages and on the facilitation of learning, assimilating, and synthesizing foreign organizing principles and best practices. Since the comparative advantages and disadvantages of organizing principles and governance mechanisms are sector- and technology-specific, *government policy should also be sector- and technology-specific*. With the increasing complexity of the economy and technology, the time has come when no single policy can universally and effectively be applied to all sectors. We need different organizing principles and governance mechanisms for different sectors in order to improve our knowledge creation capability and, thus, our economic competitiveness.

Other than assisting in the exploitation of comparative cultural advantages, government policy can be used to overcome the comparative cultural disadvantages of a nation. In the USA, the government can facilitate the formation of connectual governance in the innovation of complex technology by creating the 'government–military–industrial–university complex' in which research scientists from all fields cooperate together to push out the most advanced technologies in the world (Kash, 1989). In East Asia, government can also build a 'cultural island' (Adams, 1995) of individualism and entrepreneurship to facilitate spontaneous innovation and fusion.

In conclusion, we may call the twenty-first century the 'century of synergy' in which the welfare of human beings is greatly enhanced to a new level because of the great synergy happening everywhere all the time in our increasingly globalized world. Let us embrace this new century of great synergy with our greatest passion and enthusiasm.

References

Abo, Tetsuo (1994) *Hybrid Factory: The Japanese Production System in the United States*. New York: Oxford University Press.

Adams, Richard C. (1995) *Culture, Policy, and Technology Innovation: U.S. and Japanese Performance in Electro/Mechanical Technologies*. Ph.D. Dissertation, George Mason University, Fairfax, VA 22030.

Adler, Paul S. (1992) 'The Leaning Bureaucracy: New United Motor Manufacturing.' In: Staw, B. M. and Cummings, L. L. (eds) *Research in Organizational Behavior*. Greenwich, CT: JAI.

Adler, Paul. S., and Cole, Robert E. (1993, Spring) 'Designed for Learning: A Tale of Two Auto Plants.' *Sloan Management Review* 35: 85–94.

Alic, John A. (1993) 'Computer-Assisted Everything? Tools and Techniques for Design and Production.' *Technological Forecasting and Social Change* 44: 359–374.

Aldrich, Howard E., and Sasaki, Toshihiro (1995) 'Governance Structure and Technology Transfer in R&D Consortia in the United States and Japan.' In: Liker, Jeffrey K., Ettlie, John E., and Campbell, John C. (eds) *Engineered in Japan: Japanese Technology-Management Practices*. New York: Oxford University Press.

Allaire, Yvan, and Firsirotu, Michaela (1990) 'Strategic Plans as Contracts.' *Long Range Planning* 23: (Feb.) 102–115.

Amsden, Alice H. (1989) *Asia's Next Giant: South Korea and Late Industrialization*. New York: Oxford University Press.

Anderson, Philip, and Tushman, Michael L. (1990) 'Technological Discontinuities and Dominant Designs: A Cyclical Model of Technological Change.' *Administrative Science Quarterly* 35: 604–633.

Aoki, Masahiko (1986) 'Horizontal vs. Vertical Information Structure of the Firm.' *American Economic Review* 76: 971–983.

Aoki, Masahiko (1988) *Information, Incentives and Bargaining in the Japanese Economy*. Cambridge: Cambridge University Press.

Aoki, Masahiko (1990) 'Toward an Economic Model of Japanese Firms.' *Journal of Economic Literature* 28: 1–27.

Aoki, Masahiko (1994) 'The Japanese Firm as a System of Attributes: A Survey and Research Agenda.' In: Aoki, Masahiko, and Dore, Ronald (eds) *The Japanese Firm: The Source of Competitive Strength*. Oxford: Oxford University Press.

Aoki, Masahiro (1997) 'Unintended Fit: Organizational Evolution and Government Design of Institutions in Japan.' In: Aoki, Masahiro, and Kim, Hyung-Ki (eds) *The Role of Government in East Asian Economic Development*. Oxford: Oxford University Press.

Appelbaum, Eileen, and Batt, Rosemary (1994) *The New American Workplace: Transforming Work Systems in the United States*. Ithaca, N.Y.: ILR Press.

Arrow, Kenneth J. (1979) 'The Division of Labor in the Economy, the Polity, and Society.' In: Gerald O'Driscoll Jr., P. (ed.) *Adam Smith and Modern Political Economy*. Ames, Iowa: Iowa State University Press.

Arrow, Kenneth J. (1996) 'Invaluable Goods.' *Journal of Economic Literature* XXXV: (June) 757–765.

Arthur, W. Brian (1989) 'Competing Technologies, Increasing Returns, and Lock-in by Historical Events.' *The Economic Journal* 99(March): 116–131.

Arthur, W. Brian (1990) 'Positive Feedbacks in the Economy.' *Scientific American*: (Feb.) 92–99.

Asanuma, Banri (1989) 'Manufacturer–Supplier Relationships in Japan and the Concept of Relation-Specific Skill.' *Journal of Japanese and International Economics* 3(1): 1–30.

Ayres, R. U. (1992) 'CIM: A Challenge to Technology Management.' *International Journal of Technology Management* 7: 17–39.

Baba, Yasunori, Takai, Shinji, and Mizuta, Yuji (1995) 'The Japanese Software Industry: The 'Hub-Structure' Approach.' *Research Policy* 24: 473–486.

Baba, Yasunori, Takai, Shinji, and Mizuta, Yuji (1996) 'The User-Driven Evolution of the Japanese Software Industry: the Case of Customized Software for Mainframes.' In: Mowery, David C. (ed.) *The International Computer Software Industry*. Oxford: Oxford University Press.

Baba, Yasunori, Kuroda, Shoichi, and Yoshiki, Hiroshi (1997) 'Diffusion of the Systemic Approach in Japan: Gauge and Industrial Standards.' In: Goto, Akira, and Odagiri, Hiroyuki (eds) *Innovation in Japan*. Oxford: Clarendon Press.

Baker, Wayne E. (1990) 'Market Networks and Corporate Behavior.' *American Journal of Sociology* 96(3): 589–625.

Balassa, Bela, and Noland, Marcus (1988) *Japan in the World Economy*. Washington, D.C.: Institute of International Economics.

Baldwin, Carliss Y., and Clark, Kim B. (1994), 'Capital-Budgeting Systems and Capabilities Investments in U.S. Companies after the Second World War.' *Business History Review*: (Spring) 73–109.

Baldwin, Carliss Y., and Clark, Kim B. (1997) 'Managing in the Age of Modularity.' *Harvard Business Review*: (Sept.–Oct.) 84–93.

Baldwin, Carliss Y., and Clark, Kim B. (2000) *Design Rules: the Power of Modularity*. Cambridge, Mass.: The MIT Press.

Barley, Stephen R., and Kunda, Gideon (1992) 'Design and Devotion: Surges of Rational and Normative Ideologies of Control in Managerial Discourse.' *Administrative Science Quarterly* 37(3): 363–399.

Baron, J. N., Dobbin, F. R., and Devereaux Jennings, P. (1986) 'War and Peace: The Evolution of Modern Personal Administration in U.S. Industry.' *American Journal of Sociology* 92: 350–383.

Belderbos, Rene A. (1995) 'The Role of Investment in Europe in the Globalization Strategy of Japanese Electronics Firms.' In: Frederique Sachwald (ed.) *Japanese Firms in Europe*. Luxembourg: Harwood Academic Publishers.

Bellah, Robert N., Madsen, Richard, Sullivan, William M., Swidler, Ann, and Tipton, Steven M. (1986) *Habits of the Heart: Individualism and Commitment in*

American Life. New York: Harper & Row.

Bensaou, M., and Earl, Michael (1998) 'The Right Mind-set for Managing Information Technology.' *Harvard Business Review*: (Sept.–Oct.) 119–128.

Berger, Peter L. and Luckmann, Thomas (1966) *The Social Construction of Reality: A Treatise in the Sociology of Knowledge*. New York: Doubleday.

Berger, Peter L. and Hsiao, H. H. (1988) *In Search of an East Asia Development Model*. New Brunswick, N.J.: Transaction Books.

Berggren, Christian (1992) *Alternatives to Lean Production: Work Organization in the Swedish Auto Industry*. Ithaca, New York: ILR Press.

Berque, Augustin (1992) 'Identification of the Self in Relation to the Environment.' In: Rosenberger, Nancy R. (ed.) *Japanese Sense of Self*. New York, N.Y.: Cambridge University Press.

Best, M. (1990) *The New Competition: Institutions of Industrial Restructuring*. Cambridge, Mass: Harvard University Press.

Biggart, Nicole Woolsey (1991) 'Explaining Asian Economic Organization: Toward a Weberian Institutional Perspective.' *Theory and Society* 20: 199–232.

Biggart, Nicole Woolsey, and Hamilton, Gary G. (1994) 'On the Limits of a Firm-Based Theory to Explain Business Networks: The Western Bias of Neoclassical Economics.' In: Nohria, Nitin, and Eccles, Robert G. (eds) *Networks and Organizations: Structure, Form, and Action*. Boston, Mass: Harvard Business School Press.

Bijker, Wiebe E., Hughes, Thomas P, and Pinch, Trevor (1989) *The Social Construction of Technological Systems*. Cambridge, Mass.: The MIT Press.

Blair, John G. (1988) *Modular America: Cross-Cultural Perspectives on the Emergence of an American Way*. New York: Greenwood Press.

Bloom, Alfred (1981) *The Linguistic Shaping of Thought: A Study in the Impact of Language on Thinking in China and the West*. Hillsdale, NJ: Lawrence Erlbaum.

Bolland, Eric J., and Hofer, Charles W. (1998) *Future Firms: How America's High Technology Companies Work*. New York: Oxford University Press.

Bolton, Michele Kremen, Malmrose, Roger, and Ouchi, William G. (1994) 'The Organization of Innovation in the United States and Japan: Neoclassical and Relational Contracting.' *Journal of Management Studies* 31: 653–679.

Boothroyd, G. (1988) *American Machinists* (Aug.) 132: 54–57.

Bottoms, David T. (1993) 'GCA Dies a Slow Death.' *Electronics* 66(14): 2.

Bowles, Samuel, and Ginitis, Herbert (1993) 'The Revenge of Homo Economics: Contested Exchange and the Revival of Political Economy.' *Journal of Economic Perspectives* 7(1): 83–102.

Bowman, Scott R. (1996) *The Modern Corporation and American Political Thought*. University Park, PA: The Pennsylvania State University Press.

Branscomb, Lewis M. (1989) 'Policy for Science and Engineering in 1989: A Public Agenda for Economic Renewal.' *Business in Contemporary World* 2(1).

Branscomb, Lewis M. (1992) 'Does America Need a Technology Policy?' *Harvard Business Review*: (Mar.–Apr.) 24–31.

Brooks and Maccoby (1987) *Corporations & the Work Force* (unpublished mimeo).

Brophy, David (1996) 'United States Venture Capital Markets: Changes and Challenges.' In: OECD (ed.) *Venture Capital and Innovation*. OECD, Paris.

Brown, Clair, and Reich, Michael (1997) 'Developing Skills and Pay through Career

Ladders: Lessons from Japanese and U.S. Companies.' *California Management Review* 39(2): 124–144.

Bryer, R. A. (1993) 'The Late Nineteenth-Century Revolution in Financial Reporting: Accounting for the Rise of Investor or Managerial Capitalism?' *Accounting, Organizations and Society* 18(7/8): 649–690.

Buigues, Pierre and Jacquemin, Alexis (1994) 'Foreign Direct Investment and Exports to the European Community.' In: Mason, Mark, and Encarnation, Dennis (eds) *Does Ownership Matter?*. Oxford: Oxford University Press.

Callon, Scott (1995) *Divided Sun: MITI and the Breakdown of Japanese High-Tech Industrial Policy, 1975–1993*. Stanford, CA: Stanford University Press.

Carlsson, Bo, and Jacobsson, Staffan (1993) 'Technological Systems and Economic Performance: The Diffusion of Factory Automation in Sweden.' In: Foray, Dominique, and Freeman, Christopher (eds) *Technology and the Wealth of Nations: The Dynamics of Constructed Advantage*. London: Pinter Publisher.

Case, John (1992) *From the Ground Up: The Resurgence of American Entrepreneurship*. New York: Simon & Schuster.

Caudill, William, and Weinstein, Helen (1969/1986) 'Maternal Care and Infant Behavior in Japan and America.' In: Lebra, T. S., and Lebra, W. P. (eds) *Japanese Culture and Behavior*. Honolulu: University of Hawaii Press.

Chandler, Alfred D. (1977) *The Visible Hand: The Managerial Revolution in American Business*. Cambridge: Harvard University Press.

Chandler, Alfred. D. (1990) *Scale and Scope*. Cambridge, Mass.: Harvard University Press.

Chia, Robert (1995) 'From Modern to Postmodern Organizational Analysis.' *Organization Studies* 16(4): 579–604.

Choi, Thomas Y., and Behling, Orlando (1997) 'Top Managers and TQM Success: One More Look after all These Years.' *The Academy of Management Executive* 11(1): 37–47.

Choi, Young Back (1993) *Paradigms and Conventions: Uncertainty, Decision Making, and Entrepreneurship*. Ann Arbor: The University of Michigan Press.

Chow, Chee W., Shields, Michael D., and Chan, Yoke Kai (1991) 'The Effects of Management Controls and National Culture on Manufacturing Performance: An Experimental Investigation.' *Accounting, Organization and Society* 16(3): 209–226.

Christensen, Clayton M. (1997) *The Innovator's Dilemma: When New Technologies Cause Great Firms to Fail*. Boston, Mass.: Harvard Business School Press.

Clark, Kim B., and Fujimoto, Takahiro (1990) 'The Power of Product Integrity.' *Harvard Business Review* (Nov.–Dec.): 107–118.

Clark, Kim B., and Fujimoto, Takahiro (1991) *Product Development Performance: Strategy, Organization, and Management in the World Auto Industry*. Boston, Mass.: Harvard Business School Press.

Clark, Kim B., Chew, W. B., and Fujimoto, Takahiro (1992) 'Manufacturing for Design: Beyond the Production/R&D Dichotomy.' In: Susman, G. I. (ed.) *Integrating Design and Manufacturing for Competitive Advantage*. New York: Oxford University Press.

Clark, Peter A. (1987) *Anglo-American Innovation*. Berlin: Walter de Gruyter.

Cohen, M. D., March, J. G., and Olsen, J. P. (1972) 'A Garbage Can Model of Organizational Choice.' *Administrative Science Quarterly* 17: 1–15.

Cohen, Patricia Cline (1982) *A Calculating People: The Spread of Numeracy in Early America*. Chicago: The University of Chicago Press.

Cohen, Stephen S., and Fields, Gary (1999) 'Social Capital and Capital Gains in Silicon Valley.' *California Management Review* 41(2): 108–130.

Cole, Robert E. (1995a) *The Death and Life of the American Quality Movement*. New York: Oxford University Press.

Cole, Robert E. (1995b) 'Reflections on Organizational Learning in U.S. and Japanese Industry.' In: Liker, J. K., Ettlie, J. E., and Campbell, J. C. (eds) *Engineered in Japan: Japanese Technology-Management Practices*. New York: Oxford University Press.

Cole, Robert E. (1998) 'Learning from the Quality Movement: What Did and Didn't Happen and Why?' *California Management Review* 41(1): 43–73.

Cottrell, Tom (1994) 'Fragmented Standards and the Development of Japan's Microcomputer Software Industry.' *Research Policy* 23: 143–174.

Crosby, Alfred W. (1997) *The Measure of Reality: Quantification and Western Society, 1250–1600*. New York: Cambridge University Press.

Cusumano, Michael A. (1985) *The Japanese Automobile Industry: Technology: Technology and Management at Nissan and Toyota*. Cambridge, Mass.: Harvard University Press.

Cusumano, Michael A. (1989) 'The Software Factory: A Historical Interpretation.' *IEEE Software* 6(2): 23–30.

Cusumano, Michael A. (1991) *Japan's Software Factories: A Challenge to U.S. Management*. New York: Oxford University Press.

Cusumano, Michael A. (1992) 'Shifting Economies: From Craft Production to Flexible Systems and Software Factories.' *Research Policy* 21: 453–480.

Cusumano, Michael A. (1997) 'How Microsoft Makes Large Teams Work Like Small Teams.' *Sloan Management Review* 39(1): 9–20.

Cusumano, Michael A., and Nobeoka, Kentaro (1992) 'Strategy, Structure and Performance in Product Development: Observations from the Auto Industry.' *Research Policy* 21: 265–293.

Cusumano, Michael A., and Selby, Richard W. (1995) *Microsoft Secrets*. New York: The Free Press.

Cutler, Robert S. (1991) 'A Comparison of Japanese and U.S. High-Technology Transfer Practices.' In: Kingery, W. David (ed.) *Japanese/American Technological Innovation: The Influence of Cultural Differences on Japanese/American Innovation in Advanced Materials*. New York: Elsevier.

Czinkota, Michael R. (1985) 'Distribution in Japan: Problems and Changes.' *Columbia Journal of World Business* 20 (Fall) .

Czinkota, Michael R., and Kotabe, Masaaki (1998) 'Product Development the Japanese Way.' In: Czinkota, Michael R., and Kotabe, Masaaki (eds) *Trends in International Business: Critical Perspectives*. New York: Blackwell Business.

Dattel, Eugene R. (1994) *The Sun That Never Rose: The Inside Story of Japan's Failed Attempt at Global Financial Dominance*. Chicago, Illinois: Probus Publishing Company.

Davenport, Thomas H. (1998) 'Putting the Enterprise into the Enterprise System.' *Harvard Business Review*: (July–Aug.) 121–131.

de Bono, E. (1991) *I am Right, You are Wrong*. London: Penguin.

de Bono, E. (1994) *Parallel Thinking – From Socrates to de Bono Thinking*. London: Viking.

Deming, W. Edwards (1986) *Out of Crisis*. Cambridge, MA: MIT Center for Advanced Engineering Study.

Dennis, William J. Jr. (1997) 'More Than You Think: An Inclusive Estimate of Business Entries.' *Journal of Business Venturing* 12(3): 175–196.

Dertouzos, Michael L., Lester, Richard K., and Solow, Robert M. (1989) *Made in America: Regaining the Productive Edge*. Cambridge, Mass.: The MIT Press.

DiMaggio, P., and Powell, W. W. (1983) 'The Iron-Cage Revisited: Institutional Isomorphism and Collective Rationality in Organizational Fields.' *American Sociological Review* 48: 147–160.

Doi, Takeo (1971/1981) *The Anatomy of Dependency*. Tokyo, Kodansha International.

Dore, Ronald P. (1983) 'Goodwill and the Spirit of Market Capitalism.' *British Journal of Sociology* 34: 459–482.

Dore, Ronald P. (1987) *Taking Japan Seriously: A Confucian Perspective on Leading Economic Issues*. Stanford, CA: Standard University Press.

Dore, Ronald P.(1994) 'Japanese Capitalism, Anglo-Saxon Capitalism: How Will the Darwinian Contest Turn Out?' In: Campbell, Nigel, and Burton, Fred (eds) *Japanese Multinationals: Strategies and Management in the Global Kaisha*. London: Routledge.

Dosi, Giovanni (1988) 'Sources, Procedures and Microeconomic Effects of Innovation.' *Journal of Economic Literature* 26: 1120–1171.

Dosi, Giovanni, and Kogut, Bruce (1993) 'National Specificities and the Context of Change: The Coevolution of Organization and Technology.' In: Kogut, Bruce (ed.) *Country Competitiveness: Technology and the Organizing of Work*. New York: Oxford University Press.

Dosi, Giovanni, Teece, David J., and Chytry, Josef (1998) *Technology, Organization, and Competitiveness: Perspective on Industrial and Corporate Change*. New York: Oxford University Press.

Doyle, Peter, Saunders, John, and Wong, Veronica (1992) 'Competition in Global Markets: A Case Study of American and Japanese Competition in the British Market.' *Journal of International Business Studies* 23: 419–442.

Drucker, Peter F. (1990) 'The Emerging Theory of Manufacturing.' *Harvard Business Review*: (May–June) 94–102.

Drucker, Peter F. (1993) *Post-Capitalist Society*. New York: Harper Business.

Duenyas, Izak, Fowler, John W., and Schruben, Lee (1995) 'Japan's Development of Scheduling Methods for Manufacturing Semiconductors.' In: Liker, Jeffrey K. *et al.* (eds) *Engineered in Japan*. New York: Oxford University Press.

Duimeering, P. Robert, Safayeni, Frank, and Purdy, Lyn (1993) 'Integrated Manufacturing: Redesign the Organization before Implementing Flexible Technology.' *Sloan Management Review*: (Summer) 47–56.

Dunning, John (1994) 'The Strategy of Japanese and U.S. Manufacturing Investment in Europe.' In: Mason, Mark, and Encarnation, Dennis (eds) *Does Ownership Matter?* Oxford: Oxford University Press.

Duvall, Lorraine M. (1995) 'A Study of Software Management: The State of Practice in the Practice in the United States and Japan.' *Journal of Systems Software* 31:

109–124.

Dyer, Jeffrey H. (1996) 'How Chrysler Created an American Keiretsu.' *Harvard Business Review* 74(4): 42–53.

Dyer, Jeffrey H., and Ouchi, William G. (1993) 'Japanese-Style Partnership: Giving Companies a Competitive Edge.' *Sloan Management Review* (Fall) 35: 51–63.

Fallows, James. M. (1994) *Looking at the Sun: The Rise of the New East Asian Economic and Political System*. New York: Pantheon Books.

Ferguson, Charls H. (1990) 'Computers and the Coming of the U.S. Keiretsu.' *Harvard Busines Review*: (July–Aug.) 55–70.

Fichman, Robert G., and Kemerer, Chris (1993) 'Adoption of Software Engineering Process Innovations: The Case of Object-Orientation.' *Sloan Management Review*: (Winter) 7–22.

Finegold, David *et al.* (1994) *The Decline of the U.S. Machine-Tool Industry and Prospects for its Recovery*. RAND, 1700 Main Street, P.O. Box, Santa Monica, CA 90407–2138.

Flamm, Kenneth (1988) *Creating Computers: Government, Industry, and High Technology*. Washington, D.C.: The Brookings Institution.

Florida, Richard, and Browdy, David (1991) 'The Invention that Got Away.' *Technology Review*: (August/September) 43–54.

Florida, Richard, and Kenney, Martin (1990) *The Breakthrough Illusion: Corporate America's Failure to Move from Innovation to Mass Production*. New York: Basic Books.

Fodor, Jerry A. (1983) *The Modularity of Mind: An Essay of Faculty Psychology*. Cambridge, Mass.: The MIT Press.

Forrest, Janet E. (1996) 'Japanese/U.S. Technological Competitiveness and Strategic Alliances in the Biotechnology Industry.' *R&D Management* 26(2): 141–153.

Francis, Arthur (1994) 'The Design-Manufacturing Interface.' In: John Storey (ed.) *New Wave Manufacturing Strategies: Organizational and Human Resource Management Dimensions*. London: Paul Chapman Publishing.

Franko, Lawrence G. (1996) 'The Japanese Juggernaut Rolls on.' *Sloan Management Review*: (Winter) 103–109.

Fransman, Martin (1995) *Japan's Computer and Communication Industry: The Evolution of Giants and Global Competitiveness*. New York: Oxford University Press.

Fruin, W. Mark (1992) *The Japanese Enterprise System: Competitive Strategies and Cooperative Structure*. New York: Oxford University Press.

Fruin, W. Mark (1997) *Knowledge Works: Managing Intellectual Capital at Toshiba*. New York: Oxford University Press.

Fujimoto, Takahiro (1997) 'The Dynamic Aspect of Product Development Capabilities: An International Comparison in the Automobile Industry.' In: Goto, Akira, and Odagiri, Hiroyuki (eds) *Innovation in Japan*. Oxford: Clarendon Press.

Fukutake, Tadashi (1989) *The Japanese Social Structure: Its Evolution in the Modern Century*. Translated by Ronald P. Dore. Tokyo: University of Tokyo Press.

Fukuyama, Francis (1992) *The End of History and the Last Man*. New York: Avon Books.

Fukuyama, Francis (1995) *Trust: The Social Virtues and the Creation of Prosperity*.

New York: The Free Press.

Gagnon, Joseph E., and Rose, Andrew K. (1995) 'Dynamic Persistence of Industry Trade Balances: How Pervasive is the Product Cycle?' *Oxford Economic Papers* 47: 229–248.

Galbraith, Jay R. (1973) *Designing Complex Organizations*. Reading, Mass.: Addison-Wesley.

Gardner, Howard (1999) *Intelligence Reframed: Multiple Intelligence for the 21st Century*. New York: Basic Books.

Garfield, Jay L. (1987) (ed.) *Modularity in Knowledge Representation and Natural-Language Understanding*. Cambridge, Mass.: The MIT Press.

Geertz, Clifford (1973) *The Interpretation of Cultures*. New York: Basic Books.

Gerlach, Michael L. (1992) *Alliance Capitalism: The Social Organization of Japanese Business*. Berkeley: University of California Press.

Gertler, Meric S. (1995) ' "Being There": Proximity, Organization, and Culture in the Development and Adoption of Advanced Manufacturing Technologies.' *Economic Geography* 71(1): 1–26.

Giddens, Anthony (1990) *The Consequences of Modernity*. Stanford, CA: Stanford University Press.

Gillespie, Richard (1991) *Manufacturing Knowledge: A History of Hawthorne Experiments*. Cambridge: Cambridge University Press.

Goldman, Alan (1994) *Doing Business with the Japanese: A Guide to Successful Communication, Management, and Diplomacy*. New York: State University of New York.

Gordon, A. (1985) *The Evolution of Labor Relations in Japan: Heavy Industry: 1853–1950*. Cambridge, Mass.: Harvard University Press.

Graham, Otis L. Jr. (1992) *Losing Time: The Industrial Policy Debate*. Cambridge, Mass.: Harvard University Press.

Granovetter, Mark (1973) 'The Strength of Weak Ties.' *American Journal of Sociology* 78: 1360–1380.

Granovetter, Mark (1985) 'Economic Action and Social Structure: The Problem of Embeddedness.' *American Journal of Sociology* 91: 481–510.

Greenstone, J. David (1986) 'Political Culture and American Political Development: Liberty, Union, and the Liberal Bipolarity.' *Studies in American Political Development: An Annual* 1: 1–49.

Hagen, James M., and Choe, Soonkyoo (1998) 'Trust in Japanese Interfirm Relations: Institutional Sanctions Matters.' *Academy of Management Review* 23(3): 589–600.

Hall, Edward T. (1976) *Beyond Culture*. New York: Anchor Books, Doubleday.

Hall, Edward T. (1990) *Understanding Cultural Differences*. Yarmouth, ME: Intercultural Press.

Hamada, Tomoko, and Yaguchi, Yujin (1994) 'The Hollowing of an Industrial Ideology: Japanese Corporate Familism in America.' In: Hamada, Tomako, and Sibley, Willis (eds) *Anthropological Perspectives on Organizational Culture*. Lanham: University Press of America.

Hambrick, Donald C. (1995) 'Fragmentation and the Other Problems CEOs have with Their Top Management Teams.' *California Management Review* 37(3): 110–127.

Hamilton, Gary G., and Feenstra, Robert C. (1998) 'Varieties of Hierarchies and Markets: An Introduction.' In: Dosi, Giovanni, Teece, David J., and Chytry, Josef (eds) *Technology, Organization, and Competitiveness: Perspectives on Industrial and Corporate Change*. New York: Oxford University Press.

Hammett, Patrick C., Hancock, Walton M, and Baron, Jay S. (1995) 'Producing a World-Class Automotive Body.' In: Liker, Jeffrey K., Ettlie, John E., and Campbell, John C. (eds) *Engineered in Japan: Japanese Technology-Management Practices*. New York: Oxford University Press.

Hampden-Turner, Charles, and Trampenaars, Alfons (1993) *The Seven Cultures of Capitalism: Value Systems for Creating Wealth in the United States, Japan, Germany, France, Britain, Sweden, and the Netherlands*. New York: Currency/Doubleday.

Hardaker, Glenn, and Ahmed, Pervaiz K. (1995) 'International Approaches to Computer-Integrated Manufacturing: Perspectives from Europe and Japan.' *European Business Review* 95(2): 28–39.

Hargadon, Andrew, and Sutton, Robert I. (1997) 'Technology Brokering and Innovation in a Product Development Firm.' *Administrative Science Quarterly* 42: 716–749.

Harrison, Bennett (1994) *Lean and Mean: The Changing Landscape of Corporate Power in the Age of Flexibility*. New York: Basic Books.

Hartz, Louis (1955) *The Liberal Tradition in America*. New York: Harcourt, Brace & Co.

Hashimoto, Masanori, and Raisian, John (1985) 'Employment Tenure and Earning Profiles in Japan and the United States.' *American Economic Review* 75(4): 721–727.

Hayashi, Shuji (1988) *Culture and Management in Japan*. Translated by Frank Baldwin. Tokyo: University of Tokyo Press.

Hayek, F. A. (1945) 'The Use of Knowledge in Society.' *American Economic Review* XXXV(4): 521–530.

Hayek, F. A. (1964) 'Kinds of Order in Society.' *New Individualist Review* 3(2): 457–466.

Hayes, Robert H., and Abernathy, William J. (1980) 'Managing Our Way to Economic Decline.' *Harvard Business Review* 5: 67–77.

Hedlund, Gunnar (1994) 'A Model of Knowledge Management and the N-form Corporation.' *Strategic Management Journal* 15: 73–90.

Helper, Susan (1991a) 'How Much Has Really Changed Between U.S Automakers and Their Suppliers.' *Sloan Management Review*: (Summer) 15–28.

Helper, Susan (1991b) 'Strategy and Irreversibility in Supplier Relations: The Case of the U.S. Automobile Industry.' *Business History Review*: (Winter) 781–824.

Hemmert, Martin, and Oberlander, Christian (1998) *Technology and Innovation in Japan: Policy and Management for the Twenty-first Century*. London: Routledge.

Henderson, Rebecca M. (1996) 'Product Development Capabilities as a Strategic Weapon: Canon's Experience in the Photolithographic Alignment Equipment Industry.' In: Nishihuchi, Tashihiro (ed.) *Managing Product Development*. New York: Oxford University Press.

Henderson, Rebecca M., and Clark, Kim B. (1990) 'Architectural Innovation: The Reconfiguration of Existing Product Technologies and the Failure of Established

Firms.' *Administrative Science Quarterly* 35: 9–30.

Henke, John W., Krachenberg, A. Richard, and Lyons, Thomas F. (1993) 'Cross-Functional Teams: Good Concept, Poor Implementation!' *Journal of Product Innovation Management* 10: 216–229.

Herbig, Paul (1995) *Innovation Japanese Style: A Cultural and Historical Perspective.* Westport, Conn.: Quarum Books.

Hiromoto, Toshiro (1988) 'Another Hidden Edge – Japanese Management Accounting.' *Harvard Business Review* 66(4): 22–26.

Hirschman, Albert O. (1970) *Exit, Voice, and Loyalty.* Cambridge, Mass.: Harvard University Press.

Hofstede, Geert (1991) *Cultures and Organizations: Software of the Mind.* London: McGraw-Hill.

Hopper, Trevor, and Armstrong, Peter (1991) 'Cost Accounting, Controlling Labor and the Rise of Conglomerate.' *Accounting, Organization, and Society* 16(5/6): 405–438.

Hounshell, David A. (1984) *From the American System to Mass Production 1800–1932: The Development of Manufacturing Technology in the United States.* Baltimore: Johns Hopkins University Press.

Hughes, Thomas P. (1989a) 'The Evaluation of Large Technological Systems.' In: Bijker, Wiebe E., Hughes, Thomas P. and Pinch, Trevor (eds) *The Social Construction of Technological Systems.* Cambridge, Mass.: The MIT Press.

Hughes, Thomas P. (1989b) *American Genesis: A Century of Invention and Technological Enthusiasm.* New York: Penguin Books.

Hughes, Thomas P. (1992) 'The Dynamics of Technological Change: Salients, Critical Problems, and Industrial Revolutions.' In: Dosi, Giovanni, Giannetti, Renato, and Toninelli, Pier Angelo (eds) *Technology and Enterprise in a Historical Perspective.* Oxford: Clarendon Press.

Hulme, David (1994) 'Venture Capital Idea.' *Asian Business* 12(8): 8–9.

Huntington, Samuel P. (1996) *The Clash of Civilizations and the Remaking of World Order.* New York: Simon & Schuster.

Iansiti, Marco, and West, Jonathan (1997) 'Technology Integration: Turning Great Research into Great Products.' *Harvard Business Review*: (May–June) 69–79.

Iansiti, Marco (1998) *Technology Integration: Making Critical Choices in a Dynamic World.* Boston, Mass.: Harvard Business School Press.

Imai, Masaaki (1986) *Kaizen: The Key to Japan's Competitive Success.* New York: Random House Business Division.

Imai, Ken-ichi, Nonaka, Ikujiro, and Takeuchi, Hirotaka (1985) 'Managing the New Product Development Process: How Japanese Companies Learn and Unlearn.' In: Clark, K. B., Hayes, R. H., and Lorenz, C. (eds) *The Uneasy Alliance.* Boston: Harvard Business School Press.

Innes, J. E. (1990) *Knowledge and Public Policy: The Search for Meaningful Indicators.* New Brunswick: Transaction Publishers.

Itoh, Hideshi (1994) 'Japanese Human Resource Management from the Viewpoint of Incentive Theory.' In: Aoki, Masahiko, and Dore, Ronald (eds) *The Japanese Firm: The Sources of Competitive Strength.* New York: Oxford University Press.

Jaikumar, Ramchandran (1986) 'Postindustrial Manufacturing.' *Harvard Business Review*: (Nov.–Dec.) 69–76.

Japan Human Relations Association (1988) *The Idea Book: Improvement Through Total Employee Involvement.* Cambridge, Mass.: Productivity Press.

Jelinek, Mariann (1979) *Institutionalizing Innovation: A Study of Organizational Learning Systems.* New York: Praeger.

Jensen, Michael C., and Mechling, William H. (1976) 'Theory of the Firm: Managerial Behavior, Agency Costs and Ownership Structure.' *Journal of Financial Economics*: (October) 305–360.

Jin, Dengjian (1995) 'Bounded Governance and Extended Order: the Confucian Advantage of Synergy Under Generalized Constitutional Rules.' *Constitutional Political Economy* 6(3): 263–280.

Jin, Dengjian (1998) 'The Dynamics of Knowledge Regimes: Culture, Technology, Governance, and Sectoral Patterns of National Competitiveness.' Ph.D. dissertation. George Mason University, Fairfax, VA 22030.

Johansson, Johny K., and Nonaka, Ikujiro (1987) 'Marketing Research the Japanese Way.' *Harvard Business Review* 65(3): (May–June) 16–19.

Johansson, Johny K., and Nonaka, Ikujiro (1993) 'Market Research the Japanese Way.' In: Durlabhji, Subhash, and Marks, Norton E. (eds) *Japanese Business: Cultural Perspective.* New York: State University of New York Press.

Johansson, Johny K., and Nonaka, Ikujiro (1996) *Relentless: The Japanese Way of Marketing.* New York: Harper Business.

Johansen, John, Karmarkar, Uday S., Nanda, Dhananjay, and Seidmann, Abraham (1995) 'Computer Integrated Manufacturing: Empirical Implications for Industrial Information Systems.' *Journal of Management Information Systems* 12(2): 59–83.

Johnson, Chalmers (1982) *MITI and The Japanese Miracle.* Stanford, CA: Stanford University Press.

Johnson, Frank A. (1993) *Dependency and Japanese Socialization: Psychoanalytic and Anthropological Investigations into Amae.* New York: New York University Press.

Johnson, H. Thomas (1992) *Relevance Regained: From Top-Down Control to Bottom-Up Empowerment.* New York: The Free Press.

Jones, Eric L. (1987) *The European Miracle: Environments, Economies, and Geopolitics in the History of Europe and Asia.* Cambridge, MA: Cambridge University Press.

Kagono, Tadao (1980) 'Comparison of Corporate Strategy and Organization between the United States and Japan.' *Japanese Business*, p. 178.

Kagono, Tadao, Nonaka, I., Okumura, A., Sakakibara, K., Komatsu, Y., and Sakashita, A. (1984) 'Mechanistic vs. Organic Management Systems: A Comparative Study of Adaptive Patterns of American and Japanese Firms.' In: Sata, Kazuo, and Hoshino, Yasuo (eds) *The Anatomy of Japanese Business.* New York: M. E. Sharpe Inc.

Kalleberg, A. L., and Lincoln, J. R. (1988) 'The Structure of Earnings. Inequality in the United States and Japan.' *American Journal of Sociology* 94: S121–153.

Kalwani, Manohar U., and Narayandas, Narakesari (1995) 'Long-term Manufacturer–Supplier Relationships: Do They Pay Off for Supplier Firms.'? *Journal of Marketing* 59(1): 1–16.

Kanter, Rosabeth Moss (1994) 'Collaborative Advantage: The Art of Alliance.'

Harvard Business Review: (July–Aug.) 96–108.

Kash, Don E. (1989) *Perpetual Innovation: The New World of Competition*. New York: Basic Books.

Kash, Don E., and Rycroft, R. W. (1999) *The Complexity Challenge: Technological Innovation for the 21st Century*. New York: Continuum International.

Kashima, Emiko S., and Kashima, Yoshihisa (1998) 'Culture and Language: The Case of Cultural Pronoun Use.' *Journal of Cross-Cultural Psychology* 29(3): 461–486.

Kato, Yutaka (1989) 'Applying Quantitative Methods to Cost and Management Accounting Practices: A U.S.–Japanese Comparison.' In: Monden, Yasuhiro, and Sakurai, Michiharu (eds) *Japanese Management Accounting: A World Class Approach to Profit Management*. Cambridge, Mass.: Productivity Press.

Keltner, Brent (1995) 'Relationship Banking and Competitive Advantage: Evidence from U.S. and Germany.' *California Management Review* 37(4): 45–73.

Kennedy, Paul (1993) *Preparing for the Twenty-First Century*. New York: Random House.

Kenney, Martin, and Florida, Richard (1993) *Beyond Mass Production: The Japanese System and Its Transfer to the U.S.* New York: Oxford University Press.

Kirzner, Israel M. (1979) *Perception, Opportunity, and Profit: Studies in the Theory of Entrepreneurship*. Chicago: The University of Chicago Press.

Kirzner, Israel M. (1985) *Discovery and the Capitalist Process*. Chicago: The University of Chicago Press.

Klein, Janice. A. (1989), 'The Human Costs of Manufacturing Reform.' *Harvard Business Review* 67(Mar.–Apr.): 87–95.

Klein, Janice. A. (1994) 'The Paradox of Quality Management: Commitment, Ownership, and Control.' In: Heckscher. C., and Donnellon A. (eds) *The Post-Bureaucratic Organization: New Perspectives on Organizational Change*. London: Sage.

Kline, Stephen J., and Nathan Rosenberg (1986) 'An Overview of Innovation.' In: Landau, Ralph, and Rosenberg, Nathan, (eds) *The Positive Strategy: Harnessing Technology for Economic Growth*. Washington, D.C.: National Academy Press.

Knight, Frank H. (1957) *Risk, Uncertainty and Profit*. New York: Kelly and Millman.

Kodama, F. (1991) *Analyzing Japanese High Technologies: The Techno-Paradigm Shift*. New York: Pinter Publishers.

Kodama, F. (1992) 'Technology Fusion and the New R&D.' *Harvard Business Review*: (July/August) 70–78.

Kodama, F. (1995) *Emerging Patterns of Innovation: Sources of Japan's Techno-logical Edge*. Boston, Mass.: Harvard Business School Press.

Kogut, Bruce (1993) (ed.) *Country Competitiveness: Technology and the Organizing of Work*. New York: Oxford University Press.

Koike, Kazuo (1988) *Understanding Industrial Relations in Modern Japan*. New York: St. Martin's Press.

Koike, Kazuo (1990) 'Intellectual Skills and the Role of Employees as Constituent Members of Large Firms in Contemporary Japan.' In: Aoki, Masahiko *et al.* (eds) *The Firm as a Nexus of Treaties*. London: Sage Publications.

Koike, Kazuo (1994) 'Learning and Incentive Systems in Japanese Industry.' In:

Aoki, Masahiko, and Dore, Ronald (eds) *The Japanese Firm: The Sources of Competitive Strength*. New York: Oxford University Press.

Koike, Kazuo, and Inoki, Takenori (1990) *Skill Formation in Japan and Southeast Asia*. Tokyo: University of Tokyo Press.

Kondo, Dorinne (1992) 'Multiple Selves: the Aesthetics and Politics of Artisanal Identities.' In: Rosenberger, Nancy R. (ed.) *Japanese Sense of Self*. New York, N.Y.: Cambridge University Press.

Kotabe, Masaaki, and Lanctot, Aldor R. Jr. (1998) 'The 'Depth' of the Japanese Market Orientation: A Comparison across Ranks and Functions with U.S. Firms.' In: Czinkota, Michael R., and Kotabe, Masaaki (eds) *Trends in International Business: Critical Perspectives*. New York: Blackwell Business.

Krugman, Paul (1991) 'Increasing Returns and Economic Geography.' *Journal of Political Economy* 99(3): 483–499.

Kuhn, Thomas S. (1962/1970) *The Structure of Scientific Revolution*. Chicago: The University of Chicago Press.

Kusunoki, Ken, Nonaka, Ikujiri, and Nagata, Akiya (1998) 'Organizational Capabilities in Product Development of Japanese Firms: A Conceptual Framework and Empirical Findings.' *Organization Science* 9(6): 699–718.

Kusunoki, Ken, and Numagami, Tsuyoshi: (1997) 'Intrafirm Transfer of Engineers in Japan.' In: Goto, Akira, and Odagiri, Hiroyuki (eds) *Innovation in Japan*. Oxford: Oxford University Press.

Lakoff, George and Johnson, Mark (1999) *Philosophy in the Flesh: The Embodied Mind and Its Challenge to Western Thought*. New York: Basic Books.

Landes, David S. (1998) *The Wealth and Poverty of Nations: Why Some Are So Rich and Some So Poor*. W. W. Norton & Company.

Langlois, Richard N. (1992) 'External Economies and Economic Progress: The Case of the Microcomputer Industry.' *Business History Review* 66 (Spring): 1–50.

Langlois, Richard N., and Robertson, Paul L. (1992) 'Networks and Innovation in a Modular System: Lessons from the Microcomputer and Stereo Component Industries.' *Research Policy* 21: 297–313.

Langlois, Richard N., and Robertson, Paul L. (1995) *Firms, Markets, and Economic Change*. London: Routledge.

Lauenstein, Milton C. (1993) 'Strategic Planning in Japan.' In: Durlabhji, Subhash, and Marks, Norton E. (eds) *Japanese Business: Cultural Perspectives*. Albany: State University of New York Press.

Lavoie, Don (1985) *National Economic Planning: What is Left*. Cambridge, Mass.: Ballinger.

Lavoie, Don, and Chamlee-Wright, Emily (1997) *Culture and the Spirit of Enterprise*. Manuscripts submitted to the Cato Institute's Project on Civil Society. Program on Social & Organizational Learning, George Mason University, Fairfax, VA 22030.

Lazonick, William (1990a) *Competitive Advantage on the Shop Floor*. Cambridge, Mass.: Harvard University Press.

Lazonick, William (1990b) 'Organizational Capabilities in American Industry: The Rise and Decline of Managerial Capitalism.' *Business and Economic History* 19: 35–54.

LeBlanc, Larry J., Nash, Robert, Gallagher, Daniel, Gonda, Kinji, and Kakizaki,

Fumihiko (1997) 'A Comparison of U.S. and Japanese Technology Management and Innovation.' *International Journal of Technology Management* 13(5/6): 601–614.

Lebra, Takie Sugiyama (1992) 'Self in Japanese Culture.' In: Rosenberger, Nancy R. (ed.) *Japanese Sense of Self*. New York: Cambridge University Press.

Lei, David, Hitt, Michael A., and Goldhar, Joel D. (1996) 'Advanced Manufacturing Technology: Organizational Design and Strategic Flexibility.' *Organization Studies* 17(3): 501–523.

Leonard, Dorothy, and Rayport, Jeffrey F. (1997) 'Spark Innovation Through Empathic Design.' *Harvard Business Review*: (Nov.–Dec.) 102–113.

Lessem, R. and Neubauer, F. (1994) *European Management Systems*. Maidenhead: McGraw-Hill.

Levitt, T. (1983) 'The Globalization of Markets.' *Harvard Business Review*: (May/June) 92–102.

Li, Chieh, Nuttall, Ronald L., and Zhao, Shuwen (1999) 'The Effect of Writing Chinese Characters on Success on the Water-Level Task.' *Journal of Cross-Cultural Psychology* 30(1): 91–105.

Liebeskind, Lulia, Porter, Oliver, Amalya, Lumerman, Zucker, Lynne, and Brewer, Marilynn (1996) 'Social Networks, Learning, and Flexibility: Sourcing Scientific Knowledge in New Biotechnology Firms.' *Organization Science* 7(4): 428–443.

Liker, Jeffrey K., Ettlie, John E., and Ward, Allen C. (1995) 'Managing Technology Systematically: Common Themes.' In: Liker, Jeffrey K., Ettlie, John E., and Campbell, John C. (eds) *Engineered in Japan: Japanese Technology-Management Practices*. New York: Oxford University Press.

Liker, Jeffrey K., Ettlie, John E., and Campbell, John C. (1995) (eds) *Engineered in Japan: Japanese Technology-Management Practices*. New York: Oxford University Press.

Liker, Jeffrey K., Fleischer, Mitchell, and Arnsdorf, David (1992) 'Fulfilling the Promises of CAD.' *Sloan Management Review*: (Spring) 74–86.

Lincoln, Edward J. (1990) *Japan's Unequal Trade*. Washington, D.C.: Brookings Institution.

Lincoln, Edward J. (1993) *Japan's New Global Role*. Washington, D.C.: Brookings Institution.

Lincoln, James R. (1989) 'Japanese Organization and Organization Theory.' In: Barry M. Staw and L. L. Cummings (eds) *Research in Organizational Behavior, vol. 12*. Greenwich, Conn.: JAI Press.

Lincoln, James R. (1993) 'Work Organization in Japan and the United States.' In: Kogut, Bruce (ed.) *Country Competitiveness: Technology and the Organizing of Work*. New York: Oxford University Press.

Lincoln, James R., and Kalleberg, Arnes (1990) *Culture, Control, and Commitment: A Study of Work Organization and Work Attitudes in the United States and Japan*. Cambridge: Cambridge University Press.

Lincoln, James R., Ahmadjian, Christina L., and Mason, Eliot (1998) 'Organizational Learning and Purchase-Supply Relations in Japan: Hitachi, Matsushita, and Toyota Compared.' *California Management Review* 40(3): 241–264.

Lipset, Seymour Martin (1990) *Continental Divide: The Value and Institutions of United States and Canada*. New York: Routledge.

Lipset, Seymour Martin (1996) *American Exceptionalism: A Double-Edged Sword.* New York: W. W. Norton & Company.

Littler, Craig R. (1978) 'Understanding Taylorism.' *British Journal of Sociology* 29(2): 185–207.

Litterer, Joseph A. (1961) 'Systematic Management: The Search for Order and Integration.' *Business History Review* 35: 461–476.

Litterer, Joseph A. (1963) 'Systematic Management: Design for Organizational Recoupling in American Manufacturing Firms.' *Business History Review* 37(4): 369–391.

Locke, John (1690/1986) *The Second Treatise on Civil Government.* Buffalo, New York: Prometheus Books.

Locke, Richard, Kochan, Thomas, Piore, Michael (1995) *Employment Relations in a Changing World Economy.* Cambridge, Mass.: The MIT Press.

Locke, Robert (1996) 'The Limitations of America's *Pax Oeconomica*: Germany and Japan after World War II.' In: Glover, Ian, and Hughes, Michael (eds) *The Profession-Managerial Class.* Aldershot: Avebury.

Lodge, George C., and Vogel, Ezra F. (1987) *Ideology and National Competitiveness: An Analysis of Nine Countries.* Boston, Mass.: Harvard University Press.

Longenecker, Justin G., McKinney, Joseph A., and Moore, Carlos W. (1988) 'Egoism and Independence: Entrepreneurial Ethics.' *Organizational Dynamics* 16(3): 64–72.

Lynch, Lisa (1990) 'The Private Sector and Skill Formation in the United States: A Survey.' Working Paper 3125–90-BPS. Cambridge, Mass.: Massachusetts Institute of Technology.

Lynn, Leonard H., Piehler, Henry R., and Kieler, Mark (1993) 'Engineering Careers, Job Rotation, and Gatekeepers in Japan and the United States.' *Journal of Engineering and Technology Management* 10: 53–72.

McCartney, Laton (1997) 'The Rising Son.' *Upside* 9(4): 108–110.

McKinsey Global Institute (1993) *Manufacturing Productivity.* Washington, D.C.

McNeil, William H. (1995) 'The Rise of the West After Twenty-Five Years.' In: Sanderson, Stephen K. (ed.) *Civilizations and World Systems: Studying World-Historical Change.* London: Altamira Press.

Macaulay, Stewart (1963) 'Non-Contractual Relations in Business: A Preliminary Study.' *American Sociological Review* 28: 55–69.

Macduffie, John Paul (1995) 'Human Resource Bundles and Manufacturing Performance: Organizational Logic and Flexible Production Systems in the World Auto Industry.' *Industrial and Labor Relations Review* 48(2): 197–221.

Macduffie, John Paul, and Kochan, Thomas A. (1995) 'Do U.S. Firms Invest Less in Human Resources? Training in the World Auto Industry.' *Industrial Relations* 34(2): 147–168.

Main, Jeremy (1994) *Quality Wars: The Triumphs and Defeats of American Business.* New York: The Free Press.

Macher, Jeffrey T., Mowery, David C., and Hodges, David A. (1998) 'Reversal of Fortune? The Recovery of the U.S. Semiconductor Industry.' *California Management Review* 41(1): 107–136.

Magretta, Joan (1998) 'The Power of Virtual Integration: An Interview with Dell Computer's Michael Dell.' *Harvard Business Review*: (Mar.–Apr.) 73–84.

Majchrzak, Ann, and Wang, Qianwei (1996) 'Breaking the Functional Mind-set in Process Organizations.' *Harvard Business Review* 74(5): 92–99.

Malerba, Franco, and Orsenigo, Luigi (1996) 'Schumpeterian Patterns of Innovation are Technology-Specific.' *Research Policy* 25: 451–478.

Mansfield, Edwin (1988a) 'Industrial R&D in Japan and the United States: A Comparative Study.' *American Economic Review* 78: 223–228.

Mansfield, Edwin (1988b) 'The Speed and Cost of Industrial Innovation in Japan and the United States: External vs. Internal Technology.' *Management Science* 34(10): 1157–1168.

Mansfield, Edwin (1989) 'The Diffusion of Industrial Robotics in Japan and the United States.' *Research Policy* 18: 183–192.

Mansfield, Edwin (1993) 'The Diffusion of Flexible Manufacturing Systems in Japan and the United States.' *Management Science* 39(2): 149–159.

March, James G. (1988) *Decisions and Organizations*. Oxford: Basil Blackwell.

Marcus, Alan I., and Segal, Howard P. (1989) *Technology in America: A Brief History*. San Diego: Harcourt Brace Jovanovich Publishers.

Markus, Hazel Rose, and Kitayama, Shinobu (1998) 'The Cultural Psychology of Personality.' *Journal of Cross-Cultural Psychology* 29(1): 63–87.

Mazzoleni, Roberto (1997) 'Learning and Path-dependence in Diffusion of Innovations: Comparative Evidence on Numerically Controlled Machine Tools.' *Research Policy* 26: 405–428.

Milkman, Ruth (1997) *Farewell to the Factory: Auto Workers in the Late Twentieth Century*. Berkeley, CA: University of California Press.

Millard, Andrew (1990) *Edison and the Business of Innovation*. Baltimore: Johns Hopkins University Press.

Mintzberg, Henry (1976) 'Planning on the Left Side and Managing on the Right.' *Harvard Business Review* (July/August).

Mintzberg, Henry (1989) *Mintzberg on Management: Inside Our Strange World of Organizations*. New York: The Free Press.

Mintzberg, Henry (1994) *The Rise and Fall of Strategic Planning: Reconceiving Roles for Planning, Plans, and Planners*. New York: The Free Press.

Mintzberg, Henry, Jorgensen, Jan, and Dougherty, Deborah (1996) 'Some Surprising Things about Collaborating – Knowing How People Connect Makes it Work Better.' *Organizational Dynamics* 25(1): 60–72.

Miwa, Yoshiro (1996) *Firms and Industrial Organization in Japan*. New York: New York University Press.

Moore, James F. (1996) *The Death of Competiton: Leadership and Strategy in the Age of Business Ecosystems*. New York: Harper Business.

Morishima, Motohiro (1991) 'Information Sharing and Collective Bargaining in Japan: Effects on Wage Negotiation.' *Industrial and Labor Relations Review* 44(3): 469–485.

Morone, Joseph, and Berg, Daniel (1993) 'Management of Technology in the Service Sector: Practices in the Banking Industry.' *The Journal of High Technology Management* 4(1): 123–137.

Morris, Charles R., and Ferguson, Charles H. (1993) 'How Architecture Wins Technology Wars.' *Harvard Business Review* (Mar.–Apr.): 86–96.

Morton, Alan Q. (1994) 'Packaging History: The Emergence of the Uniform Product

Code (UPC) in the United States, 1970–75.' *History and Technology* 11: 101–111.

Mowery, David C. (1990) 'The Japanese Commercial Aircraft Industry: Déjà Vu all Over Again?' *Technovation* 10(6): 419–435.

Mowery, David C. (1996) *The International Computer Software Industry*. Oxford: Oxford University Press.

Mowery, David C., and Nelson, Richard R. (2000) *Sources of Industrial Leadership: Studies of Seven Industries*. Boston, Mass.: Cambridge University Press.

Mowery, David C., and Rosenberg, Nathan (1985) 'Commercial Aircraft: Cooperation and Competition Between the U.S. and Japan.' *California Management Review* 27(4): 70–92.

Mowery, David C., and Rosenberg, Nathan (1998) *Paths of Innovation: Technological Change in 20th Century America*. New York: Cambridge University Press.

Mowery, David C., and Teece, David J. (1993) 'Japan's Growing Capabilities in Industrial Technology: Implications for U.S. Managers and Policymakers.' *California Management Review*: (Winter) 9–34.

Mroczkowski, Tomasz, and Hanoka, Masao (1989) 'Continuity and Change in Japanese Management.' *California Management Review* 31(2).

Nakahara, Tetsushi (1993) *The Industrial Organization and Information Structure of the Software Industry: A U.S.–Japan Comparison*. Research Paper, Center for Economic Policy Research, Stanford University.

Nakane, Chie (1972) *Japanese Society*. Berkeley, CA: University of California Press.

National Science Board (1993) *Science & Engineering Indicators 1993*. Washington, D.C.

National Science Board (1996) *Science & Engineering Indicators 1996*. Washington, D.C.

National Science Board (1998) *Science & Engineering Indicators 1998*. Washington, D.C.

Needham, Joseph (1956) *The Great Titration*. Toronto: Toronto University Press.

Nelson, Daniel (1995) 'Industrial Engineering and the Industrial Enterprise, 1890–1940.' In: Lamoreaux, N. R., and Raff, D. M. G. (eds) *Coordination and Information: Historical Perspectives on the Organization of Enterprise*. Chicago: The University of Chicago Press.

Nelson, Richard R. (1993) (ed.) *National Innovation Systems*. Oxford: Oxford University Press.

Nelson, Richard R., and Winter, Sidney G. (1982) *An Evolutionary Theory of Economic Change*. Cambridge, Mass.: Harvard University Press.

Nelson, R. Ryan, Weiss, Ira R., and Yamazaki, Kazumi (1992) 'Information Resource Management Within Multinational Corporations.' *International Information Systems* 1(4): 56–88.

Nishiguchi, Toshihiro (1994) *Strategic Industrial Sourcing: The Japanese Advantage*. New York: Oxford University Press.

Noble, David F. (1979) *Force of Production: A Social History of Industrial Automation*. Oxford: Oxford University Press.

Noble, David F. (1989) 'Automation Madness, or the Unautomatic History of Automation.' In: Goldman, Steven L. (ed.) *Science, Technology, and Social Progress*. Bethlehem: Lehigh University Press.

Nohria, Nitin, and Berkley, James D. (1994) 'What Happened to the Take-Charge

Manager?'. *Harvard Business Review*: (Jan.–Feb.) 128–137.

Nonaka, Ikujiro (1990) 'Redundant, Overlapping Organizations: A Japanese Approach to Managing the Innovation Process.' *California Management Review* 32(3): 27–38.

Nonaka, Ikujiro (1991) 'The Knowledge-Creating Company.' *Harvard Business Review*: (Nov.–Dec.) 96–104.

Nonaka, Ikujiro (1994) 'A Dynamic Theory of Organizational Knowledge Creation.' *Organizational Science* 5(1): 14–37.

Nonaka, Ikujiro, and Takeuchi, Hirotaka (1995) *The Knowledge-Creating Company: How Japanese Companies Create the Dynamics of Innovation*. New York: Oxford University Press.

North, Douglass C. (1990) *Institutions, Institutional Change and Economic Performance*. Cambridge: Cambridge University Press.

Numagami, Tsuyoshi (1996) 'Flexibility Trap: A Case Analysis of U.S. and Japanese Technology Choice in the Digital Watch Industry.' *Research Policy* 25: 133–162.

Odagiri, Hiroyuki, and Goto, Akira (1993) 'The Japanese System of Innovation: Past, Present, and Future.' In: Nelson, Richard R. (ed.) *National Systems of Innovation: A Comparative Analysis*. Oxford: Oxford University Press.

Odagiri, Hiroyuki, and Goto, Akira (1996) *Technology and Industrial Development in Japan: Building Capabilities by Learning, Innovation, and Public Policy*. Oxford: Clarendon Press.

OECD (1993) *Economic and Trade Issues in the Computerized Database Market*. OECD, Paris.

OECD (1996) *Venture Capital and Innovation*. OECD, Paris. OCDE/GD(96)168.

OECD (1997a) *Information Technology Outlook, 1997*. OECD, Paris.

OECD (1997b) *The Software Sector: A Statistical Profile for Selected OECD Countries*. OECD, Paris. DSTI/ICCPAH(97)4/REV1.

OECD (1998) Measuring Electronic Commerce: International Trade in Software. OECD, Paris. DSTI/ICCP/IE(98)3/FINAL.

Ogden, Joan (1997) 'Non-US Companies Must Play Catch-up in Finance Technology.' *Global Finance* 11(5): (May) 50–52.

Ohmae, Kenichi (1996) *The End of Nation State: The Rise of Regional Economics*. New York: The Free Press.

Okimoto, Daniel I. (1989) *Between MITI and The Market: Japanese Industrial Policy and High Technology*. Stanford, CA: Stanford University.

Okimoto, Daniel I., and Saxonhouse, Gary R. (1987) 'Technology and the Future of the Economy.' In: Yamamura, K., and Yusuba, Y. (eds) *The Political Economy of Japan, volume i, The Domestic Transformation*. Stanford, CA: Stanford University Press.

Okuno-Fujiwara, Masahiro (1997) 'Toward a Comparative Institutional Analysis of the Government-Business Relationship.' In: Aoki, Masahiro, and Kim, Hyung-Ki (eds) *The Role of Government in East Asian Economic Development*. Oxford: Oxford University Press.

Oliver, N., and Wilkinson, B. W. (1992) *The Japanization of British Industry: New Development in the 1990s*. Cambridge, Mass.: Blackwell.

Orlikowski, Wanda J. (1992) 'The Duality of Technology: Rethinking the Concept of Technology in Organization.' *Organization Science* 3(3): 398–427.

Ornatowski, Gregorg K. (1998) 'The End of Japanese-style Human Resource

Management?' *Sloan Management Review* 39(3): 73–84.

Ornstein, Robert (1975) *The Psychology of Consciousness*. San Francisco: Freeman.

Ornstein, Robert (1991) *Evolution of Consciousness – The Origins of the Ways We Think*. New York: Simon & Schuster.

O'Shea, James, and Madigan, Charles (1997) *Dangerous Company: The Secret Story of the Consulting Powerhouses and the Corporations They Save and Ruin*. New York: Times Business.

Osterman, Paul (1994) 'How Common is Workplace Transformation and Who Adopts It?' *Industrial and Labor Relations Review* 47(2): 173–188.

Osterman, Paul (1995) 'Skill, Training, and Work Organization in American Establishments.' *Industrial Relations* 34(2): 125–146.

Ouchi, W. G. (1980) 'Markets, Bureaucracies and Clans.' *Administrative Science Quarterly* 25: 129–141.

Ouchi, W. G. (1981) *Theory Z: How American Business Can Meet the Japanese Challenge*. Reading, Mass.: Addison-Wesley.

Ouchi, W. G. (1984) *The M-Form Society: How American Teamwork Can Recapture the Competitive Edge*. Reading, Mass.: Addison-Wesley.

Pake, George E. (1985) 'Research at Xerox PARC: A Founder's Assessment.' *IEEE Spectrum*: (Oct.) 54–61.

Parker, Kevin (1992) 'System Integrators Seek Limits to 'Creeping Elegance.' *Manufacturing Systems* 10(12): 12–18.

Parsons, T. (1937) *The Structure of Social Action*. New York: The Free Press.

Pascale, Richard T. (1984) 'Perspectives on Strategy: the Real Story Behind Honda's Success.' *California Management Review*: (Spring) 47–72.

Patel, Pari (1996) 'Are Large Firms Internationalizing the Generation of Technology? Some New Evidence.' *IEEE Transaction on Engineering Management* 43(1): 41–47.

Patel, Parimal, and Pavitt, Keith (1998) 'Uneven (and Divergent) Technological Accumulation among Advanced Countries: Evidence and a Framework of Explanation.' In: Dosi, Giovanni *et al.* (eds) *Technology, Organization, and Competitiveness: Perspectives on Industrial and Corporate Change*. New York: Oxford University Press.

Pavitt, Keith (1984) 'Sectoral Patterns of Technological Change: Towards a Taxonomy and Theory.' *Research Policy* 13(6): 343–374.

Perrow, Charles (1986) *Complex Organizations*. 3rd edn. New York: Random House.

Perry, Tekla S., and Wallich, Paul (1985) 'Inside the PARC: the "Information Architechs".' *IEEE Spectrum*: (Oct.) 62–87.

Peters, Tom, and Waterman, Robert H. (1982) *In Search of Excellence*. New York: Harper & Row.

Petersen, Donald, and Hillkirk, John (1991) *A Better Idea: Redefining the Way Americans Work*. Boston, Mass.: Houghton Mifflin Company.

Pfeffer, Jeffrey (1994) *Competitive Advantage through People: Unleashing the Power of the Work Force*. Boston, Mass.: Harvard Business School Press.

Pilkington, Alan (1998) 'Manufacturing Strategy Regained: Evidence for the Demise of Best-Practice.' *California Management Review* 41(1): 31–42.

Pine II, Joseph (1993) *Mass Customization: The New Frontier in Business*

Competition. Boston, MA: Harvard Business School Press.

Pinker, Steven (1997) *How the Mind Works.* New York: W. W. Norton & Company.

Piore, Michael J. (1996) 'Review of the Handbook of Economic Sociology.' *Journal of Economic Literature* XXXIV: 741–754.

Piore, Michael J., and Sabel, Charles. F. (1984) *The Second Industrial Divide: Possibilities for Prosperity.* New York: Basic Books.

Polanyi, Karl (1944/1957) *The Great Transformation.* Boston: Beacon Press.

Polanyi, Karl (1957) 'The Economy as Instituted Process.' In: Karl Polanyi, Arensberg, Conrad M., and Pearson, Harry W. (eds) *Trade and Market in the Early Empires.*

Polanyi, Michael (1958/1964) *Personal* Chicago: The Free Press. *Knowledge: Towards a Post-Critical Philosophy.* New York: Harper & Row.

Polanyi, Michael (1969) *Knowing and Being.* Chicago: University of Chicago Press.

Pollack, A. (1992) 'Software: Japan's Little Nightmare-in-the-making.' *New York Times*: Oct. 11, F5.

Porter, Michael E. (1985) *Competitive Advantage: Creating and Sustaining Superior Performance.* New York: The Free Press.

Porter, Michael E. (1990) *The Competitive Advantage of Nations.* New York: The Free Press.

Porter, Michael E. (1992) 'Capital Disadvantage: America's Failing Capital Investment System.' *Harvard Business Review*: (Sept.–Oct.) 65–82.

Porter, Michael E. (1996) 'What is Strategy.' *Harvard Business Review*: (Nov.–Dec.) 61–78.

Porter, Theodore M. (1995) *Trust in Numbers: the Pursuit of Objectivity in Science and Public Life.* Princeton, NJ: Princeton University Press.

Prahalad, C.K., and Hamel, Gary (1990) 'The Core Competence of the Corporation.' *Harvard Business Review* (May–June): 79–91.

Prestowitz, Clyde V. Jr. (1988) *Trading Places: How We are Giving Our Future to Japan and How to Reclaim It.* New York: Basic Books,

Putnam, Robert D. (1995) 'Bowling Alone: America's Declining Social Capital.' *Journal of Democracy* 6: 65–78.

Pye, Lucian W. (1985) *Asian Power and Politics: The Cultural Dimensions of Authority.* Cambridge, Mass.: Harvard University Press.

Quinn, James Brian, Anderson, Philip, and Finkelstein, Sydney (1996) 'Managing Professional Intellect: Making the Most of the Best.' *Harvard Business Review* 74(2): 71–80.

Rackoff, N., Wiseman, C., and Ulrich, W. (1985) 'Information Systems for Competitive Advantage: Implementation of a Planning Process.' *MIS Quarterly* 9: (Dec.) 285–294.

Randazzese, Lucien P. (1994) *GCA and Domestic Lithography: Managing Procurement Incentives in SEMATECH and Vertical Consortia.* Critical Technologies Institute, Washington, D.C. (February).

Rasmus, Daniel W. (1994) 'The Once and Future CIM.' *Manufacturing Systems* 12(3): 62–67.

Rawls, John (1971) *A Theory of Justice.* Boston, Mass.: Harvard University Press.

Ritzer, George (1995) *The McDonaldization of Society: An Investigation into the Changing Character of Contemporary Social Life.* Thousand Oaks, CA: Pine

Force Press.

Robinson, Alan G., and Schroeder, Dean M. (1993) 'Training, Continuous Improvement, and Human Relations: the U.S. TWI Programs and the Japanese Management Style.' *California Management Review* (Winter) 36: 35–57.

Roehl, Thomas, and Truitt, Frederick (1987) 'Japanese Industrial Policy in Aircraft Manufacturing.' *International Marketing Review*: 4 (Summer) 21–32

Rohwer, Jim (1998) 'Japan's Quiet Corporate Revolution.' *Fortune* 137(6): 82–90.

Romer, Paul (1990) 'Endogenous Technological Change.' *Journal of Political Economy* 8(1): 71–102.

Rosenberg, Nathan, and Birdzell, L. E. Jr. (1986) *How the West Grew Rich: The Economic Transformation of the Industrial World.* New York: Basic Books.

Rosenberger, Nancy R. (1992) (ed.) *Japanese Sense of Self.* New York: Cambridge University Press.

Rosenblatt, Alfred, and Watson, George F. (1991) 'Concurrent Engineering.' *IEEE Spectrum* (July): 22–37.

Rush, Howard, and Bessant, John (1992) 'Revolution in Three-quarter Time: Lessons from the Diffusion of Advanced Manufacturing Technologies.' *Technology Analysis & Strategic Management* 4(1): 3–19.

Sabel, Charles F. (1987) 'The Resurgence of Regional Economics.' In: Hirst, P., and Zeitlin, J. (eds) *Revising Industrial Decline?* Oxford: Berg Publishers.

Sabel, Charles F. (1994) 'Learning by Monitoring: The Institutions of Economic Development.' In: Smelser, Neil, and Swedberg, Richard (eds) *Handbook of Economic Sociology.* Princeton, NJ: Princeton University Press.

Sachwald, Frederique (1995) 'Japanese Chemical Firms: A Limited Internationalization.' In: Sachwald, Frederique (ed.) *Japanese Firms in Europe.* Luxembourg: Harwood Academic Publishers.

Sakakibara, Kiyonori, and Westney, D. Eleanor (1992) 'Japan's Management of Global Innovation: Technology Management Crossing Borders.' In: Rosenberg, Nathan *et al.* (eds) *Technology and the Wealth of Nations.* Stanford, CA: Stanford University Press.

Sakurai, Michihru, Killouhg, Larry N., and Brown, Robert M. (1989) 'Performance Measurement Techniques and Goal Setting: A Comparison of the U.S. and Japanese Practices.' In: Monden, Yasuhiro, and Sakurai, Michiharu (eds) *Japanese Management Accounting: A World Class Approach to Profit Management.* Cambridge, Mass.: Productivity Press.

Samuels, Richard (1994) 'Pathways of Technological Diffusion in Japan.' *Sloan Management Review*: (Spring) 21–34.

Sarah, Cliffe (1998) 'Knowledge Management: The Well-Connected Business.' *Harvard Business Review* 76(4): 17–21.

Sarathy, Ravi (1989) 'The Interplay of Industrial Policy and International Strategy: Japan's Machine Tool Industry.' *California Management Review* 31(3): 130–160.

Sawinski, D. M., and Mason, W. H. (1996) (eds) *Encyclopedia of Global Industries.* New York: Gale Research.

Saxenian, Annalee (1994) *Regional Advantage: Culture and Competition in Silicon Valley and Route 128.* Cambridge, MA: Harvard University Press.

Schmitt, Richard (1995) *Beyond Separateness: The Social Nature of Human Beings – Their Autonomy, Knowledge, and Power.* Boulder: Westview Press.

Schonberger, Richard J. (1994) 'Human Resource Management Lessons from a Decade of Total Quality Management and Reengineering.' *California Management Review* 36(4): 109–123.

Schuler, Randall S., and Rogovsky, Nikolai (1998) 'Understanding Compensation Practice Variations across Firms: The Impact of National Culture.' *Journal of International Business Studies* 29(1): 159–177.

Scott, A. J., and Storper, M. (1990) *Pathways to Industrialization and Regional Development.* London: Pion.

Senge, Peter M. (1990) *The Fifth Discipline: The Art and Practice of the Learning Organization.* New York: Doubleday/Currency.

Serling, Robert J. (1992) *Legend and Legacy: The Story of Boeing and Its People.* New York: St. Martin's Press.

Shani, A.B., Grant, Robert M., Krishnan, R., and Thompson, E. (1992) 'Advanced Manufacturing Systems and Organizational Choices: Sociotechnical Systems Approach.' *California Management Review* 34(4): 91–112.

Shapiro, Eileen C., Eccles, Robert G., and Soske, Trina L. (1993) 'Consulting: Has the Solution Become Part of the Problem?' *Sloan Management Review*: (Summer) 89–95.

Shenhav, Yehouda (1995) 'From Chaos to Systems: The Engineering Foundations of Organization Theory, 1879–1932.' *Administrative Science Quarterly* 40: 557–585.

Shichihei, Yamamoto (1992) *The Spirit of Japanese Capitalism and Selected Essays.* Translated by Lynne E. Riggs and Takechi Manabu. Lanham: Madison Books.

Shook, Carrie, and Shook, Robert L. (1993) *Franchising: The Business Strategy that Changed the World.* Englewood Cliffs, NJ: Prentice Hall.

Simon, Herbert A. (1957) *Models of Man.* New York: John Wiley.

Simon, Herbert A. (1962) 'The Architecture of Complexity.' *Proceeding of the American Philosophical Society* 106(6): 467–482.

Simon, Herbert A. (1976) *Administrative Behavior: A Study of Decision-making Processes in Administrative Organization.* New York: The Free Press.

Siwek, Stephen E., and Furchtgott-Roth, Harold W. (1993) *International Trade in Computer Software.* Westport, Conn.: Quarum Books.

Smith, Hedrick (1995) *Rethinking America.* New York: Random House.

Sobol, Marion G., and Lei, David (1994) 'Environment, Manufacturing Technology, and Embedded Knowledge.' *The International Journal of Human Factors in Manufacturing* 4(2): 167–189.

Someya, Kyojiro (1996) *Japanese Accounting: A Historical Approach.* Oxford: Oxford University Press.

Song, X. Michael, and Parry, Mark E. (1992) 'The R&D-Marketing Interface in Japanese High-Technology Firms.' *Journal of Product Innovation Management* 9: 91–112.

Souder, William E., Song, X. Michael, and Kawamura, Kazuhiko (1998) 'America's Edge in New Product R&D.' *Research Technology Management*: (Mar.–Apr.) 49–56.

Spencer, William J. (1990) 'Research to Product: A Major U.S. Challenge.' *California Management Review* 33: (Winter) 45–53.

Stalk, George, Evans, Philip, and Shulman, Lawrence (1992) 'Competing on

Capabilities: The New Rules of Corporate Strategy.' *Harvard Business Review*: (Mar–Apr) 57–69.

Staudenmaier, John M. S. J. (1989) 'U.S. Technological Style and the Atrophy of Civic Commitment.' In: Gelpi, Donald (ed.) *Beyond Individualism*. Notre Dame, Indiana: University of Notre Dame Press.

Sternberg, Rolf G. (1996) 'Government R&D Expenditure and Space: Empirical Evidence from Five Industrialized Countries.' *Research Policy* 25: 741–758.

Storper, Michael (1993) 'Regional 'Worlds' of Production: Learning and Innovation in Technology Districts of France, Italy and the USA.' *Regional Studies* 27: 443–455.

Suh, N. P. (1990) *The Principles of Design*. New York: Oxford University Press. Pp. 40–42.

Sullivan, Jeremiah J. (1995) *The Innovation of the Salarymen: The Japanese Business Presence in America*. Westport, Conn.: Praeger.

Susman, Gerald I. (1992) (ed.) *Integrating Design and Manufacturing for Competitive Advantage*. New York: Oxford University Press.

Suzuki, Daisetz T. (1959) *Zen and Japanese Culture*. New York: MJF Books.

Suzuki, Kazuyuki (1997) 'Production Technology and Productive Growth in the Japanese Electrical Machinery Industry.' In: Goto, Akira, and Odagiri, Hiroyuki (eds) *Innovation in Japan*. Oxford: Oxford University Press.

Tai, H. C. (1989) *Confucianism and Economic Development: An Oriental Alternative?* Washington, D.C.: The Washington Institute Press.

Takahashi, Dean (1998) 'Hand-held Combat: How the Competition Got Ahead of Intel in Maning Cheap Chips – Giant's PC Focus Blinded It to Burgeoning Market in Consumer Electronics – Digital's Ace in the Hole.' *Wall Street Journal*, Feb. 12, A1.

Takezawa, S., and Whitechill, A. M. (1981) *Work Ways: Japan and America*. Tokyo: The Japan Institute of Labor.

Tall, Spencer (1995) 'Venture Capital, Tokyo Style.' *Upside* 7(2): 22–24.

Tapscott, Don (1996) *Digital Economy: Promise and Peril in the Age of Networked Intelligence*. New York: McGraw-Hill.

Thurow, Lester (1992) *Head to Head: The Coming Economic Battle Among Japan, Europe, and America*. New York: William Morrow and Company, Inc.

Trompenaars, Alfrons (1993) *Riding the Waves of Culture in Global Business*. London: The Economics Books.

Tsutsui, William M. (1998) *Manufacturing Ideology: Scientific Management in Twentieth-Century Japan*. Princeton, NJ: Princeton University Press.

Tyson, Laura D'Andrea (1993) *Who is Bashing Whom? Trade Conflicts in High Technology Industries*. Washington, D.C.: Institute for International Economics.

Tu, Wei-ming (1996) (ed.) *Confucian Traditions in East Asian Modernity: Moral Education and Economic Culture in Japan and the Four Mini-Dragons*. Cambridge, Mass.: Harvard University Press.

Ulrich, Karl (1995) 'The Role of Product Architecture in the Manufacturing Firm.' *Research Policy* 24: 419–440.

Ulrich, Karl, and Tung, Karen (1991) 'Fundamentals of Product Modularity.' Proceedings of the 1991 ASME Winter Annual Meeting Symposium on Issues in Design/Manufacturing Integration, Atlanta.

Upton, David (1995) 'What Really Makes Factories Flexible.' *Harvard Business Review*: (July–Aug.) 74–84.

US Congressional and Office of Technology Assessment (1990) *Making Things Better: Competing in Manufacturing*. OTA-ITE-443. Washington, D.C.: US Government Printing Office, February.

US Department of Commerce, International Trade Administration (1994) *The U.S. Global Trade Outlook: 1995–2000*. US Government Printing Office, Washington, D.C. 20402.

US Department of Commerce (1998) *The Emerging Digital Economy*. http://www.ecommerce.gov.

US Department of Commerce (2000) Online Database: http://www.ita.doc.gov/industry/otea/usfth.

Van Ark, Bart, and Pilat, Dirt (1993) 'Productivity Levels in Germany, Japan, and the United States: Differences and Causes.' *Brookings Papers on Economic Activity: Microeconomics* 2: 1–69.

Vernon, Raymond (1966) 'International Trade in the Product Cycle.' *Quarterly Journal of Economics* 80: 315–337.

Vogel, Ezra F. (1979) *Japanese as Number One*. New York: Harper & Row.

Vogel, Ezra F. (1987) 'Conclusion.' In: Lodge, George C., and Vogel, Ezra F. (eds) *Ideology and National Competitiveness: An Analysis of Nine Countries*. Boston, Mass.: Harvard University Press.

von Hippel, Eric (1990) 'Task Partitioning: An Innovation Process Variable.' *Research Policy* 19: 407–418.

Waldrop, M. M. (1992) *Complexity: The Emerging Science of the Edge of Order and Chaos*. New York: Simon & Schuster.

Warner, Malcolm (1994) 'Japanese Culture, Western Management: Taylorism and Human Resources in Japan.' *Organization Studies* 15(4): 509–533.

Weber, Max (1983) *Max Weber on Capitalism, Bureaucracy and Religion*, edited by Stanislav Andreski. London: George Allen & Unwin.

Weinstein, Marc, and Kochan, Thomas (1995) 'The Limits of Diffusion: Recent Developments in Industrial Relations and Human Resource Practices.' In: Locke, Richard, Locke, Kochan, Thomas and Piore, Michael (eds) *Employment Relations in a Changing World Economy*. Cambridge, Mass.: The MIT Press.

Westney, Eleanor (1993) 'Country Patterns in R&D Organization: The United States and Japan.' In: Kogut, Bruce (ed.) *Country Competitiveness: Technology and Organizing of Work*. New York: Oxford University Press.

Westney, D. Eleanor (1994) 'The Evolution of Japan's Industrial Research and Development.' In: Aoki, Masahiko, and Dore, Ronald (eds) *The Japanese Firm: The Sources of Competitive Strength*. New York: Oxford University Press.

Whitehill, Arthur M. (1991) *Japanese Management: Tradition and Transition*. London: Routledge.

Whitelock, Jeryl, and Pimblett, Carole (1997) 'The Standardization Debate in International Marketing.' *Journal of Global Marketing* 10(3): 45–66.

Whitley, Richard (1992) *Business Systems in East Asia: Firms, Markets and Societies*. London: Sage Publications.

Whitney, Daniel E. (1992) 'State of the Art in Japanese CAD Methodologies for Mechanical Products – Reports on Individual Visits to Companies and

Universities. *Office of Naval Research Asia Scientific Information Bulletin* 17: (July–Sept.) 83–172.

Whitney, Daniel E. (1995) 'Nippondenso Co. Ltd: A Case Study of Strategic Product Design.' In: Liker, Jeffrey K., Ettlie, John E., and Campbell, John C. (eds) *Engineered in Japan: Japanese Technology-Management Practices*. New York: Oxford University Press.

Whittaker, D. Hugh (1994) 'SMEs, Entry Barriers; and Strategic Alliances.' In: Aoki, Masahiko, and Dore, Ronald (eds) *The Japanese Firm: The Sources of Competitive Strength*. New York: Oxford University Press.

Williamson, Oliver E. (1979) 'Transaction-cost Economics: The Governance of Contractual Relationships.' *Journal of Law and Economics* 22(2): 233–261.

Williamson, Oliver E. (1985) *The Economic Institutions of Capitalism*. New York: The Free Press.

Williamson, Oliver. E. (1996) *The Mechanisms of Governance*. New York: Oxford University Press.

Wilson, James Q. (1989) *Bureaucracy: What Government Agencies Do and Why They Do It*. New York: Basic Books.

Winner, Langdon (1977) *Autonomous Technology: Technics-out-of-Control as a Theme in Political Thought*. Cambridge, Mass.: The MIT Press.

Winter, Sidney G. (1991) 'On Coase, Competence, and the Corporation.' In: Williamson, Oliver E., and Winter, Sidney G. (eds) *The Nature of the Firm: Origins, Evolution, and Development*. New York: Oxford University Press.

Womack, J. P., Jones, D. T., and Roos, D. (1990) *The Machine That Changed the World*. New York: Rawson Associates.

World Bank (1992) *Governance and Development*. Washington, D.C.: The World Bank.

World Bank (1993) *The East Asian Miracle: Economic Growth and Public Policy*. New York: Oxford University Press.

Yamada, Haru (1997) *Different Games, Different Rules: Why Americans and Japanese Misunderstand Each Other*. New York: Oxford University Press.

Yamashita, Shoichi (1991) (ed.) *Transfer of Japanese Technology and Management to the Asian Countries*. Tokyo: University of Tokyo Press.

Yasui, Masaya (1996) 'Venture Capital in Japan.' In: OECD (eds) *Venture Capital and Innovation*. Publication # 45312, OECD, Paris.

Yoshimura, Noboru, and Anderson, Philip (1997) *Inside the Kaisha: Demystifying Japanese Business Behavior*. Cambridge, Mass.: Harvard Business School Press.

Young, Scott T., Kwong, K. Kern, Li, Cheng, and Fok, Wing (1992) 'Global Manufacturing Strategies and Practices: A Study of Two Industries.' *International Journal of Operation & Production Management* 12(9): 5–17.

Zider, Bob (1998) 'How the Venture Capital Works.' *Harvard Business Review*: (Nov.–Dec.) 131–139.

Ziemke, M. Carl, and Spann, Mary S. (1993) 'Concurrent Engineering's Roots in the World War II Era.' In: Parsaei, Hamid R., and Sullivan, William G. (eds) *Concurrent Engineering: Contemporary Issues and Modern Design Tools*. London: Chapman & Hall.

Zuckerman, Mortimer B. (1998) 'A Second American Century.' *Foreign Affairs* 77(3): 18–31.

Index

Abernathy, William J. 171, 221
abstract connectivity 223, 231–2, 237, 261
abstract rules and systems 95–6, 120, 134, 250
abstraction, design principle of 230
accounting 161, 165, 172, 174
Adams, Richard C. 19, 126–7
Adler, Paul S. 155, 183, 236, 283
agency theory of firm behavior 75
Ahmed, Pervaiz K. 277–8
aircraft industry 257–61
Alic, John A. 246
Allaire, Yvan 169
alliance capitalism 64, 153
Amazon.com 199
American Airlines 262
American Electronics Association 141
American exceptionalism 41–2, 74, 105
American Express 263
American Hospital Supply 262
American Marketing Association 138
Amsden, Alice H. 42
Anderson, Philip 174
Andersen Consulting 200
Andreesen, Mark 123–4
Aoki, Masahiko 131, 148
AOL (America Online) 123–4, 187, 199
Appelbaum, Eileen 124
Apple (company) 123, 200
architectural knowledge 91, 195, 207, 237, 247–8, 255
Arthur Andersen (company) 165
Arthur, W. Brian 184
Asanuma, Banri 248
AT&T (company) 190
Austrian economics 49, 75, 90, 155
automation 245–6
automobile industry 15–17, 20–1, 70, 94, 138, 143, 146, 151, 184, 221, 224–7, 253, 273
autonomy
  of firms 76, 107, 113, 115
  of individuals 62, 73–5, 81, 84, 87, 106, 160–4
  of machines 241
  of management and stockholders 114, 169, 250
  of subsystems 82, 223
  of workers 114

Baba, Yasunori 149, 232, 261, 271
Baker, Wayne E. 118
Baldwin, Carliss Y. 215
banking 151–2, 174–5, 263
Barley, Stephen R. 124
Baron, J. N. 148
Batt, Rosemary 124
Behling, Orlando 141
Bell Lab 189–90, 195
Bensaou, M. 239, 264–5, 269, 272–5
Berkley, James D. 110
Berque, Augustin 84–5, 242–3
Biggart, Nicole Woolsey 74–9, 113
Blair, John G. 73, 214, 219
Boeing (company and aircraft) 253, 258–60, 267
Bolton, Michele Kremen 118
Boston Consulting Group 170
bounded rationality 184, 255–6, 259–60
Bowman, Scott R. 75
brain hemispheres 216–17
Branscomb, Lewis B. 208
Buchanan, James 75
Buiges, Pierre 20
business angels 199

Canon (company) 206–7
capitalism 64, 79, 90, 105–6, 113, 131–2, 153–4, 161
Case, John 201
Caterpillar Inc. 180
Caudill, William 80
Chandler, Alfred D. 16, 103, 105, 183–4
chaos theory 52, 104, 127
Chia, Robert 217
China 55, 76–9, 92, 96–7, 161–2, 172, 217, 240, 262, 283–8
Choi, Thomas Y. 141
Chow, Chee W. 215
Christensen, Clayton M. 191
Chrysler 10, 125–6, 147, 150
Cisco 123, 187
Citibank 262

Citicorp 268
clan structures 62–5, 79, 122–3, 135, 147
Clark, Jim 123–4
Clark, Kim B. 91, 247–8, 144, 146, 215, 224–6, 255, 273
closed-loop system design 276–7
closed technological systems 192, 224
Coca-Cola 58, 117
Cohen, Patricia Cline 163
Cohen, Stephen S. 200
Cole, Robert E. 91, 98, 121, 155, 183, 236, 283
communitarianism 54–5, 79, 90–1
Compaq 189
competitiveness, sectoral pattern of 2, 5, 9–10, 23, 39–43, 47, 61, 88, 129–30, 156, 185, 282
complexity 47, 50, 52, 103, 177, 181–2, 191, 214–15, 238, 248, 255–8
computer-aided design (CAD) 244, 267–8
concurrent engineering 88, 91, 96, 98, 109, 124, 133, 144–8, 155–6, 181, 184–6, 226, 231, 260, 269, 274, 284
connectivity 216–17, 232–4, 261
connectual governance 66–7, 70–1, 104, 119, 124, 126, 130–5, 140–3, 148–56, 171, 184, 205, 207, 212, 233, 274, 276, 283, 287, 289
connectual knowing 81–98 passim, 133, 139–40, 149, 181–5, 204–11, 224–7, 234, 239, 247, 253–61, 271–8, 284
connectual man 54, 61, 63, 67, 73, 76–81, 87, 89, 92–4, 97, 103–4, 148, 162, 179, 231, 233, 287
connectualization of systems 214–15, 218
consulting services 56–7, 83, 88–9, 96, 109–11, 200, 204, 268
consumer preferences 151, 163, 168, 176, 206
contextual knowledge 82–3, 87–8, 108, 139, 153, 162, 166, 177–82, 185, 206, 222, 225, 227, 236, 247–9, 272, 276
continuous improvement 117, 148, 206, 237, 248, 269–70
contractual governance 61–71, 97, 103–6, 112, 117–19, 124–8, 135, 142, 144, 147, 152, 171, 174, 190, 200, 235, 249, 276, 283, 287
contractual man 54–5, 61, 67, 73–6, 81, 86–97, 103, 113–14, 127–8, 139–40, 184, 229, 284, 287
convergence hypothesis in economics 2–3, 42, 50
copyrights 92, 111, 121
cost accounting 165–6
Critical Technology Institute 276

Crosby, Alfred W. 161
cross-functional teams 64, 66, 70, 87, 96, 109, 122–5, 143, 147–9, 155, 181, 205, 211, 231, 238, 269, 279
culture 51–2, 55, 61, 73, 97, 103, 105, 124–7, 149, 217–18, 285, 289
customization 179–80, 207–8, 232–4, 244, 267, 272–3
Cusumano, Michael A. 233, 281
Czinkota, Michael R. 38, 151

Dattel, Eugene R. 174
Davenport, Thomas H. 271–2
Dell Computer 187, 265, 267
demand articulation 177, 224
Deming, J. Edwards 136, 147–8, 182, 184
dependency structures 75, 78, 114, 126–7, 134, 139, 142, 194, 220, 251, 254
Dertouzos, Michael L. 166
Descartes, René 81
design 144–5, 206, 220–6, 230, 250, 259
of system architecture 223, 239, 269
see also computer-aided design
design for assembly (DFA) and for manufacture (DFM) 146–9, 226–7, 231, 237, 260, 269, 284
detachment, principle of 169
Dewey, John 163
Digital Equipment Corporation (DEC) 123, 189
DiMaggio, P. 60–1
division of labor 69, 84, 87, 96, 149, 205, 221, 249–50
Dore, Ronald P. 79–80
Dosi, Giovanni 280
Doyle, Peter 180
Drucker, Peter F. 166
Duimering, P. Robert 274–5
Dunning, John 180
Dyer, Jeffrey H. 150

Earl, Michael 239, 264–5, 269, 272–5
Edison, Thomas 186–7
electronic data interchange (EDI) 262, 264–5
empathetic knowing 180, 224
Engels, Friedrich 164
entertainment products 235
entrepreneurship 58–9, 90–1, 99, 204, 224
individualistic 197, 211–12, 224, 287
Ernst & Young (company) 165
experimentation 252–3

'fabless' firms 191, 209
family relationships 76, 79, 92, 132, 151
fault tree analysis 261

Federal Express 262–4
Ferguson, Charles H. 281
Fichman, Robert G. 230
Fields, Gary 200
financial information 165–6, 171
firms
  functional divisions in 116, 138, 220
  purpose of 131–2, 135–6
  workers' relationships with 67–8, 80, 132
Firsirotu, Michaela 169
flexible production 57, 109, 125–6, 130, 141, 143, 169, 183–4, 237, 283, 285
  see also manufacturing
Florida, Richard 131, 140–1, 184, 194, 198, 200
Fodor, Jerry A. 215
Ford, Henry 147, 161, 242
Ford Motors 10, 108, 126, 147, 285
Fordism 62, 76, 88, 106, 108, 117, 155, 221, 239, 283–4
franchising 107, 117
Francis, Arthur 144
Fruin, W. Mark 133–4, 206–7
Fujimoto, Takahiro 144, 146, 224–7, 255, 273
Fujitsu 207
Fukutake, Tadashi 79–80
Fukuyama, Francis 80, 89, 119, 280

Gagnon, Joseph E. 9
Galbraith, J. K. 134
games software 236
garbage can model 195–7, 201–3, 259
Gardner, Howard 217
General Motors (GM) 10, 108, 126, 147, 183, 221, 246
generalists 69, 83–4, 87, 93–4, 137–9, 211, 214, 229, 233, 247
Gerlach, Michael L. 152–3
Gertler, Meric S. 242
Giddens, Anthony 95–6
Gillespie, Richard 220
globalization 175, 280, 285–6
Gordon, A. 148
Goto, Akira 258, 261
Graham, Otis L. Jr. 127
Granovetter, Mark 118
Greenstone, J. David 74–5
groupism 53–4, 215, 257

Hall, Edward T. 52, 160–1
Hamada, Tomoko 140
Hamilton, Gary G. 74, 77–9, 113
Hammett, Patrick C. 253
Hampden-Turner, Charles 52, 54–5
Hardaker, Glenn 277–8

Hargadon, Andrew 186–7, 200
Harrison, Bennett 125–6
Hartz, Louis 74–5
Hayek, F. A. 49, 90, 103, 188, 196
Hayes, Robert H. 171
Hedlund, Gunnar 258
Hegel, G. W. F. 169, 280
Helper, Susan 150
Henderson, Rebecca M. 91, 247–8
Henke, John W. 124–5
Herbig, Paul 203
Hewlett-Packard 200
high-tech sectors 10–20, 23–7, 186–7
Hitachi 176, 206–7, 288
Hofstede, Geert 52
Honda 146, 170, 225, 244
Hughes, Thomas P. 242, 251, 259, 262
human capital 49–50, 56, 121
'human design' 239, 269
human error, avoidance of 238–40, 249, 253–4
Huntington, Samuel P. 280, 286

Iansiti, Marco 95, 190, 253–4
IBM 122, 124, 189, 195, 219, 229, 260
IDEO (company) 200
Imai, Ken-ichi 205
Imai, Masaaki 181, 248
imbedding mechanisms 96
incremental improvement 181–4, 209, 226–7, 247–8, 255
'independent model of personhood' 53–4, 217
individualism 53–5, 63, 69, 74–5, 79, 81, 90, 109, 125, 161, 215, 257
industrial policy 1, 10, 127–8, 133, 155, 204, 211
information technology, use of 156, 240, 251, 262–74
Innes, J. E. 163
innovation *see* technological innovation
insurance 167–8
Intel 120–7, 187, 189, 193, 195, 254, 288
interaction and interdependence 70–1, 76–8, 116, 133–4, 139, 142, 145, 149, 160, 171, 174, 223, 231, 237, 239, 242–3
'interdependent model of self' 53–4, 57–8, 217
Internet, the 37, 70, 110, 264–5
inter-subjective knowing 87, 89, 91
isomorphism 48, 51, 60, 66, 71–2, 98–9, 103–5, 124–31, 148–9, 156, 193, 223, 256, 282–3

Jacquemin, Alexis 20
Jaikumar, Ramchandran 235

Japan
  economic successes and failures   129,
    286–7
  Ministry of International Trade and
    Industry (MITI)   10, 154–5, 282
  unique competitiveness of   41–2
Jelinek, Mariann   168, 170, 220, 251
job classifications, broadness of   140, 233
job rotation   58, 66, 68, 70, 87, 93, 96, 98,
    133, 136–40, 143, 145, 148, 181–2, 205,
    211, 251, 271
Johansson, Johny K.   175–6
Johnson, Chalmers   1, 42, 166, 221
Johnson, Frank   75
just-in-time (JIT) production and
    delivery   58, 68, 96, 98, 109, 124, 126,
    130, 133–4, 142–3, 148–9, 155–6, 181,
    184–5, 231, 237, 265, 270, 274, 284

Kagono, Tadao   117
kaizen   98, 141, 181
Kanter, Rosabeth Moss   118
Kash, Don E.   90, 187, 191, 257
Kashima, Emiko S. and Yoshihisa   217
keiretsu   63–4, 152–3, 204, 211, 281
Kemerer, Chris   230
Kenney, Martin   131, 140–1, 184, 194, 198,
    200
Kirzner, Israel M.   90
Kitayama, Shinobu   53, 217
Klein, Janice A.   236
Knight, Frank H.   106
knowledge
  commodification and encapsulation
    of   92–3
  cumulativeness and continuity over
    time   59
  decontextualization of   162–4, 167
  deepening and widening of   88
  externalization of   109, 134–5
  firm-specific   93, 110, 114, 136–9, 150,
    153–4, 272
  genuine   172
  public and private   57–8, 76, 111, 127
knowledge creation   3–5, 42, 47–72, 76,
    87–92, 96–7, 103, 106, 111–13, 116, 119,
    127, 144, 154, 169, 181–2, 287
  American system of   76, 90, 96, 104, 194,
    196, 287–8
  Japanese system of   90, 104, 129–30, 161,
    277, 282
knowledge regime perspective   3–4, 47–8,
    51, 71–2, 89, 130–1, 141, 148, 152–4, 160,
    163, 169, 192, 205, 207, 219–22, 233, 236,
    258, 277, 280–2, 286–7
Kochan, Thomas   113

Kodama, Fumio   19, 177, 186, 205–8, 224
Kogut, Bruce   280
Koike, Kazuo   250, 270
Kondo, Dorinne   85, 243
Kotabe, Masaaki   138
Kuhn, Thomas S.   130
Kunda, Gideon   124
Kusunoki, Ken   89, 94, 179, 206, 273

Lanctot, Aldo R., Jr.   138
Langlois, Richard N.   120, 192
Lauenstein, Milton C.   170
Lavoie, Don   196
lawyers and litigation   77, 92
Lazonick, William   136
lean production   16, 124, 130, 149, 155, 183,
    185, 227, 282
learning   142, 180, 192, 285–6
  organizational   91, 110, 184
LeBlanc, Larry J.   242
Lehman Brothers   268
Lei, David   275
Liebeskind, Lulia Porter   91, 112, 120
lifetime employment   64, 66, 94, 96, 133,
    136–7, 148, 156, 211
Liker, Jeffrey K.   225
limited partnerships   198, 203
Lincoln, Edward   20, 67
Lincoln, James R.   137–8
Lipset, Seymour Martin   9, 49, 53–4, 74–5,
    105
Litterer, Joseph A.   243
Littler, Craig R.   220
lock-in   47, 50, 105, 155, 202, 232, 237, 283
Locke, John   74–5, 105
Long-Term Capital Management   268
loosely-coupled systems   70, 202–3, 235,
    287–8
Lynn, Leonard H.   94, 109

M-form organization   76, 96, 113, 116–17,
    165, 219
McDonald's and McDonaldization   58, 115,
    117, 161, 163, 166–7, 231
Macduffe, John Paul   141–2
Macher, Jeffrey T.   191
McKinsey & Company   141
McKinsey Global Institute   17–18, 26, 38,
    146
Madigan, Charles   109
management fads   2, 98, 109–10, 124, 155
management information systems   115, 169,
    240–1
Mansfield, Edwin   144, 209–10
manufacturing   21–3, 211
  American system of   108, 220

flexible systems of (FMS) 234–5, 239–41, 246
Japanese system of 130, 184
March, James G. 52
Marcus, Alan I. 239
market research 168, 172–8
marketing associations, membership of 138
Markus, Hazel Rose 53, 217
Marx, Karl 164
mass production 57, 65, 105–9, 117, 142, 144, 150, 169–72, 183–4, 220, 251, 284
Matsushita 175, 207, 244
Mazda 146, 225
Mazzoleni, Roberto 276–7
Merrill Lynch 262, 268
Microsoft 117, 120–4, 187–90, 193, 200
Mikuni, Akio 174
Milkman, Ruth 126
Mintzberg, Henry 108, 122, 169, 171–2, 240
Mitsubishi 180, 207
mobility of knowledge workers 200–1, 204, 209–12, 239, 249
modular design 226, 246–8
modular thinking 216–18
modularization 62, 116, 144, 192–3, 202–3, 214–16, 219–29, 254–7, 260–1
  flexible or rigid 236–7, 255–6, 273–6
  of knowledge and skills 66, 76, 106–7, 219
money, use of 163–4
Moore, James F. 120
Morita, Akio 175
Motorola 122, 285
Mowery, David C. 253, 257

Nakahara, Tetsushi 233
Nakane, Chie 77, 79, 87, 132
NEC (company) 187, 207, 288
Needham, Joseph 77, 84
Nelson, Daniel 220
Nelson, R. 115
neoclassical economics 47, 61, 75, 106, 150, 164
Netscape Corporation 123–4, 190
networks 62, 118–21
Nippondenso 244
Nishiguchi, Toshihiro 94
Nishikawa, Toru 176
Nissan 244
Noble, David F. 239–40, 246
Nohria, Nitin 110
Nonaka, Ikujiro 87, 161, 175–8, 180, 182, 206, 272
Numagami, Tsuyosh 94, 179, 206, 273
numerical control machine tools 234, 239, 276

object-oriented information technologies 229–30
objectivity 87, 163, 172, 176
Odagiri, Hiroyuki 258, 261
Ogden, Joan 266
Okimoto, Daniel I. 154–5, 204
Okuno-Fujiwara, Masahiro 154
Oliver, N. 134, 142
open-loop system architecture 276–7
Oracle 123, 187, 195, 223
organizing principles 47–61, 65–73, 76, 96, 103, 128, 148–9, 156, 169, 186, 189–93, 207, 214–15, 218–19, 228–35, 249, 279–89
Orlikowski, Wanda J. 244
Ornstein, Robert 216–17
O'Shea, James 109
Osterman, Paul 125, 136
Ouchi, William G. 122, 150

Pake, George E. 194
Parry, Mark E. 144
Parsons, Talcott 52, 54, 78, 82, 218
Patel, Parimal 28–9
patents 27–32, 92, 111, 121, 187–8, 207, 210
path-dependence 50–1, 277
Pavitt, Keith 28–9
people-(in)dependent systems integration 6, 57–60, 65, 67, 69, 76, 96, 99, 238–40, 248–57, 261–78, 285, 287
PeopleSoft 223, 265
Perrow, Charles 259
Perry, Tekla S. 190
Peters, Tom 171
Pfeffer, Jeffrey 249
Pilat, Dirt 26–7
Pilkington, Alan 17
Pimblett, Carole 167
Pinker, Steven 275
Piore, Michael J. 105, 218
Polanyi, Michael 85–6, 172, 178–9
Porter, Michael E. 18–19, 38, 47, 163, 166, 170
Porter, Theodore M. 165
Powell, W. W. 60–1
Prestowitz, Clyde V. Jr. 1, 12, 21
product development 89, 141, 144–7, 205, 244, 260
product integrity 146, 224–7, 237, 273
productivity 17–18, 26, 38, 115
professional associations 119–20, 201
professionalization 83, 92–3, 104, 108, 140, 222, 251–2
propositional knowledge 82–5, 88, 141, 172, 182, 185
Putnam, Robert D. 119

Pye, Lucian   78, 92

quality circles (QC)   58, 64, 68, 87, 91, 96,
    124, 140–1, 148, 181–2, 205, 237
quantification   161–3, 168–75

Rasmus, Daniel W.   277
Rawls, John   75
redundancies in design   259, 261
relational contracting   80, 118
research and development (R&D)   49–52,
    56, 94–6, 111–13, 118, 133, 144–5, 156,
    209, 242
   public component of   58, 111–12, 259
revealed comparative advantage   11–18,
    28–32
Robertson, Paul L.   192
robotics   244, 275
Roehl, Thomas   258
Rose, Andrew K.   9
Rosenberg, Nathan   257
Rosenberger, Nancy R.   80
Rycroft, R. W.   187, 191, 257

Sabel, Charles F.   105, 142
Sachwald, Frederique   25
Sakurai, Michihru   183
SAP (company)   195, 265
Saturn (company)   122, 124, 285
Saxenian, Annalee   201
Saxonhouse, G.   204
Schmitt, Richard   74, 81–4, 163
Schumpeter, Joseph   90, 186
scientific management   76, 116, 124, 141,
    144, 148–9, 168, 246
Segal, Howard P.   239
self, sense of   53–4, 73, 78, 81, 84–5, 243
Sematech   10, 153
semiconductors   118, 190–1, 208–9, 239,
    252–3
Senge, Peter M.   184
separate knowing   81–99 *passim*, 111, 115,
    134, 139–41, 160–2, 168–70, 174, 176,
    180, 183, 191–4, 197, 205, 208, 214,
    222–9, 239, 246–50, 254–9, 276, 284, 287
'separate system'   250, 270
sequential engineering   144–8, 226, 260
Serling, Robert J.   258–9
Shichihei, Yamamoto   79, 129
Shook, Carrie and Robert L.   107
shop-floor workers   85, 91, 110, 115–16,
    136–44, 181, 184, 220, 226–9, 234, 239,
    250, 254, 270–7
Silicon Graphics   123, 190
Silicon Valley   106, 120, 187, 190, 194–202,
    224, 285

Simon, Herbert A.   52, 184, 218
Sloan, Alfred   226
Sobol, Marion G.   275
social capital and social systems   82, 119–20
socialization   64–9, 73, 80–1, 86–7, 134–7,
    180, 182, 217, 272–3
software products   32–7, 70, 120–1, 212,
    223, 228–9, 232, 242, 271
Song, X. Michael   155
Sony   175, 187, 207, 235–6, 244
Souder, William E.   89
Spann, Mary S.   147
specialists, knowledge of   83–4, 94–6, 138–9
Spence, Janet   53–4
spin-off ventures   66, 195, 208, 232
stakeholder capitalism   131–2
standardization   114–15, 166–7, 184, 193,
    220, 271–2
   of knowledge and skills   108, 249, 251
   of procedures   114–15, 141, 271
   of products   58, 107–8, 167, 219
Stanford University   194
state, the, role of   92, 127–8, 133, 154, 289
statistics, use of   167–8, 182
Storper, Michael   195
strategic alliances   118, 120, 156
strategic planning   169–72
styling of products   221, 226
subcontracting   96, 125, 134, 149, 211
Sun Microsystems (company)   123, 195
supplier relationships   125–6, 149–50, 211,
    219, 261–5, 269
Sutton, Robert I.   186–7, 200
synergy   98–9, 120, 137, 140, 155, 182, 185,
    236, 280, 283–5, 289
systemic approach   261, 271

tacit knowledge   42, 56–9, 64–7, 71, 81–93,
    108, 121, 134–7, 144, 153, 160–2, 166–72,
    180–5, 239, 248–51, 268–77
   Japanese competitive advantage in
    178–80
tacitly agreed rules and procedures   118
tacitly perceived obligations   95–6
Takeuchi, Hirotaka   178, 180, 182, 206
Takezawa, S.   80
Taoism   84–5, 172, 218
Taylor, Frederick   116, 141, 161, 168–9, 238,
    242, 251, 254
Taylorism   62, 76, 88, 106, 109, 144, 149,
    155, 162, 168–9, 183, 220–1, 239, 250–4,
    265, 271, 278–9, 283–4
   dynamic   236
technological innovation   154, 189, 191,
    208–9, 215
   American and Japanese styles of   186–7

linear model of   111–12, 116–17, 193–4, 219
  spontaneous   58–9, 63, 65, 69–70, 121–2
technology breakthroughs   186, 190, 202
technology brokers   200
technology fusion   186–93, 273
  organized   188–9, 203–12, 255
  spontaneous   188–96, 199–205, 211, 216, 229, 259–60, 289
tightly coupled systems   70, 130, 153, 202, 211, 231–2, 254, 259, 287–8
Toshiba   134, 187, 207
total quality management (TQM)   98, 109, 121, 133–6, 140–1, 148–9, 155, 182–5, 269–70, 274, 279, 284
Toyota   145, 151, 175, 181, 244, 273
Toyotarism   130, 183, 284
trade barriers   12, 20–1, 280, 288
Training Within Industries (TWI)   147–8
training, on-the-job-   66, 87, 93–6, 133, 136–8, 179, 205, 229, 233, 251, 269–72, 278
transaction costs   103, 134–5, 150, 152, 176, 183
Trompenaars, Alfrons   52, 54–5
Truitt, Frederick   258
trust   89–99, 134–5, 154
  in numbers   163
Tsutsui, William M.   155

United Airlines   262
United Kingdom   177, 180, 278, 283, 286
universal product code   262
universal rules   54–5, 78, 95
UPS (company)   263–4
Upton, David   274
usual and unusual operations   270

Van Ark, Bart   26–7
venture capital   175, 197–9, 203–4, 211–12, 232
Vogel, Ezra F.   1
voluntary associations   119–21
Volvo   183

Wallich, Paul   190
Wal-Mart   117, 231, 262–4
Waterman, Robert H.   171
weak ties   119–21
Weber, Max   104, 161
Weinstein, Helen   80
Weinstein, Marc   113
West, Jonathan   95
Whitehill, A. M.   80–1
Whitelock, Jeryl   167
Wilkinson, B. W.   134, 142
Williamson, Oliver E.   50, 61, 103, 112, 114, 150, 162, 183–4
Wilson, James Q.   115
Wintel system   120–1, 193
Winter, Sidney G.   183
Womack, J. P.   144, 151

Xerox   122, 124, 189–90, 194–5, 260, 285

Yaguchi, Yujin   140
Yahoo!   123, 187, 199
Yasui, Masaya   204
Yoshimura, Noboru   174

Zider, Bob   197
Ziemke, M. Carl   147